D1315124

WOMEN AND THE NATIONAL EXPERIENCE

CONTENTS

PREFACE

The expansion of the third edition of **Women and the National Experience** from one to two volumes has made possible a more inclusive range of women's voices, an increased number of topics, and a geographic lens with significant focus on the American West. The new two-volume edition also permits greater documentary coverage of little-known women who, along with those who are more familiar and famous, demonstrate the dynamic interaction between diverse women and the national experience. Primary documents include private letters, diary entries, cartoons, photographs, newspaper accounts, songs, public speeches, records from Supreme Court decisions, and excerpts from memoirs and autobiographies. Chapter introductions and document headnotes provide historical context and biographical information. Although the chapters are arranged chronologically, each chapter focuses on a particular topic of significance within the field of women's history but also relates to major national developments. Chapter introductions incorporate current scholarship and historiography. The intersection of gender, race, class, religion, and sexual identity illuminates the complexities of identity, but as the voices of women past and present testify, individual experience and achievement express more than composite identity. As in previous editions, all documents demonstrate the centrality of women's history to the national experience. New documents expand the earlier emphasis on the multiplicity of women's voices. A wide range of documents focus on women who crossed gender barriers and widened women's roles. Sources also include the views of women who resisted change and upheld prescribed norms. Also included are the voices of women such as Catharine Beecher and Sarah Josepha Hale, editor of the popular *Godey's Lady's Book* who struggled to preserve domestic norms for women but still facilitated increased opportunity.

Fortunately, more primary sources are now available than when the earlier editions of *Women and the National Experience* were published, including translations of Spanish and Mexican women's voices. The inclusion of primary sources from New Spain allows students to compare the nun Sor Juana's experience of convent life in Mexico to that of Anne Hutchinson, a Puritan dissident, wife, and mother from the Massachusetts Bay Colony. The differences between the two women spanned geography, culture, language, status, and religion, yet both encountered persecution because of their subversion of gender roles and refusal to accept intellectual subordination. Cross-cultural comparisons of documents also illuminate the dysfunctional marriage of a Spanish woman, Eulalia Callis, who married Pedro Fages, the military governor of California and the marital misery of Puritan New Englander, Abigail Abbott Bailey, whose decades of wifely endurance ended in divorce only after she found that her husband had committed incest with their daughter.

Mohawk Indian Molly Brant's partnership with British imperial official Sir William Johnson, superintendent of Indian affairs, fostered coexistence of American Indians and the British imperial administration prior to and during the American Revolution. Brant's letters to British officials as well as the documents of Indian women, including Nancy Ward (Cherokee) and Sarah Winnemucca (Piute) provide further evidence of the role of American Indian women as negotiators and mediators in cross-cultural encounters. Although documents focus on women's agency, primary sources also reveal the grim consequences of oppression. A labor contract illustrates the coercive terms dictated to Chinese immigrant women, many of whom were brought to California as prostitutes. Autobiographical accounts and interviews of enslaved women demonstrate successful acts of defiance, but also the impact of abusive power. Generations of diverse American Indian women used a variety of strategies in pursuit if their own and tribal interest, yet others fell victim to rape, sexual exploitation, and disease.

Documents also highlight little-known women such as African American Elizabeth Jennings Graham, who put her safety at risk when she refused to leave a New York City racially segregated horse-drawn omnibus in 1854, a century before Rosa Parks's well-publicized resistance to segregation. Pioneers for racial equality also included white schoolmistress Prudence Crandall, who was imprisoned and put on trial for disobeying a town law and admitting black students to her newly opened school for girls in 1834. Far removed from Crandall's small Connecticut town of Canterbury, Chinese immigrants Mary Tape and her husband sued the San Francisco Board of Education for its refusal to allow their daughter to attend their all-white neighborhood school. Writing in 1885 to the school board, Mary Tape defended integration and spared no words condemning the racist objectives of the white school board.

WHAT'S NEW TO THIS EDITION

The third edition has been expanded with more than one hundred new documents and seven new chapters into a two-volume collection of primary sources in American women's history. Approximately one hundred new documents accompany the new chapters and are supplemented by biographical information and questions that focus student attention on key aspects of the sources. Extensive revisions, updated research, and approximately thirty-five additional documents enrich the chapters that bridge the second and third editions. Photographs, cartoons and illustrations add visual source material.

HIGHLIGHTS OF THE NEW EDITION

- Two new chapters on the multicultural West cover the entire sweep of nineteenth-century American settlement; expand the geographic reach of previous editions and the range of diverse voices.
- A new thematic chapter provides an overview of the intersection of environmental and women's history, a field that until recently has received limited attention.
- Reaching beyond national borders to the wider context of an interrelated global world, a new chapter focuses on the campaign for women's rights on a national and global stage.
- A wide range of documents and a new chapter examine the personal side of women's experience as well as the overlap between personal lives and public policy, particularly with reference to reproductive issues. Documents in different chapters address changing sexual standards, and the social construction of heterosexual and lesbian identity. Lesbian voices include pioneer blues singer Ma Rainey, Audre Lorde, and Mab Segrest.
- New documents illuminate the diverse ways women from the colonial period to the present have struggled for empowerment in marriage, the workplace, recreation and education.
- Two new chapters on enslavement and abolitionism highlight the voices of enslaved women such as Harriet Jacobs, Elizabeth Keckley, and Bethany Veney as well as the dual objective of African American women (Sarah Mapps Douglas, Sarah Remond, and Frances Ellen Watkins Harper) to achieve abolition and racial equality. White counterparts in the struggle include the iconic Angelina Grimké and the less well-known Prudence Crandall and Lydia Maria Child.
- Greater inclusion of the voices of young women include teenaged Lowell Mills factory worker Barilla Taylor and 1920's "flapper" Ellen Welles Page as well as the wartime gender role-crossing of Revolutionary war soldier Deborah Sampson and World War II air force transport pilot, Ann Baumgartner Carl.
- New documents illuminate the less well-known voices of women from diverse religious groups such as Mormon women Fanny Stenhouse and Emmeline Wells, whose outspoken voices present contradictory views on polygamy. New documents also depict the activist resistance of Catholic nuns to the patriarchal suppression of gender equality.

NEW CHAPTERS:

Chapter 4 From Moral Reform to Free Love and Voluntary Motherhood: Issues of Vulnerability and Sexual Agency (8 new documents)

A new chapter discusses female empowerment from a variety of perspectives including moral reform, voluntary motherhood, and free love. This chapter focuses on the struggle of women to limit male sexual entitlement to the female body. The growing exercise of female agency embedded in the language of nineteenth-century moral reform ranged from the chastisement of men who had sex outside of marriage to increasing efforts to suppress prostitution. Over time women also began to support the right of married women to exercise reproductive choice. Primary sources include Paulina Wright Davis and Harriot Stanton Blatch's advocacy of voluntary motherhood, as well as Victoria Woodhull's bold assertion of a woman's right to freely choose her sexual partners.

Chapter 5 Enslaved Women: Race, Gender, and the Plantation Patriarchy (6 new documents)

Narratives of former slaves Harriet Jacobs and Elizabeth Keckley, as well as little-known Bethany Veney, testify to the multiple examples of enslaved women's agency but also depict their gender-specific vulnerability. In addition to the evidence from slave narratives, the journal of plantation mistress Ella Gertrude Clanton Thomas provides evidence of sexual exploitation of enslaved women. The firsthand observations of Fanny Kemble, an abolitionist married to a plantation owner, depicts the miserable conditions enslaved women confronted on a routine basis.

Chapter 6 Abolitionist Women and the Controversy over Racial Equality (8 new documents)

The chapter introduces students to little-known African American women whose focus on civil rights accompanied their antislavery struggle. Advocates such as African American Maria Stewart, Sarah Mapps Douglas, and Sarah Remond combined their crusade for abolition with a call for racial justice and equality. Elizabeth Jennings Graham was the unacknowledged Rosa Parks of her era. Primary sources also demonstrate that some white women such as the Grimké sisters, Prudence Crandall and Lydia Maria Child supported not just the abolition of slavery, but also racial equality.

Chapter 8 Western Expansion: Different Viewpoints, Diverse Stories (11 new documents)

The pre–Civil War West provides the historical context for a wide range of new documents emphasizing divergent perspectives and multicultural voices. Anglo-Americans migrating to the West joined a multiracial, multicultural population. Documents illuminate the voices of Mexican and American Indian women such as Eulalia Perez, a chief administrator of the San Gabriel mission during Spanish rule, as well as Isadora Filomena, a member of the Churucto tribe of California Indians. The experiences of Anglo-American settlers in California such as Luzena Wilson and Mary Ballou sharply contrasted with that of women such as Rosalia Vallejo Leese who, many years after the United States took control of California, expressed enduring hostility to American acculturation. Biddy Mason, brought to California as a slave successfully sued for her freedom, in contrast to Chinese immigrant women who arrived in San Francisco as prostitutes bound to indentured labor contracts. Servitude rather than opportunity molded their experience.

Chapter 11 Women's Roles: Americanization and the Multicultural West (10 new documents)

Homestead Act legislation promoted population growth and over the decades provided settlers including Mattie Oblinger and her family as well as the German-Jewish immigrant family of Sarah Thal with the opportunity for land and home ownership. Government-supported Americanization or assimilation programs targeted American Indians. Pioneer anthropologist Alice Fletcher promoted Americanization programs ranging from instruction in appropriate gender norms to private landownership. For Johanna July, a black Seminole Indian and horse trainer, her lifestyle expressed her determination to forge an identity in defiance of appropriate middle-class gender norms. Chinese born. Mary Tape's crusade to end the segregation of Chinese students in California expresses the fierce determination of a mother who also was a pioneer advocate for equality of educational opportunity.

Chapter 17 From Municipal House Keeping to Environmental Justice (11 new documents)

The chapter provides students with an overview of the significance of women and gender assumptions in shaping the nation's environmental history from the nineteenth through the early twenty-first centuries. Long before the 1962 publication of Rachel Carson's *Silent Spring,* women environmentalists such as Ellen Swallow Richards and Alice Hamilton struggled against male-imposed barriers in pursuit of educational and career opportunity. Lois Gibbs became a politically involved activist who led her upstate New York, Love Canal community in a fight for justice against Hooker Chemical's toxic dumping. More recently, women of color, including African American Margie Eugene Richard, have assumed leadership roles in the fight the chemical contamination of communities of color.

Chapter 21 Women's Rights: National and Global Perspectives (10 new documents)

In recent years, American women's history has moved beyond national borders to consider transnational and global connections. This new field of inquiry reflects contemporary globalization as well as the greater overlap but contested construct of women's rights as human rights on a worldwide scale. From Hillary Clinton's Beijing speech in 1995 equating women's rights with human rights to the present, documents highlight the national and international effort and the role of American activists such as Robin Morgan and Eleanor Smeal to end multiple forms of violence against women, including trafficking and the Taliban violence in Afghanistan. Efforts to end gender-specific violence frequently collide with cultural norms as in the asylum case of Fauziya Kasinga who fled her country for America to prevent culturally prescribed genital cutting. A range of primary sources express the polarized policy positions of Presidents Bush and Obama on issues such as pay equity and reproductive rights and also demonstrate the dramatic divergence between women's rights activists and their conservative opponents.

ACKNOWLEDGMENTS

I would like to thank my friend and colleague Professor Marilyn Weigold for her invaluable suggestions. Her guidance rescued me more than once. My husband's computer skills also provided timely rescue and kept me on an even keel. Professor Bridget Crawford, Pace University Law School, provided insights and her manuscript with reference to third-wave feminism. Many thanks also to Steve Feyl and the Pace University Library Research and Information team for helping me locate the voices of colonial Spanish women and Mohawk Molly Brown and civil rights activist Elizabeth Jennings Graham.

Major thanks to Linda Benson, copy editor, for meticulous scrutiny and excellent suggestions. I would also like to acknowledge Lynn Hawley, San Joaquin Delta College; Sara Lee, American River College; and Paula Wheeler Carlo, Nassau Community College, who took the time to review the manuscript. Thanks also to Maureen Diana, editorial assistant for support and patience incorporating my revisions. Debra Wechsler's project supervision and guidance and Shiny Rajesh's assistance helped me navigate electronic hurdles. Thanks to Shiny's patience and expertise in dealing with my daily updates, I was able to reach the finish line on time. Above all, thanks to Charlyce Jones Owen, publisher, Prentice Hall, for providing the opportunity to develop this project. Your support, encouragement, and understanding made the third edition happen.

ABOUT THE AUTHOR

A graduate of Smith College, Ellen Skinner received a master of arts degree from Columbia University and a Ph.D. from New York University. She chaired the history department at Pace University's Westchester campus from 1987 to 2006. Her teaching career spanned four decades and in 2008 she was appointed professor emerita. In both her teaching and writing, she strives to make women's history accessible to students and relevant to their lives. Now in its third edition, **Women and the National Experience** was first published in 1996. Professor Skinner continues to teach women's history online and to search the archives for women's lost voices. Her current research focuses on women's human rights as well as the connections between women's history and the environment.

CHAPTER 9

The Civil War, Reconstruction:
Gender and Racial Issues

Hardship and the labor scarcity during the Civil War cast women in untraditional roles, and the construction of female gender norms was modified to meet wartime needs. Throughout the divided nation, women assumed the management of farms and plantations. Eager to do more than support the war effort from the home front, on both sides of the Civil War, a number of women disguised as men with assumed names entered the army. Rose O'Neal Greenhow, a passionate defender of the Confederacy, became a spy, as did other women for both the Union and the Confederacy, providing valuable information about enemy operations. The role of spy placed women at risk as they crossed geographic lines into enemy territory. Precisely because the idea of a women spy presented such a contradiction to feminine gender norms of delicacy and docility, women engaging in espionage created less suspicion than a man would.

The Civil War also propelled thousands of women into service as hospital and battlefield nurses and providers of medical supplies. Women in both the North and the South responded to the need for provisions and nursing care, and women's participation was lifesaving. In the North, they played a central role in the work of the U.S. Sanitary Commission. Nursing the wounded soldiers was very different from a woman's household role of caring for sick family members. Some battlefield nurses, such as Clara Barton, struggled to overcome nagging doubts about the "impropriety" of woman nursing wounded men and witnessing the carnage of battle. Women who entered the hospitals confronted the hostility of male doctors, who found them annoying and intrusive; however, like Phoebe Yates Levy Pember, they persevered. Nursing subsequently gained recognition as an appropriate female occupation. Yet until the Civil War, it was considered "unladylike" for women to nurse wounded men.

Even so, male doctors continued to exclude women from the medical profession. In 1873, Dr. Edward H. Clarke, a Harvard Medical School trustee, wrote a scathing report allegedly based on case studies providing multiple examples of how the inadequacies of the female brain and reproductive system made women unsuitable to pursue higher education. Until 1945, Harvard refused to grant women admission to its medical school. Similar gender barriers shaped the legal profession. In the Bradwell decision of 1873, the U.S. Supreme Court upheld the right of the state of Illinois to deny Myra Bradwell admission to the legal profession, despite the fact that she met the qualifications, because the Court claimed that the practice of law and the qualities of womanhood were incompatible. Despite continuation of professional barriers, during the Civil War, the labor scarcity opened the field of clerical work to women, and growing numbers of women were employed as clerks after peace was restored. The expanding field of teaching also offered women occupational opportunities. During Reconstruction, educated African Americans such as Charlotte Forten as well as white women left their homes in the North and moved to the South to meet the educational needs of newly freed slaves.

Although gender roles proved elastic in response to wartime needs, little had changed with reference to underlying structural inequality and a wife's legal nonexistence and subordination to her husband's authority. The case of Elizabeth Packard made clear that continued defiance of a husband's beliefs, in this particular case the husband was a Protestant minister, could result in a declaration of insanity and confinement in a mental institution.

During the Civil War, women suffragists, many of whom were also abolitionists, set aside the fight for women's rights to devote their full attention to campaigning for the emancipation of slaves. With the passage of the Thirteenth Amendment and emancipation achieved, women's rights leaders resumed their struggle for the ballot. Their suffragist crusade was far removed from the experiences of newly freed black women, who joined their husbands in the subsistence life of sharecroppers. Many took in laundry or worked as domestics to supplement their husbands' marginal wages. For the vast majority of married African American women, the norm of the sole male breadwinner was a myth. Work—combined with family care—remained the focus of their lives.

The passage of the Fifteenth Amendments gave African American men the right to vote. To Elizabeth Cady Stanton and Susan B. Anthony, the exclusion of women from the amendment was an inexcusable betrayal on the part of male abolitionists who formerly had linked women's rights to emancipation. Abolitionist men now urged women to be patient as it was the "negro's" hour. Dismissing patience, Stanton and Anthony severed ties with their former comrades. Embittered and defiant, they opposed the Fifteenth Amendment and in 1869 organized the National Woman's Suffrage Association (NWSA), open only to female members. Through their radical publication, *The Revolution,* Stanton and Anthony promoted a wide range of economic and social reforms for women, as well as the right to vote. To enable women to leave abusive marriages, Stanton advocated liberalized divorce laws.

Stanton and Anthony conducted massive petition drives and repeatedly and unsuccessfully sought congressional approval for women's suffrage. In 1872, Anthony tested the right of women as citizens to vote—she was arrested and brought to trial for unlawful voting. In *Minor v. Happersett,* in 1875, the U.S. Supreme Court rejected the suffragist argument that women, as U.S. citizens, had a constitutional right to vote. The Court alleged that only individual states could grant suffrage.

Women less radical than Stanton and Anthony followed Lucy Stone and Julia Ward Howe and joined the American Woman's Suffrage Association (AWSA). Organized in 1869 in opposition to the Stanton-Anthony NWSA, the AWSA included abolitionist men and recognized the Fifteenth Amendment. African American female abolitionists such as Frances Watkins Harper joined the AWSA. In a speech to the Women's Rights Convention in 1866, Watkins had emphasized the need for a biracial coalition of women to move ahead on the dual issues of civil rights and women's rights.

A more moderate organization, the AWSA also enjoyed greater support than the NWSA. Focusing its efforts completely on the right to vote, the AWSA campaigned for women's suffrage on the state level. For more than twenty years, the rival associations pursued their separate objectives and strategies. However, deeply rooted gender assumptions, similar to those of Catharine Beecher and Harriet Beecher Stowe as well as Amelia Barr, about women's special feminine traits making them unfit for public roles, made it difficult for women's rights leaders of either faction to secure a constituency for the vote. Both organizations proved ineffectual in building a mass base of support. Reunited in 1890 as the National American Woman's Suffrage Association (NAWSA), suffragists continued to lack significant public support until the 1900s. Only in the West, in Wyoming, Idaho, Utah, and Colorado, had women gained the right to vote.

Alternative approaches to suffrage also emerged. The Women's Christian Temperance Union (WCTU) supported suffrage as the means to achieving a broad-based agenda of social purity concerns that focused on temperance and privileged women's alleged moral authority. Increasingly over time, suffragists not explicitly concerned with Christian values also emphasized women's moral and maternal qualities, their allegedly unique qualities, rather than women's equality as citizens in their justification of voting rights.

ROSE O'NEAL GREENHOW, *Letter to the Hon. William H. Seward* (Nov. 1, 1861)

Women spies were employed by both the Union and the Confederacy. Women's roles expanded and gender restrictions were temporarily suspended in response to wartime needs. Many women sought to do more than home-based wartime service roles. Most dramatic was the role of female spies. Rose O'Neal Greenhow (1817–1864) was a member of the plantation elite, well known in Washington society and one of the Confederacy's most successful spies. Imprisoned twice by the Union, she was exiled to the South and resumed her wartime work with an official visit to Britain and France to secure support for the Confederate cause. Unfortunately, on her return, her ship, a blockade-runner supplied by the British, ran aground near the North Carolina coast, and she was not able to reach shore. How would you describe the tone of this letter of appeal?*

To the Hon. Wm. H. Seward,

Secretary of State:

Sir—For nearly three months I have been confined, a close prisoner, shut out from air and exercise, and denied all communication with family and friends.

"Patience is said to be a great virtue," and I have practised it to my utmost capacity of endurance. . . .

I therefore most respectfully submit, that on Friday, August 23d, without warrant or other show of authority, I was arrested by the Detective Police, and my house taken in charge by them; that all my private letters, and my papers of a life time, were read and examined by them; that every law of decency was violated in the search of my house and person, and the surveilance over me.

---

* In the public domain.

We read in history, that the poor Maria Antoinette had a paper torn from her bosom by lawless hands, and that even a change of linen had to be effected in sight of her brutal captors. It is my sad *experience* to record even more revolting outrages than that, for during the first days of my imprisonment, whatever *necessity* forced me to seek my chamber, a detective stood sentinel at the open door. And thus for a period of seven days, I, with my little child, was placed absolutely at the mercy of men without character or responsibility; that during the first evening, a portion of these men became brutally drunk, and boasted in my hearing of the *"nice times"* they expected to have with the female prisoners; and that rude violence was used towards a colored servant girl during that evening, the extent of which I have not been able to learn. For any show of decorum afterwards was practiced toward me, I was indebted to the detective called Capt. Dennis. . . .

You have held me, sir, to man's accountability, and I therefore claim the right to speak on subjects usually considered beyond a woman's ken, and which you may class as "errors of opinion." I offer no excuse for this long digression, as a three months' imprisonment, without formula of law, gives me authority for occupying even the precious moments of a Secretary of State.

My object is to call your attention to the fact: that during this long imprisonment, I am yet ignorant of the causes of my arrest; that my house has been seized and converted into a prison by the Government; that the valuable furniture it contained has been abused and destroyed; that during some periods of my imprisonment I have suffered greatly for want of proper and sufficient food. Also, I have to complain that, more recently, a woman of bad character, recognized as having been seen on the streets of Chicago as such, by several of the guard, calling herself Mrs. Onderdonk, was placed here in my house, in a room adjoining mine.

In making this exposition, I have no object of appeal to your sympathies, if the justice of my complaint, and a decent regard for the world's opinion, do not move you, I should but waste your time to claim your attention on any other score.

I may, however, recall to your mind, that but a little while since you were quite as much proscribed by public sentiment here, for the opinions and principles you held, as I am now for mine.

I could easily have escaped arrest, having had timely warning. I thought it impossible that your statesmanship might present such a proclamation of weakness to the world, as even the fragment of a once great Government turning its arms against the breasts of women and children. You have the power, sir, and may still further abuse it. You may prostrate the physical strength, by confinement in close rooms and insufficient food—you may subject me to harsher, ruder treatment than I have already received, but you cannot imprison the soul. Every cause worthy of success has had its martyrs. . . . My sufferings will afford a significant lesson to

Rosie O'Neal Greenhow and her Daughter
(Library of Congress)

the women of the South, that sex or condition is no bulwark against the surging billows of the "irrepressible conflict."

The "iron heel of power" may keep down, but it cannot crush out, the spirit of resistance in a people armed for the defence of their rights; and I tell you now, sir, that you are standing over a crater, whose smothered fires in a moment may burst forth.

It is your boast, that thirty-three bristling fortifications now surround Washington. The fortifications of Paris did not protect Louis Phillippe when his hour had come.

In conclusion, I respectfully ask your attention to this protest, and have the honor to be, &c, (Signed)

Rose O. N. Greenhow

JULIA WARD HOWE, *Battle Hymn of the Republic*

Overshadowed by the more dynamic Stanton and Anthony, in her own lifetime Julia Ward Howe (1819-1910) was celebrated as the author of the lyrics for *The Battle Hymn of the Republic,* the defining Civil War song that memorialized the righteousness of the Union cause. Howe wrote the lyrics in 1861 and the song was published a year later. The song still resonates in the present era. The chorus was not part of the song as first published. Although a contemporary of Stanton and Anthony, Howe did not join the suffrage struggle until after the Civil War. With her colleagues Lucy Stone and Thomas Wentworth Higginson in 1869 she helped organize the American Woman's Suffrage Association, (AWSA) the cautious rival of the Stanton and Anthony, National Woman's Suffrage Association (NWSA) founded earlier in the same year. For many years Howe served as one of the editors of the organization's *Woman's Journal.* Abolitionist men such as Higginson and Frederick Douglas played key roles in the AWSA, promoted African American male voting rights and also supported their female associates in the campaign for women's suffrage.

Howe advocated other reforms including pacifism and a mother's day celebration that would link women across national borders in the cause of universal peace. She also played a key role in the repudiation of Dr. Edward H. Clarke's medical misinformation that served to frighten women from attending college. The lyrics of her famous hymn appear below. In what ways did Howe fuse religion with the Union cause?*

Mine eyes have seen the glory
Of the coming of the Lord;
He is trampling out the vintage
Where the grapes of wrath are stored;
He hath loosed the fateful lightning
Of His terrible swift sword;
His truth is marching on.

Chorus
Glory! Glory! Hallelujah!
Glory! Glory! Hallelujah!
Glory! Glory! Hallelujah!
His truth is marching on.

I have seen Him in the watchfires
Of a hundred circling camps
They have builded Him an altar
In the evening dews and damps;

I can read His righteous sentence
By the dim and flaring lamps;
His day is marching on.

Chorus
Glory! Glory! Hallelujah!
Glory! Glory! Hallelujah!
Glory! Glory! Hallelujah!
His truth is marching on.

I have read a fiery gospel writ
In burnished rows of steel:
"As ye deal with My contemners,
So with you My grace shall deal":
Let the Hero born of woman
Crush the serpent with His heel,
Since God is marching on.

* *The Battle Hymn of the Republic,* lyrics originally published *The Atlantic Monthly,* 1862, did not include the chorus.

Chorus
Glory! Glory! Hallelujah!
Glory! Glory! Hallelujah!
Glory! Glory! Hallelujah!
His truth is marching on.

He has sounded forth the trumpet
That shall never call retreat;
He is sifting out the hearts of men
Before His judgement seat;
Oh, be swift, my soul, to answer Him;
Be jubilant, my feet;
Our God is marching on.

Chorus
Glory! Glory! Hallelujah!
Glory! Glory! Hallelujah!

Glory! Glory! Hallelujah!
His truth is marching on.

In the beauty of the lilies
Christ was born across the sea,
With a glory in His bosom
That transfigures you and me;
As He died to make men holy,
Let us die to make men free;
While God is marching on.

Chorus
Glory! Glory! Hallelujah!
Glory! Glory! Hallelujah!
Glory! Glory! Hallelujah!
His truth is marching on.

CLARA BARTON, *Nursing on the Firing Line* (c. 1870)

In this document, Clara Barton (1821–1912) described the ordeals she faced as a battlefield nurse caring for wounded Union soldiers. Although she won national acclaim for her nursing, her contribution also involved fund-raising and collecting and distributing medical supplies. Like other Civil War women nurses, Barton had to overcome enormous resistance. How did Barton deal with the argument that nursing wounded soldiers was inappropriate and "unseemly for a woman"?*

I was strong and thought I might go to the rescue of the men who fell. The first regiment of troops, the old 6th Mass. that fought its way through Baltimore, brought my playmates and neighbors, the partakers of my childhood; the brigades of New Jersey brought scores of my brave boys, the same solid phalanx; and the strongest legions from old Herkimer brought the associates of my seminary days. They formed and crowded around me. What could I do but go with them, or work for them and my country? The patriot blood of my father was warm in my veins. The country which he had fought for, I might at least work for, and I had offered my service to the government in the capacity of a double clerkship at twice $1400 a year, upon discharge of two disloyal clerks from its employ—the salary never to be given to me, but to be turned back into the U.S. Treasury then poor to beggary, with no currency, no credit. But there was no law for this, and it could not be done, and I would not draw salary from our government in such peril, so I resigned and went into direct service of the sick and wounded troops wherever found.

But I struggled long and hard with my sense of propriety—with the appalling fact that I was only a woman whispering in one ear, and thundering in the other the groans of suffering men dying like dogs—unfed and

---

* From Perry Epler, *Life of Clara Barton* (New York: Macmillan, 1915), 31–32, 35–43, 45, 59, 96–98.

unsheltered, for the life of every institution which had protected and educated me!

I said that I struggled with my sense of propriety and I say it with humiliation and shame. I am ashamed that I thought of such a thing.

When our armies fought on Cedar Mountain, I broke the shackles and went to the field. . . .

Five days and nights with three hours sleep—a narrow escape from capture—and some days of getting the wounded into hospitals at Washington, brought Saturday, August 30. And if you chance to feel, that the positions I occupied were rough and unseemly for a *woman*—I can only reply that they were rough and unseemly for *men*. But under all, lay the life of the nation. I had inherited the rich blessing of health and strength of constitution—such as are seldom given to woman—and I felt that some return was due from me and that I ought to be there. . . .

You generous thoughtful mothers and wives have not forgotten the tons of preserves and fruits with which you filled our hands. Huge boxes of these stood beside that railway track. Every can, jar, bucket, bowl, cup or tumbler, when emptied, that instant became a vehicle of mercy to convey some preparation of mingled bread and wine, or soup or coffee to some helpless famishing sufferer who partook of it with the tears rolling down his bronzed cheeks, and divide his blessings between the hands that fed him and his God. I never realized until that day how little a human being could be grateful for, and that day's experience also taught me the utter worthlessness of that which could not be made to contribute directly to our necessities. The bit of bread which would rest on the surface of a gold eagle was worth more than the coin itself.

But the most fearful scene was reserved for the night. I have said that the ground was littered with dry hay and that we had only two lanterns, but there were plenty of candles. The wounded were laid so close that it was impossible to move about in the dark. The slightest misstep brought a torrent of groans from some poor mangled fellow in your path.

Consequently here were seen persons of all grades, from the careful man of God who walked with a prayer upon his lips, to the careless driver hunting for his lost whip—each wandering about among this hay with an open flaming candle in his hands.

The slightest accident, the mere dropping of a light could have enveloped in flames this whole mass of helpless men.

How we watched and pleaded and cautioned as we worked and wept that night! How we put socks and slippers upon the cold, damp feet, wrapped your blankets and quilts about them, and when we had no longer these to give, how we covered them in the hay and left them to their rest!

Clara Barton (Matthew Brady/National Archives and Records Administration)

PHOEBE YATES LEVY PEMBER, *A Southern Woman's Story* (1879)

Phoebe Yates Levy Pember (1823–1913) was a member of an elite Southern Jewish family. In 1862, she was appointed to the position of matron of the Confederate Chimborazo Hospital in Richmond, Virginia. In the following excerpt, Pember recounts the activism of Southern women on behalf of the Confederacy. Her story serves as a reminder that men governed hospital nursing. The presence of women in hospitals was bitterly resented although desperately needed. What information does Pember's account supply about male resentment? What role did southern women play?*

The women of the South had been openly and violently rebellious from the moment they thought their states' rights touched. They incited the men to struggle in support of their views, and whether right or wrong, sustained them nobly to the end. They were the first to rebel—the last to succumb. Taking an active part in all that came within their sphere, and often compelled to go beyond this when the field demanded as many soldiers as could be raised; feeling a passion of interest in every man in the gray uniform of the Confederate service; they were doubly anxious to give comfort and assistance to the sick and wounded. In the course of a long and harassing war, with port blockaded and harvests burnt, rail tracks constantly torn up, so that supplies of food were cut off, and sold always at exorbitant prices, no appeal was ever made to the women of the South, individually or collectively, that did not meet with a ready response. There was no parade of generosity; no published lists of donations, inspected by public eyes. What was contributed was given unostentatiously, whether a barrel of coffee or the only half bottle of wine in the giver's possession.

About this time one of these large hospitals was to be opened, and the wife of George W. Randolph, Secretary of War, offered me the superindendence—rather a startling proposition to a woman used to all the comforts of luxurious life. Foremost among the Virginia women, she had given her resources of mind and means to the sick, and her graphic and earnest representations of the benefit a good and determined woman's rule could effect in such a position, settled the result in my mind. The natural idea that such a life would be injurious to the delicacy and refinement of a lady—that her nature would become deteriorated and her sensibilities blunted, was rather appalling. But the first step only costs, and that was soon taken.

A preliminary interview with the surgeon-in-chief gave necessary confidence. He was energetic—capable—skillful. A man with ready oil to pour upon troubled waters. Difficulties melted away beneath the warmth of his ready interest, and mountains sank into mole-hills when his quick comprehension had surmounted and leveled them. However troublesome daily increasing annoyances became, if they could not be removed, his few and ready words sent applicants and grumblers home satisfied to do the best they could. Wisely he decided to have an educated and efficient woman at the head of his hospital, and having succeeded, never allowed himself to forget that fact.

The day after my decision was made found me at "headquarters," the only two-story building on hospital ground, then occupied by the chief surgeon and his clerks. He had not yet made his appearance that morning, and while awaiting him, many of his

* From Phoebe Yates Pember, *A Southern Woman's Story: Life in Confederate Richmond,* Bell Irwin Wiley, ed. (Jackson, TN: McCowat-Mercer, 1959). Reprinted by permission of Broadfoot Publishing Company.

corps, who had expected in horror the advent of female supervision, walked in and out, evidently inspecting me. There was at the time a general ignorance on all sides, except among the hospital officials, of the decided objection on the part of the latter to the carrying out of a law which they prognosticated would entail "petticoat government"; but there was no mistaking the stage-whisper which reached my ears from the open door of the office that morning, as the little contract surgeon passed out and informed a friend he met, in a tone of ill-concealed disgust, that *"one of them had come."*

CHARLOTTE FORTEN, *Letter to William Lloyd Garrison* (1862)

A member of one of the nation's most prominent free African American families, Charlotte Forten (1837–1914) joined other women who served as teachers to contraband slaves under the protection of the Union army. In what ways did Forten find in her teaching experience "great happiness" but also that it was "more fatiguing than at the North"?*

St. Helena's Island, South Carolina

November 20, 1862

My Dear Friend:

St. Helena's Island, on which I am, is about six miles from the mainland of Beaufort. I must tell you that we were rowed hither from Beaufort by a crew of negro boatmen, and that they sang for us several of their own beautiful songs. There is a peculiar wildness and solemnity about them which cannot be described, and the people accompany the singing with a singular swaying motion of the body which seems to make it more effective.

As far as I have been able to observe, the negroes here rejoice in their new-found freedom. It does me good to see how *jubilant* they are over the downfall of their "secesh" masters. I do not believe that there is a man, woman, or even a child that would submit to be made a slave again. They are a truly religious people. They speak to God with a loving familiarity. Another trait that I have noticed is their natural courtesy of manner. There is nothing cringing about it, but it seems inborn, and one might almost say elegant. It marks their behavior toward each other as well as to the white people.

My school is about a mile from here, in the little Baptist church, which is in a grove of white oaks. These trees are beautiful—evergreen—and every branch heavily draped with long, bearded moss, which gives them a strange, mournful look. There are two ladies in the school besides myself—Miss T and Miss M—both of whom are most enthusiastic teachers. At present, our school is small—many of the children being ill with whooping cough—but in general it averages eighty or ninety. It is a great happiness to teach them. I wish some of those persons at the North who say the race is hopelessly and naturally inferior could see the readiness with which these children, so long oppressed and deprived of every privilege, learn and understand.

I have some grown pupils—people on our own plantation—who take lessons in the evenings. It will amuse you to know that one of them,—our man-of-all-work—is name *Cupid*. (Venuses and Cupids are very

_____

* From Charlotte Forten, "Letter to William Lloyd Garrison." Reprinted in *We Are Your Sisters: Black Women in the Nineteenth Century,* edited by Dorothy Sterling, copyright © 1984 by Dorothy Sterling. Used by permission of W. W. Norton & Company, Inc.

common here.) He told me he was "feared" he was almost too old to learn, but I assured him that that was not the case, and now he is working diligently at the alphabet. One of my people—Harry—is a scholar to be proud of. He makes most wonderful improvement. I never saw anyone so determined to learn. . . .

These people have really a great deal of musical talent. It is impossible to give you any idea of their songs and hymns. They are so wild, so strange, and yet so invariably harmonious and sweet. There is one of their hymns—"Roll Jordan Roll"—that I never listen to without seeming to hear, almost to feel, the rolling of waters. There is a great rolling wave of sound through it all. . . .

After the lessons, we talk freely to the children, often giving them slight sketches of some of the great and good men. Before teaching them the "John Brown" song, which they learned to sing with great spirit, Miss T. told them the story of the brave old man who had died for them. I told them about Toussaint, thinking it well they should know what one of their own color had done. They listened attentively and seemed to understand. We found it rather hard to keep their attention in school. It is not strange, as they have been so entirely unused to intellectual concentration. It is necessary to interest them every moment, in order to keep their thoughts from wandering. Teaching here is consequently far more fatiguing than at the North.

ELIZABETH PACKARD, Excerpt from *The Prisoner's Hidden Life or Insane Asylums Unveiled* (1868)

Elizabeth Packard (1816–1897) had the audacity to question her minister husband's religious beliefs privately as well as in a Bible study group. When she refused to submit to her husband's pressure to repudiate her views, he declared her insane and had her committed to an asylum where she remained imprisoned for three years. At the time of her commitment, she had six children and had been married more than twenty years. Her youngest child was only eighteen months old. Her husband alleged that her religious beliefs endangered her children and demonstrated her insanity.

This was the Civil War era and little had changed in the husband's legal right to control his wife. Elizabeth Packard's defiance was a smaller-scale reenactment of resistance to orthodoxy and male authority and subsequent punishment that Anne Hutchinson had endured two hundred years earlier. Fortunately for Packard, her ordeal had a happier resolution. A courtroom trial in 1864 led to a verdict in her favor. The trial focused on whether her husband, after her release from three years in the asylum, had the legal right to imprison her in a room. This was carrying even a husband's power too far. Her personal freedom secured, Packard spent the rest of her life engaged in a struggle to rally support for laws that would limit a husband's power to have his wife committed to an insane asylum. What significance does Packard give to the loss of a married woman's identity? How did this loss of identity relate to Packard's personal ordeal?*

XII Introduction

It is to delineate these spiritual wrongs of woman, that I have given my narrative to the public, hoping that my more tangible experiences may draw the attention of the philanthropic public to a more just consideration of married woman's legal disabilities; for since the emancipation of the negro, there is no class of American citizens, who so much need legal protection, and who receive so little, as this class.

As their representative, I do not make complaint of physical abuses, but it is the usurpation of our natural rights of which we complain; and it is our legal position of

---

* In the public domain.

nonentity, which renders us so liable and exposed to suffering and persecution from this source.

In the following narrative of my experiences, the reader will therefore find the interior of woman's life delineated through the exterior surroundings of her bitter experiences. I state facts through which the reader may look in to woman's soul, as through a mirror, that her realm of suffering may be thus portrayed.

I therefore commence my narrative where my persecution commenced, with the marital usurpation of my rights of opinion and conscience, and as I progress, will note such incidents as I can best employ to portray my feelings, rather than the recital of the physical abuses I witnessed; since my Coadjutors and the Committee have so graphically described the exterior life of the prisoner, it is unnecessary for me to enlarge on this feature of prison life in Insane Asylums. . . .

I have been Illinois State's Prisoner three years in Jacksonville Insane Asylum, for simply expressing religious opinions in a community who were unprepared to appreciate and understand them. I was incarcerated June 18, 1860, and liberated June 18, 1863. Fortunately for me, all these obnoxious views were presented in writing, and are now in my own possession, although they were, secretly taken from me, at the time of my abduction, and retained for years in the hands of my persecutor, Rev. Theophilus Packard, who was at that time the pastor of the Old School Presbyterian Church at Manteno, Kankakee County, Illinois.

He had been my husband for twenty-one years, and was the father of my six children, five of whom are boys, and one girl. At the time he forced me from my dear little ones, my daughter was ten years old and my babe eighteen months. I was in perfect health and of sound mind, and cheerfully and faithfully performing the duties of wife and mother to the entire satisfaction of my family and society, so far as I know. And, since the only plea Mr. Packard makes in defence of this course is,

that my religious views were dangerous to the spiritual interests of his children and the community, I feel called upon to present these views, frankly and candidly, that my readers may judge for themselves whether my imprisonment can be justified on this basis.

As an Introduction therefore to my "Hidden Life" in my prison, I shall present these views just as I presented them to the bible class in Manteno, a few weeks before my incarceration. I became connected with this class at the special request of Deacon Abijah Dole, the teacher of the class, and with the full and free consent of my husband. Mr. Dole gave as his reason for wishing me to join his class, that he found it impossible to awaken any interest, and he fondly hoped that I might bring forward some views which might elicit the attention he desired. I seated myself among his pupils, who then numbered only six men in all, as a sincere seeker after the truth. Mr. Dole allowed his pupils to be regarded as mutual teachers, so that all were allowed to ask questions and offer suggestions. Availing myself of this license, others were encouraged to follow my example, so that our class soon became the place of animating discussions, and as our tolerant teacher allowed both sides of a question to be discussed I found it became to me a great source of pleasure and profit. Indeed, I never can recollect a time when my mind grew into a knowledge of religious truths faster, than under the influence of these free and animated discussions. The effect of these debates was felt throughout the whole community, so that our class of seven soon increased to forty-six, including the most influential members of the community.

About this time a latent suspicion seemed to be aroused, lest the church creed be endangered by this license of free inquiry and fair discussion; and a meeting of some of the leading church-members was called, wherein this bible-class was represented as being a dangerous influence, involving the exposure of the creed to the charge of fallibility.

> **FRANCES WATKINS HARPER,** *"We Are All Bound Up Together," Address to the 11th National Women's Convention, New York* (1866)

Frances Watkins Harper (1825–1911) worked for years as a domestic, despite her literary gifts and education. Almost all doors of employment were closed to freeborn African American women. Harper was an abolitionist, a crusader for civil rights, and as she described in the following address, a supporter of women's rights who joined the cause as the result of her own experiences as a widow. African American women linked racial equality and women's rights because of their experience of interlocking racial and gender oppression. White women addressed the need for gender equality and rights in a universal language that ignored or glossed over the racial discrimination women of color confronted. Supporting the ballot for African American men, Harper rejected Stanton's and Anthony's bitter denunciation of the omission of women from voting rights. In the following speech to the Women's Rights Convention in 1866, Harper tried to alert her mainly white audience to the need to address racial injustice. In her speech, she refers to the hostile environment of racial segregation that African American women, including the iconic Harriet Tubman, confronted in the North as well as the South. In the last paragraph, her reference to "Moses" refers to Tubman, who was known as the Moses of her people, for leading them out of slavery (see Chapter 5). What events in Harper's life awakened her to the need to support women's rights as a gender-based reform? Why does Harper devote a significant part of her speech to woman's "wrongs"? What does her title "We Are All Bound Up Together" mean?*

I feel I am something of a novice upon this platform. Born of a race whose inheritance has been outrage and wrong, most of my life had been spent in battling against those wrongs. But I did not feel as keenly as others, that I had these rights, in common with other women, which are now demanded. About two years ago, I stood within the shadows of my home. A great sorrow had fallen upon my life. My husband had died suddenly, leaving me a widow, with four children, one my own, and the others stepchildren. I tried to keep my children together. But my husband died in debt; and before he had been in his grave three months, the administrator had swept the very milk crocks and wash tubs from my hands. I was a farmer's wife and made butter for the Columbus market; but what could I do, when they had swept all away? They left me one thing and that was a looking glass! Had I died instead of my husband, how different would have been the result! By this time he would have had another wife, it is likely; and no administrator would have gone into his house, broken up his home, and sold his bed, and taken away his means of support. I took my children in my arms, and went out to seek my living. While I was gone; a neighbor to whom I had once lent five dollars, went before a magistrate and swore that he believed I was a non resident, and laid an attachment on my very bed. And I went back to Ohio with my orphan children in my arms, without a single feather bed in this wide world, that was not in the custody of the law. I say, then, that justice is not fulfilled so long as woman is unequal before the law.

We are all bound up together in one great bundle of humanity, and society cannot trample on the weakest and feeblest of its members without receiving the curse in its own soul. You tried that in the case of the negro. You pressed him down for two centuries; and in so doing you crippled the moral strength and paralyzed the spiritual

---

*Frances Ellen Watkins Harper, *We Are All Bound Up Together: Proceedings of the Eleventh Women's Rights Convention* (New York: Robert J. Johnston, 1866), pp. 45–48.

energies of the white men of the country. When the hands of the black were fettered, white men were deprived of the liberty of speech and the freedom of the press. Society cannot afford to neglect the enlightenment of any class of its members. At the South, the legislation of the country was in behalf of the rich slaveholders, while the poor white man was neglected. What is the consequence to day? From that very class of neglected poor white men, comes the man who stands to day, with his hand upon the helm of the nation. He fails to catch the watchword of the hour, and throws himself, the incarnation of meanness, across the pathway of the nation. . . .

This grand and glorious revolution which has commenced, will fail to reach its climax of success, until throughout the length and brea[d]th of the American Republic, the nation shall be so color-blind, as to know no man by the color of his skin or the curl of his hair. It will then have no privileged class, trampling upon outraging the unprivileged classes, but will be then one great privileged nation, whose privilege will be to produce the loftiest manhood and womanhood that humanity can attain.

I do not believe that giving the woman the ballot is immediately going to cure all the ills of life. I do not believer that white women are dew-drops just exhaled from the skies. I think that like men they may be divided into three classes, the good, the bad, and the indifferent. The good would vote according to their convictions and principles; the bad, as dictated by preju[d]ice or malice; and the indifferent will vote on the strongest side of the question, with the winning party. You white women speak here of rights. I speak of wrongs. I, as a colored woman, have had in this country an education which has made me feel as if I were in the situation of Ishmael, my hand against every man, and every man's hand against me. Let me go to-morrow morning and take my seat in one of your street cars—I do not know that they will do it in New York, but they will in Philadelphia—and the conductor will put up his hand and stop the car rather than let me ride.

A Lady—They will not do that here.

Mrs. Harper—They do in Philadelphia. Going from Washington to Baltimore this Spring, they put me in the smoking car. (Loud Voices—"Shame.") Aye, in the capital of the nation, where the black man consecrated himself to the nation's defence, faithful when the white man was faithless, they put me in the smoking car! They did it once; but the next time they tried it, they failed; for I would not go in. I felt the fight in me; but I don't want to have to fight all the time. To-day I am puzzled where to make my home. I would like to make it in Philadelphia, near my own friends and relations. But if I want to ride in the streets of Philadelphia, they send me to ride on the platform with the driver. (Cries of "Shame.") Have women nothing to do with this? Not long since, a colored woman took her seat in an Eleventh Street car in Philadelphia, and the conductor stopped the car, and told the rest of the passengers to get out, and left the car with her in it alone, when they took it back to the station. One day I took my seat in a car, and the conductor came to me and told me to take another seat. I just screamed "murder." The man said if I was black I ought to behave myself. I knew that if he was white he was not behaving himself. Are there no wrongs to be righted? . . .

We have a woman in our country who has received the name of "Moses," not by lying about it, but by acting out (applause)—a woman who has gone down into the Egypt of slavery and brought out hundreds of our people into liberty. The last time I saw that woman, her hands were swollen. That woman who had led one of Montgomery's most successful expeditions, who was brave enough and secretive enough to act as a scout for the American army, had her hands all swollen from a conflict with a brutal conductor, who undertook to eject her from her place. That woman, whose courage and bravery won a recognition from our army and from every black man in the land, is excluded from every thoroughfare of travel. Talk of giving women the ballot-box? Go on. It is a normal school, and the white women of this country need it. While there exists this brutal element in society which tramples upon the feeble and treads down the weak, I tell you that if there is any class of people who need to be lifted out of their airy nothings and selfishness, it is the white women of America. (Applause.)

CATHARINE BEECHER AND HARRIET BEECHER STOWE, *Why Women Should Not Seek the Vote* (1869)

Suffragists combated women's acceptance of their submissive roles and their resistance to identifying with the need to vote. In the following document, two of the nation's best-known women—Catharine Beecher (1800–1878), the advocate of teaching as a woman's profession, and Harriet Beecher Stowe (1811–1896), the author of the enormously successful abolitionist novel, *Uncle Tom's Cabin*—expressed their views on women's suffrage. The sisters' personal achievements testified to the expansion of women's roles, yet both rejected voting rights for women. Which specific aspects of their argument support women's subordinate roles? Why did they believe that the entire suffrage effort was doomed to failure?*

Many intelligent and benevolent persons imagine that the grand remedy for the heavy evils that oppress our sex is to introduce woman to political power and office, to make her a party in primary political meetings, in political caucuses, and in the scramble and fight for political offices; thus bringing into this dangerous *melée* the distinctive tempting power of her sex. Who can look at this new danger without dismay? . . .

Let us suppose that our friends have gained the ballot and the powers of office: are there any real beneficent measures for our sex, which they would enforce by law and penalties, that fathers, brothers, and husbands would not grant to a united petition of our sex, or even to a majority of the wise and good? Would these not confer what the wives, mothers, and sisters deemed best for themselves and the children they are to train, very much sooner than they would give power and office to our sex to enforce these advantages by law? Would it not be a wiser thing to *ask* for what we need, before trying so circuitous and dangerous a method? God has given to man the physical power, so that all that woman may gain, either by petitions or by ballot, will be the gift of love or of duty; and the ballot never will be accorded till benevolent and conscientious men are the majority—a millennial point far beyond our present ken.

---

* From Catharine Beecher and Harriet Beecher Stowe, "Why Women Should Not Seek the Vote," 1869. Reprinted in *Major Problems in American Women's History*, 2d ed., Mary Beth Norton and Ruth M. Alexander, eds., copyright © 1996 by Houghton Mifflin Company.

ELIZABETH CADY STANTON, *On Marriage and Divorce* (c1870)

Elizabeth Cady Stanton (1815–1902) the mother of seven children, combined motherhood with a life-long commitment to a wide range of women's rights reforms. The author of the Declaration of Sentiments, (Chapter 7) her half-century friendship and collaboration with Susan B. Anthony added to the momentum of women's rights reforms. In an era when it was difficult for a women to obtain a divorce, Stanton advocated liberal divorce laws. She addressed the New York State Senate Judiciary on the subject of divorce reform in 1861 and returned to the issue on different occasions, including the Women's Rights Convention in 1870 that contains the following excerpt. Divorce reform was a radical idea at a time when marriage was regarded as a life-time arrangement and for many a religious sacrament. Stanton argued that marriage was a civil contract that for a variety of reasons could be dissolved. Her views on marriage and divorce alienated more cautious women reformers. How did Stanton link the power of men to the abuse of women? On what grounds did she advocate divorce?*

All this talk about the indissoluble tie and the sacredness of marriage, irrespective of the character and habits of the husband, is for its effect on woman. She never could have been held the pliant tool she is today but for the subjugation of her religious nature to the idea that in whatever condition she found herself as man's subject, that condition was ordained of Heaven; whether burning on the funeral pile of her husband in India, or suffering the slower torture of bearing children every year in America to drunkards, diseased, licentious men, at the expense of her own life and health, and the enfeebling of both the mind and body of her progeny. Women would not live as they now do in this enlightened age in violation of every law of their being, giving the very hey-day of their existence to the exercise of one an-imal function, if subordination to man had not been made through the ages the cardinal point of their religious faith and daily life. It requires but little thought to see that . . . the indissoluble tie was found to be necessary in order to establish man's authority over woman. The argument runs thus:

Men all admit that if two cannot be agreed they must part. This may apply to partners in business, pastor and people, physi-cian and patient, master and servant, and many other relations in life; but in the case of parent and child, husband and wife, as their relations cannot be dissolved, there must be some alternate authority to decide all matters on which they cannot agree, hence man's headship. These cases should be distin-guished, however; the child is free to act on his own opinions, by law, at a certain age, and the tie is practically dissolved between him and the parent so soon as he earns his own bread. The child is under the parent's control only during its minority; but the wife's condi-tion is perpetual minority, lifelong subjection to authority, with no appeal, no hope on the indissoluble tie theory. The practical effect of this is to make tyrants of men and fools of women. There never was a human being yet on this footstool godlike enough to be trusted with the absolute control of any living thing. Men abuse each other. Look in your prisons, jails, asylums, battle-fields and camps, they abuse their horses, dogs, cats. . . . They abuse their own children, and of course they will abuse their wives, taught by law and gospel that they own them as property, especially as a wife can vex and thwart a man, as no other living thing can . . .

---

*From Elizabeth Cady Stanton, "On Marriage and Divorce," reprinted in Paulina Wright Davis, *History of the National Woman's Rights Movement for Twenty Years . . . From 1850 to 1870* (New York: Journeymen Printers' Cooperative Association, 1871), 62–83.

SUSAN B. ANTHONY, *Proceedings of the Trial* (1873)

No woman in American history did more for the suffrage cause than Susan B. Anthony (1820–1906). Her decision to vote in the 1872 presidential election put into action suffragists' hope that women already possessed the right to vote under the Fourteenth Amendment. This strategy failed. Women, including Virginia Minor, were turned away at the polls. Anthony managed to cast a ballot but was subsequently arrested by a U.S. marshal and brought to trial.

The following excerpt from the trial documents Anthony's defiant outrage. How does her speech illuminate feminist demands for equal rights? In what ways does her defense echo the rationale for equality found in the Declaration of Sentiments (see Chapter 7). Ultimately the U.S. Supreme Court resolved the issue of whether the Fourteenth Amendment gave women the right to vote. The negative decision was expressed in *Minor v. Happersett* (1875). Women possessed citizenship but only the individual states could determine suffrage eligibility. For women, the Reconstruction-era promise of suffrage ended with this Supreme Court decision.*

JUDGE HUNT [*Ordering the defendant to stand up*]: Has the prisoner anything to say why sentence shall not be pronounced?

MISS ANTHONY: Yes, your honor, I have many things to say; for in your ordered verdict of guilty, you have trampled under foot every vital principle of our government. My natural rights, my civil rights, my political rights, my judicial rights, are all alike ignored. Robbed of the fundamental privilege of citizenship, I am degraded from the status of a citizen to that of a subject; and not only myself individually, but all of my sex, are, by your honor's verdict, doomed to political subjection under this, so-called, form of government.

JUDGE HUNT: The Court cannot listen to a rehearsal of arguments the prisoner's counsel has already consumed three hours in presenting.

MISS ANTHONY: May it please your honor, I am not arguing the question, but simply stating the reasons why sentence cannot, in justice, be pronounced against me. Your denial of my citizen's right to vote, is the denial of my right of consent as one of the governed, the denial of my right of representation as one of the taxed, the denial of my right to a trial by a jury of my peers as an offender against law, therefore, the denial of my sacred rights to life, liberty, property and—

JUDGE HUNT: The Court cannot allow the prisoner to go on.

MISS ANTHONY: But your honor will not deny me this one and only poor privilege of protest against this high-handed outrage upon my citizen's rights. May it please the Court to remember that since the day of my arrest last November, this is the first time that either myself or any person of my disfranchised class has been allowed a word of defense before judge or jury—

JUDGE HUNT: The prisoner must sit down—the Court cannot allow it.

MISS ANTHONY: All of my prosecutors, from the 8th ward corner grocery politician, who entered the compliant, to the United States Marshal, Commissioner, District Attorney, District Judge, your honor on the bench, not one is my peer, but each and all are my political sovereigns; and had your honor submitted my case to the jury, as was clearly your duty, even then I should have had just cause of protest, for

---

* From An Account of the Proceedings of the Trial of Susan B. Anthony, on the Charge of Illegal Voting, at the Presidential Election in Nov., 1872, and on the Trial of Beverly W. Jones, Edwin T. Marsh and William B. Hall, The Inspectors of Election by whom her Vote was Received (Rochester, NY: 1874).

not one of those men was my peer; but, native or foreign born, white or black, rich or poor, educated or ignorant, awake or asleep, sober or drunk, each and every man of them was my political superior; hence, in no sense, my peer. Even, under such circumstances, a commoner of England, tried before a jury of Lords, would have far less cause to complain than should I, a woman, tried before a jury of men. Even my counsel, the Hon. Henry R. Selden, who has argued my cause so ably, so earnestly, so unanswerably before your honor, is my political sovereign. Precisely as no disfranchised person is entitled to sit upon a jury, and no woman is entitled to the franchise, so, none but a regularly admitted lawyer is allowed to practice in the courts, and no woman can gain admission to the bar—hence, jury, judge, counsel, must all be of the superior class.

JUDGE HUNT: The Court must insist—the prisoner has been tried according to the established forms of law.

MISS ANTHONY: Yes, your honor, but by forms of law all made by men, interpreted by men, administered by men, in favor of men, and against women; and hence, your honor's ordered verdict of guilty; against a United States citizen for the exercise of *"that citizen's right to vote,"* simply because that citizen was a woman and not a man. But, yesterday, the same man made forms of law, declared it a crime punishable with $1,000 fine and six months imprisonment, for you, or me, or you of us, to give a cup of cold water, a crust of bread, or a night's shelter to a panting fugitive as he was tracking his way to Canada. And every man or woman in whose veins coursed a drop of human sympathy violated that wicked law, reckless of consequences, and was justified in so doing. As then, the slaves who got their freedom must take it over, or under, or through the unjust forms of law, precisely so, now, must women,

to get their right to a voice in this government, take it; and I have taken mine, and mean to take it at every possible opportunity.

JUDGE HUNT: The Court orders the prisoner to sit down. It will not allow another word.

MISS ANTHONY: When I was brought before your honor for trial, I hoped for a broad and liberal interpretation of the Constitution and its recent amendments, that should declare all United States citizens under its protecting gis—that should declare equality of rights the national guarantee to all persons born or naturalized in the United States. But failing to get this justice—failing, even, to get a trial by a jury *not* of my peers—I ask not leniency at your hands—but rather the full rigors of the law."

JUDGE HUNT: The Court must insist—

[*Here the prisoner sat down.*]

JUDGE HUNT: The prisoner will stand up.

[*Here Miss Anthony arose again.*]

The sentence of the Court is that you pay a fine of one hundred dollars and the costs of the prosecution.

MISS ANTHONY: May it please your honor, I shall never pay a dollar of your unjust penalty. All the stock in trade I possess is a $10,000 debt, incurred by publishing my paper—*The Revolution*—four years ago, the sole object of which was to educate all women to do precisely as I have done, rebel against your manmade, unjust, unconstitutional forms of law, that tax, fine, imprison and hang women, while they deny them the right of representation in the government; and I shall work on with might and main to pay every dollar of that honest debt, but not a penny shall go to this unjust claim. And I shall earnestly and persistently continue to urge all women to the practical recognition of the old revolutionary maxim, that "Resistance to tyranny is obedience to God."

Excerpt from *MINOR V. HAPPERSETT,* (1875)

The *Minor v. Happersett* Supreme Court decision from the perspective of women's history was an infamous obstruction that erased all hope of women as citizens gaining the right to vote under the terms of the Fourteenth Amendment. Virginia Minor (1824–1894), in a manner similar to that of Susan B. Anthony, also attempted to vote in the election of 1872. Unlike Anthony who actually managed to vote, Minor's attempt to register to vote was thwarted by the registrar. With the support of her husband, she filed a lawsuit against Happersett, the St. Louis, Missouri, voting official who refused to allow her to register. Her lawsuit expressed the hope of many suffragists that the Fourteenth Amendment could be interpreted to include women's right to vote. The case ultimately resulted in a hearing before the Supreme Court. In a unanimous decision the Court ruled against the claim that women as citizens possessed a constitutional right to vote.

Although Virginia Minor's name is linked to this Supreme Court decision, she also was a leading advocate for suffrage in her home state of Missouri and helped to organize and to serve as president of the Missouri Woman's Suffrage Association. She remained a suffrage activist until her death. On what grounds did the Supreme Court rule against the right of women to vote? The following document is an excerpt from the Supreme Court decision.*

ERROR to the Supreme Court of Missouri; the case being thus:

The fourteenth amendment to the Constitution of the United States, in its first section, thus ordains;

"All persons born or naturalized in the United States, and subject to the jurisdiction thereof, are citizens of the United States, and of the State wherein they reside. No State shall make or enforce any law, which shall abridge the privileges or immunities of citizens of the United States. Nor shall any State deprive any person of life, liberty, or property, without due process of law; nor deny to any person within its jurisdiction, the equal protection of the laws."

And the constitution of the State of Missouri thus ordains:

"Every male citizen of the United States shall be entitled to vote."

Under a statute of the State all persons wishing to vote at any election, must previously have been registered in the manner pointed out by the statute, this being a condition precedent to the exercise of the elective franchise.

In this state of things, on the 15th of October, 1872 (one of the days fixed by law for the registration of voters), Mrs. Virginia Minor, a native born, free, white citizen of the United States, and of the State of Missouri, over the age of twenty-one years, wishing to vote for electors for President and Vice-President of the United States, and for a representative in Congress, and for other officers, at the general election held in November, 1872, applied to one Happersett, the registrar of voters, to register her as a lawful voter, which he refused to do, assigning for cause that she was not a "male citizen of the United States," but a woman. She thereupon sued him in one of the inferior State courts of Missouri, for wilfully refusing to place her name upon the list of registered voters, by which refusal she was deprived of her right to vote.

The registrar demurred, and the court in which the suit was brought sustained the demurrer, and gave judgment in his favor; a judgment which the Supreme Court affirmed. Mrs. Minor now brought the case here on error.

CHIEF JUSTICE WAITE delivered the opinion of the court.

The question is presented in this case, whether, since the adoption of the fourteenth amendment, a woman, who is a citizen of the United States and of the State of Missouri, is a voter in that State, notwithstanding the provision of the constitution and laws of the State, which confine the right of suffrage to men alone. We might, perhaps, decide the case

---

* *Minor v. Happersett,* Supreme Court of the United States, 1875, 21 Wall (88 U.S.) 162.

upon other grounds, but this question is fairly made. From the opinion we find that it was the only one decided in the court below, and it is the only one which has been argued here. The case was undoubtedly brought to this court for the sole purpose of having that question decided by us, and in view of the evident propriety there is of having it settled, so far as it can be by such a decision, we have concluded to waive all other considerations and proceed at once to its determination . . .

In this condition of the law in respect to suffrage in the several States it cannot for a moment be doubted that if it had been intended to make all citizens of the United States voters, the framers of the Constitution would not have left it to implication. So important a change in the condition of citizenship as it actually existed, if intended, would have been expressly declared.

But if further proof is necessary to show that no such change was intended, it can easily be found both in and out of the Constitution. By Article 4, section 2, it is provided that "the citizens of each State shall be entitled to all the privileges and immunities of citizens in the several States." If suffrage is necessarily a part of citizenship, then the citizens of each State must be entitled to vote in the several States precisely as their citizens are. This is more than asserting that they may change their residence and become citizens of the State and thus be voters. It goes to the extent of insisting that while retaining their original citizenship they may vote in any State. This, we think, has never been claimed. And again, by the very terms of the amendment we have been considering (the fourteenth), "Representatives shall be apportioned among the several States according to their respective numbers, counting the whole number of persons in each State, excluding Indians not taxed. But when the right to vote at any election for the choice of electors for President and Vice-President of the United States, representatives in Congress, the executive and judicial officers of a State, or the members of the legislature thereof, is denied to any of the male inhabitants of such State, being

twenty-one years of age and citizens of the United States, or in any way abridged, except for participation in the rebellion, or other crimes, the basis of representation therein shall be reduced in the proportion which the number of such male citizens shall bear to the whole number of male citizens twenty-one years of age in such State." Why this, if it was not in the power of the legislature to deny the right of suffrage to some male inhabitants? And if suffrage was necessarily one of the absolute rights of citizenship, why confine the operation of the limitation to male inhabitants? Women and children are, as we have seen, "persons." They are counted in the enumeration upon which the apportionment is to be made, but if they were necessarily voters because of their citizenship unless clearly excluded, why inflict the penalty for the exclusion of males alone? Clearly, no such form of words would have been selected to express the idea here indicated if suffrage was the absolute right of all citizens.

And still again, after the adoption of the fourteenth amendment, it was deemed necessary to adopt a fifteenth, as follows: "The right of citizens of the United States to vote shall not be denied or abridged by the United States, or by any State, on account of race, color, or previous condition of servitude." The fourteenth amendment had already provided that no State should make or enforce any law which should abridge the privileges or immunities of citizens of the United States. If suffrage was one of these privileges or immunities, why amend the Constitution to prevent its being denied on account of race, &c.? Nothing is more evident than that the greater must include the less, and if all were already protected why go through with the form of amending the Constitution to protect a part?

It is true that the United States guarantees to every State a republican form of government. It is also true that no State can pass a bill of attainder, and that no person can be deprived of life, liberty, or property without due process of law. All these several provisions of the Constitution must be construed in connection with the other parts of the instrument, and in the light of the surrounding circumstances.

The guaranty is of a republican form of government. No particular government is designated as republican, neither is the exact form to be guaranteed, in any manner especially designated. Here, as in other parts of the instrument, we are compelled to resort elsewhere to ascertain what was intended.

The guaranty necessarily implies a duty on the part of the States themselves to provide such a government. All the States had governments when the Constitution was adopted. In all the people participated to some extent, through their representatives elected in the manner specially provided. These governments the Constitution did not change. They were accepted precisely as they were, and it is, therefore, to be presumed that they were such as it was the duty of the States to provide. Thus we have unmistakable evidence of what was republican in form, within the meaning of that term as employed in the Constitution.

As has been seen, all the citizens of the States were not invested with the right of suffrage. In all, save perhaps New Jersey, this right was only bestowed upon men and not upon all of them. Under these circumstances it is certainly now too late to contend that a government is not republican, within the meaning of this guaranty in the Constitution, because women are not made voters.

The same may be said of the other provisions just quoted.Women were excluded from suffrage in nearly all the States by the express provision of their constitutions and laws. If that had been equivalent to a bill of attainder, certainly its abrogation would not have been left to implication. Nothing less than express language would have been employed to effect so radical a change. So also of the amendment which declares that no person shall be deprived of life, liberty, or property without due process of law, adopted as it was as early as 1791. If suffrage was intended to be included within its obligations, language better adapted to express that intent would most certainly have been employed. The right of suffrage, when granted, will be protected. He

who has it can only be deprived of it by due process of law, but in order to claim protection he must first show that he has the right.

But we have already sufficiently considered the proof found upon the inside of the Constitution. That upon the outside is equally effective.

The Constitution was submitted to the States for adoption in 1787, and was ratified by nine States in 1788, and finally by the thirteen original States in 1790. Vermont was the first new State admitted to the Union, and it came in under a constitution which conferred the right of suffrage only upon men of the full age of twenty-one years, having resided in the State for the space of one whole year next before the election, and who were of quiet and peaceable behavior. This was in 1791. The next year, 1792, Kentucky followed with a constitution confining the right of suffrage to free male citizens of the age of twenty-one years who had resided in the State two years or in the county in which they offered to vote one year next before the election. Then followed Tennessee, in 1796, with voters of freemen of the age of twenty-one years and upwards, possessing a freehold in the county wherein they may vote, and being inhabitants of the State or freemen being inhabitants of any one county in the State six months immediately preceding the day of election. But we need not particularize further. No new State has ever been admitted to the Union which has conferred the right of suffrage upon women, and this has never been considered a valid objection to her admission. On the contrary, as is claimed in the argument, the right of suffrage was withdrawn from women as early as 1807 in the State of New Jersey, without any attempt to obtain the interference of the United States to prevent it. Since then the governments of the insurgent States have been reorganized under a requirement that before their representatives could be admitted to seats in Congress they must have adopted new constitutions, republican in form. In no one of these constitutions was suffrage conferred upon women, and yet the States have all been restored to their original position as States in the Union.

Besides this, citizenship has not in all cases been made a condition precedent to the enjoyment of the right of suffrage. Thus, in Missouri, persons of foreign birth, who have declared their intention to become citizens of the United States, may under certain circumstances vote. The same provision is to be found in the constitutions of Alabama, Arkansas, Florida, Georgia, Indiana, Kansas, Minnesota, and Texas.

Certainly, if the courts can consider any question settled, this is one. For nearly ninety years the people have acted upon the idea that the Constitution, when it conferred citizenship, did not necessarily confer the right of suffrage. If uniform practice long continued can settle the construction of so important an instrument as the Constitution of the United States confessedly is, most certainly it has been done here. Our province is to decide what the law is, not to declare what it should be.

We have given this case the careful consideration its importance demands. If the law is wrong, it ought to be changed; but the power for that is not with us. The arguments addressed to us bearing upon such a view of the subject may perhaps be sufficient to induce those having the power, to make the alteration, but they ought not to be permitted to influence our judgment in determining the present rights of the parties now litigating before us. No argument as to woman's need of suffrage can be considered. We can only act upon her rights as they exist. It is not for us to look at the hardship of withholding. Our duty is at an end if we find it is within the power of a State to withhold.

Being unanimously of the opinion that the Constitution of the United States does not confer the right of suffrage upon any one, and that the constitutions and laws of the several States which commit that important trust to men alone are not necessarily void, we affirm the judgment.

EDWARD H. CLARKE, *Sex in Education; Or a Fair Chance for the Girls* (1873)

A Harvard Medical School trustee, Dr. Edward H. Clarke argued against higher education for women at a time when increasing numbers of young women were applying to medical schools. At Harvard, Clarke voted against opening admission to women. In Clarke's medical opinion, intellectual effort ruined the mental and reproductive health of college women. Arising out of a combination of medical ignorance and a lengthy tradition of patriarchal control that argued for women's limited intellectual capacity, Clarke's views also expressed the increasing cultural emphasis on the need to safeguard the female reproductive function. What "evidence" did Clarke provide that a college education puts women's "complicated reproductive mechanisms" at risk? What purpose would this fear serve?*

This case needs very little comment: its teachings are obvious. Miss D— went to college in good physical condition. During the four years of her college life, her parents and the college faculty required her to get what is popularly called an education. Nature required her, during the same period, to build and put in working order a large and complicated

reproductive mechanism, a matter that is popularly ignored—shoved out of sight like a disgrace. She naturally obeyed the requirements of the faculty, which she could see, rather than the requirements of the mechanism within her that she could not see. Subjected to the college regimen, she worked four years in getting a liberal education. Her way of work was sustained

---

* From Edward H. Clark, M.D., *Sex in Education, or A Fair Chance for the Girls* (Boston: James R. Osgood and Co., 1873), 78–87.

and continuous, and out of harmony with the rhythmical periodicy of the female organization. The stream of vital and constructive force evolved within her was turned steadily to the brain, and away from the ovaries and their accessories. The result of this sort of education was, that these last-mentioned organs, deprived of sufficient opportunity and nutriment, first began to perform their functions with pain, a warning of error that was unheeded; then, to cease to grow; next, to set up once a month a grumbling torture that made life miserable; and, lastly, the brain and the whole nervous system, disturbed, in obedience to the law, that, if one member suffers, all the members suffer, became neuralgic and hysterical. And so Miss D—— spent the next few years succeeding her graduation in conflict with dysmenorrhea, headache, neuralgia, and hysteria. Her parents marveled at her ill health; and she furnished another text for the often-repeated sermon on the delicacy of American girls.

It may not be unprofitable to give the history of one more case of this sort. Miss E—— had an hereditary right to a good brain and to the best cultivation of it. Her father was one of our ripest and broadest American scholars, and her mother one of our most accomplished American women. They both enjoyed excellent health. Their daughter had a literary training— an intellectual, moral, and aesthetic half of education, such as their supervision would be likely to give, and one that few young men of her age receive. Her health did not seem to suffer at first. She studied, recited, walked, worked, stood, and the like, in the steady and sustained way that is normal to the male organization. She *seemed* to evolve force enough to acquire a number of languages, to become familiar with

the natural sciences, to take hold of philosophy and mathematics, and to keep in good physical case while doing all this. At the age of twenty-one she might have been presented to the public, on Commencement Day, by the president of Vassar College or of Antioch College or of Michigan University, as the wished-for result of American liberal female culture. Just at this time, however, the catamenical function began to show signs of failure of power. No severe or even moderate illness overtook her. She was subjected to no unusual strain. She was only following the regimen of continued and sustained work, regardless of Nature's periodical demands for a portion of her time and force, when, without any apparent cause, the failure of power was manifested by moderate dysmenorrhea and diminished excretion. Soon after this the function ceased altogether, and up to this present writing, a period of six or eight years, it has shown no more signs of activity than an amputated arm. In the course of a year or so after the cessation of the function, her head began to trouble her. First there was headache, then a frequent congested condition, which she described as a "rush of blood" to her head; and, by and by, vagaries and foreboding and despondent feelings began to crop out. Coincident with this mental state, her skin became rough and coarse, and an inveterate acne covered her face. She retained her appetite, ability to exercise, and sleep. A careful local examination of the pelvic organs, by an expert, disclosed no lesion or displacement there, no ovarian or other inflammation. Appropriate treatment faithfully persevered in was unsuccessful in recovering the lost function. I was finally obliged to consign her to an asylum.

Excerpt from *Bradwell v. Illinois* (1873)

Law was even more of a male preserve than medicine. In *Bradwell v. Illinois,* the U.S. Supreme Court upheld traditional gender roles. As with other restrictive arguments made in the post–Civil War period, women's feminine nature and reproductive function were used to deny them the right to practice law.

The last lines of the document refer to the fact that the plaintiff was married. Apparently, the Court found married women pursuing careers "repugnant." In what ways did the concept of gender influence the Court's decision?*

In regard to that amendment, counsel for plaintiff in this court truly says that there are certain privileges and immunities which belong to a citizen of the United States as such; otherwise it would be nonsense for the XIV Amendment to prohibit a State from abridging them, and he proceeds to argue that admission to the bar of a State of a person who possesses the requisite learning and character is one of those which a State may not deny.

In this latter proposition we are not able to concur with counsel. We agree with him that there are privileges and immunities belonging to citizens of the United States, in that relation and character, and that it is these, and these alone, which a State is forbidden to abridge. But the right to admission to practice in the courts of a State is not one of them. The right in no sense depends on citizenship of the United States. . . .

[From a Concurring Opinion]

The claim that, under the XIV Amendment of the Constitution, which declares that no State shall make or enforce any law which shall abridge the privileges and immunities of citizens of the United States, the statute law of Illinois, or the common law prevailing in that State, can no longer be set up as a barrier against the right of female to pursue any lawful employment for a livelihood (the practice of law included) assumes that it is one of the privileges and immunities of women as citizens to engage in any and every profession, occupation, or employment in civil life.

It certainly can not be affirmed, as a historical fact, that this has ever been established as one of the fundamental privileges and immunities of the sex. On the contrary, the civil law, as well as nature herself, has always recognized a wide difference in the respective spheres and destinies of man and woman. Man is, or should be, woman's protector and defender. The natural and proper timidity and delicacy which belongs to the female sex evidently unfits it for many of the occupations of civil life. The constitution of the family organization, which is founded in the divine ordinance, as well as in the nature of things, indicates the domestic sphere as that which properly belongs to the domain and functions of womanhood. The harmony, not to say identity, of interests and views which belong, or should belong, to the family institution is repugnant to the idea of a woman adopting a distinct and independent career from that of her husband.

AMELIA BARR, *Discontented Women* (1896)

Amelia Barr (1831–1919) was a novelist who wrote romantic stories about love and married life. Before she was forty years old, three of her six children and her husband died from Yellow Fever. Her success as an author provided the family's sole source of income. Although well aware of the many injustices women had to overcome in pursuing a career, she identified with the opponents of women's suffrage. Her argument against suffrage provides an excellent example of how anti-suffragists used gendered assumptions to deny women the ballot. Note how Barr contrasts "virile virtues" with "feminine softness." She claims that men possess reason, but women cannot go beyond their feminine natures, which "substitute sentiment for reason." Anti-suffragists viewed women's desire to vote as unnatural.

---

* *Bradwell v. Illinois,* Supreme Court of the United States, 1873, 83 U.S. (16 Wallace) 130, 141.

Barr linked women's discontent to Eve and believed it was necessary for women to control their own discontent. Her stress on women's "original sin" contradicted the conventional nineteenth-century emphasis on womanly virtue. How would you evaluate this gendered argument against women's suffrage? Discuss whether any part of Barr's argument would have relevance today?*

Discontent is a vice six thousand years old, and it will be eternal; because it is in the race. Every human being has a complaining side, but discontent is bound up in the heart of woman; it is her original sin. For if the first woman had been satisfied with her conditions, if she had not aspired to be "as gods," and hankered after unlawful knowledge, Satan would hardly have thought it worth his while to discuss her rights and wrongs with her. That unhappy controversy has never ceased; and, without reason, woman has been perpetually subject to discontent with her conditions and, according to her nature, has been moved by its influence. Some, it has made peevish, some plaintive, some ambitious, some reckless, while a noble majority have found in its very control that serene composure and cheerfulness which is granted to those who conquer, rather than to those who inherit.

Finally, women cannot get behind or beyond their nature, and their nature is to substitute sentiment for reason—a sweet and not unlovely characteristic in womanly ways and places; yet reason, on the whole, is considered a desirable necessity in politics. . . . [Women may cease to be women, but they can never learn to be men and feminine softness and grace can never do the work of the virile virtues of men.] Very fortunately this class of discontented women have not yet been able to endanger existing conditions by combinations analogous to trades unions; nor is it likely they ever will; because it is doubtful if women, under any circumstances, could combine at all. Certain qualities are necessary for combination, and these qualities are represented in women by their opposites. . . .

The one unanswerable excuse for woman's entrance into active public life of any kind, is *need* and alas! need is growing daily, as marriage becomes continually rare, and more women are left adrift in the world without helpers and protectors. But this is a subject too large to enter on here, though in the beginning it sprung from discontented women, preferring the work and duties of men to their own work and duties. Have they found the battle of life any more ennobling in masculine professions, than in their old feminine household ways? Is work done in the world for strangers, any less tiresome and monotonous, than work done in the house for father and mother, husband and children? If they answer truly, they will reply "the home duties were the easiest, the safest and the happiest."

Of course all discontented women will be indignant at any criticism of their conduct. They expect every one to consider their feelings without examining their motives. Paddling in the turbid maelstrom of life, and dabbling in politics and the most unsavory social questions, they still think men, at least, ought to regard them as the Sacred Sex. But women are not sacred by grace of sex, if they voluntarily abdicate its limitations and its modesties, and make a public display of unsexed sensibilities, an unabashed familiarity with subjects they have nothing to do with. If men criticize such women with asperity it is not to be wondered at; they have so long idealized women, that they find it hard to speak moderately. They excuse them too much, or else they are too indignant at their follies, and unjust and angry in their denunciation. Women must be criticized by women; then they will hear the bare uncompromising truth, and be the better for it.

---

* From Amelia Barr, "Discontented Women," in *North American Review* 162 (February 1896), 201, 205–7, 209.

CHAPTER 10

Separate Sisterhoods:
Identity and Division

The last decades of the nineteenth century were characterized by the founding of women's institutions and organizations. These separate institutions expressed the contested but still popular view that men and women needed a separate sphere or social space in which to fulfill their distinctive roles. Separate institutions resulted in part because male-dominated institutions excluded women but also enabled women to forge positive identities, strengthen the bonds of sisterhood, and create supportive networks. The refusal of men to grant women an opportunity for higher education in the colleges and universities that they controlled, provided the impetus for the establishment of separate female colleges, which had rigorous academic standards comparable to those of male institutions. In pursuit of a college education, M. Carey Thomas and other women of her generation had to surmount the pervasive perception that women were intellectually inferior, as well as the dismal medical warnings of "experts" such as Edward. Clarke (Chapter 9) that intellectual activity strained the weak female brain and nervous system, leading to the eventual collapse of the reproductive organs.

The proliferation of women's clubs expressed the need to create an environment in which women could gather socially and participate in cultural and intellectual activities. Club objectives quickly widened and became community oriented. Club women promoted projects such as kindergartens, libraries, playgrounds, and civic beautification. They lobbied for uncontaminated food and milk, clean streets, and better "municipal housekeeping." In 1890, thousands of local clubs formed the General Federation of Women's Clubs (GFWC). The GFWC played a major role in securing the passage of the Pure Food and Drug Act and promoted protective legislation for women and children. Club women's activism indicated how permeable the boundaries were between public and private spheres. As housewives, women responded to a wide range of public issues that affected the security of their homes and neighborhoods and the well-being of their families.

Activism grew out of traditional community service and the women's associations that had flourished since the 1800s. Club membership reached two million by 1915. Women's clubs expressed no concern for gender inequities, and the GFWC did not support the suffrage movement until 1914. Yet, critics such as former president Grover Cleveland, who took the ideology of separate spheres literally, viewed club involvement as the abandonment of motherhood and predicted national calamity if women continued their "club habit."

One of the most popular female organizations of the era, the Women's Christian Temperance Union (WCTU) was determined to rid the nation of alcohol. Unlike the pre–Civil War temperance activists who were auxiliaries in a male-directed movement, women led and managed the WCTU. Prohibition of alcohol was an infinitely more popular cause than women's rights. WCTU chapters sprang up throughout the United States. The WCTU sought to end drunken husbands' abuse of their wives. Under Frances Willard's leadership, the WCTU linked women's suffrage to the protection of the nation's homes and families from alcoholic abuse. With a focus on white Christian, more accurately, Protestant women, the organization was a prime example of identity based sisterhood. Non Christian women lacked appropriate religious affiliation. Efforts to recruit African American women collided with white racist views, including Willard's lack for support for the struggle of African American women such as Ida B. Wells against lynching.

The WCTU selective sisterhood was representative of a wider trend. Women's institutions were exclusive rather than inclusive; colleges, clubs, and organizations rarely crossed racial, class, religious or ethnic lines. Cultural and racial diversity undermined the development of an inclusive sisterhood. Newly opened women's colleges became enclaves for elite, white Protestant women. Jewish women were denied admission to Bryn Mawr college despite meeting the rigorous academic standards by anti Semitic policies upheld by the the college's first woman president M. Carey Thomas. Anna Julia Cooper's vision of a women's rights coalition across lines of difference did not occur. Within the social homogeneity of the women's suffrage organization, conformist thinking became the norm. Elizabeth Cady Stanton's feminist attack on religious orthodoxy presented in her book *The Bible and Church Degrade Women,* proved too radical for the growing conservatism of her suffragist colleagues, who sought her ostracism. Only Susan B. Anthony's intervention prevented an official denunciation.

African American middle-class women launched their own club movement. In their commitment to community service and female sociability, African American clubs paralleled those of white women. However, African American club women also sought to eradicate the racist stereotyping of women of color as sexually promiscuous—a racial and gender stereotype that justified white male sexual exploitation. Recognizing the intersection of race, class, and gender—the multiple burdens African American women confronted—club women adopted the motto "lifting as we climb." They emphasized that improved conditions for African American women could be gained only in the context of greater racial equality and opportunities for all African Americans. In organizing the National Association of Colored Women (NACW) in 1896, African American women created the first nationally organized civil rights association.

The late nineteenth century was characterized by heightened racism, fear of foreigners, a rising tide of anti Semitism and increasing class conflict. Jim Crow laws and segregated social patterns prevailed throughout the South and were validated by the U.S. Supreme Court in the 1896 *Plessy v. Ferguson* decision. Not only in the South, but throughout the nation, white supremacist values molded social behavior. Defying racial hostility, outspoken African American women followed the example of Ida B. Wells and Mary Church Terrell (Chapter 12) and opposed both the injustice and daily indignities of segregation as well as the deadly practice of lynching. The government effort to privatize tribal holdings and assimilate indigenous people demonstrated little concern or respect for Indian culture and ethnic identity. Zitkala–Sa's recollections of her school days relate the trauma of coerced Americanization (Chapter 11).

ANNA JULIA COOPER, *Address to the World's Congress of Representative Women, Chicago* **(1893)**

Born into slavery, the child of an enslaved mother and her owner, Anna Julia Cooper (1858–1964) had a lifelong dedication to learning. She received a B.A. and M.A. from Oberlin College. In her middle sixties, she completed a Ph.D. degree from the Sorbonne in Paris. Deeply intellectual, she was for most of her long life a teacher and educator, as well as during the 1930s the president of Frelinghuysen College. An advocate for racial justice and educational opportunity for African American women, she struggled against the increasing racism that blanketed the nation after Reconstruction ended. In the following speech, she charted the educational and intellectual progress of African American women since the end of slavery. She advocated racial and gender power equity to displace Anglo-American male privilege that denied equality to women as well as to African American men. The Congress of Representative Women was a forum for African Americans that met in Chicago separately from the city's Columbian Exposition, which excluded blacks from equitable representation and recognition. Despite explicit manifestations of racist policies on the part of white women, Cooper still hoped that racial inclusion would prevail. Unfortunately her hopes were not fulfilled, and the Supreme Court's *Plessey v. Ferguson* decision in 1896 acknowledged the constitutionality of racial segregation.

What evidence does Cooper provide of the accomplishments of black women? What aspects of their achievement merit her particular praise? How does her appeal to human rights relate to the objective of racial equality?*

The higher fruits of civilization can not be extemporized, neither can they be developed normally, in the brief space of thirty years. It requires the long and painful growth of generations. Yet all through the darkest period of the colored women's oppression in this country her yet unwritten history is full of heroic struggle, a struggle against fearful and overwhelming odds, that often ended in a horrible death, to maintain and protect that which woman holds dearer than life. The painful, patient, and silent toil of mothers to gain a free simple title to the bodies of their daughters, the despairing fight, as of an entrapped tigress, to keep hallowed their own persons, would furnish material for epics. That more went down under the flood than stemmed the current is not extraordinary. The majority of our women are not heroines but I do not know that a majority of any race of women are heroines. It is enough for me to know that while in the eyes of the highest tribunal in America she was deemed no more than a chattel, an irresponsible thing, a dull block, to be drawn hither or thither at the volition of an owner, the Afro American woman maintained ideals of womanhood unshamed by any ever conceived. Resting or fermenting in untutored minds, such ideals could not claim a hearing at the bar of the nation. [The white woman could least plead for her own emancipation; the black woman, doubly enslaved, could but suffer and struggle and be silent. I speak for the colored

---

* Anna Julia Cooper, in May Wright Sewell, ed., *The World's Congress of Representative Women* (Chicago: Rand, McNally, 1894), pp. 711–15.

women of the South, because it is there that the millions of blacks in this country have watered the soil with blood and tears, and it is there too that the colored woman of America has made her characteristic history, and there her destiny evolving. Since emancipation the movement has been at times confused and stormy, so that we could not always tell whether we were going forward or groping in a circle. We hardly knew what we ought to emphasize, whether education or wealth, or civil freedom and recognition. We were utterly destitute. Possessing no homes nor the knowledge of how to make them, no money nor the habit of acquiring it, no education, no political status, no influence, what could we do? But as Frederick Douglass had said in darker days than those, "One with God is a majority," and our ignorance had hedged us in from the fine spun theories of agnostics. We had remaining at least a simple faith that a just God is on the throne of the universe, and that somehow—we could not see, nor did we bother our heads to try to tell how—he would in his own good time make all right that seemed most wrong.

Schools were established, not merely public day schools, but home training and industrial schools, at Hampton, at Fisk, Atlanta, Raleigh, and other stations, and later, through the energy of the colored people themselves, such schools as the Wilberforce, the Livingstone, the Allen, and the Paul Quinn were opened. These schools were almost without exception co-educational. Funds were too limited to be divided on sex lines, even had it been ideally desirable; but our girls as well as our boys flocked in and battled for an education. Not even then was that patient, untrumpeted heroine, the slave-mother, released from self sacrifice, and many an unbuttered crust was in silent content that she might eke out enough from her poverty to send her young folks off to school. She "never had the chance," she would tell you, with tears on her withered cheek, so she wanted them to get all they could. The work

in these schools, and in such as these, has been like the little leaven hid in the measure of meal, permeating life throughout the length and breadth of the Southland, lifting up ideals of home and of womanhood; diffusing a contagious longing for higher living and purer thinking, inspiring woman herself with a new sense of her dignity in the eternal purposes of nature. To day there are twenty five thousand five hundred and thirty colored schools in the United States with one million three hundred and fifty-three thousand three hundred and fifty two pupils of both sexes. This is not quite the thirtieth year since their emancipation, and the color people hold in landed property for churches and schools twenty five million dollars. Two and one half million colored children have learned to read and write, and twenty two thousand nine hundred and fifty six colored men and women (mostly women) are teaching in these schools. According to Doctor Rankin, President of Howard University, there are two hundred and forty seven colored students (a large percentage of whom are women) now preparing themselves in the universities of Europe. Of other colleges which give the B.A. course to women, and are broad enough not to erect barriers against colored applicants, Oberlin, the first to open its doors to both woman and the negro, has given classical degrees to six colored women, one of whom, the first and most eminent, Fannie Jackson Coppin, we shall listen to tonight. Ann Arbor and Wellesley have each graduated three of our women; Cornell University one, who is now professor of sciences in a Washington high school. A former pupil of my own from the Washington High School who was snubbed by Vassar, has since carried off honors in a competitive examination in Chicago University. The medical and law colleges of the country are likewise bombarded by colored women, and every year some sister of the darker race claims their professional award of "well done." Eminent in their profession are Doctor Dillon and Doctor

James, and there sailed to Africa last month a demure little brown woman who had just outstripped a whole class of men in a medical college in Tennessee.

In organized efforts for self help and benevolence also our women have been active. The Colored Women's League, of which I am at present corresponding secretary, has active, energetic branches in the South and West. The branch in Kansas City, with a membership of upward of one hundred and fifty, already has begun under their vigorous president, Mrs. Yates, the erection of a building for friendless girls. Mrs. Coppin will, I hope, herself tell you something of her own magnificent creation of an industrial society in Philadelphia. The women of the Washington branch of the league have subscribed to a fund of about five thousand dollars to erect a woman's building for educational and industrial work, which is also to serve as headquarters for gathering and disseminating general information relating to the efforts of our women. This is just a glimpse of what we are doing.

Now, I think if I could crystallize the sentiment of my constituency, and deliver it as a message to this congress of women, it would be something like this: Let woman's claim be as broad in the concrete as in the abstract. We take our stand on the solidarity of humanity, the oneness of life, and the unnaturalness and injustice of all special favoritisms, whether of sex, race, country, or condition. If one link of the chain be broken, the chain is broken. A bridge is no stronger than its weakest part, and a cause is not worthier than its weakest element. Least of all can woman's cause afford to decry the weak. We want, then, as toilers for the universal triumph of justice and human rights, to go to our homes from this Congress, demanding an entrance not through a gateway for ourselves, our race, our sex, or our sect, but a grand highway for humanity. The colored woman feels that woman's cause is one and universal; and that not till the image of God, whether in parian or ebony, is sacred and inviolable; not till race, color, sex, and condition are seen as the accidents, and not the substance of life; not till the universal title of humanity to life, liberty, and the pursuit of happiness is conceded to be inalienable to all; not till then is woman's lesson taught and woman's cause won—not the white woman's, nor the black woman's, not the red woman's, but the cause of every man and of every woman who has writhed silently under a mighty wrong. Woman's wrongs are thus indissolubly linked with undefended woe, and the acquirement of her "rights" will mean the final triumph of all right over might, the supremacy of the moral forces of reason, and injustice, and love in the government of the nations of earth.

M. CAREY THOMAS, *Present Tendencies in Women's Education* (1908)

The following document was written by M. Carey Thomas (1857–1935) a Cornell college graduate and a recipient of a doctoral degree from a European university. Gender barriers had made it impossible for Thomas to attain a PH.D in the United States. Thomas served as the president of Bryn Mawr, one of the nation's most prestigious women's colleges, which opened in 1885. What did Thomas mean by her statement that when women first began to attend college, little was known about the effect higher education would have on their health?*

---

* From M. Carey Thomas, "Present Tendencies in Women's Education," *Publications of the Association of Collegiate Alumnae,* 3, February 1908.

The passionate desire of the women of my generation for higher education was accompanied throughout its course by the awful doubt, felt by women themselves as well as by men, as to whether women as a sex were physically and mentally fit for it. I think I can best make this clear to you if I refer briefly to my own experience. I cannot remember the time when I was not sure that studying and going to college were the things above all others which I wished to do. I was always wondering whereto it could be really true, as everyone thought, that boys were cleverer than girls. Indeed, I cared so much that I never dared ask any grown-up person the direct question, not even my father or mother, because I feared to hear the reply. I remember often praying about it, and begging God that if it were true that because I was a girl I could not successfully master Greek and go to college and understand things, to kill me at once, as I could not bear to live in such an unjust world. When I was a little older I read the Bible entirely through with passionate eagerness, because I had heard it said that it proved that women were inferior to men. Those were not the days of the higher criticism. I can remember weeping over the account of Adam and Eve because it seemed to me that the curse pronounced on Eve might imperil girls' going to college; and to this day I can never read many parts of the Pauline epistles without feeling again the sinking of the heart with which I used to hurry over the verses referring to women's keeping silence in the churches and asking their husbands at home. I searched not only the Bible, but all other books I could get for light on the woman question. I read Milton with rage and indignation. Even as a child I knew him for the woman-hater he was. The splendor of Shakespeare was obscured to me then by the lack of intellectual power in his greatest woman characters. Even now it seems to me that only Isabella in *Measure for Measure* thinks greatly, and weights her actions greatly, like Hamlet or a Brutus. . . .

But how vast the difference between then and now in my feeling, and in the feelings of every woman who has had to do with the education of girls! Then I was terror-struck lest I, and every other woman with me, were doomed to live as pathological invalids in a universe merciless to woman as a sex. Now we know that it is not we, but the man who believes such things about us, who is himself pathological, blinded by neurotic mists of sex, unable to see that women for one-half of the kindly race of normal, healthy human creatures in the world; that women, like men, are quickened and inspired by the same great traditions of their race by the same love of learning, the same love of science, the same love of abstract truth; that women, like men, are immeasurably bene-fited, physically, mentally, and morally, and are made vastly better mothers, as men are made vastly better fathers, by subordinating the distracting instincts of sex to the simple human fellowship of similar education, and similar intellectual and social ideals.

It was not to be wondered at that we were uncertain in those old days as to the ultimate result of women's education. Before I myself went to college I had seen only one college woman. I had heard that such a woman was staying at the house of an acquaintance. I went to see her with fear. Even if she had appeared in hoofs and horns I was determined to go to college all the same. But it was a relief to find this Vassar graduate tall and handsome and dressed like other women. When, five years later, I went to Leipzig to study after I had graduated from Cornell, my mother used to write me that my name was never mentioned to her by the women of her acquaintance. I was thought by them to be as much of a disgrace to my family as if I had eloped with the coachman. Now, women who have been to college are as plentiful as black-berries on summer hedges. . . .

We did not know when we began whether woman's health could stand the strain of college education. We were haunted in those days by the clanging chains of that gloomy little specter, Dr. Edward H. Clarke's *Sex in Education.* With trepidation of spirit, I made my mother read it, and was much cheered by her remark that, as neither she, nor any of the women she knew, had ever seen girls or women of the kind described in Dr. Clarke's book, we might as well act as if they did not exist. Still we did not *know* whether colleges might not produce a crop of just such invalids. Doctors insisted that they would. We women could not be sure until we had tried the experiment. Now we have tried it, and tried it for more than a generation, and

we know that college women are not only not invalids, but that they are better physically than other women in their own class of life. . .

We did not really know anything about even the ordinary everyday intellectual capacity of women when we began to educate them. We were not even sure that they inherited their intellects from their fathers as well as their mothers. We were told that their brains were too light, their foreheads too small, their reasoning powers too defective, their emotions too easily worked upon to make good students. None of these things has proved to be so.

ANNA MANNING COMFORT, *Only Heroic Women Were Doctors Then* (1916)

Even before the Civil War, a few women became doctors. Elizabeth Blackwell was the first woman in the United States to earn a medical degree in 1849. In 1857, she joined her sister and another female doctor and opened the New York Infirmary for Women and Children. Some years later, they established the New York Medical College and Hospital for Women, from which Anna Manning Comfort (1845–1931) graduated. Comfort's testimony emphasized the vital role that women's medical institutions played in providing women with an opportunity to practice medicine. Why were male doctors so resistant to women entering the medical profession?*

Changes in the position of women in the world of the last fifty years were emphasized by Dr. Anna Manning Comfort, graduate of the New York Medical College and Hospital for Women in its first class in 1865, at a luncheon in her honor, given by the Faculty and Trustees of the college at Delmonico's yesterday. Dr. Comfort was graduated at the age of 20, and she is only in the early seventies, alert and well preserved, though she has had a vigorous career, has been married, and is the mother of three children.

"Students of today have no idea of conditions as they were when I studied medicine," said Dr. Comfort. "It is difficult to realize the changes that have taken place. I attended the first meeting when this institution was proposed, and was graduated from the

first class. We had to go to Bellevue Hospital for our practical work, and the indignities we were made to suffer are beyond belief. There were 500 young men students taking post-graduate courses, and we were jeered at and catcalled, and the 'old war horses,' the doctors, joined the younger men.

"We were considered aggressive. They said women did not have the same brains as men and were not trustworthy. All the work at the hospital was made as repulsively unpleasant for us as possible. There were originally six in the class, but all but two were unable to put up with the treatment to which we were subjected, and dropped out. I trembled whenever I went to the hospital and I said once that I could not bear it. Finally the women went to the authorities, who said that if we

---

* From "Only Heroic Women Were Doctors Then," *The New York Times,* April 9, 1916.

were not respectfully treated they would take the charter from the hospital!

"As a physician there was nothing that I could do that satisfied people. If I wore square-toed shoes and swung my arms they said I was mannish, and if I carried a parasol and wore a ribbon in my hair they said I was too feminine and if I smiled they said I had too much levity.

"They tore down my sign when I began to practice, the drugstores did not like to fill my prescriptions, and the other doctors would not consult with me. But that little band of women made it possible for the other women who have come later into the field to do their work. When my first patients came and saw me they said I was too young, and they asked in horrified tones if I had studied dissecting just like the men. They were shocked at that, but they were more shocked when my bills were sent in to find that I charged as much as a man.

"I believe in women entering professions," said Dr. Comfort, "but I also believe in motherhood. For the normal woman it is no more of a tax to have a profession as well as a family life, than it is for man to carry on the multitudinous duties he has outside the family. I had three sons of my own and two adopted ones, and I am as proud of my motherhood as of my medical career. I gave as much of my personality to my children in an hour than some mothers do in ten. My children honored me and have been worthwhile in the world."

There were many expressions of esteem for Dr. Comfort, and she was overcome when it was announced that money had been raised for an Anna Manning Comfort scholarship at the hospital.

MARTHA E.D. WHITE, *Work of the Woman's Club* (1904)

In this document, Martha E.D. White described how the club movement helped shape public opinion. Even without the vote, club women successfully publicized community needs and increasingly gained a political voice. What specific evidence does White offer about the way club activity shaped community life and influenced national policy?*

But even without the personal enlightenment that counts for so much, women's clubs have been a potent factor in determining public opinion. As organizations, they have realized that "in public opinion we are all legislators by our birthright." And in practice, they have found that they could actually legislate by means of this power. Legislative work is undertaken by all the state federations, in urging and securing the passage of laws that deal with the conditions of women and children. In Massachusetts, Connecticut, and Illinois, the state federations have promoted the passage of a bill giving joint and equal parental guardianship to minor children. The Juvenile Court Law has been secured in California, Illinois, Maryland and Nebraska. The Louisiana Federation has worked successfully for the Probationary Law, and in Texas an industrial school has been established. Laws to raise the standard of public morality, to segregate and classify defective and delinquent classes, to secure the services of women as factory inspectors, police matrons, and on boards of control, are other measures for which women's clubs have successfully worked.

But it is in the work for the extension of libraries that women's clubs have more fully demonstrated their ability to further an

---

* From Martha E.D. White, "Work of the Woman's Club," *Atlantic Monthly,* 93, May 1904.

educational project. Many states in the Union have made no provision for the establishment of free libraries, and in others, where there is the necessary legislation, local conditions prevent their adequate establishment. Realizing keenly what a dearth of books means to a community, women's clubs have promptly initiated in many states systems of traveling libraries to satisfy the needs of the people until free libraries could be established on a permanent basis. In Oklahoma and Indian territory the federation collected one thousand volumes. These were classified and divided into fifty libraries, and each was sent on its enlightening pilgrimage. Kansas is sending to its district schools and remote communities 10,000 books divided into suitable libraries. The women of Ohio circulate 900 libraries; Kentucky is sending sixty-four to its mountaineers. In Maine the traveling library has become a prized educational opportunity. Its success has secured the appointment of a Library Commission and the enactment of suitable library legislation. This movement is extensive, and as an indication of what organized women can do, when the issue is concrete and appealing, it is significant. At a recent federation meeting in Massachusetts, no orator of the day made so eloquent an appeal as did the neat and convenient case of good books that invited our inspection before it should be sent to a remote community in the Tennessee Mountains. . . .

Six years ago the General Federation undertook to help solve certain industrial problems, notably to further organization among working-women; to secure and enforce child labor legislation where needed; to further attendance at school; and to secure humane conditions under which labor is performed. State federations have acted in accordance with the General Federation's plans to appoint standing industrial committees, procure investigations, circulate literature, and create a public sentiment in favor of these causes. In Illinois this indirect power was of much aid in securing a Child Labor Law. In other communities something has been accomplished by way of enacting new laws or enforcing existing ones, showing that organized women readily avail themselves of the chance for indirect service in promoting the intelligent efforts of the federations.

GROVER CLEVELAND, *Woman's Mission and Woman's Clubs* (1905)

Former president Grover Cleveland's attack on women's clubs reflected an outpouring of anxiety over any activity that took women away from complete concentration on their domestic and maternal concerns. Cleveland considered motherhood to be part of the divine and natural order. His effort to link club membership with the destruction of family life and the nation's well-being typified conservative fears that any departure of women from their God-ordained roles would result in national ruin.

How did Cleveland link the suffrage movement with the "club habit"? Why did he believe that club membership subverted "true womanhood"? In what ways were his views similar to those of John Abbott (see Chapter 2). How does Cleveland define "true womanhood"? What, if any, relevance, would his views have today? In view of White's summary of women's clubs' achievements, how would you present an argument that women's clubs, rather than being a "menace," were a benefit to the nation?*

The restlessness and discontent to which I have referred is most strongly manifested in a movement which has for a long time been on foot for securing women the right to vote and otherwise participate in public affairs. Let it here be distinctly understood that no sensible man

---

has fears of injury to the country on account of such participation. It is its dangerous, undermining effect on the characters of the wives and mothers of our land that we fear. This particular movement is so aggressive, and so extreme in its insistence, that those whom it has fully enlisted may well be considered as incorrigible. At a very recent meeting of these radicals a high priestess of the faith declared: "No matter how bad the crime a woman commits, if she can't vote, and is classed with idiots and criminals and lunatics, she should not be punished by the same laws as those who vote obey." This was said when advocating united action on the part of the assembled body to prevent the execution of a woman proved guilty of the deliberate and aggravated murder of her husband. The speaker is reported to have further announced as apparently the keynote of her address: "If we could vote we'd be willing to be hanged." It is a thousand pities that all the wives found in such company cannot sufficiently open their minds to see the complete fitness of the homely definition which describes a good wife as "a woman who loves her husband and her country with no desire to run either;" and what a blessed thing it would be if every mother, and every woman, whether mother, wife, spinster or maid, who either violently demands or wildly desires for women a greater share in the direction of public affairs, could realize the everlasting truth that "the hand that rocks the cradle is the hand that rules the world."

There is comfort in the reflection that, even though these extremists may not be amenable to reformation, there is a fair prospect that their manifest radicalism and their blunt avowal of subverting purposes will effectively warn against a dangerously wide acceptance of their theories.

The real difficulty and delicacy of our topic becomes more apparent when we come to speak of the less virulent and differently directed club movements that have crossed the even tenor of the way of womanhood. I do not include those movements which amount to nothing more than woman's association or cooperation in charitable, benevolent and religious work, largely local in its activities, and in all its qualities and purposes entirely fitted to a woman's highest nature and best impulses. I speak more especially of the woman's clubs of an entirely different sort which have grown up in all sections of our land, and which have already become so numerous that in the interest of their consolidated management a "National Federation of Woman's Clubs" has been created. I speak also of the vast number of associations less completely organized, but no less exacting of time and attention, whose professed purposes are in many instances the intellectual improvement or entertainment of the women composing their membership. Doubtless in numerous cases the objects of these clubs and associations are shown in such a light and are made to appear so good, or at least so harmless, that a conscientious woman, unless she make a strong fight against self-delusion, may quite easily persuade herself that affiliation with them would be certainly innocent and perhaps even within her dictates of duty. The danger of self-delusion lies in her supposition that she is consulting the need of relaxation, or the duty of increased opportunity for intellectual improvement, when in point of fact, and perhaps imperceptibly to herself, she is taking counsel of her discontent with the humdrum of her home life. . . .

Woman's Danger of the Club Habit

No woman who enters upon such a retaliatory course can be sure that the man she seeks to punish will be otherwise affected than to be made the more indifferent to home, and the more determined to enlarge the area of his selfish pleasures. She can be sure, however, that cheerlessness will invade her home, and that if children are there they will be irredeemably deprived of the mysterious wholesomeness and delight of an atmosphere which can only be created by a mother's loving presence and absorbing care. She can also be certain that, growing out of the influence which her behavior and example are sure to have upon the conduct of the wives and mothers within the range of her companionship, she may be directly responsible for marred happiness in other households, and that as an aider and abettor of woman's clubs she must bear her share of liability for the injury they may inflict upon the domestic life of our land. It must be abundantly evident that, as agencies for retaliation or man's punishment, woman's clubs are horribly misplaced and miserably vicious.

To the honest-minded women who are inclined to look with favor upon such of these clubs as indicate beneficent purposes or harmless relaxation, it is not amiss to suggest that these purposes and characteristics are naturally not only of themselves expansive, but that membership in one such organization is apt to create a club habit which, if it does not lead to other smaller affiliations, induces toleration and defense of club ideas in general. It is in this way that many conscientious women, devoted to their home duties and resentful of any suspicion to the contrary, through apparently innocent club membership, subordinate their household interests, and are lost to the ranks of the defenders of home against such club influences and consequences as the unbiased judgment of true womanhood would unhesitatingly condemn. The woman is fortunate and well poised who, having yielded to whatever allurements there may be in a single club membership, can implicitly rely upon her ability to resist persuasion to additional indulgence, and can fix the exact limit of her surrender to its infatuation. It is quite evident that she ought not take the first step toward such membership before considering the matter with a breadth of view sufficient to take in all its indirect possibilities, as well as its immediate and palpable consequences.

Woman's Clubs Not Only Harmful, but a Menace

I am persuaded that without exaggeration of statement we may assume that there are woman's clubs whose objects and intents are not only harmful, but harmful in a way that directly menaces the integrity of our homes and the benign disposition and character of our wifehood and motherhood; that there are others harmless in intent, but whose tendency is toward waster of time and perversion of effort, as well as toward the formation of the club habit, and the toleration or active patronage of less innocent organizations; that there are also associations of women whose purposes of charity, religious enterprise or intellectual improvement are altogether laudable and worthy. Leaving this latter class out of account, and treating the subject on the theory that only the other organizations mentioned are under consideration, I believe that it should be boldly declared that the best and safest club for a woman to patronize is her home. American wives and American mothers, as surely as "the hand that rocks the cradle is the hand that rules the world," had, through their nurture of children and their influence over men, the destinies of our Nation in their keeping to a greater extent than any other single agency. It is surely not soft-hearted sentimentalism which insists that, in a country where the people rule, a decisive share in securing the perpetuity of its institutions falls upon the mothers who devote themselves to teaching their children who are to become rulers, lessons of morality and patriotism and disinterested citizenship. Such thoughts suggest how supremely great is the stake of our country in woman's unperverted steadfastness, and enjoin in the necessity of its protection against all risks and temptations.

The Real Path of True Womanhood

I am in favor of according to women the utmost social enjoyment; and I am profoundly thankful that this, in generous and sufficient measure, is within their reach without encountering the temptations or untoward influences so often found in the surroundings of woman's clubs.

For the sake of our country, for the sake of our homes, and for the sake of our children,

I would have our wives and mothers loving and devoted, though all others may be sordid and heedless; I would have them disinterested and trusting, though all others may be selfish and cunning; I would have them happy and contented in following the Divinely appointed path of true womanhood, though all others may grope in the darkness of their own devices.

An Angry Susan B. Anthony Chasing President Cleveland
(Courtesy of the Library of Congress)

NATIONAL ASSOCIATION OF COLORED WOMEN, *Club Activities* (1906)

The following excerpt is from an annual NACW report that documents African American women's club activities. In an era when government provided nominal attention to the needs of poor blacks, clubs provided social services that sustained the lives of the community's poorest members. What were some of the causes club women supported?*

Women's Christian, Social and Literary Club of Peoria, Ill

We, the Women's Christian, Social and Literary Club of Peoria, Ill. beg leave to submit the following report for 1905–1906: We have a membership of 15 active members and 7 honorary members. . . . Our motto is "For God and Humanity." . . . Last year we had a good school for the little ones, and did much good and realized $5.50 for the work. . . . We have seventeen pupils. We have donated to the Baptist Church $15 and

---

* From the National Association of Colored Women's Annual Report, 1906.

to the A.M.E. Church $17. . . . Assisted 44 different persons. We meet every Monday afternoon. . . .

On June 28, 1906, we made arrangements to purchase 5½ acres of land on which we will erect an industrial home and school for all ages of our people. This piece of land cost us $6000. It is a handsome place, and it is now laid out in 36 lots, thirty by one hundred twenty-five feet. After paying all expenses and $150 on the place, we will have left in the bank $5. Respectfully submitted, Mrs. Anna R. Fields, Founder and President.

Phillis Wheatley Home Association of Detroit

The Phillis Wheatley Home Association of Detroit, Michigan was organized in 1897, the object being the establishment of a home for our aged colored women. In 1897 a few earnest women met . . . and they were without funds but each one contributed her mite and the Committee rented a building. Furnishings were solicited . . . applications were received and on our opening day seven old ladies were received in the Phillis Wheatley Home. In 1901 the Phillis Wheatley Home Association was incorporated under the state laws, and seeing the necessity of having a permanent building, we purchased the property at 176 East Elizabeth Street at a cost of $4000, paying $1300 cash. We have at present 12 inmates. . . . We have 24 members, regular meetings are held every Tuesday evening. Cash receipts (from donations for the past two years, 1904–1906) includes $1847. Respectfully submitted, Eliza Wilson, President.

Sojourner Truth Club of Montgomery, Ala

The Sojourner Truth Club of Montgomery, Alabama furnished a reading room, this being the only one of its kind available for colored people in our city. It has six tables, two bookcases, three sets of bookshelves, one and a half dozen chairs, stove pictures, floor coverings of linoleum, rugs, twelve to fifteen current periodicals, 300 or more books. The room is lighted by shaded Incandescent lights. The librarian is hired and the hours are from 3 p.m. to 9 p.m. Back of the reading room we had recently furnished a club room with a small table, two dozen chairs, matting, rugs, curtains, stove and pictures. It makes quite a cozy appearance. A third room we hope to furnish is a kitchen. Here we hope to have cooking lessons given for the benefit of the public. All this is paid for by 25¢-per-month membership dues and fundraising affairs held by the club. They have also invited guest speakers, such as Dr. Booker T. Washington, W. E. B. DuBois and Kelly Miller. The membership is 29.

FRANCES WILLARD, *On Behalf of Home Protection* (1884)

Under Frances Willard's (1839–1898) leadership, the Women's Christian Temperance Union (WCTU) supported the effort for suffrage. Although WCTU women avoided the confrontational issues of gender equity involved in the crusade for women's rights, Willard directly linked women's right to vote to the issues of home protection and temperance. Within this context, the vote became a means to extend a mother's protection of her sons to the maternal protection of the nation. Why would this argument for the vote be less threatening than those found in the earlier "Declaration of Sentiments" (see Chapter 7)?*

---

* From Frances Willard, "On Behalf of Home Protection," in *Women and Temperance or The Work and Workers of the Women's Christian Temperance Union* (Hartford, CT: Park Publishing Co., 1884), 457–59.

Dear Christian women who have crusaded in the rum shops, I urge that you begin crusading in halls of legislation, in primary meetings, and the offices of excise commissioners. Roll in your repetitions, burnish your arguments, multiply your prayers. Go to the voters in your town—procure the official list and see them one by one—and get them pledged to a local ordinance requiring the votes of men and women before a license can be issued to open rum shop doors beside your homes; go to the Legislature with the same; remember this may be just as really Christian a work as praying in saloons was in those other glorious days. Let us not limit God, whose modes of operation are so infinitely varied in nature and grace. I believe in the correlation of spiritual forces, and that the heat which melted hearts to tenderness in the Crusade is soon to be the light which shall reveal our opportunity and duty as the Republic's daughters.

Longer ago than I shall tell, my father returned one night to the far-off Wisconsin home where I was reared; and, sitting by my mother's chair, with a child's attentive ear, I listened to their words. He told us of the news that day had brought about Neal Dow and the great fight for prohibition down in Maine, and then he said: "I wonder if poor, rum-cursed Wisconsin will ever get a law like that?" And mother rocked a while in silence in the dear old chair I love, and then she gently said:

"YES, JOSIAH, THERE'LL BE SUCH A LAW OVER THE LAND SOME DAY, WHEN WOMEN VOTE."

My father had never heard her say so much before. He was a great conservative; so he looked tremendously astonished, and replied, in his keen, sarcastic voice: "And pray, how will you arrange it so that women shall vote?" Mother's chair went to and fro a little faster for a minute, and then, looking not into his face, but into the flickering flames of the grate, she slowly answered: "Well, I say to you, as the apostle Paul said to his jailer, 'You have put us into prison, we being Romans, and you must come and take us out.'"

That was a seed-thought in a girl's brain and heart. Years passed on, in which nothing more was said upon this dangerous theme. My brother grew to manhood, and soon after he was twenty-one years old he went with his father to vote. Standing by the window, a girl of sixteen years, a girl of simply, homely face, not at all strong-minded, and altogether ignorant of the world, I looked out as they drove away, my father and my brother, and as I looked I felt a strange ache in my heart, and tears sprang to my eyes. Turning to my sister Mary, who stood beside me, I saw that the dear little innocent seemed wonderfully sober, too. I said: "Don't you wish we could go with them when we are old enough? Don't we love our country just as well as they do?" and her little frightened voice piped out: "Yes, of course we ought. Don't I know that? but you mustn't tell a soul—not mother, even; we should be called strong-minded."

In all the years since then I have kept these things, and many others like them, and pondered them in my heart; but two years of struggle in this temperance reform have shown me, as they have ten thousand other women,

Frances Willard (Courtesy of the Library of Congress)

so clearly and so impressively, my duty, that I HAVE PASSED THE RUBICON OF SILENCE and am ready for any battle that shall be involved in this honest declaration of the faith that is within me . . . Ah, it is women who have given the costliest hostages to fortune. Out into the battle of life they have sent their best beloved, with fearful odds against them, with snares that men have legalized and set for them on every path. Beyond the arms that held them so long, their boys have gone forever. Oh! by the danger they have dared; by the hours of patient watching over beds where helpless children lay; by the incense of ten thousand prayers wafted from their gentle lips to Heaven, I charge you give them power to protect, along life's treacherous highway, those whom they have so loved. Let it no longer be that they must sit back among the shadows, hopelessly mourning over their strong staff broken, and their beautiful rod; but when the sons they love shall go forth into life's battle, still let their mothers walk beside them, sweet and serious, and clad in the garments of power.

Elizabeth Cady Stanton, *Bible and Church Degrade Women* (1898)

Suffragists of the late nineteenth century distanced themselves from the liberty rhetoric and feminist outrage against male power that had characterized the pre–Civil War women's reform movement. In contrast to this growing conservatism, Elizabeth Cady Stanton retained her earlier conviction that if women were to achieve equality, they would have to transform male-centered institutions and privileges, including religion. In 1895, at age eighty, she published *The Woman's Bible,* a feminist interpretation that provides examples of the ways in which Scripture and religious teachings denied equality and according to Stanton "degraded" women. She shocked most of her suffragist colleagues, who found her interpretations blasphemous. In 1898, *The Woman's Bible* was reprinted, accompanied by three essays that added to her critique of patriarchal religious control. The excerpt that follows is from one of these essays. What evidence does Stanton offer that religious teachings "degrade" women and prevent them from attaining equality? How does Stanton account for the improved status of American women in the late nineteenth century?*

The Pentateuch makes woman a mere afterthought in creation; the author of sin; cursed in her maternity; a subject in marriage; and claims divine authority for this fourfold bondage, this wholesale desecration of the mothers of the race. While some admit that this invidious language of the Old Testament is disparaging to woman, they claim that the New Testament honors her. But the letters of the apostles to the churches, giving directions for the discipline of women, are equally invidious, as the following texts prove:

"Wives, obey your husbands. If you would know anything, ask your husbands at home. Let your women keep silence in the churches, with their heads covered. Let not your women usurp authority over the man, for as Christ is the head of the church so is the man the head of the woman. Man was prior in creation, the woman was of the man, therefore shall be in subjection to him."

No symbols or metaphors can twist honor or dignity out of such sentiments. Here, in plain English, woman's position is as degraded as in the Old Testament.

As the Bible is in every woman's hands, and she is trained to believe it "the word of

---

* From Elizabeth Cady Stanton, "The Degraded Status of Woman in the Bible," 1898.

God," it is impossible to describe her feelings of doubt and distrust, as she awakes to her status in the scale of being; the helpless, hopeless position assigned her by the Creator, according to the Scriptures.

Men can never understand the fear of everlasting punishment that fills the souls of women and children. The orthodox religion, as drawn from the Bible and expounded by the church, is enough to drive the most imaginative and sensitive natures to despair and death. Having conversed with many young women in sanatoriums, insane asylums, and in the ordinary walks of life, suffering with religious melancholia; having witnessed the agony of young mothers in childbirth, believing they were cursed of God in their maternity; and with painful memories of my own fears and bewilderment in girlhood, I have endeavored to dissipate these religious superstitions from the minds of women, and base their faith on science and reason, where I found for myself at last that peace and comfort I could never find in the Bible and the church. I saw the first step to this end was to convince them that the Bible was neither written nor inspired by the Creator of the Universe, the Infinite Intelligence, the soul and center of Life, Love and Light; but that the Bible emanated, in common with all church literature, from the brain of man. Seeing that just in proportion as women are devout believers in the dogmas of the church their lives are shadowed with fears of the unknown, the less they believe, the better for their own happiness and development. It was the religious devotee that threw her child under the car of Juggernaut, that gave her body a living sacrifice on the funeral pyre of her husband, to please God and save souls; for the same reason the devotees of our day build churches and parsonages, educate young men for the ministry, endow theological seminaries, make surplices and embroider slippers for the priesthood.

It may not be amiss for man to accept the Bible, as it honors and exalts him. It is a title deed for him to inherit the earth. According to the Pentateuch he communes with the gods, in performing miracles he is equal in power and glory with his Creator, can command the sun and moon to stand still to lengthen the day and lighten the night, if need be, to finish his battles.

He can stand in the most holy places in the temples, where woman may never enter; he can eat the consecrated bread and meat, denied her; in fact, there is a suspicion of unworthiness and uncleanness seductively infused into the books of Moses against the whole female sex, in animal as well as human life. *The first born male* kid is the only fit burnt offering to the Lord; if preceded by a female it is unfit.

As the Bible gives us two opposite accounts of the creation of woman and her true position, so the church gives two opposite interpretations of the will of the God concerning her true sphere of action. When ecclesiastics wish to rouse woman's enthusiasm to lift a church debt or raise a pastor's salary, then they try to show her that she owes all she is and all the liberty she enjoys to the Bible and Christian religion; they dwell on the great honor God conferred on the sex in choosing a woman to be the mother of his only begotten son.

But when woman asks for equal rights and privileges in the church, to fill the office of pastor, elder, deacon or trustee, to be admitted as a delegate to the synods, general assemblies or conferences, then the bishops quote texts to show that all these positions are forbidden by the Bible. . . . The honor and worship accorded the ideal mother, of the ideal man, has done naught to elevate the real mother, of the real man. So far from woman owing what liberty she does enjoy, to the Bible and the church, they have been the greatest block in the way of her development. The vantage ground woman holds to-day is due to all the forces of civilization, to science, discovery, invention, rationalism, the religion of humanity chanted in the golden rule round the globe centuries before the Christian religion was known. It is not to Bibles, prayer books, catechisms, liturgies, the canon law and church creeds and organizations, that woman owes one step in her progress, for all these alike have been hostile, and still are, to her freedom and development.

Lucretia Mott, Elizabeth Cady Stanton and Susan B. Anthony
(The New York Public Library)

Ida Wells Barnett, *A Red Record* (1895)

An African American journalist from Memphis, Tennessee, Ida Wells Barnett (1862–1931) witnessed the increased racial violence of the post-Reconstruction era. A leading civil rights advocate, she led a national crusade against lynching. In the following excerpt from her writings, Barnett addressed the subject of interracial sexual relationships. She argued that these voluntary relationships served as the pretext for allegations of rape and subsequent lynching of African American men. What did Barnett mean by "true chivalry"? How did she regard the "white women of the South"?*

A word as to the charge itself. In considering the third reason assigned by the Southern white people for the butchery of blacks, the question must be asked, what the white man means when he charges the black man with rape. Does he mean the crime which the statutes of the states describe as such? Not by any means. With the Southern white man, any misalliance existing between a white woman and a colored man is a sufficient foundation for the charge of rape. The Southern white man says that it is impossible for a voluntary alliance to exist between a white woman and a colored man, and therefore, the fact of an alliance is a proof of force. In numerous instances where colored men have been

* From Ida Wells Barnett, *A Red Record* (Chicago: Donohue & Henneberry, 1895), 8–15.

lynched on the charge of rape, it was positively known at the time of lynching, and indisputably proven after the victim's death, that the relationship sustained between the man and the woman was voluntary and clandestine, and that in no court of law could even the charge of assault have been successfully maintained.

It was for the assertion of this fact, in the defense of her own race, that the writer hereof became an exile; her property destroyed and her return to her home forbidden under penalty of death, for writing the following editorial which was printed in her paper, the *Free Speech,* in Memphis, Tenn., May 21, 1892:

"Eight Negroes lynched since last issue of the *Free Speech*: one at Little Rock, Ark., last Saturday morning where the citizens broke (?) into the penitentiary and got their man; three near Anniston, Ala., one near New Orleans; and three at Clarksville, Ga.; the last three for killing a white man, and five on the same old racket—the new alarm about raping white women. The same programme of hanging, then shooting bullets into the lifeless bodies was carried out to the letter. Nobody in this section of the country believes in the old threadbare lie that Negro men rape white women. If Southern white men are not careful, they will overreach themselves and public sentiment will have a reaction; a conclusion will then be reached which will be very damaging to the moral reputation of their women."

But threats cannot suppress the truth, and while the Negro suffers the soul deformity, resultant from two and a half centuries of slavery, he is no more guilty of this vilest of all vile charges than the white man who would blacken his name.

During all the years of slavery, no such charge was ever made, not even during the dark days of the rebellion. . . . While the master was away fighting to forge the fetters upon the slave, he left his wife and children with no protectors save the Negroes themselves. . . .

Likewise during the period of alleged "insurrection," and alarming "race riots," it never occurred to the white man that his wife and children were in danger of assault. Nor in the Reconstruction era, when the hue and cry was against "Negro Domination," was there ever a thought that the domination would ever contaminate a fireside or strike toward the virtue of womanhood. . . .

It is not the purpose of this defense to say one word against the white women of the South. Such need not be said, but it is their misfortune that the . . . white men of that section . . . to justify their own barbarism . . . assume a chivalry which they do not possess. True chivalry respects all womanhood, and no one who reads the record, as it is written in the faces of the million mulattos in the South, will for a minute conceive that the southern white man had a very chivalrous regard for the honor due the women of his race, or respect for the womanhood which circumstances placed in his power. . . . Virtue knows no color line, and the chivalry which depends on complexion of skin and texture of hair can command no honest respect.

When emancipation came to the Negroes . . . from every nook and corner of the North, brave young white women . . . left their cultured homes, their happy associations and their lives of ease, and with heroic determination went to the South to carry light and truth to the benighted blacks. . . . They became the social outlaws in the South. The peculiar sensitiveness of the southern white men for women, never shed its protecting influence about them. No friendly word from their own race cheered them in their work; no hospitable doors gave them the companionship like that from which they had come. No chivalrous white man doffed his hat in honor or respect. They were "Nigger teachers"—unpardonable offenders in the social ethics of the South, and were insulted, persecuted and ostracized, not by Negroes, but by the white manhood which boasts of its chivalry toward women.

And yet these northern women worked on, year after year. . . . Threading their way through dense forests, working in school-houses, in the cabin and in the church, thrown at all times and in all places among the unfortunate and lowly Negroes, whom they had come to find and to serve, these northern women, thousands and thousands of them, have spent more than a quarter of a century in giving the colored people their splendid lessons for home and heart and soul. Without protection, save that which innocence gives to every good woman, they went about their work, fearing no assault and suffering none. Their chivalrous protectors were hundreds of miles away in their northern homes, and yet they never feared any "great dark-faced mobs." . . . They never complained of assaults, and no mob was ever called into existence to avenge crimes against them. Before the world adjudges the Negro a moral monster, a vicious assailant of womanhood and a menace to the sacred precincts of home, the colored people ask the consideration of the silent record of gratitude, respect, protection and devotion of the millions of the race in the South, to the thousands of northern white women who have served as teachers and missionaries since the war. . . .

These pages are written in no spirit of vindictiveness. . . . We plead not for the colored people alone, but for all victims of the terrible injustice which puts men and women to death without form of law. During the year 1894, there were 132 persons executed in the United States by due form of law, while in the same year, 197 persons were put to death by mobs, who gave the victims no opportunity to make a lawful defense. No comment need be made upon a condition of public sentiment responsible for such alarming results.

CHAPTER 11

Women's Roles:
Americanization and the Multicultural West

The process of expansion and nation building accelerated after the Civil War. The U.S. Army and government funding facilitated the last phase of the conquest and the Americanization of the West. In about thirty years, the federal government displaced the remaining American Indians from their tribal lands and achieved their containment on reservations. Subsidies to railroads quickened the pace of settlement and the commercialization of agriculture. The rapid expansion of the railroads and massive emigration and settlement of territories transformed both the natural and Indian environments. By century's end, the United States, fulfilling Manifest Destiny's geographic dream, stretched from the Atlantic to the Pacific oceans.

Highly critical of government mismanagement and the living conditions of Indians on tribal reservations, during the 1880s reformers proposed the end of the reservation system and the substitution of an Americanization or assimilation program that would transform every aspect of American Indian culture including gender roles. Within the context of women's history, unequal power relationships dominated the interaction between Euro-American and American Indian women. Pioneer anthropologist Alice Fletcher, supported boarding schools and the Dawes Act of 1887 as the major strategies for the assimilation or Americanization of Indians. The Dawes Act forced the privatization of land ownership and the end of tribal land-use patterns. Although hailed as a reform, the Dawes' Act further damaged Indian rights and resulted in even greater loss of land for American Indians and significant land acquisition for whites. The boarding schools, often many miles away from the children's homes, intentionally uprooted children and immersed them in the English language and American cultural norms. The objective was to create a new generation of assimilated children. Indian women would be trained to assume domestic roles by white women, who had new career opportunities for employment as boarding school matrons and teachers.

Reformers also sought to bring Indian gender roles into closer alignment with Anglo-American middle-class norms. Although gender roles varied among different tribes, they generally diverged from accepted norms of female domesticity, monogamous marriages, and patriarchal patterns of authority. Under the provisions of the Dawes Act, Indian men would give up hunting and become sedentary farmers. Education for women would focus on housekeeping skills and gender-based, middle-class norms of appropriate female behavior. In terms of cultural interaction, Euro-American women, once called the "gentle tamers of the West," appear more as agents of colonization, interacting with Mexican and American Indians from a perspective of their own cultural and moral superiority. Reformers such as, Fletcher, and the empathetic writer Helen Hunt Jackson believed that assimilation of the American Indians expressed beneficial change and were anxious to end the oppressive mismanagement of the U.S. government's reservation policy. In her book *A Century of Dishonor,* published in 1883, Jackson accused the federal government of dishonorable and unjust policies. A political activist as well as a writer, Jackson was appointed by Congress to investigate the plight of the Mission Indians in California.

Indians were not passive recipients of government policies, cultural assimilation, or religious conversion. Many struggled to express their own identity and some like Johanna July continued an independent lifestyle, unhampered by cultural intrusion. Others such as Sarah Winnemucca Hopkins sought to preserve their culture, and accommodate to changed circumstances. Hopkin's English language skills facilitated her mediation with the federal government. The granddaughter of a Piute Indian chief, she was an outspoken defender of Piute rights and opened a school that would preserve Indian culture and language. Ironically, boarding schools' Americanization programs in some children fostered the opposite result: defiance and cultural persistence. Zikala–Sa's immersion in cultural assimilation programs led to her bitter resentment of cultural coercion and a lifelong commitment to improve Indian conditions.

Although a significant number of female teachers, boarding school matrons, and missionaries became involved with the education and assimilation of Indian children, the majority of women who settled in the newly opened Indian lands made family and home care the major focus of their lives. The search for farmland supplied the primary motive for relocation, and thousands of families took advantage of the Homestead Act to acquire land on the Great Plains. German Jewish Sarah Thal and her husband left Europe in the early 1880s for their new homestead in North Dakota, where they would encounter physical hardship not dissimilar from Mattie Oblinger's experience in Nebraska. The unremitting labor of women characterized work patterns on farms in the Great Plains. Women's domestic and physical labor was vital not only to the family economy and community building, but to survival itself. Although the Homestead Act permitted single women to file claims, the major objective of government land-use programs was to promote the settlement of white American families. By the 1880s, railroad construction accelerated the rate of settlement. The overland trails were still used, but the comfort and speed of the train lured even more settlers to the West.

Did the unsettled environment of the West facilitate expanded roles for women? For many years, the debate over women's rights in the West focused on whether gender norms relaxed and women found new opportunities. Although there were women gold miners, single-woman homesteaders, and sharp shooters such as Annie Oakley, conventional gender assumptions about correct womanly conduct coexisted with the expansion of women's roles to meet unsettled conditions and labor needs. White women such as the nun, Sister Blandina Segale, became teachers in Indian and Mexican American schools, as well as in newly opened schools for the children of settlers. Women had a greater chance than in the

East to become school principals and even county superintendents. In the West, as in the East, the feminization of teaching was accompanied by low pay and viewed as an extension of women's maternal role.

White women's belief in their own moral authority also moved west, as did the struggle for suffrage. Suffrage victories in Wyoming, Idaho, Utah, and Colorado years in advance of eastern states suggest that the western environment was more conducive to the expansion of political rights. Certainly there are examples of an expanded role for women in western politics, particularly in the Populist Party, the political wing of the grassroots Farmer's Alliance. Mary Elizabeth Lease (see Chapter 12), the flamboyant Populist speaker, was known for her fiery rhetoric in defense of the small farmer against Wall Street and banking interests. Third-party Populist strength in Colorado was decisive in the 1893 victory for suffrage.

It is tempting to view the early suffrage victories in the West as examples of the region's hospitality to women's rights and settlement. Closer examination reveals a far more complex picture and indicates that suffrage success served agendas that involved more than women's rights. What made suffrage for women easier to accomplish in the West might be linked to the writing of constitutions in the newly formed states. The lack of preexisting restrictive conditions against women may have facilitated the inclusion of voting rights in new state constitutions. In Wyoming, men granted women suffrage when Wyoming was still a territory. The major reason may have been to lure more women to an area where males outnumbered females six to one. Even in newer communities of the West, segregation followed the flag. Although the debate over why the West was more open to voting rights for women still continues, the fact remains that thirteen of sixteen states granting women the vote prior to the Nineteenth Amendment were in the West.

Nowhere was the suffrage struggle more complex than in Utah, where Mormonism, polygamy, and the issue of suffrage and statehood became interwoven. Although they shared their Euro-American background with the majority of the nation's population, Mormons proved defiant of cultural and social values, including monogamy and nuclear family formation. Based on a revelation of the prophet and founder of the religion, Joseph Smith, polygamy known as "The Principle" was a fundamental cornerstone of the Mormon belief system. In 1856, the Republican Party described polygamy as barbaric and degrading. The practice of polygamy placed the Mormons on a collision course with the U.S. government and dominated political discourse for decades. Utah's territorial legislature granted suffrage to women in 1870. Non-Mormon female suffrage advocates wrongly assumed Mormon women would renounce polygamy. They found it difficult to understand how women such as Emmeline Wells, an ardent defender of plural marriages and herself a seventh wife, could combine women's rights with support for polygamy.

In an era of cultural assimilation and Americanization objectives, Mormon commitment to plural wives defied deeply rooted values and challenged the growing trend toward more egalitarian marriages. Fanny Stenhouse, who left Britain with her husband to join the Mormon community in Utah, found her husband's choice of a second wife to be a denial of her own agency. Congress passed laws outlawing polygamy, and official renunciation of the doctrine became a prerequisite for Utah's admission to the Union. Congress also nullified Utah women's right to vote. Utah became part of the Union after the Mormons officially renounced the practice of plural wives, and women's voting rights were reinstituted in the new state constitution of 1896.

During the same time period that Indian tribes confronted coercive Americanization policies, Congress passed the Chinese Exclusion Act, which, with few exceptions, restricted further immigration from China. The act expressed the incessant racism and hostility that the Chinese experienced, which was particularly virulent in California. There the Chinese faced racist restrictions, including antimiscegenation laws forbidding intermarriage with whites. California laws also prevented Chinese children from attending school with white students. Mary Tape's protest against school segregation failed to sway the San Francisco Board of Education, even though the California Supreme Court had ruled in favor of her daughter Mamie's admission to an all-white school. Subverting the decision, the San Francisco School Board drew up new racist legislation that expressed the board's continued objective to segregate Chinese students.

MARTHA (MATTIE) VIRGINIA OBLINGER, *Letter to her Family* (June 16, 1873)

Martha (Mattie) Virginia Oblinger (1844–1873) and her husband Uriah took advantage of the Homestead Act to acquire land in Nebraska. Oblinger's experience of the rigors and sacrifices of pioneer homesteading is representative of life on the Great Plains. Yet optimism molds this letter written to family members. Above all else, she emphasizes that despite hardship, her family and her neighbors are no longer renters. Her delight in the independence of home and land ownership underlies much of her upbeat assessment of the Great Plains living conditions. Perhaps her letter also sought to reassure her family and encourage them to relocate. What adds poignancy to this letter is that Mattie's hopes for the future would not be realized. At age thirty-six, she died in childbirth.

In her letter, Mattie uses the phrase we are "not entirely out of civilization." What does she mean by this? Mattie also makes an argument in favor of sod homes. Why does she consider them superior to frame houses? What factors did Mattie stress as the justification for the hardship and deprivation of homesteading? What motives might she have for emphasizing the positive rather than the negative aspects of her existence?*

Letter from Mattie V. Oblinger to Thomas Family, May 19, 1873

May 19th 1873

At Home in our own house and a sod at that And just eat dinner

Dear friends as I have an opportunity to send a letter to the office I will send you a few hastly composed lines Billie Mote come to our house Saturday . . . [morning] he is going to Grafton this afternoon so I will not have time to write much We have considerable of rain since I came here Saturday night it rained very hard It is too wet to plant corn some are ready but have to wait a day or so for the ground to dry off The plants and shrubery that I brought I put on Giles place I was looking at them last evening they look very promising the Dialetre especialy We went to Mr Cambels yesterday to church and sabbath school They live seven miles south of here The minister failed to come so there was society meeting Mr Cambels are real Kentuckians wish you could hear them talk We took dinner with them Uriah & Billie are talking U A C is lying on the [Lounge] and Ella is teasing him for his book We moved in to our house last Wednesday (U. W. O birthday) I suppose you would like to see us in our sod house It is not quite so convenient as a nice frame but I would as soon live in it as

---

* In the public domain.

the cabins I have lived in and then we are at home which makes it more comfortable I ripped our Waggon sheet in too have it arround too sides and have several papers up so the boys think it looks real well the Uriahs made a bed stead and a Lounge so could have some thing to sleep on The only objection I have we have no floor yet will be better this fall I got one tea cup & saucer and the corner of the glass on the little hero picture broken Pretty good luck I think my goods got here two days before I did Uriah had taken them out to Mr Houks Uriah was plowing sod this fore noon talks of planting some this after noon he has twenty acres surounded have ten of it broke Doc & Billie & Uriah C stayed with us I know you would have laughed to see us fixing their bed we set boxes the side of the Lounge and enlarged Uriahs bed for all of them We enjoyed the fun and they enjoyed their bed as much as if they had been in a nice parlor bed room U. C. & Doc sung while I got supper They call Doc Sam out here sounds very odd to me wish you could see his whiskers shaved all off but what is on his chin an lip I told him I wanted some to send you but he could not see it He has worked one day at his house I have got acquainted with some here They are not hard to get acquainted The boys went to Sutton Saturday after noon I went along to see the town and country on our way we seen three Antelopes U C shot at them for fun Charlie if you was here you would never get done looking for you can see ever so far comeing from Sutton we could see the Co seat which was eleven miles from us We got a letter from you U C says tell Kate D that he gloreis in her spunk and for peace and joy to go with her but She must not do so when she comes to Neb There is some here looks as though they would like if some girls would come . . .

I am washing to day This after noon is little cloudy with the sun shineing occasionaly Ella is as hearty as she can be and has an appetite like a little horse I never cooked for such appetites as I have since I been here some times I think I will cook enough of some things for two meals but the boys clean them every time

We are all well I must close for this I am as ever your sister & daughter Our love to all

M V O

Mattie Oblinger (Courtesy of the Library of Congress)

SARAH THAL, *Recollections of a German-Jewish Woman in North Dakota, Edited by Martha Thal* (1882)

Sarah Thal and her husband Solomon left Germany to homestead in the North Dakota Territory. A German Jewish immigrant, Thal's experience as a pioneer exhibits many characteristics shared by diverse ethnic and religious groups. Her description of isolation and the blizzard that prevented the arrival of a doctor who might have been able to save her son's life were unfortunately not uncommon experiences. For pioneer women, endurance and adaptation characterized life on the Great Plains. Deprivation and hardship were representative experiences.

What evidence does Thal give of her ability to adapt to a new environment? How does she assess the growing number of amenities? How does her account of adaptation to the harsh conditions of the Great Plains compare to that of Mattie Oblinger?*

When a child attending the religious school the story of The Sojourn of the Israelites in the Wilderness stirred my imagination. I too longed for a sojourn in the wilderness. I did not know that my dreams would become a reality, a reality covering long years of hardship and privation. My husband had brothers in Milwaukee who sent home glowing reports of conditions in America. We wished to tell our luck in that wonderful land. When my daughter, Elsie, was fourteen months old we left to make our fortune fully confident of our undertaking.

We sailed from Antwerp and landed in Boston. I brought with me my linen chest, feather beds, pillows, bedding, etc. My brother-in-law, Sam Thal advised us to go to Dakota Territory. He had been out there and thought highly of the prospects. My husband was anxious to get started and as soon as he could leave me he went out there. Six weeks later I followed. I had never seen frame houses until we reached America. Everything I saw from the train window was interesting and new. We reached Grand Forks late at night. Being unable to speak English I could not make my wants known so I went to bed without supper. I reached Larimore hungry but safely. Here I met my husband. He was wearing a buffalo skin coat, the first I had ever seen. With him was Sol Mendelson, the manager of the Sam Thal farm.

A newcomer must of course experience much embarrassment. My worst one day was when Mr. Mendelson brought in a crate of pork and asked me, a piously reared Jewess, to cook it. In time I consented. However, I never forgot my religious teachings. In the spring of

'83 we homesteaded land in Dodds Township along the supposed railroad right of way. Here we planted our first garden. My, how I loved to watch things grow in that newly broken land.

That fall I would look out of the window and see fires in the distance. These I believe were far off factories. I was still unable to realize the completeness of our isolation. That fall my second baby, Jacob, was born. I was attended by a Mrs. Saunders, an English woman. It was in September. The weather turned cold and the wind blew from the north. It found its way through every crack in that poorly built house. I was so cold that during the first night they moved my bed into the living room by the stove and pinned sheets around it to keep the draft out and so I lived through the first child birth in the prairies. I liked to think that God watched out for us poor lonely women when the stork came.

In the spring our baby was taken very ill. I wanted a doctor so badly. There was a terrific storm and when it cleared the snow was ten feet deep. My husband couldn't risk a trip to Larimore. On the fourth day my baby died unattended. I never forgave the prairies for that. He was buried in the lot with Mrs. Seliger and a child of the Mendelson's. For many years we kept up the lonely graves. In time the wolves and elements destroyed them. They are unmarked in all save my memory.

In winter we killed our meats and froze them, in summer we bought fresh meat from the market and kept it by tying it to a rope and lowering it into the well where it kept as though on ice. Fresh fruit of any sort was almost unknown. We used Arbuckles coffee, paying a dollar for eight pounds. Our fare was

---

* Jewish Women's Archive.

meat and potatoes, bread and vegetables. The only fruit obtainable were dried. Syrup and jelly came in large wooden pails. Biscuits and jelly, pancakes and syrup constituted the favorite breakfast.

I never learned to milk a cow. On one occasion when my husband and the hired man went threshing and did not return at night I waited until dark. The cows came home to be milked. I tried my hand at milking. I sat under a gentle and patient cow for nearly an hour and succeeded in getting only a few drops of milk. I grew desperate, and drove my cows to the nearest neighbor. The man was away and Mrs. Fahey milked the cows for me and I carried home the heavy pails, a distance of about three-fourths of a mile. Card playing was

a favorite winter pastime. The neighbors would gather in each others homes. When extra men were needed a lantern was hung out and left there until they came. I can't remember that this signal ever failed.

By this time most of the sod houses and barns have been replaced by frame buildings and such luxuries as buggies and driving horses became common. There were schools in every district. Then came hanging lamps, upholstered furniture, carpets and curtains and when the cream separator came into common use I felt that the pioneer's days were gone and that the land was tamed forever. Year by year wild ducks and geese became scarcer, the storms become fewer and less severe and the Northern Lights less mysterious.

HELEN HUNT JACKSON, Excerpt from *A Century of Dishonor* (1883)

An outspoken critic of the government's treatment of Indians, Helen Hunt Jackson (1830–1885) demanded that the government end its dishonorable treatment of American Indians. In her account of the government's Indian policies, *A Century of Dishonor,* she became one of the fiercest and earliest advocates for American Indian rights. Highly critical of federal policies, she wanted protection for the remaining Mission Indians in California. Through her writing and political activism, Jackson appealed to the U.S. government to acknowledge and abandon its inhumane treatment of the Indians. Yet even Jackson's commitment to American Indians incorporated her belief in Anglo-American cultural superiority. In the following excerpt from her book, she describes the interaction between the Cheyenne and government officials.

What role did Jackson assign to the government in terms of the mistreatment of the Indians? How does she describe the conditions the Cheyenne Indians faced?*

The ration allowed to these Indians is reported as being "reduced and insufficient," and the small sums they have been able to earn by selling buffalo hides are said to have been "of material assistance" to them in "supplementing" this ration. But in this year there have been sold only $657 worth of skins by the Cheyennes and Arapahoes together. In 1876 they sold $17,600 worth. Here is a falling off enough to cause very great suffering in a little community of five thousand people. But this was only the beginning of

their troubles. The summer proved one of unusual heat. Extreme heat, chills and fever, and "a reduced and insufficient ration," all combined, resulted in an amount of sickness heart-rending to read of "It is no exaggerated estimate," says the agent, "to place the number of sick people on the reservation at two thousand. Many deaths occurred which might have been obviated had there been a proper supply of anti-malarial remedies at hand. Hundreds applying for treatment have been refused medicine."

---

* In the public domain.

The Northern Cheyennes grew more and more restless and unhappy. "In council and elsewhere they profess an intense desire to be sent North, where they say they will settle down as the others have done," says the report; adding, with an obtuseness which is inexplicable, that "no difference has been made in the treatment of the Indians," but that the "compliance" of these Northern Cheyennes has been "of an entirely different nature from that of the other Indians," and that it may be "necessary in the future to compel what so far we have been unable to effect by kindness and appeal to their better natures."

If it is "an appeal to men's better natures" to remove them by force from a healthful Northern climate, which they love and thrive in, to a malarial Southern one, where they are struck down by chills and fever—refuse them medicine which can combat chills and fever, and finally starve them there indeed, might be said to have been most forcible appeals made to the "better natures" of these Northern Cheyennes. What might have been predicted followed.

Early in the autumn, after this terrible summer, a band of some three hundred of these Northern Cheyennes took the desperate step of running off and attempting to make their way back to Dakota. They were pursued, fought desperately, but were finally overpowered, and surrendered. They surrendered, however, only on the condition that they should be taken to Dakota. They were unanimous in declaring that they would rather die than go back to the Indian Territory. This was nothing more, in fact, than saying that they would rather die by bullets than of chills and fever and starvation.

These Indians were taken to Fort Robinson, Nebraska. Here they were confined as prisoners of war, and held subject to the orders of the Department of the Interior. The department was informed of the Indians' determination never to be taken back alive to Indian Territory. The army officers in charge reiterated these statements, and implored the department to permit them to remain at the North; but it was of no avail. Orders came—explicit, repeated, finally stern—insisting on the return of these Indians to their agency. The commanding officer at Fort Robinson has been censured severely for the course he pursued in his effort to carry out those orders. It is difficult to see what else he could have done, except to have resigned his post. He could not take three hundred Indians by sheer brute force and carry them hundreds of miles, especially when they were so desperate that they had broken up the iron stoves in their quarters, and wrought and twisted them into weapons with which to resist. He thought perhaps he could starve them into submission. He stopped the issue of food; he also stopped the issue of fuel to them.

It was midwinter; the mercury froze in that month at Fort Robinson. At the end of two days he asked the Indians to let their women and children come out that he might feed them. Not a woman would come out. On the night of the fourth day—or, according to some accounts, the sixth—these starving, freezing Indians broke prison, overpowered the guards, and fled, carrying their women and children with them. They held the pursuing troops at bay for several days; finally made a last stand in a deep ravine, and were shot down—men, women, and children together. Out of the whole band there were left alive some fifty women and children and seven men, who, having been confined in another part of the fort, had not had the good fortune to share in this outbreak and meet their death in the ravine. These, with their wives and children, were sent to Fort Leavenworth to be put in prison; the men to be tried for murders committed in their skirmishes in Kansas on their way to the north. Red Cloud, a Sioux chief, came to Fort Robinson immediately after this massacre and entreated to be allowed to take the Cheyenne widows and orphans into his tribe to be cared for. The Government, therefore, kindly permitted twenty-two Cheyenne widows and thirty-two Cheyenne children—many of them orphans—to be received into the band of the Ogallalla Sioux.

An attempt was made by the Commissioner of Indian Affairs, in his Report for 1879, to show by tables and figures that these Indians were not starving at the time of their flight from Indian Territory. The attempt only redounded to his own disgrace; it being proved, by the testimony given by a former clerk of the Indian Bureau before the Senate committee appointed to investigate the case of the Northern Cheyennes, that the commissioner had been guilty of absolute dishonesty in his estimates, and that the quantity of beef actually issued to the Cheyenne Agency was hundreds of pounds less than he had reported it, and that the Indians were actually, as they had claimed, "starving."

The testimony given before this committee by some of the Cheyenne prisoners themselves is heart-rending. One must have a callous heart who can read it unmoved. When asked by Senator Jon T. Morgan, "Did you ever really suffer from hunger?" one of the chiefs replied, "We were always hungry; we never had enough. When they that were sick once in awhile felt as though they could eat something, we had nothing to give them."

"Did you not go out on the plains sometimes and hunt buffalo, with the consent of the agent?"

"We went out on a buffalo-hunt, and nearly starved while out; we could not find any buffalo hardly; we could hardly get back with our ponies; we had to kill a good many of our ponies to eat, to save ourselves from starving."

"How many children got sick and died?"

"Between the fall of 1877 and 1878 we lost fifty children. A great many of our finest young men died, as well as many women."

"Old Crow," a chief who served faithfully as Indian scout and ally under General George Crook for years, said: "I did not feel like doing anything for awhile, because I had no heart. I did not want to be in this country. I was all the time wanting to get back to the better country where I was born, and where my children are buried, and where my mother and sister yet live. So I have laid in my lodge most of the time with nothing to think about but that, and the affair up north at Fort Robinson, and my relatives and friends who were killed there. But now I feel as though, if I had a wagon and a horse or two, and some land, I would try to work. If I had something, so that I could do something, I might not think so much about these other things. As it is now, I feel as though I would just as soon be asleep with the rest."

The wife of one of the chiefs confined at Fort Leavenworth testified before the committee as follows: "The main thing I complained of was that we didn't get enough to eat; my children nearly starved to death; then sickness came, and there was nothing good for them to eat; for a long time the most they had to eat was corn-meal and salt. Three or four children died every day for awhile, and that frightened us."

When asked if there were anything she would like to say to the committee, the poor woman replied: "I wish you would do what you can to get my husband released. I am very poor here, and do not know what is to become of me. If he were released he would come down here, and we would live together quietly, and do no harm to anybody, and make no trouble. But I should never get over my desire to get back north; I should always want to get back where my children were born, and died, and were buried. That country is better than this in every respect. There is plenty of good, cool water there—pure water—while here the water is not good. It is not hot there, nor so sickly. Are you going where my husband is? Can you tell when he is likely to be released?" . . .

It is stated also that there was not sufficient clothing to furnish each Indian with a warm suit of clothing, "as promised by the treaty," and that, "by reference to official correspondence, the fact is established that the Cheyennes and Arapahoes are judged as having no legal rights to any lands, having forfeited their treaty reservation by a failure to settle thereon," and their "present reservation not having been, as yet, confirmed by Congress. Inasmuch as the Indians fully understood, and were assured that this reservation was given to them in lieu of their treaty reservation, and have commenced farming in the belief that there was no uncertainty about the matter it is but common justice that definite action be had at an early day, securing to them what is their right."

It would seem that there could be found nowhere in the melancholy record of the experiences of our Indians a more glaring instance of confused multiplication of injustices than this. The Cheyennes were pursued and slain for venturing to leave this very reservation, which, it appears, is not their reservation at all, and they have no legal right to it. Are there any words to fitly characterize such treatment as this from a great, powerful, rich nation, to a handful of helpless people?

SARAH WINNEMUCCA HOPKINS, *Life Among the Piutes: Their Wrongs and Claims* (1883)

A northern Piute, Sarah Winnemucca Hopkins (1844–1891) was the first American Indian woman to write her autobiography. In her own lifetime, the American government reduced Piute lands from what had been open access to the Nevada Territory to a reservation in California. The Piutes, like other tribes before them, were forced to relocate. Hopkins was and to a degree still is judged by some to be an outstanding defender of her tribal heritage and by others to have betrayed Piute interests. She used her language skills and leadership to alert Indian reformers to the plight of her tribe. In her own day, she served as a mediator between the U.S. government and the Piutes. Broken promises of the federal government compromised her integrity as negotiator, and government removal thwarted her efforts to protect the Piutes. Nonetheless she spent most of her life fighting to protect the rights of her people. Near the end of her life, she opened a school that would continue to use the Piute language rather than enforce English usage.

How does Hopkins describe the Piutes first encounter with whites? How would you evaluate her childhood experience?*

Chapter I

First Meeting of Piutes and Whites

I WAS born somewhere near 1844, but am not sure of the precise time. I was a very small child when the first white people came into our country. They came like a lion, yes, like a roaring lion, and have continued so ever since, and I have never forgotten their first coming. My people were scattered at that time over nearly all the territory now known as Nevada. My grandfather was chief of the entire Piute nation, and was camped near Humboldt Lake, with a small portion of his tribe, when a party travelling eastward from California was seen coming. When the news was brought to my grandfather, he asked what they looked like? When told that they had hair on their faces, and were white, he jumped up and clasped his hands together, and cried aloud,—

"My white brothers,—my long-looked for white brothers have come at last!" . . .

The next year came a great emigration, and camped near Humboldt Lake. The name of the man in charge of the trains was Captain Johnson, and they stayed three days to rest

---

* In the public domain.

their horses, as they had a long journey before them without water. During their stay my grandfather and some of his people called upon them, and they all shook hands, and when our white brothers were going away they gave my grandfather a white tin plate. Oh, what a time they had over that beautiful gift,—it was so bright! They say that after they left, my grandfather called for all his people to come together, and he then showed them the beautiful gift which he had received from his white brothers. Everybody was so pleased; nothing like it was ever seen in our country before. My grandfather thought so much of it that he bored holes in it and fastened it on his head, and wore it as his hat. He held it in as much admiration as my white sisters hold their diamond rings or a sealskin jacket. So that winter they talked of nothing but their white brothers. The following spring there came great news down the Humboldt River, saying that there were some more of the white brothers coming, and there was something among them that was burning all in a blaze. My grandfather asked them what it was like. They told him it looked like a man; it had legs and hands and a head, but the head had quit burning, and it was left quite black. There was the greatest excitement among my people everywhere about the men in a blazing fire. They were excited because they did not know there were any people in the world but the two,—that is, the Indians and the whites; they thought that was all of us in the beginning of the world, and, of course, we did not know where the others had come from, and we don't know yet. Ha! ha! oh, what a laughable thing that was! It was two negroes wearing red shirts!

The third year more emigrants came, and that summer Captain Fremont, who is now General Fremont.

My grandfather met him, and they were soon friends. They met just where the railroad crosses Truckee River, now called Wadsworth, Nevada. Captain Fremont gave my grandfather the name of Captain Truckee, and he also called the river after him. <u>Truckee is an Indian word, it means *all right,* or *very well.*</u> A party of twelve of my people went to California with Captain Fremont. I do not know just how long they were gone. . . .

The following spring, before my grandfather returned home, there was a great excitement among my people on account of fearful news coming from different tribes, that the people whom they called their white brothers were killing everybody that came in their way, and all the Indian tribes had gone into the mountains to save their lives. So my father told all his people to go into the mountains and hunt and lay up food for the coming winter. Then we all went into the mountains. There was a fearful story they told us children. Our mothers told us that the whites were killing everybody and eating them. So we were all afraid of them. Every dust that we could see blowing in the valleys we would say it was the white people. In the late fall my father told his people to go to the rivers and fish, and we all went to Humboldt River, and the women went to work gathering wild seed, which they grind between the rocks. The stones are round, big enough to hold in the hands. The women did this when they got back, and when they had gathered all they could they put it in one place and covered it with grass, and then over the grass mud. After it is covered it looks like an Indian wigwam.

Oh, what a fright we all got one morning to hear some white people were coming. Every one ran as best they could. My poor mother was left with my little sister and me. Oh, I never can forget it. My poor mother was carrying my little sister on her back, and trying to make me run; but I was so frightened I could not move my feet, and while my poor mother was trying to get me along my aunt overtook us, and she said to my mother: "Let us bury our girls, or we shall all be killed and eaten up." So they went to work and buried us, and told us if we heard any noise not to cry out, for if we did they would surely kill us and eat us. So our mothers buried me and my cousin, planted sage bushes over our faces to keep the sun from burning them, and there we were left all day.

Oh, can any one imagine my feelings *buried alive,* thinking every minute that I was to be unburied and eaten up by the people that my grandfather loved so much? With my heart throbbing, and not daring to breathe, we lay there all day. It seemed that the night would never come. Thanks be to God! the night came at last. Oh, how I cried and said: "Oh, father, have you forgotten me? Are you never coming for me?" I cried so I thought my very heartstrings would break.

At last we heard some whispering. We did not dare to whisper to each other, so we lay still. I could hear their footsteps coming nearer and nearer. I thought my heart was coming right out of my mouth. Then I heard my mother say, "'T is right here!" Oh, can any one in this world ever imagine what were my feelings when I was dug up by my poor mother and father? My cousin and I were once more happy in our mothers' and fathers' care, and we were taken to where all the rest were.

I was once buried alive; but my second burial shall be for ever, where no father or mother will come and dig me up. It shall not

be with throbbing heart that I shall listen for coming footsteps. I shall be in the sweet rest of peace,—I, the chieftain's weary daughter.

Well, while we were in the mountains hiding, the people that my grandfather called our white brothers came along to where our winter supplies were. They set everything we had left on fire. It was a fearful sight. It was all we had for the winter, and it was all burnt during that night. My father took some of his men during the night to try and save some of it, but they could not; it had burnt down before they got there.

These were the last white men that came along that fall. My people talked fearfully that winter about those they called our white brothers. My people said they had something like awful thunder and lightning, and with that they killed everything that came in their way.

This whole band of white people perished in the mountains, for it was too late to cross them. We could have saved them, only my people were afraid of them. We never knew who they were, or where they came from. So, poor things, they must have suffered fearfully, for they all starved there. The snow was too deep.

ALICE FLETCHER, *"Our Duty to Dependent Races," Transactions of the National Council of Women* **(1891)**

Alice Fletcher (1838–1923) was the first female anthropologist to actually live with the American Indian tribes that she studied. She shared Helen Hunt Jackson's negative evaluation of American treatment of Indians. She also shared with the Women's National Indian Association, a belief in the superiority of white, Christian, Euro-American civilization. In common with many white Americans, Fletcher was guided in her perception of American Indians by racial and ethnocentric assumptions. As a late-nineteenth-century anthropologist, she also accepted the prevalent assumption that progress toward civilization, which she defined in ethnocentric terms, evolved over time. She believed that total immersion of Indians in Americanization programs would accelerate their evolutionary progress and their ability to assimilate into American civilization. In the following document, Fletcher promotes the Women's National Indian Association agenda and also praises the work of Protestant missionaries.

How would you evaluate Fletcher's agenda for Indian assimilation? How did the Women's National Indian Association support Americanization policies?*

* In the public domain.

We use the term "Dependent Races" in an historic sense, and apply it solely to the race problem which confronts the people of the United States.

There are in our country a considerable number of people belonging to two races, each distinct from the other, and from our own race, physiologically and linguistically, having but a few points in common in their folk-lore and religious beliefs, which points seem to touch the whole human family. There are therefore gathered under one system of law the representatives of three diverse races, and their relations to each other present many phases of study new in the history of nations.

In a republic the interests of all citizens are indissolubly bound together; the cords of trade, of mutual dependence, make of many members but one body; if a portion suffer, all suffer, and safety for the republic is to be found only in those provisions which afford security and prosperity to each one of these many members; so, in the list of qualifications for citizenship, race differences should not be called in question, since before the law all should enjoy equal rights "to life, liberty, and the pursuit of happiness." In theory this is conceded, but human nature and its prejudices are stronger than the enactments of legislative bodies, and the facts of to-day read,—that one's race does augment or reduce one's chances of enjoying these theoretic and legal rights.

The causes which lie at the root of the feeling of repulsion so common between individuals of different races cannot be fairly or authoritatively stated with our present knowledge of the history of man. Race integrity has its claims. It is right that a race should insist upon being allowed to keep on its way towards a full development; that it should have open to it all knowledge which has been gained by other races; that it should appropriate its share of the earth's surface, and perform its part of the world's labor; and that no other race should declare that it shall cease to exist, or pronounce its destruction by war, pestilence, or absorption. . . .

The Indian holds towards us quite different historic relations from those of the negro, but our ignorance of him is equally profound. We have learned to fear the Red Man, and our fears, often well founded, have so disturbed our vision that it is hard to get a sight of the man as he really is. We have fought him with guns, with whiskey, with disease. We have sought to get him out of our way, regardless of the moral consequences to ourselves. He has fought us, and he has bred evil among us by turning loose the lightly-leashed savage element of our nature,—our greed, our hatred, our contempt. The conduct of white men at home here in the East, contrasted with the conduct of the same men in the West among the Indians, shows how slight a hold our race civilization has over our primitive savagery, how strong the tendency to atavism. We are not yet all civilized; in our onward march the rear column straggles far behind and often reverts to types that exceed in cruelty those we call barbarians. Happily, the better element is now strong enough to prevail, and Christian sentiment finds cordial reinforcement from governmental authority. The present Commissioner of Indian Affairs is whole-hearted in his efforts to set the Indian upon his land in severalty, to provide him with educational facilities, to open the way for his self-support and entrance into the rights of citizenship.

The landed wealth of the Indian has been his bane; it is now being made as rapidly as possible to serve him in his efforts towards self-maintenance in a new and a difficult future. It is a cause for gratulation that at this crisis so fearless, tireless, and conscientious an officer as General Morgan is at the head of Indian affairs. Let but the public uphold him in his work, and he will soon solve the vexed Indian problem.

Much of the difficulty in dealing with the Indian has arisen out of our profound ignorance of him, and it has been a hard and a slow task to penetrate that ignorance. Much has been done by missionaries from the time of John Eliot to the present, but the great work of enlightenment has come down to the philanthropic of our own day. Much credit should be given the Woman's National Indian Association for their persistent efforts in this direction. Twelve years ago a few earnest practical women determined to attack the public ignorance, and, if it might be, change that ignorance to an enlightened public sentiment working towards justice and humanity. The diluted Christian feeling over the land concentrated and crystallized about these women, and to-day its numbers are among the thousands; there is hardly a State or Territory without its branch society, while in the larger cities and towns their organizations are in full working order. What these women have done cannot be tabulated. They have largely helped to make possible the carrying out of the great work now being done by the government, supplemented by private enterprise.

The Woman's National Indian Association is composed of eight departments:

- 1st. The Legislative Department. State and local Secretaries and Press Committees all over the country publish facts in the papers, periodicals, and magazines. These are also sent to officials, and when important relevant matters are pending in Congress or elsewhere, careful and concise statements are furnished, and many a victory for the right has been thus quietly gained.
- 2d. Mission Department. Many of our Indian tribes have ever had a mission among them, and it has been the care of this department to collect money to build a house or chapel, to secure requisite land and establish a mission among the people, turning it over to some organized religious body at the earliest day. Several such stations have been already started, and of them four chapels and four cottages have been given up to the management of different denominations.
- 3d. Home-Building Department. This department makes small loans to Indians desirous of building houses or opening up farms, or to those in need of a wagon, horses, mowing- or sewing-machine, in fact, for anything that will help to make or keep the home. Some fifty cottages have been erected by Indians with the aid of this department, and the helpfulness that has gone out from it cannot be estimated. Men, women, and children from Alaska to the Gulf of Mexico have felt the kindly touch, and to-day are better and happier and more useful by reason of it.
- 4th. Department of Special Indian Education. There are many young men and women in different tribes possessing promising talents and desirous of using them to benefit their people. The means towards a higher education are often lacking. This department has educated young people in the law and in medicine, some of whom are already in this field of work, doing brave service.
- 5th. The Young People's Department. Various bands of children are instructed to lend the might of their little hands to help their elders in the task of uplifting the Indian; the aid which they give, welcome as it is, is of far less moment than the development of character resulting to these little helpers from their interested efforts. In helping others we all help ourselves.
- 6th. Indian Civilization Department. This department aims to establish labor bureaus on reservations through which work may be obtained at self-supporting wages by returned students and other Indians. Its practical worth is self-evident.
- 7th. Library Department. Books, periodicals, and papers are sent to returned students and reading-rooms furnished on the reservations.

• 8th. Hospital Department. The building and equipping of hospitals and the furnishing of trained nurses is the charge of this department.

Such, in brief, is the manner in which this organization of women carries forward its work, timely and practical in all its lines.

ZITKALA–SA, *The School Days of an Indian Girl* (1900)

Founder and first president of the National Council of American Indians, Zitkala–Sa (1876–1938) described the pain of her disrupted identity. In the article that follows, she described how Americanization left her in a cultural void. Even though she was uprooted from her native beliefs, she failed to fully adapt to American culture. How does this article add to our knowledge of power relationships between American Indians and European Americans? How did Zitkala–Sa evaluate the effort to exchange her Indian identity with an American one?*

The first turning away from the easy, natural flow of my life occurred in an early spring. It was in my eighth year; in the month of March, I afterward learned. At this age I knew but one language, and that was my mother's native tongue. . . .

The Cutting of My Long Hair

The first day in the land of apples was a bitter cold one; for the snow still covered the ground, and the trees were bare. A large bell rang for breakfast, its loud metallic voice crashing through the belfry overhead and into our sensitive ears. The annoying clatter of shoes on bare floors gave us no peace. The constant clash of harsh noises, with an undercurrent of many voices murmuring an unknown tongue, made a bedlam within which I was securely tied. And though my spirit tore itself in struggling for its lost freedom, all was useless.

A paleface woman, with white hair, came up after us. We were placed in a line of girls who were marching into the dining room. These were Indian girls, in stiff shoes and closely clinging dresses. The small girls wore sleeved aprons and shingled hair. As I walked noiselessly in my soft moccasins, I felt like sinking to the floor, for my blanket had been stripped from my shoulders. I looked hard at the Indian girls, who seemed not to care that they were even more immodestly dressed than I, in their tightly fitting clothes. While we marched in, the boys entered at an opposite door. I watched for the three young braves who came in our party. I spied them in the rear ranks, looking as uncomfortable as I felt.

A small bell was tapped, and each of the pupils drew a chair from under the table. Supposing this act meant they were to be seated, I pulled out mine and at once slipped into it from one side. But when I turned my head, I saw that I was the only one seated, and all the rest at our table remained standing. Just as I began to rise, looking shyly around to see how chairs were to be used, a second bell was sounded. All were seated at last, and I had to crawl back into my chair again. I heard a man's voice at one end of the hall, and I looked around to see him. But all the others hung their heads over their plates. As I glanced at the long chain of tables, I caught the eyes of a paleface woman upon me.

---

* From Zitkala–Sa (Gertrude Simmons Bonnin), "The School Days of an Indian Girl," *Atlantic Monthly* 89, January–March 1900.

Immediately I dropped my eyes, wondering why I was so keenly watched by the strange woman. The man ceased his mutterings, and then a third bell was tapped. Everyone picked up his knife and fork and began eating. I began crying instead, for by this time I was afraid to venture anything more.

But this eating by formula was not the hardest trial in that first day. Late in the morning, my friend Judéwin gave me a terrible warning. Judéwin knew a few words of English; and she had overheard the paleface woman talk about cutting our long, heavy hair. Our mothers had taught us that only unskilled warriors who were captured had their hair shingled by the enemy. Among our people, short hair was worn by mourners, and shingled hair by cowards!

We discussed our fate for some moments, and when Judéwin said, "We have to submit, because they are strong," I rebelled.

"No, I will not submit! I will struggle first!" I answered.

I watched my chance, and when no one noticed I disappeared. I crept up the stairs as quietly as I could in my squeaking shoes—my moccasins had been exchanged for shoes. Along the hall I passed, without knowing whither I was going. Turning aside to an open door, I found a large room with three white beds in it. The windows were covered with dark green curtains, which made the room very dim. Thankful that no one was there. I directed my steps toward the corner farthest from the door. On my hands and knees I crawled under the bed, and cuddled myself in the dark corner.

From my hiding place I peered out, shuddering with fear whenever I heard footsteps nearby. Though in the hall loud voices were calling my name, and I knew that even Judéwin was searching for me, I did not open my mouth to answer. Then the steps were quickened and the voices became excited. The sounds came nearer and nearer. Women and girls entered the room. I held my breath and watched them open closet doors and peep behind large trunks. Someone threw up the curtains, and the room was filled with sudden light. What caused them to stoop and look under the bed I do not know. I remember being dragged out, though I resisted by kicking and scratching wildly. In spite of myself, I was carried downstairs and tied fast in a chair.

I cried aloud, shaking my head all the while until I felt the cold blades of the scissors against my neck, and heard them gnaw off one of my thick braids. Then I lost my spirit. Since the day I was taken from my mother I had suffered extreme indignities. People had stared at me. I had been tossed about in the air like a wooden puppet. And now my long hair was shingled like a coward's! In my anguish I moaned for my mother, but no one came to comfort me. Not a soul reasoned quietly with me, as my own mother used to do, for now I was only one of many little animals driven by a herder.

Zikala-Sa (© Bettmann/CORBIS All Rights Reserved)

Sɪsᴛᴇʀ Bʟᴀɴᴅɪɴᴀ Sᴇɢᴀʟᴇ, **Excerpt from** *At the End of the Santa Fe Trail* **(1932)**

A member of the Cincinnati, Ohio, Sisters of Charity, Sister Blandina Segale (1850–1941) was born in Italy and came to Cincinnati with her family at age four. As a young woman, she represented the Sisters of Charity first in Colorado's Trinidad mining frontier and then in Santa Fe and Albuquerque, New Mexico. Her autobiographical narrative covers events from 1872 through the 1890s and was published in 1932. Not a member of a cloistered order, Sister Blandina moved freely through the community, mixing with culturally diverse people and taking care of seriously ill individuals regardless of religious affiliation. For more than twenty years, she was both teacher and educator, promoting the building of schools in the still relatively undeveloped environments of Colorado and New Mexico. After her return to Ohio, she was instrumental in developing the Santa Maria Institute that offered Cincinnati immigrants settlement house support services.

In the following excerpt, she expresses her concept of protection for the Indians. How would you describe her views? How did Segale contrast her approach to the Indians with that of the anthropologist Bandelier? How might this difference of approach relate not only to their different fields of work but also to the gender norms of the era?*

"I told you, Sister, when I was about to go to the Indians, who were supposed to worship snakes, that I would remain with them until I could prove the truth or falsity of snake worship. Here are my proofs (unfolding sketches of an estufa and some snakes)—no doubt whatever, these Indians are snake worshippers."

"Knowing the Indians' tenacity to hold secrets, I am curious to know how you managed to get into their *estufa*." (Council Chamber).

"I will tell you, Sister. The first day I approached these Indians they gave me plainly to understand I was not wanted. They saw I was not armed. I only carry my whittling knife, water colors and material for sketching. I made sketches of my own surroundings, which pleased those who saw them and who were trying to find out why I came among them.

"The day passed and night came. I made a bed of leaves and cedar and was content. The next day other Indians of the same clan came and treated me about the same—only I spoke more in order to get them to answer as I wanted to familiarize myself with their particular language. The interchange of speech pleased them, but their attitude toward me remained the same. In a few days the small amount of my edible provisions gave out, so I ate what the Indians threw to the dogs—after the dogs were satiated."

I could only look at the man and wonder. He continued:

"For fully five months this was the routine. I sketched and spoke to those of the clan who came to see and watch me and talk to me. I did many little services for those who came near me which I could see pleased them. At last I was invited to eat and sleep among them though the Chief gave me some of the squaws' work to do. I knew this was the last test before they gave me their confidence. Little by little the old men came to ask advice, then at last I was admitted to their Council in the *Estufa*. This was the seventh month among them. As they had seen me daily sketching, my doing so in the Councilroom did not alarm them—in fact they were pleased to see the snakes on paper; they compared them and were satisfied they were good.

---

* In the public domain.

"Altogether I remained nine months to make sure those Indians worship snakes. I left the clan on friendly terms."

"Thank you so much for the information."

"I understand, Sister, you have had some encounters with the Apaches and other tribes of Indians. Would you mind telling me anything that would be of interest in my research work?"

"Mr. Bandelier, contacts made by me with any Indian tribe, were, and are, of a protective type. On several occasions I gave ample reasons to prove that the government agents were defrauding the tribes they were paid for assisting. I once reconciled the Apaches—in an act of injustice toward them—convincing them that one white man doing wrong to them did not mean that all white men would do as he did. In Trinidad,

Colorado, in the early seventies we were all expecting an attack from the Utes. The whole tribe was camped a few miles from Trinidad. The citizens made full preparation for defense. Our convent was to be the fort. Meanwhile, I made some of the Indians—who came in to reconnoiter—understand that we (all of the inhabitants) were friendly. Maybe they didn't test me in their own Indian way! But they soon recognized I was friendly and sincere. Their Chief at the time was Rafael, whose son was dying of pneumonia. Rafael asked if he should bury him like a dog. I said: 'No. I will send for him and bury him like a Christian.' He had been baptized. After the son's burial, the tribe moved on. You see, Mr. Bandelier, all of my contacts with the Indians partook of protectiveness and nothing of a scientific nature."

JOHANNA JULY, *Interview, Federal Writers' Project* (1936–1940)

A descendent of slaves and Seminole Indians, Johanna July (c. 1857–c.1946) supplied this autobiographical information when she was interviewed as part of the Federal Writers' Project. Her nonconformist lifestyle and independent spirit infused the interview. July was a member of the Seminole tribe that fled to Mexico and subsequently returned to Texas. The woman who interviewed July interweaves her own commentary with July's narrative.

Using her own unique methods of taming wild horses, July described her life as a horse "breaker" and how she tamed horses for the U.S. Army. In what ways does the description of July's physical appearance visually highlight this interview? How did July's relationships to her three husbands demonstrate her independent spirit? How did she deal with her abusive first husband? What reasons might account for the fact that the life of Johanna July, an example of independent womanhood, is not better known?*

One of the most interesting characters of the so-called Seminole tribe to ever cross the border from Mexico was Johanna July, a horsebreaker. She came across to Eagle Pass with her family as members of the band who signed a contract in '71 with Major Perry of the U. S. Army to help clear the Texas side of the Rio Grande of depredating Indians.

This tribe of Seminole Indians was a mixture of the Seminole Indians with the

Negro. Fleeing from Florida after the Seminole War, a number of Negro slaves came with the Indians into Mexico. After crossing into Mexico they became so thorough in clearing their territory of the marauders, their fame spread into the U.S. which prompted the invitation from the army. They were first brought across the Rio Grande to Fort Duncan at Eagle Pass, then to Fort Clark at Brackettville, where a tract

---

* In the public domain.

of land was assigned them to live on adjoining the post.

Johanna was a colorful girl, whose Indian blood was dominant. Her love of horses, her wily and daring ways, her bright dresses and ornaments were that of an Indian. Her quick, darting eyes, aquiline nose, thin lips and high cheek bones showed more Indian blood than Negro.

Her horsemanship was her pride. Being practically forced into the job of breaking horses after her father died and her brother "runned away," Johanna lived the life of a carefree Indian boy. She scorned a saddle, preferring to ride bareback and sideways.

"I couldn't ride a hoss like dey do dese days," she said. "I couldn't straddle 'em. I didn't use no bridle either, just a rope around deir necks and looped over de nose. We called it a 'nosin.'—same as a half-hitch. Old man Adam Wilson learned me how to ride. He was an old scout. Right today I don't like a saddle an' I don't like shoes. I can sure get over de ground barefooted."

As a girl, Johanna was not required to do a woman's work about the place. Her meals were always ready for her and her clothes were washed. Her job was to break horses, take them to water, cut grass for them, look after the other stock and ride, ride, ride.

Dressed in a bright homespun dress, ropes of beads around her slender neck, long gold earrings nearly touching her shoulders, her hair in thick, black braids and her feet bare, she flashed among her horses like a bright bird, soothing them with a masterful hand and soft words. A shuck cigarette of Black Horse tobacco between her lips, Johanna rode as well as a boy, her eye always quick and her senses alert.

The horses were there to break and Johanna, being dextrous and nimble, was quite able to accomplish the task, though she devised her own means of doing so.

"I could break a hoss myself, me and my Lawd," she declared soberly. "Many a narrow scrape I've been through wid hosses and mules. I'll tell you how I broke my hosses. I would pull off my clothes and get into de clothes I intended to bathe in and I would lead 'em right into de Rio Grande and keep 'en in dere till dey got pretty well worried. When dey was wild, wild, I would lead 'im down to de river and get 'im out in water where he couldn't stan' up and I would swim up and get 'im by de mane an' ease up on 'im. He couldn't pitch and when I did let 'im out of dat deep water he didn't *want* to pitch. Sometimes dey wasn't so wore out an' would take a runnin' spree wid me when dey got out in shallow water where dey could get deir feet on de ground, and dey would run clear up into de corral. But I was young and I was havin' a good time.

"I was used to hard ridin'. I've been chased by de Indians. One day it was cloudy and I went out to cut hey for de hosses, and as de Lawd should have it, I got so sleepy I said, 'Suppose I lay down here an' take myself a nap an' den finish cuttin, my hay,' but I thought 'No, I better go on and cut my hay,' an' about den, I seen de hosses gettin' nervous an' dey had deir ears up lookin' at somet'ing an' actin' scared. I had a big bay an' I could call 'im up to me so I hollered to 'im, 'Come Bill, come Bill!' An' all de hosses come runnin'. I jumped on a little gray hoss named Charley, an' when I cut my eye aroun' here come a Indian in full gallop, leanin' over on his hoss, en' I started runnin' an' run clear by de army post, me and all dem hosses. The post sent the scout out and dey took up de trail. Dey was two Indians an' dey followed 'em clear into Mexico and brought 'em back. But dat didn't break me. I was always out wid dem hosses."

Johanna knew nothing of housekeeping, sewing or cooking, when, at eighteen, she married a Seminole scout named Lesley. Her life had been as free and untamed as a bird's. She could judge a horse's age, endurance and speed, she knew where the eagles nested and the coyote kept her whelps and she could point out the dark pools where the yellow cat fed in the Rio Grande.

But that wasn't the knowledge she needed when she married the scout who brought her to live at Fort Clark away from the Rio Grande and her horses. However, she tried hard to be a dutiful wife. There were days when she attempted to sew and the thread knotted, the material was cut wrong and the whole garment wouldn't fit. She scorched her beans and rice, got the stew too dry and forgot to put the corn to soak. The husband came in with harsh words, and a hard fist. Instead of the kindness she had known, she was intro- duced to a life that seemed more like a pris- oner's. At length, her tears dried and her cunning brain began to deliberate on escape. She was not capricious for life in the open had prepared her to face facts with an open mind, and her grief was genuine.

Thus, her fearlessness and endurance were to be put to the test. After a particularly stormy encounter with her husband one day, in which she felt that his cruelty had passed the limit of her endurance, she slipped quietly from the house and stole into a neighbor's field where a work horse was kept. Having no rope, she took a small, worn pocketknife she carried and cut strips of pite (Spanish dagger) into strings and made a rope. As she rode out from the post toward Eagle Pass where her mother was living, she heard the cannon fire at sunset.

"I couldn't get dat old pony out of a trot," she remembers, "and I rode dat forty-five miles dat night. As I got to Fort Duncan I heard de sentry call out, 'Four o'clock an' all is well!' I know I said to myself, 'All may be well, but I don't feel so well after dis ride!' I met two batches of men an' I guess day tole I was a woman 'cause dey heard me talk. Dey tole me, 'Who comes dere?' and I said, 'Frien!' Den dey said, 'Whar you headed for?' and I tole 'em, 'Fort Duncan,' an' dey let me pass an' didn't offer to hurt me. I guess dey was rangers. De next bunch I met was about a mile from de fort. Dey didn't speak an' I didn't either.

"I never did go back to 'im. He come down dere three or four times to get me but I wouldn't go. He shot at me two different times but he missed me, den he tried to rope me, but de Lawd fixed it so my head was too low and de rope went over. I got to de brush an' he never could find me. He would have killed me, an' I knowed it!

"After he died I married twice mo'. I helped my last husband break hosses an' mules. I 'member one bad mule. He was the meanest one I ever had any dealin's wid. He was 'hip-shotten.' I had to tie his good front leg to his good back leg an', don't you know, he'd catch me by de clothes and toss me and shake me if he could get hold of me. I never did break 'im, I got 'fraid of 'im. I've had some awful scrapes. I hunted and trapped wid my las' husband and sold many a hide. I could get out and cut a cord and a half of wood, easy. Down here on de Fadillas ranch I've had mules run away wid me an' sometimes tear de wagon to pieces.

"My last husband has been dead eight years now. My first husband was so mean to me I suppose dat was why de Lawd fixed it so I didn't divo'ce 'im an' he didn't divo'ce me, an' now what little bread I'm gettin', I'm gettin' it right off of him."

Johanna lives on a hill in the northeast part of Brackettville. She, like the others who were moved from the post, resents the government's having moved them from Fort Clark. With only two of the original scouts who signed the contract still living, and only three of the oldest woman who were wives or sisters of the first scouts, it would seem that the government had fulfilled its contract with them long and well.

Active and nimble at 77, Johanna moves about her small place on the hill, tending a garden, keeping house, gliding over the rocks barefooted and rolling her cigarettes with a steady hand.

EMMELINE WELLS, *"Is It Ignorance?" The Woman's Exponent* (July 1, 1883)

Emmeline Wells (1828–1921) was born in Massachusetts. As a young married woman, she moved with the Mormon community first to Illinois and then to Utah. After her first husband's desertion, she entered into a polygamous marriage with a much older man only to become widowed a short time later. Her subsequent and final marriage occurred when she became the seventh wife of Daniel Wells, a prominent Mormon leader. She lived separately from Wells and his other wives. In her writing, she expresses loneliness and sorrow that her husband did not love her. However, she turned these marital deficiencies into strengths and developed self-reliance and a pro–women's rights perspective. Within the Mormon community, she edited the women's journal, *The Woman's Exponent,* and advocated polygamy, suffrage, and women's rights. She participated in national suffrage activity and was acquainted with both Elizabeth Cady Stanton and Susan B. Anthony.

What defense does Wells provide about the qualities of Mormon women and the reasons for their defense of polygamy?*

It seems a very common thing with people unacquainted with the facts to say, it is the ignorance of "Mormon" women "that keeps them in bondage," that "makes them submit to plural marriage," when in truth the very contrary is the case. It is because of the intelligence they possess on subjects connected with their existence here and hereafter, as well as that of their posterity and kindred, the hopes entertained, and the actual knowledge concerning the future that causes them to embrace a doctrine so unpopular and so objectionable in the eyes of the world. Such paragraphs as the following and similar ones abound in the newspapers and journals of the day: "It was hoped by giving the women of Utah the ballot they would use it for the destruction of the monster, which keeps them under its iron heel, in hopeless misery." These people may be well meaning, but they talk nonsense and folly in the extreme. Who are the "Mormon" women, who accepted plural marriage when the principle was first revealed to the Prophet Joseph, and taught to a few of the people called Latter-day Saints?

They were just such sound, practical, intelligent women as the foremothers of New England and the women pioneers of those Eastern States. Women prepared to encounter hardships and privation, perils by land and sea for the sake of the religion in which they devoutly and implicitly believed. Aye, more! Determined not only to make the sacrifices incident to all those sufferings, but still further to prove their integrity to God by denying themselves that others might be benefited and exalted. . . . The women who entered into these sacred covenants of marriage for time and all eternity accepted this holy order as a divine revelation and commandment, and in all sincerity, with the purest motives obeyed the same. . . .

Mormon girls and women have as sensible ideas upon marriage as any people in the civilized world. They are thoroughly taught and instructed to consider well before accepting this sacred rite, and to choose wisely. More particularly are they cautioned in this regard, because, the covenants they make are not only for time, but reach into eternity. It is an important matter to make the choice of a companion for this life, but how much more so does it become when the union is an eternal one. In order to investigate the "Mormon" question it is essentially necessary to know the people themselves, and not accept testimony of reporters, tourists and sensational writers nor yet of political demagogues, whose sole aim is to make

---

* In the public domain.

capital by the votes of the Territory, and turn everything into the hands of their own party. "Mormon" people have rights under the Constitution, and they will seek to maintain them, women as well as men. If anyone supposes these same women citizens to be ignorant of the rights the ballot gives them, then they know very little about the women of this Territory, and our advice to them is, let the matter rest until you have an opportunity of solving the problem by thorough investigation, and not from one side, and remember the words of the Savior, "Judge not, lest ye be judged."

FANNY STENHOUSE, *Tell It All: A Woman's Life in Polygamy* (1875)

In complete contrast to Emmeline Wells's ardent commitment, Fanny Stenhouse (1828–unknown) renounced polygamy and the Mormon religion. Even before Eliza Young, Brigham Young's nineteenth wife, divorced him and proceeded to go on a confessional lecture tour, Stenhouse wrote *Tell It All: A Woman's Life in Polygamy.* In one of the book's most compelling episodes, she describes her emotional ordeal when after fifteen years of marriage and six children, her husband decided to take a second wife. First wives who denied their husband's request for a second wife were considered "rebels." Moreover, a first wife's denial of plural wives lessened her husband's chance for celestial happiness. Stenhouse felt compelled to accept her husband's decision regardless of her own feelings.

Stenhouse received encouragement to publish her writing about her ordeal as a plural wife from Harriet Beecher Stowe, who wrote the book's introduction. Like many non-Mormons, Stowe considered polygamy a form of female enslavement. For a wife unwilling to accept polygamy, and Stenhouse was one of them, membership in the Mormon religion became impossible. Hugely popular, her book and lecture tour provided the curious with a firsthand account of Mormon polygamy. How does Stenhouse attempt to undermine the Mormon belief that plural marriage is a man's religious duty? Many of the anti-polygamy writings exposed sensationalist details. How would you assess Stenhouse's commentary? How would you describe the tone of her criticism of Mormon men?*

Any idea of mutual obligation between husbands and wives has, I believe, never entered the mind of Brigham Young and the leaders who most nearly imitate him. He himself has forsaken wife after wife, giving them no love, no companionship; nay, scarcely even a thought. They have gone out of his life as completely as if they had never possessed the slightest interest in his eyes. He has, however, continued to give them "breadstuffs," clothing and shelter, which he could so well afford; but it was for appearance sake, and certainly not for love.

When a man has more than one wife, his affections must of necessity be divided; he really has no home in the truest sense of the word; his houses are simply boarding-places.

Should he have all his wives in one house, as is often the case, they are then all slaves to the system, each one is watching the others—and they know it—trying to discover something that can be secretly told to the husband to draw away his affections from the rest. What more miserable position could be imagined?

There is, however, no fixed principle regulating Mormon men in the management of their families—every one is at liberty to do as he thinks best, and scarcely two families are governed alike. When Salt Lake City was first settled, the people had to live as best they could, and a man was glad to get even one roof under which he and all his wives might be sheltered. Now, when the husband is wealthy he generally provides separate homes

---

* In the public domain.

for his wives. Some wealthy men, however, still have all their wives and families together.

I have in my mind, as I write, a very prominent Mormon, who has half a dozen wives; and he divides his time among them after this fashion. The first week he stays with the first wife; the next week he is with the second; then he goes back to the first. The fourth week he passes with the third wife; then he returns for another week to the first. And thus he continues to give one week to the first wife, and the next to one of the other five in turn, until he has blessed them all with his presence. Now, it would at a casual glance appear that this first wife has by far the largest share of her husband's society; but if the truth must be told, it must be admitted that the husband is not quite so generous as he appears. The last wife of this good man is a young and pretty girl, and she lives with the first wife, and thus his devotion to the latter is rewarded by the presence of the former. Each of the other wives has one week of his society and attentions in every eleven—about five weeks apiece of companionship with their husband in the course of a whole year. Other men with the same number of wives pass constantly between one house and another; they can never be found when wanted; their lives are one eternal round, and they may be said to have no real abiding place.

In every settlement in Utah, long, low-roofed houses may be seen with a row of doors and windows alternating. Even in Salt Lake City, much as it has changed of late years, such houses may still be found. To every door and window there is, of course, a wife; and the furniture of her room consists of a bed, three chairs, and a table. Then, if the man is a very devout Mormon and wishes to increase his kingdom by adding another wife to the inhabitants of the long many-doored house, a wagon-box is so arranged as to form a sleeping apartment for the new comer; or, what is more likely, one of the old wives is put into the wagon-box, and the new one takes her place.

A house with two wings is rather a favorite style with those men, who, to silence their conscience and the priesthood, conclude to take "just *one* extra wife," and no more. The wives, with their children, occupy, respectively, each a wing; and the entrance-door opens into a parlor, which serves as a reception-room for both families. The husband in this case spends a week on one side of the house and a week on the other, alternately; and thus, by an impartial division of his attentions, he preserves peace in his family. A man who is comfortably off can, of course, arrange his domestic affairs so as to avoid, as far as is possible, the inconveniences of the system, but a poor man is forced to submit to circumstances. Many men have entered into Polygamy, with two, three, and even four wives, all, with their children, living together under one roof—in one room—in the most disgraceful and barbarous manner; but even for this the leaders were really more to blame than the poor deluded men themselves; for the command to " Build up the Kingdom!—build up the Kingdom !"—in other words, take many wives and raise up large families —has been so constantly and imperatively insisted upon that good sense and propriety have at last been entirely overlooked.

MARY MCGLADERY TAPE, *Letter to School Board, A Chinese Mother Protests School Segregation in San Francisco* (1885)

The issues that Mary McGladery Tape (1857–1934) raises in her letter to the San Francisco School Board exposed the racist core of Chinese segregation and exclusion. Tape and her husband were born in China and arrived in California at a time of growing anti-Chinese public sentiment. An orphan, Tate lived for five years in a California Christian rescue home for Chinese females. The exclusion of her daughter Mamie from the public school in their neighborhood outside of Chinatown resulted in a landmark anti-segregation case against the San Francisco Board of Education. Despite a court decision favorable to the Tapes, the school board continued to embrace anti-Chinese legislation. The Tapes were a Chinese Christian family of middle-class status, assimilated in terms of language and customs. Assimilation, however, did not protect them from racial classification and oppression.

Tape's letter demonstrated her ability to negotiate gender norms and defy the stereotype of Chinese as well as Anglo-American female docility. In what ways does Tape's letter address the racism that motivated the San Francisco School Board's refusal to admit her daughter to a school with white children? How would you describe the tone of this letter? How would you evaluate Tape's protest?*

San Francisco, April 8, 1885.

To the Board of Education—dear sirs: I see that you are going to make all sorts of excuses to keep my child out of the Public schools. Dear sirs, Will you please to tell me! Is it a disgrace to be Born a Chinese? Didn't God make us all!!! What right have you to bar my children out of the school because she is a Chinese Decend. They is no other worldly reason that you could keep her out, except that. I suppose, you all goes to churches on Sundays! Do you call that a Christian act to compel my little children to go so far to a school that is made in purpose for them. My children don't dress like the other Chinese. They look just as phunny amongst them as the Chinese dress in Chinese look amongst you Caucasians. Besides, if I had any wish to send them to a Chinese school I could have sent them two years ago without going to all this trouble. You have expended a lot of the Public money foolishly, all because of a one poor little Child. Her playmates is all Caucasians ever since she could toddle around. If she is good enough to play with them! Then is she not good enough to be in the same room and studie with them? You had better come and see for yourselves. See if the Tape's is

not same as other Caucasians, except in features. It seems no matter how a Chinese may live and dress so long as you know they Chinese. Then they are hated as one. There is not any right or justice for them.

You have seen my husband and child. You told him it wasn't Mamie Tape you object to. If it were not Mamie Tape you object to, then why didn't you let her attend the school nearest her home! Instead of first making one pretense Then another pretense of some kind to keep her out? It seems to me Mr. Moulder has a grudge against this Eight-year-old Mamie Tape. I know they is no other child I mean Chinese child! care to go to your public Chinese school. May you Mr. Moulder, never be persecuted like the way you have persecuted little Mamie Tape. Mamie Tape will never attend any of the Chinese schools of your making! Never!!! I will let the world see Sir What justice there is When it is govern by the Race prejudice men! just because she is of the Chinese decend, not because she don't dress like you because she does. just because she is decended of Chinese parents I guess she is more of a American then a good many of you that is going to prewent her being Educated.

Mrs. M. Tape.

---

* Alta *(16 April 1885)*

CHAPTER 12

Gilded Age Protest and Women Activists

After the Civil War and through the early 1900s, rapid industrial and business expansion provided women with new opportunities to enter the workplace. Widening opportunity was not the same as equal opportunity: Gender bias pervaded the workplace. Sex-segregated jobs restricted women from most employment fields that were reserved for men. Women encountered limited choices and low wages, and many remained locked in entry-level positions because gender discrimination denied them promotions. Race proved an even more formidable obstacle, and African American women were hired for neither office nor even factory jobs. For the great majority of African American women, domestic and agricultural work provided the only employment opportunities. Within segregated school systems, better-educated African American women found their best employment opportunities in teaching. Industrial and business expansion provided even educated African American women with few if any jobs. Mary Church Terrill, a leading African American advocate of civil rights, provides multiple examples of exclusionary racial policies that prevented access to entry-level jobs for skilled as well as unskilled African American women. In contrast, immigrant women from Europe crowded into urban areas, providing factory owners with a major source of cheap labor.

Although the West did not provide women with equal economic opportunity, labor scarcity and the desire to increase population muted gender discrimination. Single women as well as families made the journey west. Development of the railroad facilitated late-nineteenth-century travel. Although teaching provided women with a major employment opportunity, some single women took advantage of the gender-neutral requirements of the Homestead Act and became homesteaders. Mary Elizabeth Lease gained prominence in the West as a Populist Party leader and as an advocate of farm and labor reform as well as women's suffrage (see Chapter 11). Many farm women expressed their resentment of the unremitting burden of women's farm work. Although machinery had eased some of the burdens of male-designated farmwork, women working on late-nineteenth-century farms still performed household work without laborsaving machinery. Countless other women were actively involved in the agrarian protest movements that coexisted with major industrial strikes and labor militancy.

Agrarian and labor unrest characterized the late nineteenth and early twentieth centuries. Women of Irish or Eastern European Jewish background such as Irish-born Leonora Barry, Mother Jones, and Russian-born Rose Schneiderman played key roles in protest and reform as organizers, strike leaders, and union recruiters. The tragedy of the New York City Triangle factory fire that caused the death of 146 women garment workers furthered Schneiderman's determination to devote her life to a crusade for workplace justice and women's rights. Schneiderman and many other immigrant labor reform leaders had limited education but direct experience of poverty and the grueling workplace conditions of the late nineteenth and early twentieth centuries. Their workplace and life experiences were in contrast to those of the affluent, native-born, college-educated women who became the dominant leaders of Progressive reforms (see Chapter 13).

White women, usually native born, entered the expanding fields of office work and retail sales as typists, secretaries, and sales clerks. By the late-nineteenth-century, magazine articles, such as Clara Lanza's, promoted (white) women's newfound employment opportunities, even as they upheld gendered assumptions that served to further legitimize women's subordinate workplace status. The invention of the telegraph and telephone opened additional areas of employment to white women as telephone operators and clerks. Similar expansion of opportunity occurred in the retail sector and post–Civil War construction of department stores provided increased employment options. Expanded opportunity rarely translated into financial success, however. Even when women performed work identical to that of men, for example, in teaching or clerical work, their paychecks were approximately half that of their male counterparts.

The factory also was structured in accordance with cultural beliefs about gender and race. The garment industry was numerically dominated by women and, as was true even before the Civil War, paid women a barely survival wage. A Massachusetts labor report noted that the living conditions of most women workers were unhealthy and overcrowded. Garment factories of the late nineteenth and early twentieth centuries undervalued women's work. Throughout the industry, gender gap divisions favored men. Men entered skilled fields such as tailoring and pattern making. Denied choice, women clustered in the lower paid area of sewing. Gender and racial discrimination precluded African American women from even entering factory work.

With the exception of the Knights of Labor, unions refused to accept female members. The Knights separated women into their own division, and as Leonora Barry, the leader of the Women's Department would learn, male leadership remained indifferent if not hostile to women's issues. Despite difficulty in organizing women, Irish-born Barry crossed the nation organizing women for membership in the separate women's division of the Knights of Labor. Not constrained by genteel middle-class norms, many immigrant working-class women embraced workplace activism and militant protest. Labor militants' primary emphasis was on union organizing. Although the Knights of Labor had recruited women workers, the successor union, the American Federation of Labor, resented their presence in the workplace and generally refused assistance.

Susan B. Anthony lectured extensively on the link between the ballot and economic independence. She tried unsuccessfully in most cases to convince working-class women that they needed to become politically active and gain the right to vote if they were to achieve higher wages and better conditions. Many working-class women believed the vote would do little to help them. They placed their faith in marriage and their husbands' ability to support and protect them. For such women, the basic priority was to have their husbands secure a "family wage" that would allow mothers to care for their families full time. In the context of the exploitation of women's labor and her growing despair that workplace conditions would not improve for women, Leonora Barry hoped women's work in factories would be temporary and end when they married. Poor widows also needed employment and Barry had returned to work after her husband died. When she remarried, she continued to lecture for suffrage, but her paid employment with the Knights of Labor ended. The termination of her employment coincided with the organization's downward spiral and also appears to have expressed the male leadership's dissatisfaction with Barry's increasingly pro-women's rights advocacy. In contrast, the fiery labor radical, Mary Harris Jones, known as Mother Jones, dedicated her life to militant activism on behalf of working-class men and children was an outspoken opponent of women's suffrage. She believed the suffrage cause diverted attention from the crusade for workers' rights. Not until the early twentieth century would middle-class suffragists successfully cross class lines and forge an alliance with working-class women. Coalition building began with the organization of the National Women's Trade Union League (NWTUL) formed in 1903. Activist immigrant women played a key role in its founding with overlapping support from settlement house leaders, and suffragists.

Some of the nation's wealthiest women, such Alva Belmont, and J. P. Morgan's daughter Anne, crossed class lines to join immigrant women workers in the uprising of mainly Jewish immigrant women in the 1909 New York City garment workers' strike. The *New York Times* ran a series of articles dealing with the strike and the unusual alliance of the elite and the impoverished. A massive strike of roughly 20,000 women, it remains the largest strike by women that the country has ever witnessed.

Mary Church Terrell, *What It Means to Be Colored in the Capital of the United States* (1906)

At a time when industrial expansion widened workplace opportunities for white women, women of color faced racist barriers that prevented their entry into most of the newly opened factory and office jobs. This was true not only in the South, but also throughout the United States. Mary Church Terrell (1863–1954) was one of the nation's most outspoken advocates for civil rights. In the following article, she recounts her personal oppression and also shows how racism limited educational and economic equality for African Americans. What evidence does Terrell give that for African American women, race not gender was the primary barrier? What specific educational and employment opportunities were open to women of color? What type of constraints and indignities did Terrell face in her daily life?*

_____

* From *The Independent*, January 24, 1907, 181–86.

Washington, D.C., has been called "The Colored Man's Paradise." Whether this sobriquet was given to the national capital in bitter irony by a member of the handicapped race, as he reviewed some of his own persecutions and rebuffs, or whether it was given immediately after the war by an ex-slaveholder who, for the first time in his life saw colored people walking about like freemen, minus the overseer and his whip, history saith not. It is certain that it would be difficult to find a worse misnomer for Washington than "The Colored Man's Paradise," if so prosaic a consideration as veracity is to determine the appropriateness of a name.

For fifteen years I have resided in Washington, and while it was far from being a paradise for colored people, when I first touched these shores it has been doing its level best ever since to make conditions for us intolerable. As a colored woman I might enter Washington any night, a stranger in a strange land, and walk miles without finding a place to lay my head. Unless I happened to know colored people who live here, or ran across a chance acquaintance who could recommend a colored boardinghouse to me, I should be obliged to spend the entire night wandering about. Indians, Chinamen, Filipinos, Japanese and representatives of any other dark race can find hotel accommodations, if they can pay for them. The colored man alone is thrust out of the hotels of the national capital like a leper.

As a colored woman I may walk from the Capitol to the White House, ravenously hungry and abundantly supplied with money with which to purchase a meal, without finding a single restaurant in which I would be permitted to take a morsel of food, if it was patronized by white people, unless I were willing to sit behind a screen. As a colored woman I cannot visit the tomb of the Father of this country, which owes its slavery existence to the love of freedom in the human heart, and which stands for equal opportunity for all, without being forced to sit in the Jim Crow section of an electric car, which starts from the very heart of the city, midway between the Capitol and the White House. If I refuse thus to be humiliated, I am cast into jail and forced to pay a fine for violating the Virginia laws. Every hour in the day Jim Crow cars, filled with colored people, many of whom are intelligent and well to do, enter and leave the national capital.

As a colored woman I may enter more than one white church in Washington without receiving that welcome which as a human being I have a right to expect in the sanctuary of God. Sometimes the color blindness of the usher takes on that particular form which prevents a dark face from making any impression whatsoever upon his retina, so that it is impossible for him to see colored people at all. If he is not so afflicted, after keeping a colored man or woman waiting a long time, he will ungraciously show these dusky Christians who have had the temerity to thrust themselves into a temple where only the fair of face are expected to worship God, to a seat in the rear, which is named in honor of a certain personage, well known in this country, and commonly called Jim Crow.

Unless I am willing to engage in a few menial occupations, in which the pay for my services would be very poor, there is no way for me to earn an honest living, if I am not a trained nurse or a dressmaker, or can secure a position as teacher in the public schools, which is exceedingly difficult to do. It matters not what my intellectual attainments may be or how great is the need for the services of a competent person, if I try to enter many of the numerous vocations in which my white sisters are allowed to engage, the door is shut in my face.

From one Washington theater I am excluded altogether. In the remainder certain seats are set aside for colored people, and it is almost impossible to secure others. I once telephoned to the ticket seller just before a matinee and asked if a neat-appearing colored nurse would be allowed to sit in the parquet with her little white charge, and the answer rushed quickly and positively through the receiver—NO. When I remonstrated a bit and told him that in some of the theaters colored nurses were allowed to sit with the white children for whom they cared, the ticket seller told me that in Washington it was very poor policy to employ colored nurses, for they were excluded from many places where white girls would be allowed to take children for pleasure.

If I possess artistic talent, there is not a single art school of repute which will admit me. A few years ago a colored woman who possessed great talent, submitted some drawings to the Concoran Art School of Washington, which were accepted by the committee of awards, who sent her a ticket entitling her to a course in this school. But when the committee discovered that the young woman was colored, they declined to admit her and told her that if they had suspected that her drawings had been made by a colored woman, they would not have examined them at all. The efforts of Frederick Douglass and a lawyer of great repute who took a keen interest in the affair were unavailing. In order to cultivate her great talent, this young woman was forced to leave her comfortable home in Washington and incur the expense of going to New York. Having entered the Woman's Art School of Cooper Union, she graduated with honor, and then went to Paris to continue her studies, where she achieved signal success and was complimented by some of the greatest living artists in France.

With the exception of the Catholic University, there is not a single white college in the national capital to which colored people are admitted, no matter how great their ability, how lofty their ambition, how unexceptionable their character or how great their thirst for knowledge may be.

A few years ago the Columbia Law School admitted colored students, but in deference to the Southern white students the authorities have decided to exclude them altogether. . . .

Not only can colored women secure no employment in the Washington stores, department and otherwise, except as menials, and such positions, of course, are few, but even as customers they are not infrequently treated with discourtesy by both the clerks and the proprietor himself. Following the trend of the times, the senior partner of the largest and best department store in Washington, who originally hailed from Boston, once the home of Wm. Lloyd Garrison, Wendell Phillips and Charles Sumner, if my memory serves me right, decided to open a restaurant in his store. Tired and hungry after her morning's shopping, a colored schoolteacher, whose relation to her African progenitors is so remote as scarcely to be discernible to the naked eye, took a seat at one of the tables in the restaurant of this Boston store. After sitting unnoticed a long time the colored teacher asked a waiter who passed her by if he would not take her order. She was quickly informed that colored people could not be served in that restaurant, and was obliged to leave in confusion and shame, much to the amusement of the waiters and the guests who had noticed the incident. Shortly after that a teacher in Howard University, one of the best schools for colored youth in the country, was similarly insulted in the restaurant of the same store.

In one of the Washington theaters from which colored people are excluded altogether, members of the race have been viciously assaulted several times, for the proprietor well knows that colored people have no redress for such discriminations against them in the District courts. Not long ago a colored clerk in one of the departments, who looks more like his paternal ancestors who fought for the lost cause, than his grandmothers who were victims of the peculiar institution, bought a ticket for the parquet of this theater in which colored people are nowhere welcome, for himself and mother, whose complexion is a bit swarthy. The usher refused to allow the young man to take the seats for which his tickets called and tried to snatch from him his coupons. A scuffle ensued and both mother and son were ejected by force. A suit was brought against the proprietor, and the damages awarded the injured man and this mother amounted to the munificent sum of one cent. One of the teachers in the Colored High School received similar treatment in the same theater.

Mary Church Terrell (Courtesy of the Library of Congress)

Susan B. Anthony, *Bread Not Ballots* (c. 1867)

Susan B. Anthony (1820–1906) led the suffragist effort to recruit working-class women during the post–Civil War era. She addressed the following remarks to those women whose wages were their only means of survival. Anthony attempted to convince working women that the vote would give them a political voice and the means to greater economic security. What specific arguments did Anthony offer to prove that voting rights for working women would lessen capitalist abuse? Why did many working women believe "capital, not the vote, regulates labor"?*

It is said women do not need the ballot for their protection because they are supported by men. Statistics show that there are 3,000,000 women in this nation supporting themselves. In the crowded cities of the East they are compelled to work in shops, stores and factories for the merest pittance. In New York alone, there are over 50,000 of these women receiving less than fifty cents a day. Women wage-earners in different occupations have organized themselves into trades unions, from time to time, and made their strikes to get justice at the hands of their employers just as men had done, but I have yet to learn of a successful strike of any body of women. The best organized one I ever knew was that of the collar laundry women of the city of Troy, N.Y., the great emporium for the manufacture of shirts, collars and cuffs. They formed a trades union of several hundred members and demanded an increase of wages. It was refused. So one May morning in 1867, each woman threw down her scissors and her needle, her starch-pan and flat-iron, and for three long months not one returned to the factories. At the end of that time they were literally starved out, and majority of them were compelled to go back, but not at their old wages, for their employers cut them down to even a lower figure.

---

* From Ida Harper, *The Life and Work of Susan B. Anthony* (Arno, 1969).

In the winter following I met the president of this union, a bright young Irish girl, and asked her, "Do you not think if you had been 500 carpenters or 500 masons, you would have succeeded?" "Certainly," she said, and then she told me of 200 bricklayers who had the year before been on strike and gained every point with their employers. "What could have made the difference? Their 200 were but a fraction of that trade, while your 500 absolutely controlled yours." Finally she said, "It was because the editors ridiculed and denounced us." "Did they ridicule and denounce the bricklayers?" "No." "What did they say about you?" "Why, that our wages were good enough now, better than those of any other workingwoman except teachers; and if we weren't satisfied, we had better go and get married. . . . It must have been because our employers bribed the editors.". . . In the case of the bricklayers, no editor, either Democrat or Republican, would have accepted the proffer of a bribe, because he would have known that if he denounced or ridiculed those men, not only they but all the trades union men of the city at the next election would vote solidly against the nominees advocated by the editor. If those collar laundrywomen had been voters, they would have held, in that little city of Troy, the "balance of political power.". . .

There are many women equally well qualified with men for principals and superintendents of schools, and yet, while three-fourths of the teachers are women, nearly all of them are relegated to subordinate positions on half or at most two-thirds the salaries paid to men . . . sex alone settles the question. . . .

And then again you say, "Capital, not the vote, regulates labor." Granted, for the sake of argument, that capital does control the labor of women . . . but no one with eyes to see and ears to hear, will concede for a moment that capital absolutely dominates the work and wages of the free and enfranchised men of this republic. It is in order to lift the millions of our wage earning women into a position of as much power over their own labor as men possess, that they should be invested with the franchise. This ought to be done not only for the sake of justice to the women, but to the men with whom they compete; for, just so long as there is a degraded class of labor in the market, it always will be used by the capitalists to checkmate and undermine the superior classes.

Now that as a result of the agitation for equality of chances, and through the invention of machinery, there has come a great revolution in the world of economics, so that wherever a man may go to earn an honest dollar, a woman may go also, there is no escape from the conclusion that she must be clothed with equal power to protect herself. That power is the ballot, the symbol of freedom and equality, without which no citizen is sure of keeping even that which he hath, much less of getting that which he hath not.

MASSACHUSETTS BUREAU OF STATISTICS OF LABOR, *The Working Girls of Boston* **(1884)**

This document, part of a Massachusetts state report that compiled labor statistics, recounts the unhealthy living conditions of women workers, who barely made a subsistence wage. Overcrowding and unhealthy conditions characterized most working-class housing of the era. In general, wages were too low to allow for better conditions. How would you describe the living conditions of female workers described in this report?*

---

* From "The Working Girls of Boston," in Carroll Wright, *15th Annual Report of the Massachusetts Bureau of Statistics of Labor,* 1884 (Boston: 1889).

The population of the city of Boston, according to the Tenth United States Census, in 1880, was 362,839; of this number 172,368 were males and 190,571 were females. The whole number of persons engaged in that year in all occupations was 149,194, the males numbering 110,313 and the females 38,881; out of this latter number of females employed in all occupations, there were, in round numbers, 20,000 employed in occupations other than domestic service, and these constitute the body of the working girls of Boston. . . .

In numerous cases . . . girls were found living for the sake of economy in very limited quarters, which could not be conducive to good sanitary conditions. In some instances, girls were found living in small attic rooms, lighted and ventilated by the skylight only; the furnishing generally consisted of a small single bed, bureau and chair, with no wardrobe, except one curtained in the corner. In other cases, girls were forced to content themselves with small side rooms without a chance for a fire, which in some cases was sadly needed. One girl had a small side room in the third story of a respectable house, but said she could not expect much more at the present cost of living; still others were reported as living together with other members of the family in a tenement of one back room and side bedroom; another, as one of 18 families in a single building with hardly the necessary articles of furniture; another, occupying the third story of a house which seemed the poorest on the street. On the other hand, girls were found living in large rooms, quite well and sometimes handsomely furnished, in some instances with side rooms adjoining, not perhaps because they could really afford such quarters, but because they preferred to economize in other ways, in order to have some of the comforts, in looks at least, of home.

In a few cases where girls reported their health as being poor, or not good, they also complained of the poor board provided, as well as of the unpleasant surroundings at home; one girl made the statement that her home was pleasant and healthy, but to the agent of the bureau, the reverse seemed to be the case, for the hall was dirty, the floor covered with a worn-out rag carpet, while the air was filled with disagreeable odors; the girl appeared to be in poor health, untidily dressed, and dirty. Another was found living in the upper story of a cheap tenement house, directly in the rear of a kerosene factory having a tall chimney that constantly puffed out thick black smoke, which, together with the offensive smell of the kerosene, forced the occupants always to have the kitchen windows closed. In another case, one of the girls said that she spent all her spare time and Sundays with her sister in another part of the city, as her home was very unpleasant and uncomfortable; she also said the Board of Health had visited the house last year and recommended many alterations, but she did not know whether they were attended to or not. Another girl was found living in four small rooms as one of a family of 12, in a house located very near a stable and having bad drainage. One other girl complained of the odor from the waterclosets in the halls, and said it was anything but agreeable.

In a house where a considerable number of girls are cared for, it was found that there was no elevator in the building, and some of the girls were obliged to go up five flights of stairs to reach their rooms, two or three girls being placed in each room; the upper story of the building was without heat, and in the winter was said to be like an ice house; radiators are placed at the ends of halls, and transoms open into the rooms, but these have no particular effect on the temperature of the rooms, and there are no other ways of heating; extra charge is made for rooms heated directly by the register, and even then such rooms are not always to be obtained, they being generally occupied, and there being but a few of them.

Leonora Barry, *Investigator for the Knights of Labor* (1888)

The Knights of Labor was the nation's first major union. Established in 1869, the union began to organize women workers in 1881. Leonora Barry (1849–1930), a widow and former factory worker, led the effort to recruit women and reported to the Knights on working conditions. Although dedicated to female empowerment, Barry met with little success in her effort to organize female factory women. After she left the Knights she lectured on behalf of women's suffrage. What evidence does Barry provide about worsening conditions for women factory workers?*

During our stay at Minneapolis, I addressed two public meetings, visited the Woman's Local, whose numerical strength and progress in the work of Knighthood was sufficient evidence of the clear brain and honest heart of its members. From October 22 to 31, I filled an engagement under the auspices of D.A. 72 at Toledo, Ohio. There are two Locals of women in this city. A few are organized from the many industries in which they are employed, such as tailoring, knitting mills, box factories, pin factory, etc. The earnestness and activity of the officials of D.A. 72 will surely have its reward. After my address in Findlay, Ohio, a Woman's Local was organized. November 18 I delivered an address in Allentown, Pa. Here I found women employed in shoe, silk, shirt, stocking and cigar factories, none of which were organized, except about half of the three hundred employed in the silk mill. It is stated on good authority that of the eight hundred people employed in this factory, about one hundred and fifty are children under 14 years of age—another proof of the great need of a state factory inspection law in the Keystone State, many parts of which are known as the Europe of America by the products of its cheap labor. . . .

December 7 to 20—filled dates with D.A. 68 of Troy, N.Y. There is not a city in the Empire State, excepting New York City, which stands so much in need of thorough organization as Troy. Women are employed principally in manufacturing shirts, collars, cuffs and laundering, with one or two knitting mills. In the shirt industry, Troy has a governing influence throughout the State. This is also true of laundering. At the first inception of the Order in Troy, women flocked into the Order until their membership numbered thousands, but closely following their membership with the order, came the Ide's strike and lockout, with which all our members are familiar. Had the strike been successful, they might have remained members until disappointed in some other demand; its injudicious precipitation and consequent failure caused disruption in their ranks, although a faithful few still remain at the helm. . . .

On January 30 held a meeting of the hat workers in Brooklyn.

On February 10 held a public meeting in Harrisburg, Pa. One Woman's Local Assembly in the city, which was not as flourishing as it should be, owing, it was claimed, to some injudicious and illegal action on the part of some men, officials at the time of its formation. . . .

On May 2 and 3 I was at Sandy Hill, N.Y., and from May 5 to 9 at Cohoes, N.Y. (D.A. 104). The unsuccessful termination of a strike in the Harmony Cotton Mills of that city caused the almost total disruption of the woman's organization; and it is a pity that such is the fact, as there is no city in the Union more in need of organized effort on the part of workingmen to protect themselves

---

* From "Report of the General Investigator," *Proceedings of the General Assembly of the Knights of Labor,* 1887.

from wrongs that are suicidal to life, liberty and happiness. The effect of the employment of foreign labor, child labor, together with cutdowns and fines, the large number of married women who are obliged to seek employment to support their families owing to the inability, incapacity or dissipation of their husbands, is seen in the fact that in twelve years the reduction in the wages of the cotton operatives of Cohoes has been 45 percent by actual cut-downs—to say nothing of the injustice of holding back their earnings by shortage in measurement. And in these twelve years the amount of work required of the individual has been increased. The number of women employed in the six cotton mills, known as the Harmony Mills, and conducted by Garner & Co., is 1,617—married women, 500, single, 1,117—about 250 of whom as widow's children (321 from 11 years of age and upward). Notwithstanding the repeated and continuous efforts of the State Factory Inspector, through the conniving of parents and employers, the child-labor law is violated. The large number of women and children employed is owing chiefly to there being no work for men at living wages. Fines are reported to be excessively large. In the twenty-one woolen mills of Cohoes, the number of women employed is 2,449; children, from 12 years upward, 117.

The box-making industry of this city employs 100 women—married, 5; single 85; widows, 4; children, from 12 to 16 years; 25. In all three of these industries the prevalence of diseases among women is very great, being mostly of consumption and complaints peculiar to women only, brought on by constant confinement and close application to their work, defective sanitary condition and inability through small wages to secure sufficient home comforts. The effect of all this on future generations will be a progeny wanting in development and health of body and mind.

Leonora Barry (Catholic University of America)

MARY ELIZABETH LEASE, *Speech to the Woman's Christian Temperance Union,* 1890

A political activist long before women received the vote, Mary Elizabeth Lease (1850–1933) was a leader in the Populist farm protest movement. In the Populist campaign of 1890, she traveled and lectured extensively throughout the state of Kansas. A fiery speaker, she was best known for her protest against capitalism's perceived exploitation of farmers and laborers. Her views reflected the growing chasm between capitalism and farmers that characterized late-nineteenth-century industrial and agricultural expansion. She was also a feminist with a strong commitment to voting rights for women. Why did Lease believe farm women joined the Farmers' Alliance? What role did they play?*

---

* In the public domain.

. . . Yet, after all our years of toil and privation, dangers and hardships upon the Western frontier, monopoly is taking our homes from us by an infamous system of mortgage foreclosure, the most infamous that has ever disgraced the statutes of a civilized nation. It takes from us at the rate of five hundred a month the homes that represent the best years of our life, our toil, our hopes, our happiness. How did it happen? The government, at the bid of Wall Street, repudiated its contracts with the people; the circulating medium was contracted in the interest of Shylock from $54 per capita to less than $8 per capita; or, as Senator Plumb tells us, "Our debts were increased, while the means to pay them was decreased"; or as grand Senator Steward puts it, "For twenty years the market value of the dollar has gone up and the market value of labor has gone down, till today the American laborer, in bitterness and wrath, asks which is the worst—the black slavery that has gone or the white slavery that has come?"

Do you wonder the women are joining the Alliance? I wonder if there is a woman in this broad land who can afford to stay out of the Alliance. Our loyal, white-ribbon women should be heart and hand in this Farmers' Alliance movement, for the men whom we have sent to represent us are the only men in the councils of this nation who have not been elected on a liquor platform; and I want to say here, with exultant pride, that the five farmer Congressmen and the United States Senator we have sent up from Kansas—the liquor traffic, Wall Street, "nor the gates of hell shall not prevail against them."

It would sound boastful were I to detail to you the active, earnest part the Kansas women took in the recent campaign. A Republican majority of 82,000 was reduced to less than 8,000, when we elected 97 representatives, 5 out of 7 Congressmen, and a United States Senator, for to the women of Kansas belongs the credit of defeating John J. Ingalls. He is feeling badly about it yet, too, for he said today that "women and Indians were the only class that would

scalp a dead man." I rejoice that he realizes that he is politically dead.

I might weary you to tell you in detail how the Alliance women found time from cares of home and children to prepare the tempting, generous viands for the Alliance picnic dinners; where hungry thousands and tens of thousands gathered in the forests and groves to listen to the words of impassioned oratory, oftentimes from woman's lips, that nerved the men of Kansas to forget their party prejudice and vote for "Mollie and the babies." And not only did they find their way to the voters' hearts, through their stomachs, but they sang their way as well. I hold here a book of Alliance songs, composed and set to music by an Alliance woman, Mrs. Florence Olmstead of Bulter County, Kan., that did much toward molding public sentiment. Alliance Glee Clubs composed of women, gave us such stirring melodies as the nation has not heard since the Tippecanoe and Tyler campaign of 1840. And while I am individualizing, let me call your attention to a book written also by an Alliance woman. I wish a copy of it could be placed in the hands of every woman in this land. "The Fate of a Fool" is written by Mrs. Emma G. Curtis of Colorado. This book in the hands of women would teach them to be just and generous toward women, and help them to forgive and condemn in each other the sins so sweetly forgiven when committed by men.

Let no one for a moment believe that this uprising and federation of the people is but a passing episode in politics. It is a religious as well as a political movement, for we seek to put into practical operation the teachings and precepts of Jesus of Nazareth. We seek to enact justice and equity between man and man. We seek to bring the nation back to the constitutional liberties guaranteed us by our forefathers. The voice that is coming up today from the mystic chords of the American heart is the same voice that Lincoln heard blending with the guns of Fort Sumter and the Wilderness, and it is breaking into a clarion cry today that will be heard around the world.

Crowns will fall, thrones will tremble, kingdoms will disappear, the divine right of kings and the divine right of capital will fade away like the mists of the morning, when the Angel of Liberty shall kindle the fires of justice in the hearts of men. "Exact justice to all, special privileges to none." No more millionaires, and no more paupers; no more gold kings, silver kings and oil kings, and no more little waifs of humanity starving for a crust of bread. No more gaunt faced, hollow-eyed girls in the factories, and no more little boys reared in poverty and crime for the penitentiaries and the gallows. But we shall have the golden age of which Isaiah sang and the prophets have so long foretold; when the farmers shall be prosperous and happy, dwelling under their own vine and fig tree; when the laborer shall have that for which he toils; when occupancy and use shall be the only title to land, and everyone shall obey the divine injunction, "In the sweat of thy face shalt thou eat bread." When men shall be just and generous, little less than gods, and women shall be just and charitable toward each other, little less than angels; when we shall have not a government of the people by capitalists, but a government of the people, by the people.

CLARA LANZA, *Women as Clerks in New York* (1891)

When Betsy Cowles filed her labor report for the 1851 Women's Rights Convention, women had few opportunities beyond needlework and clothing manufacture or being maids and teachers. As the following magazine article by Clara Lanza demonstrates, forty years later the field of office work provided women with an impressive array of opportunities; they could be bookkeepers, cashiers, typists, and stenographers. Although Lanza applauds the increased opportunity for employment, she also upholds conventional gender norms that constrained workplace equality and even exerted control over women's personal lives. What reasons does Lanza give for the preference of women as cashiers and bookkeepers? Why was it considered necessary for female clerks to live at home with their families? How does the author account for women's failure to advance in their careers?*

The close of the nineteenth century brings us face to face with many noteworthy progressive movements that point triumphantly to the promotion of free thought; but perhaps none is more vital and significant than the progress that is based upon a high standard of womanly independence and is the direct outcome of a purely feminine inspiration. With the increase of educational advantages has come a corresponding evolution in habits and manners. Old-time prejudices lie buried. Work has become fashionable. By work, I do not mean dilettante dalliance with the implements of labor, but actual exercise of brain and muscle as a means of livelihood. Feminine dignity is nowadays in nowise imperiled by legitimate employment used as a means of existence. It is an accepted fact, and one that is wholly in accordance with a proper American spirit of democracy, that girls should be educated with a view to earning their own living. . . .

Among the woman workers in New York there are none who afford a more interesting study than the vast army of clerks; the work of a clerk being admirably adapted to the sex. You may count almost on the fingers of one hand the number of years that have elapsed since the women clerks appeared. Yet so prevalent have they become in all our large cities, that one might say they have entirely

---

* From Clara Lanza, "Women as Clerks in New York," *Cosmopolitan* 10 (1891).

superseded the men in this particular department. Nine employers out of ten prefer women as clerks. If this statement for women as clerical workers appears to be a sweeping one, it can be verified by the fact that the demand is steadily on the increase, while men stand a comparatively poor chance of securing positions. The circumstance is amply justified by many reasons, not the least of these being the superior quality of the work performed by women.

Speaking, not long ago, to the head of a large publishing house where women were employed as cashiers and book-keepers, I ventured to ask whether the women compared favorably with men in the fulfillment of their respective duties.

"Women," was the answer, "are much to be preferred for a number of reasons. They are capable and industrious, and, so far as my personal experience goes, absolutely reliable. Besides, a women is more conscientious about her work. . . .

"Men are troublesome. They complain about trifles that a women wouldn't notice. The office boys don't suit, or the temperature of the building is too hot or cold, or the light is not properly adjusted. Then, if they have a slight headache, they stay at home. Most of them are married, and when their wives fall ill, or their mother-in-law comes on a visit, all these things are made an excuse for absence. The women come whether they have headaches or not. They never want a day off to attend a baseball match. They undertake the work with a full understanding of what is required of them, and they are steadfast in the performance of their duties. We treat them well and never refuse to grant them any trifling favor. There is only one thing we exact over and above their business qualifications. We do not employ a women unless she lives at home with her family.

"This has the appearance of injustice, but if you reflect a moment you will recollect that the temptations to which a woman living by herself is exposed in a great city are manifold

and dangerous, and for our own sake we find it necessary that our clerks, like Caesar's wife, should be above suspicion as to character and antecedents. We must know all about them and their families.". . .

The above proved conclusively that capability and a readiness to work did not in every instance insure a desirable occupation to the woman who sought it. A girl who had no "family," and who was obliged to depend upon her individual exertions for the food she ate and the clothes she wore, could not hope to get any position of trust. A woman who handles large sums of money that do not belong to her must be surrounded on all sides by a definite respectability; and while it sounds a bit quixotic to insist that she must have family connections over and above all her other virtues, it is perfectly just in the abstract. Unfortunately, respectable relations cannot be manufactured to order; therefore she who has them not would better become a typewriter, a stenographer, or a telegraph operator.

The large schools of stenography and typewriting turn out annually hundreds of women who rank easily with the most accomplished men clerks. Typewriting, being in great demand, is perhaps the most lucrative of the minor employments open to women. It is claimed that the market is decidedly overstocked with typewriters, and that there are not half enough positions for the largely increasing number of candidates. But this is a mistake. The market may be overcrowded with women who claim to be typewriters and stenographers, but in reality there is not a sufficient number of well-trained and capable clerks to supply the demand.

"By far the greatest difficulty I have to contend with," says Miss Seymour, who presides over the Union School of stenography and typewriting, "is to keep my best operators with me. Although I pay them liberal salaries and do everything I can to secure their services permanently, they are in constant receipt of offers that men would be glad to receive." Many pupils of the school receive offers of positions at salaries varying from eight to twelve dollars a week before they have finished the six months' course of instruction. I mention this for the purpose of showing how popular the employment of women clerks has become, that is, if they are properly trained for the work. It is positive that an intelligent woman is especially fitted for clerical work. If she does not succeed her failure is due to faulty training. Business men tell me they prefer women as shorthand amanuenses for one particular reason. It is because, contrary to accepted tradition, women are less likely than men to disclose the business secrets of their employers. Then, too, they are more faithful and more apt to remain for a long period in the service of one employer. . . .

From all I am able to gather the girls make good wives. There is nothing in clerical training that detracts from the finest womanly qualities, and men have outgrown their admiration for feminine helplessness and have come to look upon independence as something worth having. Clerical training educates the mind to accuracy in details, punctuality in the daily affairs of life, economy in the adjustment of time and quickness of perception. Perhaps this is the reason why so many men choose a wife amid the deft-fingered clerks in preference to the society misses. The woman clerk has studied the value of concentration, learned the lesson that incites to work when a burden bears heavily upon her strength. She knows the worth of self-reliance, and the fine courage that springs from the consciousness that a good result has been accomplished by a well-directed effort.

MOTHER JONES, *The March of the Mill Children* (1903)

This selection is an excerpt from Mother Jones's (1830–1930) autobiography. A labor radical, but not a suffrage advocate, Mother Jones spent much of her life actively involved in some of the nation's most dramatic labor strikes. Her deepest concern was to end the exploitation of children. To publicize the victimization of mill children, many of whom had missing fingers and other work-caused deformities, she led a march of child laborers from Philadelphia to President Theodore Roosevelt's home in Long Island, New York. Her activism contributed to protective legislation for children in Pennsylvania. Why did Jones hold capitalism responsible for the evils of child labor? What specific protest strategies did she use to awaken public support?*

In the spring of 1903 I went to Kensington, Pennsylvania, where seventy-five thousand textile workers were on strike. Of this number at least ten thousand were little children. The workers were striking for more pay and shorter hours. Every day little children came into Union Headquarters, some with their hands off, some with the thumb missing, some with their fingers off at the knuckle. They were stooped little things, round shouldered and skinny. Many of them were not

over ten years of age, although the state law prohibited their working before they were twelve years of age.

The law was poorly enforced and the mothers of these children often swore falsely as to their children's age. In a single block in Kensington, fourteen women, mothers of twenty-two children all under twelve, explained it was a question of starvation or perjury. That the fathers had been killed or maimed at the mines.

---

* From *The Autobiography of Mother Jones,* 3rd ed. (Chicago: Charles H. Kerr Publishing Company, 1977).

I asked the newspapermen why they didn't publish the facts about child labor in Pennsylvania. They said they couldn't because the mill owners had stock in the papers.

"Well, I've got stock in these little children," said I, "and I'll arrange a little publicity."

We assembled a number of boys and girls one morning in Independence Park, and from there were arranged to parade with banners to the courthouse where we would hold a meeting.

A great crowd gathered in the public square in front of the city hall. I put the little boys with their fingers off and hands crushed and maimed on a platform. I held up their mutilated hands and showed them to the crowd, and made the statement that Philadelphia's mansions were built on the broken bones, the quivering hearts and drooping heads of these children. That their little lives went out to make wealth for others. That neither state nor city officials paid any attention to these wrongs. That they did not care that these children were to be the future citizens of the nation. . . .

I called upon the millionaire manufacturers to cease their moral murders, and I cried to the officials in the open windows opposite, "Someday the workers will take possession of your city hall, and when we do, no child will be sacrificed on the altar of profit."

The reporters quoted my statement that Philadelphia mansions were built on the broken bones and quivering hearts of children. The Philadelphia papers and the New York papers got into a squabble with each other over the question. The universities discussed it. Preachers began talking. That was what I wanted. Public attention on the subject of child labor.

The matter quieted down for a while and I concluded the people needed stirring up again. . . . I asked some of the parents if they would let me have their little boys and girls for a week or ten days, promising to bring them back safe and sound. They consented. A man named Sweeny was marshall

for our "army." A few men and women went with me to help with the children. They were on strike and I thought they might as well have a little recreation.

The children carried knapsacks on their backs in which was a knife and fork, a tin cup and a plate. We took along a wash boiler in which to cook the food on the road. One little fellow had a drum and another had a fife. That was our band. We carried banners that said, "We want more schools and less hospitals." "We want time to play." "Prosperity is here. Where is ours!"

We started from Philadelphia where we held a great mass meeting. I decided to go with the children to see President Roosevelt to ask him to have Congress pass a law prohibiting the exploitation of childhood. I thought that President Roosevelt might see these mill children and compare them with his own little ones who were spending the summer on the seashore at Oyster Bay. . . .

The children were very happy, having plenty to eat, taking baths in the brooks and rivers every day. I thought when the strike is over and they go back to the mills, they will never have another holiday like this. All along the line of the march the farmers drove out to meet us with wagon loads of fruit and vegetables. Their wives brought the children clothes and money. The interurban trainmen would stop their trains and give us free rides.

We were on the outskirts of New Trenton, New Jersey, cooking our lunch in the wash boiler, when the conductor on the interurban car stopped and told us the police were coming to notify us that we could not enter the town. There were mills in the town and the mill owners didn't like our coming.

I said, "All right, the police will be just in time for lunch."

Sure enough, the police came and we invited them to dine with us. They looked at the little gathering of children with their tin plates and cups around the wash boiler. They just smiled and spoke kindly to the children, and said nothing at all about not going into the city.

We went in, held our meeting, and it was the wives of the police who took the little children and cared for them that night, sending them back in the morning with a nice lunch rolled up in paper napkins.

Everywhere we had meetings, showing up with living children, the horrors of child labor. . . .

I called on the mayor of Princeton and asked for permission to speak opposite the campus of the University. I said I wanted to speak on higher education. The mayor gave me permission. A great crowd gathered, professors and students and the people; and I told them that the rich robbed these little children of any education of the lowest order, that they might send their sons and daughters to places of higher education. . . . And I showed those professors children in our army who could scarcely read or write because they were working ten hours a day in the silk mills of Pennsylvania.

"Here's a text book on economics," I said, pointing to a little chap, James Ashworth, who was ten years old and who was stooped over like an old man from carrying bundles of yarn that weighed seventy-five pounds. "He gets three dollars a week.". . .

I sent a committee over to the New York Chief of Police, Ebstein, asking for permission to march up Fourth Avenue to Madison Square, where I wanted to hold a meeting. The chief refused and forbade our entrance to the city.

I went over myself to New York and saw Mayor Seth Low. The mayor was most courteous but he said he would have to support the police commissioner. I asked him what the reason was for refusing us entrance to the city, and he said that we were not citizens of New York.

"Oh, I think we will clear that up, Mr. Mayor," I said. "Permit me to call your attention to an incident which took place in this nation just a year ago. A piece of rotten royalty came over here from Germany, called Prince Henry. The Congress of the United States voted $45,000 to fill that fellow's stomach for three

weeks and to entertain him. His brother was getting $4,000,000 in dividends out of the blood of the workers in this country. Was he a citizen of this land?"

"And it was reported, Mr. Mayor, that you and all the officials of New York and the University Club entertained that chap." And I repeated, "Was he a citizen of New York?"

"No, Mother," said the mayor, "he was not." . . .

"Well, Mr. Mayor, these are the little citizens of the nation and they also produce its wealth. Aren't we entitled to enter your city?". . .

We marched to Twentieth Street. I told an immense crowd of the horrors of child labor in the mills around the anthracite region, and I showed them some of the children. I showed them Eddie Dunphy, a little fellow of twelve, whose job it was to sit all day on a high stool, handing in the right thread to another worker. Eleven hours a day he sat on the high stool with dangerous machinery all about him. All day long, winter and summer, spring and fall, for three dollars a week.

And then I showed them Gussie Rangnew, a little girl from whom all the childhood had gone. Her face was like an old woman's. Gussie packed stockings in a factory, eleven hours a day for a few cents a day.

We raised a lot of money for the strikers, and hundreds of friends offered their homes to the little ones while we were in the city.

The next day we went to Coney Island at the invitation of Mr. Bostick, who owned the wild animal show. The children had a wonderful time such as they never had in all their lives. After the exhibition of the trained animals, Mr. Bostick let me speak to the audience. . . . Right in front were the empty iron cages of the animals. I put my little children in the cages and they clung to the iron bars while I talked. . . .

"Fifty years ago there was a cry against slavery, and men gave up their lives to stop the selling of black children on the block. Today the white child is sold for two dollars a week to the manufacturers. Fifty years ago the black babies were sold C.O.D. Today the white baby is sold on the installment plan. . . .

"The trouble is that no one in Washington cares. I saw our legislators in one hour pass three bills for the relief of the railways, but when labor cries for aid for the children they will not listen.

"I asked a man in prison once how he happened to be there, and he said he had stolen a pair of shoes. I told him if he had stolen a railroad he would be a United States Senator.

"We are told that every American boy has the chance of being president. I tell you that these little boys in the iron cages would sell their chance any day for good square meals and a chance to play."

The next day we left Coney Island for Manhattan Beach to visit Senator Platt, who had made an appointment to see me at nine o'clock in the morning. The children got stuck in the sandbanks and I had a time cleaning the sand off the littlest ones. So we started to walk on the railroad track. I was told it was private property and we had to get off. Finally a saloon keeper showed us a shortcut into the sacred grounds of the hotel, and suddenly the army appeared in the lobby. The little fellows played "Hail, hail, the gang's all here" on their fifes and drums, and Senator Platt, when he saw the little army, ran away through the back door to New York.

I asked the manager if he would give the children breakfast, and charge it up to the Senator, as we had an invitation to breakfast that morning with him. He gave us a private room and he gave those children a breakfast as they had never had in all their lives. I had breakfast too, and a reporter from one of the Hearst papers and I charged it all up to Senator Platt.

We marched down to Oyster Bay, but the President refused to see us and he would not answer my letters. But our march had done its work. We had drawn the attention of the nation to the crime of child labor. And while the strike of the textile workers in Kensington was lost and the children driven back to work, not long afterward the Pennsylvania legislature passed a child labor law that sent thousands of children home from the mills, and kept thousands of others from entering the factory until they were fourteen years of age.

NEW YORK TIMES, *Miss Morgan Aids Girl Waist Strikers* (1909)

The historic strike known as the Shirtwaist Uprising involved a strike on the part of garment workers, mainly young immigrant women who manufactured the shirtwaists or blouses that were the popular attire of this era. The defiant behavior of the women proved to factory owners that, contrary to prevailing stereotypes of female passivity, exploited women factory workers could engage in militant protest. Union men had little interest in organizing women, and most women workers received subsistence pay and worked in unhealthy sweatshop conditions.

The uprising of approximately twenty thousand mostly young Jewish immigrant women and girl shirtwaist makers also provides a rare example of cross-class and cross-cultural cooperation. Some of New York City's wealthiest and socially most prominent leaders such as Alva Belmont and Anne Morgan, the daughter of the financier J. P. Morgan, actively supported the strikers. The sight of elite women helping poor immigrant workers was newsworthy and the *New York Times* gave the event major coverage. What role did the elite women play? What reasons did they give for their support of the strike? What role did Rose Schneiderman play?*

---

* From "Miss Morgan Aids Girl Waist Strikers," *The New York Times,* December 14, 1909, p. 1.

Miss Anne Morgan, daughter of J. Pierpont Morgan, is a recent applicant for membership in the Women's Trade Union League, and when her name has been passed upon she will become a regular member, paying $1 a year, which is the fee. This is the league to which the striking shirtwaist makers belong, and the application for membership means that Miss Morgan is interested in the attempt these girls are making for their own betterment. In joining the league she gives her moral support. . . .

Miss Morgan Tells of Strike

"I have only known something of this strike for a short time," said Miss Morgan to a *Times* reporter last night, "and I find other people to whose attention it has not been brought do not know anything about it. If we come to fully recognize these conditions, we can't live our own lives without doing something to help them, bringing them at least the support of public opinion.

"We can see from the general trade conditions how difficult it must be for these girls to get along. Of course, the consumer must be protected, but when you hear of a woman who presses forty dozen skirts for $8 a week something must be very wrong. And fifty-two hours a week seems little enough to ask.

"Rose Schneiderman told me of a woman who had worked in a box shop in Chicago for thirty years and could not in ten hours a day make enough to live on—she could only do it by working twelve to fourteen hours. Those conditions are terrible, and the girls must be helped to organize and to keep up their organizations, and if public opinion is on their side they will be able to do it."

Mrs. Belmont Appeals for Funds

Mrs. Alva E. Belmont, President of the Political Equality Association . . . has issued an appeal for funds to assist the striking women and girls of the Shirtwaist Makers' Union. Mrs. Belmont states that few of them are able to save anything from their wages for an emergency. Mrs. Belmont sharply criticises some of the shirtwaist manufacturers for employing inside contractors, who in turn, she adds, employ immigrants to run the machines at a weekly wage as low, sometimes, as $3.50. The following contributions to the fund were announced yesterday . . .

Contributions should be sent to Mrs. Belmont. . . . The shirtwaist makers at a mass meeting in Grand Central Palace, decided yesterday by a unanimous vote to keep up the strike.

ROSE SCHNEIDERMAN, *The Triangle Fire* (1911)

A Jewish immigrant from Russian controlled Poland, Rose Schneiderman (1882–1972) arrived with her parents in New York City when she was five years old. Poverty forced her to leave school and she began to work in the garment industry as a cap maker when she was thirteen. Her experience of the hardship immigrant women workers encountered ignited her determination to improve conditions. She played a key role in the leadership of the Women's National Trade Union League. Schneiderman made the following speech after the disastrous Triangle garment factory fire in 1911 in which an estimated 146 immigrant women lost their lives. She expressed her outrage and dismay that the lives of factory workers were so unimportant that the owners had neglected to provide even minimal fire safety precautions. Why did she advocate collective action? How was her reaction to labor abuses similar to Mother Jones?*

I would be traitor to these poor burned bodies if I came here to talk good fellowship. We have tried you good people of the public, and we have found you wanting. The old Inquisition had its rack and its thumbscrews and its instruments of torture with

---

* From "Triangle Memorial Speech," in Rose Schneiderman and Lucy Goldmaite, *All for One* (New York: Paul Erickson, 1967).

iron teeth. We know what these things are today: the iron teeth are our necessities, the thumbscrews the high-powered and swift machinery close to which we must work, and the rack is here in the "fireproof" structures that will destroy us the minute they catch on fire.

This is not the first time girls have been burned alive in the city. Each week I must learn of the untimely death of one of my sister workers. Every year thousands of us are maimed. The life of men and women is so cheap and property is so sacred. There are so many of us for one job it matters little if 143 of us are burned to death.

We tried you, citizens; we are trying you now, and you have a couple of dollars for the sorrowing mothers and daughters and sisters by way of a charity gift. But every time the workers come out in the only way they know to protest against conditions which are unbearable, the strong hand of the law is allowed to press down heavily upon us. Public officials have only words of warning to us— warning that we must be intensely orderly and must be intensely peaceable, and they have the workhouse just back of all their warnings. The strong hand of the law beats us back when we rise into the conditions that make life bearable.

I can't talk fellowship to you who are gathered here. Too much blood has been spilled. I know from my experience it is up to the working people to save themselves. The only way they can save themselves is by a strong working-class movement.

CHAPTER 13

Progressive Era:
Maternal Politics and Suffrage Victory

Well-educated, middle-class women played a central role in molding progressive era reforms. In part, their activism evolved from the women's clubs and settlement houses that were involved in community improvement and outreach to the immigrant poor. Reform objectives expressed domestic norms based on the experience of white middle-class families. The caregiver model of motherhood that developed during the nineteenth century shaped reformist goals that defined women as wives and mothers. Progressive and later New Deal reformers adhered to these norms and did not support policies that would provide greater workplace opportunities for married women workers or target the intersection of race and gender that denied equality of opportunity to African American and other women of color. For Progressive-era reformers such as Jane Addams and Lillian Wald, women's maternal, nurturing qualities provided the rationale for women's involvement as municipal housekeepers, promoting cleaner streets, purer drinking water, and safer food, as well as better health care services particularly for immigrant women and their families. Settlement house leaders Addams in Chicago and Wald in New York City spearheaded many of these reforms within their own communities. Progressive-era female reformers moved from community improvement to a national agenda focused on obtaining state and federal laws to improve, maternal welfare and provide protective legislation for workingwomen and children. They were also active in the era's conservationist movement and establishment of wilderness and national parks (see Chapter 17).

Settlement houses enabled college-educated women to participate in social work at a time when professional employment opportunities were limited. Sustained by a network of female friends, and committed to making social reform—not marriage—the central focus of their lives, settlement leaders such as Jane Addams and Lillian Wald became the caregivers of the nation's urban immigrants—they "settled" immigrants into their new environments and provided services from child care to citizenship classes. Settlement houses provided kindergarten and nursery care for the children of poor workingwomen. Child care filled a special need of the immigrant poor but contradicted the middle-class ideal of the mother at home. The "melting pot" belief of assimilation was the prevailing Progressive ideology, and immigrants were encouraged to shed their diverse cultural identities and become full-fledged Americans. The settlement house movement expressed the larger national agenda of Americanization programs for newly arrived Eastern and Southern European immigrants viewed as too alien to assimilate without structured assistance and supervision. As the document "Conquering Little Italy "makes clear, sometimes zeal for improving the standards of municipal hygiene also promoted the removal of makeshift housing and immigrant residents. A blatant departure from middle-class housing standards, the removal of the "Little Italy" immigrant community that New York City municipal reform women celebrated also was an offense not just to hygiene but to the wealthier American residents of the area.

Wald and other settlement house leaders made protective legislation for working-women a major priority. In an era of unbridled capitalism and rampant industrialization, protective legislation sought to mitigate exploitation. With a background in factory inspection and settlement work, Florence Kelley who resided at Hull House, supplied the data on women's working conditions that led to the landmark 1908 U.S. Supreme Court decision *Muller v. Oregon,* which upheld the right of states to pass protective legislation for women. Protective legislation was the major means of redress of harsh, even brutal factory conditions, including inadequate sanitary facilities, long hours standing at machines, and lifting heavy weights. But it also produced negative consequences that precluded women from working the night shift or performing work involving the lifting of heavy objects Protective legislation reaffirmed employment discrimination on the basis of gender.

Settlement house women reformers also lobbied the federal government on behalf of child welfare. The result was the establishment of the Children's Bureau in 1912. Headed by Julia Lathrop, who lived at Hull House for many years, the bureau focused on achieving a ban on child labor and increasing federal funding for maternal and infant care.

Maternal politics and factory workplace reform were not the sole current of women's activism. Women who identified with equal rights and restructured gender roles advocated alternatives to the centrality of motherhood and domesticity. To provide mothers with the time for more alternatives than continual pregnancies and healthier lives, Margaret Sanger began her crusade to make birth control available to the poor and to liberate all women from unwanted pregnancies (see Chapter 14).

Progress toward voting rights inched along during the early 1900s. Poet and humorist Alice Duer poked fun at the slow rate of progress and the persistence of timeworn, gendered arguments used by "antis" or suffrage opponents. Suffrage leader Anna Howard Shaw also ridiculed gendered clichés that justified women's exclusion from political engagement. As more Americans accepted women's limited political participation, women gained the right to vote in school and municipal elections. As a region, the West proved most receptive to women's suffrage (see Chapter 8). However, in general, women could not vote in national elections until 1920. Progressive-era female reformers struggled for the ballot as the means to gain social and moral reform, rather than as an expression of equal rights. Suffrage leaders no longer argued for the vote as a way to confront male political dominance. Leaders now described the vote as an extension of maternal concerns, female moral authority, and women's traditional civic involvement.

Suffragists of the early twentieth century emphasized that the expanding functions of government had entered the private realm of the home, making the older notion of a separate sphere of home isolated from government obsolete. Yet they also advocated voting rights for women on the grounds that their domestic and maternal roles made them ideally suited to participate in a government that was assuming the functions of child welfare, food and water safety, and educational and recreational needs.

The nineteenth-century feminists' equal rights agenda had continually provoked the outrage of advocates of women's domestic identity. The new argument for voting rights by-passed the equal rights agenda of gender equality and focused on women's mission to better society and protect the vulnerable, and it attracted increasing support. Even the cautious Confederation of Women's Clubs could identify with the link between the right to vote and women's commitment to community improvement and in 1914 endorsed suffrage.

During the 1900s, white middle-class and elite suffragists successfully crossed class lines and recruited native-born and immigrant working-class women. Harriet Stanton Blatch, the daughter of Elizabeth Cady Stanton, and other suffrage leaders reached out to working class women. Within New York State, Blatch organized the Equality League of Self-Supporting Women. Female factory workers became part of an activist political coalition, concerned with voting rights and workplace reform. Progressive reformers and affluent suffragists also promoted the unionization of working women.

In direct contrast to the effort to gain cross-class white support, suffragists were unwilling to alienate white southerners and distanced themselves from African American suffragists. By 1900, Jim Crow legislation blanketed the South, and the entire nation supported segregated social and economic institutions. Myth replaced history and southerners depicted with nostalgia an imaginary pre–Civil War past of racial harmony that gave a positive spin to slavery and stressed white supremacy. Racism, never absent in the North, grew more pronounced and residential and school segregation became normative. President Woodrow Wilson supported segregation and applauded the racist portrayals and pro-southern interpretation of the Civil War and Reconstruction depicted in W.B. Griffith's widely popular, 1913 movie, *Birth of a Nation.*

The Progressive era is commonly referred to as the "nadir of race relations," and progressive reform with few exceptions did little to offset white racist policies. African American women who left the rural South for cities in the Northeast and Midwest found that racial barriers excluded them from office work and most types of factory work. Generally confined to domestic service or share cropping on farms, they benefited neither from protective legislation nor labor organizations. African American civil rights leaders Mary Church Terrell (see Chapter 12) and Ida B. Wells (see Chapter 10) joined W.E.B. DuBois and white reformers, including Jane Addams, Lillian Wald, and Mary White Ovington to organize the National Association for the Advancement of Colored People (NAACP). Mary White Ovington provided much of the initial organizing momentum. A white woman of privileged background who graduated from the Harvard Annex (later Radcliffe College), Ovington's commitment to civil rights sprang from her abolitionist heritage; both her parents were abolitionists. A rare effort at interracial cooperation, the NAACP, would in the future launch successful legal challenges to redress racial discrimination.

The final phase of the suffrage movement occurred during America's participation in World War 1. During the war, women worked in munitions plants and as streetcar conductors and postal workers. Once again, as in the case of the Civil War, nontraditional employment dramatically demonstrated the ability and willingness of women to move beyond their prescribed gender roles. Of major significance was the contribution of nurses to the military effort. Unlike during the Civil War, their service was not resented, as the role of military nurse no longer challenged gender expectations. The significance of women's wartime participation combined with President Wilson's rhetoric that U.S. participation in the war was a means to make the world safer for democracy dramatized the contradiction of the president's continued failure to support suffrage until 1918.

In the closing years of the struggle, suffragists waged extensive campaigns on both the state and national levels. The formation of a new suffrage organization, the National Woman's Party (NWP), in 1916, further drew national attention to the suffrage crusade. Led by Alice Paul, who borrowed from the protest strategies of the militant British suffragettes, NWP staged massive demonstrations, picketed the White House, and hung banners to embarrass President Wilson. When arrested, the women endured hunger strikes in prison. NWP's militancy gained enormous media attention and served to make the National American Women's Suffrage Association (NAWSA) appear more "ladylike" and acceptable in contrast. Under Carrie Chapman Catt's leadership, membership in the NAWSA increased to two million, and NAWSA leaders secured President Wilson's support for suffrage and gained congressional approval in 1919. The requisite number of states ratified the Nineteenth Amendment in 1920.

"Conquering Little Italy," Transactions of the National Council of Women (1891)

The objectives of municipal housekeeping generally involved cleaner streets, safe drinking water, and public sanitation. All were vitally important objectives for public health and urban development. Progressive reform coincided with the arrival of large numbers of poor immigrants from Italy and Eastern Europe. Women reformers came mainly from the middle and upper-middle classes and were born in the United States. Impoverished, makeshift communities of immigrants generally impeded progressive municipal goals. As the following brief report demonstrates, municipal cleanup might also include removal of immigrant communities as well as environmental health hazards. The association mentioned in the document would refer to the women involved in municipal housekeeping objectives. In this case, clean up also meant to "invade" the slum and forcibly remove the inhabitants. What is the tone of this report? Are there any examples of ethnic or class bias? How would you interpret the use of the word "conquest"?*

During the summer of 1886 a district known as "Little Italy"—just north of Central Park and between Fifth and Madison Avenues—made it necessary for residents in adjacent fine houses to close their windows in order to escape the noisome atmosphere. Having heard of the prowess of the Association, these people made an appeal to it for help. The women's committee inspected, and found a large colony of Italians crowded in rickety, tumble-down hovels, existing without the least regard for cleanliness or decency. Their yards were a mass of corruption, and street-pickings were drying on sheds. The squalor and dirt of the interior of these places were horrible beyond description. For once the women shrank from their task. They did not dare to invade this slum without a policeman. The policeman to whom they applied thought there ought to be several policemen, and he got reinforcements. The

---

* In the public domain.

Board of Health was greatly surprised and equally enlightened when the women told that body how bad this district was. Then "Little Italy" declined, fell, and was effaced.

The women killed another bird this time with the same stone. They observed on their way to "Little Italy" that there were several cow-sheds in Eighty-Ninth Street, near Madison Avenue. They looked into the small, ill-kept,

undrained buildings and saw cans of milk standing about, liberally absorbing the prevalent effluvia. The owners of the "dairy" peddled this milk through the city as pure, fresh, and healthful. Brewers' refuse constituted the chief part of the cows' food. The Board of Health forbade the cows to be kept there, and its order was reluctantly and gradually, but finally, obeyed.

MARY WHITE OVINGTON, *How the NAACP Began* (1914)

Racial violence, hostility, and extensive segregation of the Progressive era provided the catalyst for the founding of the NAACP. White women who helped in the founding included social work and suffrage reformers and trade unionists, such as Jane Addams, Lillian Wald, Florence Kelley, Harriot Stanton Blatch, and the less well-known Mary White Ovington (1865–1951). The daughter of abolitionists, Ovington was among the first white women to emphasize that white women could not speak for women of color but must allow them to speak for themselves. She grew up in Brooklyn, New York, and attended private school and Radcliff College (known then as the Harvard Annex). Ovington remained a member of the executive board of the NAACP until 1947. During the early 1920s, she came into direct conflict with Alice Paul and the National Woman's Party's refusal to allow African American women to speak at NWP meetings. More interested in white southern support than racial inclusion, Paul did not budge and the NWP maintained its racist exclusivity.

The following excerpt is from an article Ovington wrote in 1914, in which she describes the reasons for the founding of the NAACP and her own role in it. Note that during this period of time, African Americans were referred to as "Negro" or "Colored." Neither term was considered racially demeaning. What specific racist developments did Ovington note as evidence of the need for a civil rights organization? Why would the biracial membership have significance during the early twentieth century?*

The National Association for the Advancement of Colored People is five years old—old enough, it is believed, to have a history; and I, who am perhaps, its first member, have been chosen as the person to recite it. As its work since 1910 has been set forth in its annual reports, I shall make it my task to show how it came into existence and to tell of its first months of work.

In the summer of 1908, the country was shocked by the account of the race riots at Springfield, Illinois. Here, in the home of Abraham Lincoln, a mob containing many of the town's "best citizens," raged for two days,

killed and wounded scores of Negroes, and drove thousands from the city. Articles on the subject appeared in newspapers and magazines. Among them was one in the Independent of September 3rd, by William English Walling, entitled "Race War in the North." After describing the atrocities committed against the colored people, Mr. Walling declared:

"Either the spirit of the abolitionists, of Lincoln and of Love-joy must be revived and we must come to treat the Negro on a plane of absolute political and social equality, or Vardaman and Tillman will soon have

---

*In the public domain.

transferred the race war to the North." And he ended with these words, "Yet who realizes the seriousness of the situation, and what large and powerful body of citizens is ready to come to their aid?"

It so happened that one of Mr. Walling's readers accepted his question and answered it. For four years I had been studying the status of the Negro in New York. I had investigated his housing conditions, his health, his opportunities for work. I had spent many months in the South, and at the time of Mr. Walling's article, I was living in a New York Negro tenement on a Negro Street. And my investigations and my surroundings led me to believe with the writer of the article that "the spirit of the abolitionists must be revived."

The NAACP is Born

So I wrote to Mr. Walling, and after some time, for he was in the West, we met in New York in the first week of the year of 1909. With us was Dr. Henry Moskowitz, now prominent in the administration of John Purroy Mitchell, Mayor of New York. It was then that the National Association for the Advancement of Colored People was born. It was born in a little room of a New York apartment. It is to be regretted that there are no minutes of the first meeting, for they would make interesting if unparliamentary reading. . . .

Lincoln's Birthday

Of course, we wanted to do something at once that should move the country. It was January. Why not choose Lincoln's birthday, February 12, to open our campaign? We decided, therefore, that a wise, immediate action would be the issuing on Lincoln's birthday of a call for a national conference on the Negro question. At this conference we might discover the beginnings, at least, of that "large and powerful body of citizens" of which Mr. Walling had written.

And so the meeting adjourned. Something definite was determined upon, and our next

step was to call others into our councils. We at once turned to Mr. Oswald Garrison Villard, president of the N. Y. Evening Post Company. He received our suggestions with enthusiasm, and aided us in securing the co-operation of able and representative men and women. It was he who drafted the Lincoln's birthday call and helped to give it wide publicity. I give the Call in its entirety with the signatures since it expresses, I think, better than anything else we have published, the spirit of those who are active in the Association's cause.

"The celebration of the Centennial of the birth of Abraham Lincoln, widespread and grateful as it may be, will fail to justify itself if it takes no note of and makes no recognition of the colored men and women for whom the great Emancipator labored to assure freedom. Besides a day of rejoicing, Lincoln's birthday in 1909 should be one of taking stock of the nation's progress since 1865.

"How far has it lived up to the obligations imposed upon it by the Emancipation Proclamation? How far has it gone in assuring to each and every citizen, irrespective of color, the equality of opportunity and equality before the law, which underlie our American institutions and are guaranteed by the Constitution?

Disfranchisement

"If Mr. Lincoln could revisit this country in the flesh, he would be disheartened and discouraged. He would learn that on January 1, 1909, Georgia had rounded out a new confederacy by disfranchising the Negro, after the manner of all the other Southern States. He would learn that the Supreme Court of the United States, supposedly a bulwark of American liberties, had refused every opportunity to pass squarely upon this disfranchisement of millions, by laws avowedly discriminatory and openly enforced in such manner that the white men may vote and that black men be without a vote in their government; he would discover, therefore, that taxation without representation is the lot of millions of wealth-producing American citizens, in whose hands rests the economic progress and welfare of an entire section of the country.

"He would learn that the Supreme Court, according to the official statement of one of its own judges in the Berea College case, has laid down the principle that if an individual State chooses, it may make it a crime for white and colored persons to frequent the same market place at the same time, or appear in an assemblage of citizens convened to consider questions of a public or political nature in which all citizens, without regard to race, are equally interested.

"In many states Lincoln would find justice enforced, if at all, by judges elected by one element in a community to pass upon the liberties and lives of another. He would see the black men and women, for whose freedom a hundred thousand of soldiers gave their lives, set apart in trains, in which they pay first-class fares for third-class service, and segregated in railway stations and in places of entertainment; he would observe that State after State declines to do its elementary duty in preparing the Negro through education for the best exercise of citizenship.

"Silence . . . Means Approval"

"Added to this, the spread of lawless attacks upon the Negro, North, South and West—even in the Springfield made famous by Lincoln—often accompanied by revolting brutalities, sparing neither sex nor age nor youth, could but shock the author of the sentiment that 'government of the people, by the people, for the people; should not perish from the earth.'

"Silence under these conditions means tacit approval. The indifference of the North is already responsible for more than one assault upon democracy, and every such attack reacts as unfavorably upon whites as upon blacks. Discrimination once permitted cannot be bridled; recent history in the South shows that in forging chains for the Negroes the white voters are forging chains for themselves. 'A house divided against itself cannot stand'; this government cannot exist half-slave and half-free any better today than it could in 1861.

"Hence we call upon all the believers in democracy to join in a national conference for the discussion of present evils, the voicing of protests, and the renewal of the struggle for civil and political liberty."

JANE ADDAMS, *The Clubs of Hull House* (1905)

Jane Addams (1860–1935) pioneered the settlement house movement. She co-founded Hull House in an immigrant Chicago neighborhood in 1889. The clubs of Hull House provided social services and educational opportunities to working-class immigrant families. Living within the settlement house, college-educated, affluent women, including Addams, gained firsthand knowledge of immigrant workers. Despite their elite backgrounds, these women were more open than most of their contemporaries to the needs and cultural backgrounds of immigrant working-class women and children. In what ways did the Hull House clubs promote the Americanization of the immigrants? How did the clubs address the needs of workingwomen and children?*

The two original residents of Hull House are entering upon their sixth year of settlement in the nineteenth ward. They

publish this outline that the questions daily asked by neighbors and visitors may be succinctly answered. . . . It aims not so much to

---

* From Jane Addams and Ellen Gates Starr, "Hull House: A Social Settlement," in *Hull House Maps and Papers* (Boston: Thomas Y. Crowell and Co., 1895), 207–30.

give an account of what has been accomplished, as to suggest what may be done by and through a neighborhood of working people, when they are touched by a common stimulus, and possess an intellectual and social centre about which they may group their various organizations and enterprises.

The original residents came to Hull House with a conviction that social intercourse could best express the growing sense of the economic unity of society. They wished the social spirit to be the undercurrent of the life of Hull House, whatever direction the stream might take. All the details were left for the demands of the neighborhood to determine, and each department has grown from a discovery made through natural and reciprocal social relations. . . .

The Jane Club

The Jane Club, a cooperative boarding-club for young workingwomen, had the advice and assistance of Hull House in its establishment. The original members of the club, seven in number, were a group of trades union girls accustomed to organized and cooperative action. The club has been from the beginning self-governing, without a matron or outside control, the officers being elected by the members from their own number, and serving for six months gratuitously. . . .

The club now numbers fifty members, and the one flat is increased to five. The members do such share of the housework as does not interfere with their daily occupations. There are various circles within the club for social and intellectual purposes; and while the members are glad to procure the comforts of life at a rate within their means, the atmosphere of the club is one of comradeship rather than thrift. The club holds a monthly reception in the Hull House gymnasium.

The Phalanx Club

A similar cooperative club has been started by nine young men at 245 West Polk Street, most of the members of which are members of the Typographical Union. The club has made a most promising beginning.

The Labor Movement

The connection of the House with the labor movement may be said to have begun on the same social basis as its other relations. Of its standing with labor unions, which is now "good and regular," it owes the foundation to personal relations with the organizer of the Bingery Girls' Union, who lived for some months in the House as a guest. It is now generally understood that Hull House is "on the side of the unions." Several of the women's unions have held their regular meetings at the House, two have been organized there, and in four instances men and women on strike against reduction in wages met there while the strike lasted. In one case, a strike was successfully arbitrated by the House. It is most interesting to note that a number of small and feeble unions have, from the very fact of their weakness, been compelled to a policy which has been their strength, and has made for the strength of their cause. In this policy it has been the privilege of Hull House to be of service to them.

Eight-Hour Club

After the passage of the factory and workshop bill, which includes a clause limiting women's labor to eight hours a day, the young women employees in a large factory in the near neighborhood of Hull House, formed an Eight-Hour Club for the purpose of encouraging women in factories and workshops to obey the eight-hour law.

The Working-People's Social Science Club

was formed during the first year of residence at Hull House, and has met weekly every since, with the exception of the two summer months. In the summer of 1893, however, owing to the number of interesting speakers to be secured from the World's Fair Congresses, the club met without interruption. The purpose of the club is the discussion of social and economic topics.

The Arnold Toynbee Club

meets at Hull House. The objects of the club are: (1) To offer lectures on economic subjects, (2) to ascertain and make known facts of interest to working people in the fields of economics and legislation, (3) to promote legislation for economic and social reform, especially to secure greater public control over natural monopolies.

The Chicago Question Club

meets in the Hull House Art Gallery at two o'clock every Sunday afternoon. The club was fully formed before it asked for the hospitality of Hull House. It is well organized, and each meeting is opened by presentation of two sides of a question. Occasionally, the various economic clubs meet for a common discussion. One of the most successful was led by Father Huntington, on the subject, "Can a Freethinker believe in Christ?" An audience of four hundred people followed closely the two hours' discussion, which was closed by Mr. Henry George.

The Nineteenth Ward Improvement Club

The Nineteenth Ward Improvement Club meets at Hull House the second Saturday evening of each month. The president is the district representative in the Illinois State Legislature, and one of the ward aldermen is an active member. The club is pledged to the improvement of its ward in all directions. It has standing committees on streetcleaning, etc., and was much interested in the efforts of the Municipal Order league to secure public baths.

The Hull House Women's Club

which now numbers ninety of the most able women in the ward, developed from a social meeting for purposes of tea-drinking and friendly chat. Several members of this club have done good work in street and alley inspecting through the Municipal Order League. The club has also presented to a public school in the neighborhood a fine autotype of Millet's *Knitting Shepherdess,* and hopes to do more in future for the art-in-schools movement. They have been active in the visiting and relief work which has taken so large a share of the energies of the settlement during the hard times. One winter they purchased a ticket to the lectures given to mothers in the Kindergarten College. One member attended each week, and reported to the club. They are in touch with some of the vigorous movements of the city, and have frequent lectures on philanthropic and reform questions.

Children's Clubs

Since its foundation, Hull House has had numerous classes and clubs for children. The fortunes and value of the clubs have varied, depending very much on the spirit of the leaders. An effort has always been made to avoid the school atmosphere. The children are received and trusted as guests, and the initiative and control have come from them as far as possible. Their favorite occupation is listening to stories. One club has had a consecutive course of legends and tales of chivalry. There is no doubt that the more imaginative children learn to look upon the house as a gateway into a magic land, and get a genuine taste of the delights of literature. One boy, after a winter of Charlemagne stories, flung himself half-crying, from the house, and said that "there was no good in coming anymore now that Prince Roland was dead." The boys' clubs meet every Tuesday afternoon at four o'clock, and clubs of little girls come on Friday. The latter are the Schoolgirls' Club and the Pansy Club, the

Storytelling Club and the Kindergarten Club. They sew, paint, or make paper chains during the storytelling, and play games in the gymnasium together before they go home at five o'clock. A club of Bohemian girls, called "Libuse," meets every Monday, and studies the heroic women in history. The little children meet one afternoon in the week for advanced kindergarten work. There are various children's classes for gymnastics and dancing; and two children's choruses, of two hundred and fifty each, meet weekly under the direction of Mr. William Tomlins. Dinners are served to schoolchildren, upon presentation of tickets which have been sold to their mothers for five cents each. Those children are first selected whose mothers are necessarily at work during the middle of the day; and the dinner started with children formerly in the Hull House *creche*. While it is desired to give the children nutritious food, the little diners care much more for the toys and books and the general good time, than they do for the dinners. It has been found, too, that the general attractiveness performs the function of the truant officer in keeping them at school; for no school implies no dinner. The House has had the sympathetic and enthusiastic cooperation of the principal of the Polk Street public school.

The Paderewski Club

A club of twenty children, calling themselves the Paderewski Club, has had a year of instruction on the piano, together with Sunday afternoon talks by their teacher on the lives of the great musicians. Six of the most proficient have obtained scholarships in the Chicago Conservatory.

The Hull House Men's Club

holds a reception there once a month, and an occasional banquet. This club, which rents a room in the front of the building, is composed of one hundred and fifty of the abler citizens and more enterprising young men of the vicinity. Their constitution commits them, among other things, to the "cultivation of sobriety and good-fellowship."

**LILLIAN WALD, *"Good Metal in our Melting Pot, Says Miss Wald,"*
New York Times (Nov. 16, 1913)**

Born in Cincinnati, Ohio, Lillian Wald (1867–1930) grew up in Rochester, New York, the daughter of an affluent German Jewish family. Wald embraced a progressive reform agenda that included a lifetime of commitment to improving the residential and community health of the impoverished mainly Eastern European Jewish immigrant population of New York City's lower East Side. She opened the Henry Street Settlement House in 1895. Although the settlement, with its multifaceted Americanization programs, provided educational programs, recreational activities, and citizenship training, the major objective was the provision of affordable health services with a focus on maternal and infant care. To accomplish this, Wald used her own training as a nurse to found the Visiting Nurses Association of New York City.

The Nurses Association remains a viable health care resource to the present day, and the Henry Street Settlement House also has retained its viability. True to the spirit of multifaceted progressive reform, Wald supported government meat inspections laws as well as the creation of the Children's Bureau, women's suffrage, and as this account describes assimilation programs for European immigrants. What information does Wald provide to support her belief that immigrants needed more health and educational resources to fully develop their potential and contribute to American society?*

---

* Edward Marshall, "Good Metal in Our Melting Pot, Says Miss Wald," *New York Times,* Nov. 16, 1913.

Twenty Years' Experience with the Varied Races of New York Convinces Henry Street Settlement's Founder that our Racial Outcome Will Be Worthy.

"My philosophy," Miss Wald declared, "is that the material for citizen making with which the tenements of New York provide the city and the nation is good.

"I believe and steadfastly maintain that the failures are principally our own. Emigration every year sends us an army of new youth, thus swelling that which is already here. All need guidance, hospitality, opportunity. It has been in search of these that they or their forebears have adventured to our shores. But these things we do not always furnish. The immigrant loses and we lose. Our waste of human beings on the great east side of New York is infinitely greater than our waste of natural resources in the whole of our domain.

"I went to a baby show the other day—a show of colored babies. Bright-eyed, alert, in every way attractive, they were exhilarating. But the thoughts which they inspired were not. "If any of those colored babies achieve the best of which it may be capable, if any tenement-house baby, whatever may be the color of its skin, achieves the best of which it may be capable, it will be in spite of what the city, State, and nation do not do for it, rather than because of what they do for it.

"It is my belief that we in the United States have been doing just exactly that which we pretend not to do, what we have solemnly declared we never shall do. We have denied to many very worthy human beings that dignity which, according to the theory on which our Government was founded, should be accorded to every human being. When we disregard the first and holiest tenet of our primary creed, then we are dragging down, not building up.

Individual Not Respected Enough

"We respect the individual far too little, often not at all. If this settlement has any influence, and it has been generally credited with having done something toward the betterment of conditions on the east side and to the advantage of its citizenship, it is because we here respect the individual. We never classify in herds the human beings with whom we come in contact. We hope we never will.

"Human material cannot be worked up in mass, like clay. It is even difficult to separate it into groups. The tendency to thrust the non-prosperous aside as unworthy, or, at least, uninteresting, is wholly un-American, but is so common in America that in it lies a general threat.

"We promise opportunity to all, but do not keep our promise. If newcomers really have opportunity, they usually get it only after fighting for it. And not all individuals are fighters. I know a young working girl—a really delightful creature. The other day she told me of an old woman who sells potatoes in the pushcart market with such extraordinary imagery that I listened, fascinated. I am not certain that this telling indicated genius; but it may very well have done just that.

"The point is, there is no way of finding out. She is a working girl. If she has genius now, it may be crushed. The melting pot of the east side, in spite of all that has been done, still spoils much good metal.

"Here is something to consider: The greatest men and women of the world have not been notable for physical strength, have they? Well, physical strength, resistance, and endurance have always and are still usually essential to emergence from the tenement melting pot. Of course there are exceptions, but they are truly marvelous.

"I wonder how much we may lose by this? People tell me that it is too great a task to search for human diamonds in the mud. That is exactly what is done by those who find stone diamonds. They dig in the mud—into the blue clay of South Africa—and search there for them with tremendous effort. Too little digging is done in the human diamond-bearing clay of the east side. Extraordinary spirits rise; but it is very largely through their own dynamic force. They get too little encouragement.

"But in spite of everything, what I have seen among the people—the massed people—of New York makes me an optimist. The fine material is here. In spite of the American system which spoils much of it, much good is preserved. That any of the good is wasted is a tragedy.

"Extraordinary men and women emerge from New York's tenements. Take the famous cloak and suit trade protocol, which imperatively keeps peace between employer and employed. Its operation is largely in the control of the intelligence of the east side, and stands as one of the industrial triumphs of the time!

"Such ignorance as exists among the tenements—the east side may be ignorant, that is its misfortune, and our crowded districts have many intellectuals—is not the people's fault. They could learn if they but really had the opportunity. Talk with the women of the rear tenements upon subjects touching their own lives and you will always get reactions. Even if they talk in very simple language, they sometimes have big things to say.

"It was because the tenements shocked me that, twenty years ago, I went into this work. I had been in a hospital, seeking training as a nurse.

"After that I went to the Women's Medical College, to fill my training out by studying medicine. In the hospital I began to see; later,

Lillian Wald (Visiting Nurse Service of New York)

when I was enabled to go out among the people, my vision became clearer.

"My period in the wards of the hospital gave me tremendous stimulation. The patience and pathos of the sufferers, many of whom were victims of industrial accidents or occupational diseases, fascinated and distressed me. The unnecessity of a great part of their suffering stirred me.

"After I left the hospital some one asked me to talk of nurses' training schools, and I then offered to try the experiment of teaching in the tenements the principles of home care of the sick. In the hospital I had found a training which I longed to apply in the home.

Excerpt from *Muller v. Oregon* (1908)

In this landmark decision, the U.S. Supreme Court upheld the right of the state of Oregon to establish the maximum hours for women employees. Florence Kelley helped gather the data about factory conditions used by attorney Louis Brandeis (later appointed to the U.S. Supreme Court by President Woodrow Wilson). A major victory for protective legislation, the decision later stirred enormous controversy. Alice Paul, an equal rights feminist, charged that "protection" caused women more damage than good. Social reformers and many workingwomen argued the reverse. What factors influenced the Court's decision? What role did women's maternal function play? Given the exploitive conditions of the early twentieth century, and the hostile or indifferent attitude of the American Federation of Labor toward women workers, was protective legislation necessary or were there other viable solutions?*

Delivered by Mr. Justice Brewer, February 24, 1908

That woman's physical structure and the performance of maternal functions place her at a disadvantage in the struggle for subsistance is obvious. This is especially true when the burdens of motherhood are upon her. Even when they are not, by abundant testimony of the medical fraternity, continuance for a long time on her feet at work, repeating this from day to day, tends to injurious effects upon the body, and as healthy mothers are essential to vigorous offspring, the physical well-being of women becomes an object of public interest and care in order to preserve the strength and vigor of the race.

Still again, history discloses the fact that woman has always been dependent upon man. He established his control at the outset by superior physical strength, and this control in various forms, with diminishing intensity, has continued to the present. As minors, though not to the same extent, she has been looked upon in the courts as needing especial care that her rights may be preserved. Education was long denied her, and while now the doors of the schoolroom are opened and her opportunities for acquiring knowledge are great, yet even with that and the consequent increase of capacity for business affairs, it is still true that in the struggle for subsistence she is not an equal competitor with her brother. Though limitations upon personal and contractual rights may be removed by legislation, there is that in her disposition and habits of life which will operate against a full assertion of those rights. She will still be where some legislation to protect her seems necessary to secure a real equality of right. Doubtless there are individual exceptions, and there are many respects in which she has

an advantage over him; but looking at it from the viewpoint of the effort to maintain an independent position in life, she is not upon an equality. Differentiated by these matters from the other sex, she is properly placed in a class by herself, and legislation designed for her protection may be sustained, even when like legislation is not necessary for men and could not be sustained. It is impossible to close one's eyes to the fact that she still looks to her brother and depends upon him. Even though all restrictions on political, personal, and contractual rights were taken away, and she stood, so far as statutes are concerned, upon an absolutely equal plane with him, it would still be true that she is so constituted that she will rest upon and look to him for protection; that her physical structure and a proper discharge of her maternal functions—having in view not merely her own health, but the well-being of the race—justify legislation to protect her from the greed as well as the passion of man. The limitations which this statute places upon her contractual powers, upon her right to agree with her employer as to the time she shall labor, are not imposed solely for her benefit, but also largely for the benefit of all. Many words cannot make this plainer. The two sexes differ in structure of body, in the functions to be performed by each, in the amount of physical strength, in the capacity for long-continued labor, particularly when done standing, the influence of vigorous health upon the future well-being of the race, the self-reliance which enables one to assert full rights, and in the capacity to maintain the struggle for subsistence. This difference justifies a difference in legislation and upholds that which is designed to compensate for some of the burdens which rest upon her.

---

* *Muller v. State of Oregon*, Supreme Court of the United States, 1907, 208 U.S. 412.

We have not referred in this discussion to the denial of the elective franchise in the State of Oregon, for while that may disclose a lack of political equity in all things with her brother, that is not of itself decisive. The reason runs deeper, and rests in the inherent difference between the two sexes, and in the different functions in life which they perform.

For these reasons, and without questioning in any respect the decision in *Lochner v. New York,* we are of the opinion that it cannot be adjudged that the act in question is in conflict with the Federal Constitution, so far as it respects the work of a female in a laundry, and the judgment of the Supreme Court of Oregon is *Affirmed.*

NATIONAL WOMEN'S TRADE UNION LEAGUE, *Legislative Goals* (1911)

The following document outlines the protective legislation goals of the National Women's Trade Union League (NWTUL). Affluent female reformers helped factory women organize the WTUL in 1903, during an American Federation of Labor (AFL) convention. Although AFL leaders recognized the WTUL, they offered little assistance to women workers. To further protect women workers, WTUL leaders promoted the establishment of the Women's Bureau of the Department of Labor. How would the gender-based protection objectives of WTUL's legislative goals affect women employees in ways that might be damaging as well as helpful?*

1. The eight hour day.
2. Elimination of night work.
3. Protected machinery.
4. Sanitary workshops.
5. Separate toilet rooms.
6. Seats for women and permission for their use when the work allows.
7. Prohibition of the employment of pregnant women two months before and after child-birth.
8. Pensions for working mothers during the lying-in period.
9. Factory inspection laws which make possible the enforcement of labor laws. An increased number of women inspectors . . . and the inspectors to be men and women with a practical knowledge of the work, under civil service.
10. In the states where women workers are to be examined for physical fitness, women physicians to be employed.
11. A minimum wage commission to create wage boards for each industry; having an equal representation of employers

and workers and representation from the public.
12. To provide adequate fire protection in factories, stores and offices, including compulsory fire drills.
13. Employers' Liability Law and compensation for industrial accidents.
14. Banking laws for the protection of the savings of workers. Weekly payment of wages, and prohibition of payment of wages by check.
15. Control and supervision of employment agencies, and abolition of the vampire system.
16. The enactment of a law making it compulsory . . . when advertising for employees in time of strike, to state in such advertisement that a strike is going on.
17. The initiative, referendum and recall.
18. Amendment to the child labor law that the certificate of employment shall not be granted unless the child has passed an examination in the labor laws of the State.

---

* From Gladys Boone, *The Women's Trade Union Leagues in Great Britain and the United States of America* (New York: Columbia University Press, 1911), 113–14.

ALICE DUER MILLER, *A Consistent Anti to her Son* (1915)

An 1899 graduate from Barnard, Alice Duer Miller (1874–1942) came from an affluent New York family. She was best known for her satirical verse, short stories, and the very popular White Cliffs, published in 1940. An ardent suffragist, she wrote a column for the *New York Tribune* called "Are Women People? A Book of Rhymes for Suffrage Times" that parodied many of the anti-suffrage arguments for granting women the vote.

   When Miller published her women's rights and suffrage verse, the state-by-state campaign for voting rights had already stretched over many years and time-worn, anti-suffragist arguments still remained entrenched and mired in clichés. The following poem, published in the *New York Tribune* in 1915, ridicules the anti-suffrage argument that voting would harm women. How does Miller satirize the arguments against women voting? In what ways does she use gender reversal to make her points?*

You're twenty-one to-day, Willie,
And a danger lurks at the door,
I've known about it always,
But I never spoke before;
When you were only a baby
It seemed so very remote,
But you're twenty-one to-day, Willie,
And old enough to vote.

You must not go to the polls, Willie,
Never go to the polls,
They're dark and dreadful places
Where many lose their souls;
They smirch, degrade and coarsen,
Terrible things they do
To quiet, elderly women—
What would they do to you!

Male Fear of Role Reversal (Courtesy of the Library of Congress)

* In the public domain.

If you've a boyish fancy
For any measure or man,
Tell me, and I'll tell Father,
He'll vote for it, if he can.
He casts my vote, and Louisa's,
And Sarah, and dear Aunt Clo;
Wouldn't you let him vote for you?
Father, who loves you so?

I've guarded you always, Willie,
Body and soul from harm;
I'll guard your faith and honor,
Your innocence and charm
From the polls and their evil spirits,
Politics, rum and pelf;
Do you think I'd send my only son
Where I would not go myself?

ANNA HOWARD SHAW, *NAWSA Convention Speech* (1913)

In addition to playing a central role in the suffrage movement and serving as president of the National American Woman's Suffrage Association from 1904 to 1915, Anna Howard Shaw (1847–1919) was also a medical doctor and Protestant minister. In the following speech, she ridiculed gender stereotyping. Anti-suffrage advocates repeatedly argued that men were born leaders, purposeful and rational in contrast to women who were too emotional to vote. Shaw described the behavior of men at the Democratic National Convention. What evidence does Shaw provide of men's hysterical and emotional behavior? In what ways is this argument similar to that of Alice Duer Miller?*

By some objectors women are supposed to be unfit to vote because they are hysterical and emotional, and of course men would not like to have emotion enter into a political campaign. They want to cut out all emotion and so they would like to cut us out. I had heard so much about our emotionalism that I went to the last Democratic National Convention, held at Baltimore, to observe the calm repose of the male politicians. I saw some men take a picture of one gentleman whom they wanted elected, and it was so big they had to walk sidewise as they carried it forward; they were followed by hundreds of other men screaming and yelling, shouting and singing the "Houn' Dawg;" then, when there was a lull, another set of men would start forward under another man's picture, not to be outdone by the "Houn' Dawg" melody, whooping and howling still louder. I saw men jump up on the seats and throw their hats in the air and shout: "What's the matter with Champ Clark?" Then when those hats

came down, other men would kick them back in the air, shouting at the top of their voices: "He's all right!!" Then I heard others howling for "Underwood, Underwood, first, last and all the time!!" No hysteria about it—just patriotic loyalty, splendid manly devotion to principle. And so they went on and on until 5 o'clock in the morning—the whole night long. I saw men jump up on their seats and jump down again and run around in a ring. I saw two men turn towards another man to hug him both at once, and they split his coat up the middle of his back and sent him spinning around like a wheel. All this with the perfect poise of the legal male mind in politics!

I have been to many women's conventions in my day, but I never saw a woman leap up on a chair and take off her bonnet and toss it up in the air and shout: "What's the matter with" somebody. I never saw a woman knock another woman's bonnet off her head as she screamed: "She's all right!" I never heard a body

---

* From Anna Howard Shaw, "Remarks on Emotionalism in Politics Given at the National American Women Suffrage Association Convention in 1913," in *History of Woman Suffrage*, Susan B. Anthony, ed. (Indianapolis: Hollenbeck Press: 1920), 5.

of women whooping and yelling for five minutes when somebody's name was mentioned in the convention. But we are willing to admit that we are emotional. I have actually seen women stand up and wave their handkerchiefs. I have even seen them take hold of hands and sing,

"Blest be the tie that binds." Nobody denies that women are excitable. Still, when I hear how emotional and how excitable we are, I cannot help seeing in my mind's eye the fine repose and dignity of this Baltimore and other political conventions I have attended!

NAWSA, *A Letter to Clergymen* (1912)

Although National American Woman's Suffrage Association (NAWSA) women paraded and held suffrage rallies, the organization upheld the norms of the middle class. In the following letter, what justification did the NAWSA provide for religious support for the ballot?*

Dear Sir:

"Mother's Day" is becoming more and more observed in the churches of our land, and many clergymen on that day are delivering special sermons, calling attention to the Mother's influence in the Home. . . .

In view of the fact that in the moral and social reform work of the churches, the Mothers and Women of the churches are seeking to correct serious evils that exist in our cities as a menace to the morals of their children outside the home, and in view of the fact that churchwomen are finding that much of their effort is ineffective and of no value, because they are denied the weapon of Christian warfare, the ballot . . . we ask of you, will you not in justice to the Mothers of your church choose for your topic on "Mother's Day" some subject bearing on "The need of the Mother's influence in the State?"

Women are recognized as the most religious, the most moral and the most sober portion of the American people. Why deny them a voice in public affairs when we give it for the asking to every ignorant foreigner who comes to our shores?

The women have always been the mainstay and chief supporters of the churches, and in their struggle for their civil liberty. Should not their clergymen or Christian brothers sympathize with them and "Remember those in bonds as bound with them" and help them in their struggle? On behalf of the church work committee representing Christian Mothers in every State in the Union, I would be pleased to know if you will be one to raise your voice on "Mother's Day" in favor of the extension of the Mother's influence in our land "to help those women that labored with you in the Gospel?"

CARRIE CHAPMAN CATT, *Mrs. Catt Assails Pickets* (1917)

Under Carrie Chapman Catt's (1859–1947) leadership, the National American Woman's Suffrage Association (NAWSA) participated in the achievement of women's suffrage. Catt grew up on an Iowa farm and became a superindent of schools, a position rarely opened to women in the East. Under Catt's energetic leadership, the drive for suffrage became a well-organized protest movement that still paid

* From "Report of the Church Work Committee," *Proceedings of the Forty-Fourth Annual Convention of the National American Woman Suffrage Association* (New York: National American Woman Suffrage Association, 1912), 55–57.

attention to the norms of ladylike behavior. Concerned about propriety, Catt distinguished NAWSA from the unladylike tactics of the militant National Woman's Party (NWP), in this case its heckling of President Wilson. What mistake did she believe the NWP made?*

Mrs. Carrie Chapman Catt, President of the National American Woman Suffrage Association, said yesterday that the women who were doing the picketing in Washington had made a psychological mistake.

"The pickets," Mrs. Catt said, "make the psychological mistake of injecting into this stage of the suffrage campaign tactics which are out of accord with it. Every reform, every change of idea in the world passes through three stages—agitation, argument, and surrender. We have passed through the first two stages and entered into the third. The mistake of the pickets is that they have no comprehensive idea of the movement, and are trying to work this first stage in the third. We stand on the threshold of final victory, and the only contribution these women make to it is to confuse the public mind."

Suffragist Parade (Courtesy of the Library of Congress)

ALICE PAUL, *Why the Suffrage Struggle Must Continue* (1917)

Alice Paul (1885–1977) received a Ph.D. from the University of Pennsylvania in 1912. She organized the National Woman's Party (NWP) in 1916. Having visited Britain and participated in the suffrage struggle there, she popularized the more radical strategy and tactics of the British suffrage movement. NWP women continued to picket the White House and stage demonstrations during the U.S. involvement in World War I. Do you find Paul's linking suffrage to U.S. involvement in World War I persuasive? Why?**

---

* From "Mrs. Catt Assails Pickets," *The New York Times,* November 13, 1917.
** From Alice Paul, "Why the Suffrage Struggle Must Continue," *The Suffragist,* April 21, 1917.

In our national convention in March, our members, though differing widely on the duty of the individual in war, were unanimous in voting that in event of war the National Woman's party, as an organization, should continue to work for political liberty for women and for that alone, believing, as the convention resolution stated, that in so doing the organization "serves the highest interest of the country." . . .

Never was there greater need of work for internal freedom in this country. At the very moment when democracy is increasing among nations in the throes of war, women in the United States are told that attempts at electoral reforms are out of place until war is over. The Democrats have decided in caucus that only war measures shall be included in their legislative program, and have announced that they will take up no new subjects, unless the President considers them of value for war purposes. Suffrage has not yet been included under this head. . . . No "war measure" that has been suggested would contribute more toward establishing unity in the country, than would the giving of suffrage to all the people. It will always be difficult to wage a war for democracy abroad while democracy is denied at home.

CHAPTER 14

Post-Suffrage Trends and the Limits of Liberated Behavior

In women's history, the 1920s were a period of great contrasts as the pace escalated for women's liberation from traditional social and sexual constraints. Growing numbers of women entered the workplace and college. Changes in clothing and conduct gained momentum. Eleanor Wembridge's discussions with college women recorded how nineteenth-century assumptions about male and female sexuality were collapsing. Women were no longer considered passionless; they were now perceived as sexual beings capable of sexual pleasure. The new emphasis on female sexuality did not encompass lesbian relationships, however. In fact, within middle-class society, as heterosexuality received greater emphasis, intolerance grew for the same-sex friendships characteristic of an earlier era. Dr. Irving Steinhardt was just one of many male "experts" dispensing warnings about the negative consequences of same-sex relationships. Lesbian women sought the comfort and support of other individuals who came under attack for their same-sex orientation. Some formed identity communities such as those in Greenwich Village and Harlem in New York City. Beyond the constraints of heterosexual conformity, African American blues singer Ma Rainey recorded "Prove it on Me Blues," a song about the adventures of a cross-dressing lesbian.

With her bobbed hair, scanty clothing, cosmetics, and more explicit sexuality, flappers such as Ellen Welles Page won popular attention as a symbol of heterosexual women's greater freedom. Although flapper behavior had roots in young workingwomen's nonconformist clothing and lifestyles of the late nineteenth century, with the flapper, social liberation and greater freedom of sexual expression entered the mainstream middle class. The loosening of sexual constraints did not signify a comprehensive transformation of gender roles; the majority of women continued to believe that domestic roles defined womanhood. Nor did a quest for greater economic opportunity accompany the advent of more liberated behavior. Little had changed in the sex-segregated and gender-biased workplace.

Except for a small group of feminists led by Alice Paul and organized in the National Woman's Party (NWP) (see Chapter 13), economic independence for women and workplace gender equity were not central issues. The hiring of women streetcar conductors was a brief interlude of widening opportunity for women workers during

World War I. With the soldiers' return, opportunity for women to enter nontraditional jobs abruptly terminated. Government surveys of the period expressed the deeply entrenched gender beliefs about appropriate female work that continued to limit female-designated occupations to routine employment such as clerical work. In fact, more explicit emphasis on female sexuality coexisted with a reassertion that womanly fulfillment depended on marriage and domesticity. Heightened emphasis on marriage as the path to happiness devalued alternative lifestyle options as well as women's friendships and support networks. For the majority of middle-class urban women and some farm women, mail-order catalogues and an unprecedented array of consumer goods elevated shopping into a significant housewife's responsibility. For some farm women, laborsaving appliances, electricity, and running water eased the burden of home and family care and the bitterness that had surfaced in the nineteenth century agrarian protest movements (see Chapter 12). In recognition of the reaffirmation of domestic priorities even prominent women's colleges relaxed their rigorous academic standards and offered home economics courses.

The disbanding of the suffrage movement ended the era of women's national political activism. For many women, the suffrage victory provided a satisfactory conclusion to a struggle initiated more than seventy years earlier. For others, voting represented only an initial step in the struggle for full equality. What remained of the organized suffrage movement splintered into two major groups. Alice Paul led the NWP in the struggle for an Equal Rights Amendment (ERA) to the Constitution that would end gender inequities and allow women to compete equally with men. ERA advocates campaigned against protective as well as discriminatory legislation. They promoted an Equal Rights Amendment that made no legal distinction between the rights of men and women. With a single focus on removing all gender laws that limited women's opportunity, the NWP focused its efforts on mobilizing white southern support and omitted African American women from their programs and objectives. Their equal rights campaign did not win the support of the majority of women's advocacy groups, including the League of Women Voters, settlement house leaders, and trade unionists. Women who fought against the ERA supported protective female legislation that treated women as different from men and expressed the same concerns as those upheld in the *Mueller v. Oregon* Supreme Court decision that women's special maternal functions and allegedly weaker bodies necessitated legal protection (see Chapter 13).

Although significant numbers of African American women had supported the struggle for women's suffrage, for them the right to vote remained illusory. Southern states prevented black women from voting as they had previously disenfranchised black men. Appeals made by African American women to the white NWP were rejected. The NWP, intent on securing the ERA, asserted that the disenfranchisement of black women was a racial rather than a women's issue. But denial of voting rights was only one of numerous injustices. As Charlotte Hawkins Brown's appeal to white southern women for help made abundantly clear, racism in multiple forms stalked women of color.

The ferment of reform that characterized the Progressive era declined. Negative reaction to women's rights bolstered extreme right-wing institutions such as the revived Ku Klux Klan (KKK) that had a flourishing women's division. In addition to its racist, anti-Catholic, and anti-Jewish agenda, the KKK embraced a return to traditional family values. Proudly carrying the banner of an "anti-feminist," more mainstream right-wing women such as Mary Kilbreth called for a reversal of the suffrage amendment as well as an end to Progressive-era child- and women-centered social legislation. Neither the U.S. Supreme

Court nor the conservative Republican administrations of the 1920s were hospitable to the Children's and Women's Bureau's objectives. In 1923, the Court overturned the ban on child labor and minimum wage laws for women. Despite the maternity needs of poor women reported by Ann Martin, Congress repealed the Sheppard-Towner Maternity bill in 1929. Passed in 1921, this bill made federal funds available to the states to establish clinics for prenatal and infant care. Concern about women's health was equally a part of Margaret Sanger's ongoing crusade to make contraception accessible to all women.

Although the term *feminism* gained currency in the 1920s, women did not agree about what it meant. Many younger women denied that they needed to identify with a collective group or movement. To such women, feminism came to mean greater personal autonomy and the satisfaction of individual aspirations. They believed post-suffrage women would advance in the workplace on the basis of individual merit. Optimistic that women could combine careers with marriage and motherhood, they saw no reason to continue the older feminist generation's political activism. For most women this optimism would prove illusory.

DR. IRVING STEINHARDT, *Ten Sex Talks to Young Girls* **(1914)**

Dr. Irving Steinhardt was one of a growing number of male "experts" dispensing advice about female sexuality. The emphasis on heterosexuality and acknowledgment of female passion made same-sex relationships between women increasingly unacceptable. Experts pinned deviant labels on relationships previously considered harmless. Such attitudes expressed the wider social concerns about the self-reliant, assertive, "new women" of the early twentieth century. Setting the standard for acceptable sexuality by instilling fear drove same-sex relationships into the closet and also led to the formation of communities of same-sex identity in Greenwich Village and Harlem in New York City. What examples demonstrate the manipulation of fear? How does this "expert" advice from Dr. Steinhardt relate to the "expert" advice of Dr. Edward Clark (see Chapter 9)?*

Avoid girls who are too affectionate and demonstrative in their manner of talking and acting with you; who are inclined to admire your figure and breast development; who are inclined to be just a little too familiar in their actions toward you; who are inclined to be rather free and careless in the display of themselves in your presence; who press upon you too earnestly invitations to remain at their homes all night, and to occupy the same bed they do. When sleeping in the same bed with another girl, old or young, avoid "snuggling up" close together. Avoid the touching of sexual parts, including the breasts, and, in fact, I might say avoid contact of any parts of the body at all. Keep your night robe about you so that you are as well protected from outside contact as its size will permit, and let your conversation be of other topics than sexuality. Do not lie in each other's arms when awake or falling asleep; and, after going to bed, if you are sleeping alone or with others, just bear in mind that beds are sleeping places. When you go to bed, go to sleep just as quickly as you can. If possible, avoid sleeping with anyone else. It is more healthful and sanitary to sleep in a separate bed . . . certain diseases, both those affecting the genital organs and others, are often conveyed through contaminated bed

---

* Irving D. Steinhardt, *Ten Sex Talks to Girls, 14 Years and Older* (Philadelphia: J. B. Lippincott Company, 1914).

clothes, body contact, the breath, etc. You can see for yourselves, therefore, that separate beds are good for more reasons than one. . . .

Some girls are low enough to accept pay for bringing about the moral ruin of members of their sex; . . . they are to be found everywhere, in the smallest village as well as in the largest town. Girls who have become discontented with their lot are easily influenced by the sweet, honeyed lies of these vile creatures. Beware of strange women, as well as of strange men, who seek to shower favors and other things upon you for no apparent reason except that they are strangely attracted to you. If you do not, you will live to regret it. Thousands of your sex already have, and lie in nameless graves away from home, most likely in a pauper's burying-ground, because they had become so degraded in name and fact as to be lost to "the old folks at home."

MA RAINEY (GERTRUDE PRIDGETT), *Prove it on Me Blues*

Ma Rainey's (1886–1939) song celebrates a lesbian lifestyle and cross-dressing. Rainey probably wrote the lyrics and the music. Her gender-bending and lesbian identity made her a sex rebel in an era that sought to curtail same-sex relationships. Today, Ma Rainey is remembered as the "Mother of the Blues" and musical mentor of the younger, better-known Bessie Smith. Born in Columbus, Georgia, she began her singing career at age fourteen. At sixteen, she married a singer who went by the name of Pa Rainey and she took the name Ma. She was an early-twentieth-century pioneer in the development of the African American women's blues tradition. Her major appeal was to the African American working class, although over the years her audience crossed class and racial lines. During the twenties, she made a large number of recordings for Paramount records. Mainly she sang about hard luck, hard times, and heartbreak over love gone wrong. Although other blues songs also subverted sexual and gender norms, her "Prove it on Me" blues song has enduring popularity. How does this depiction of the lesbian lifestyle contrast with the advice given by Dr. Steinhardt?*

Went out last night, had a great big fight
Everything seemed to go on wrong
I looked up, to my surprise
The gal I was with was gone

Where she went, I don't know
I mean to follow everywhere she goes
Folks say I'm crooked, I didn't know
*   where she took it*
I want the whole world to know

They said I do it, ain't nobody caught me
Sure got to prove it on me
Went out last night with a crowd of my
*   friends*

They must've been women, 'cause
*   I don't like no men*

It's true I wear a collar and a tie
Make the wind blow all the while
'Cause they say I do it, ain't nobody
*   caught me*
They sure got to prove it on me

Say I do it, ain't nobody caught me
Sure got to prove it on me
I went out last night with a crowd of
*   my friends*
They must've been women, 'cause
*   I don't like no men*

---

* Used with permission of Mary K. Roarabaugh, Executive Director of Georgia Women of Achievement.

Wear my clothes just like a fan
Talk to the gals just like any
old man

'Cause they say I do it, ain't nobody
caught me
Sure got to prove it on me.

ELLEN WELLES PAGE, *"A Flapper's Appeal to her Parents,"* **Outlook (Dec. 1922)**

Not much is known about Ellen Welles Page, although her article in *Outlook,* a popular monthly magazine, has been reprinted many times. Page's plea for parental understanding, while specific to the era of flapper defiance, spans the decades in terms of the parent/child generation gap. Eleanor Wembridge addressed the liberated behavior of young college women. Actually the emergence of freedom that flappers and liberated middle-class women exhibited had precedents in the working-class culture of the late nineteenth and early twentieth centuries. As Page noted, flapper identity did not have to go to extremes. There was a moderate flapper style that she preferred and most young women followed. Even in the moderate version, the flapper clothing and behavior represented a break from previous decades of restraint. What specific areas of misunderstanding did Page address? What aspects of this generation gap would still be meaningful today?*

If one judge by appearances, I suppose I am a flapper. I am within the age limit. I wear bobbed hair, the badge of flapperhood. (And, oh, what a comfort it is!), I powder my nose. I wear fringed skirts and bright-colored sweaters, and scarfs, and waists with Peter Pan collars, and low-heeled "finale hopper" shoes. I adore to dance. I spend a large amount of time in automobiles. I attend hops, and proms, and ball-games, and crew races, and other affairs at men's colleges. But none the less some of the most thoroughbred superflappers might blush to claim sistership or even remote relationship with such as I. I don't use rouge, or lipstick, or pluck my eyebrows. I don't smoke (I've tried it, and don't like it), or drink, or tell "peppy stories." I don't pet. And, most unpardonable infringement of all the rules and regulations of Flapperdom, I haven't a line! But then—there are many degrees of flapper. There is the semi-flapper; the flapper; the superflapper. Each of these three main general divisions has its degrees of variation. I might possibly be placed somewhere in the middle of the first class.

I think every one realizes by this time that there has been a marked change in our much-discussed tactics. Jazz has been modified, and probably will continue to be until it has become obsolete. Petting is gradually growing out of fashion through being overworked. Yes, undoubtedly our hopeless condition is improving. But it was not for discussing these aspects of the case that began this article.

I want to beg all you parents, and grandparents, and friends, and teachers, and preachers—you who constitute the "older generation"—to overlook our shortcomings, at least for the present, and to appreciate our virtues. I wonder if it ever occurred to any of you that it required brains to become and remain a successful flapper? Indeed it does! It requires an enormous amount of cleverness and energy to keep going at the proper pace. It requires self- knowledge and self-analysis. We must know our capabilities and limitations. We must be constantly on the alert. Attainment of flapperhood is a big and serious undertaking!

"Brains?" you repeat, skeptically. "Then why aren't they used to better advantage?" That

---

* Ellen Welles Page, "A Flapper's Appeal To Parents," *Outlook* 132 (6 December 1922).

is exactly it! And do you know who is largely responsible for all this energy's being spent in the wrong directions? You! You parents, and grandparents, and friends, and teachers, and preachers—all of you! "The war!" you cry. "It is the effect of the war!" And then you blame prohibition. Yes! Yet it is you who set the example there! But this is my point: Instead of helping us work out our problems with constructive, sympathetic thinking and acting, you have muddled them for us more hopelessly with destructive public condemnation and denunciation.

Think back to the time when you were struggling through the teens. Remember how spontaneous and deep were the joys, how serious and penetrating the sorrows. Most of us, under the present system of modern education, are further advanced and more thoroughly developed mentally, physically, and vocationally than were our parents at our age. We hold the infinite possibilities of the myriads of new inventions within our grasp. We have learned to take for granted conveniences, and many luxuries, which not so many years ago were as yet undreamed of. We are in touch with the whole universe. We have a tremendous problem on our hands. You must help us. Give us confidence—not distrust. Give us practical aid and advice—not criticism. Praise us when praise is merited. Be patient and understanding when we make mistakes.

We are the Younger Generation. The war tore away our spiritual foundations and challenged our faith. We are struggling to regain our equilibrium. The times have made us older and more experienced than you were at our age. It must be so with each succeeding generation if it is to keep pace with the rapidly advancing and mighty tide of civilization. Help us to put our knowledge to the best advantage. Work with us! That is the way! Outlets for this surplus knowledge and energy must be opened. Give us a helping hand.

Youth has many disillusionments. Spiritual forces begin to be felt. The emotions are frequently in a state of upheaval, struggling with one another for supremacy. And Youth

does not understand. There is no one to turn to—no one but the rest of Youth, which is as perplexed and troubled with its problems as ourselves. Everywhere we read and hear the criticism and distrust of older people toward us. It forms an insurmountable barrier between us. How can we turn to them?

In every person there is a desire, an innate longing, toward some special goal or achievement. Each of us has his place to fill. Each of us has his talent—be it ever so humble. And our hidden longing is usually for that for which nature equipped us. Any one will do best and be happiest doing that which he really likes and for which he is fitted. In this "age of specialists," as it has been called, there is less excuse than ever for persons being shoved into niches in which they do not belong and cannot be made to fit. The lives of such people are great tragedies. That is why it is up to you who have the supervision of us of less ripe experience to guide us sympathetically, and to help us find, encourage, and develop our special abilities and talents. Study us. Make us realize that you respect us as fellow human beings, that you have confidence in us, and, above all, that you expect us to live up to the highest ideals, and to the best that is in us.

It must begin with individuals. Parents, study your children. Talk to them more intimately. Respect their right to a point of view. Be so understanding and sympathetic that they will turn to you naturally and trustfully with their glowing joys or with their heartaches and tragedies. Youth has many of the latter because Youth takes itself so seriously. And so often the wounds go un-confessed, and, instead of gradually healing, become more and more gnawing through suppression until of necessity relief is sought in some way which is not always for the best.

Mothers, become acquainted with your children. Be the understanding, loving, happy comrade of your daughter. Become her ideal. And strive to live up to the ideal you set for the woman who is to become your son's wife.

Be his chum. Be young with him. Oh, what a powerful and wonderful influence you are capable of exerting if you only will!

Fathers, find out what is within the minds and hearts and souls of your children. There is a wonderful, an interesting, and a sacred treasure-house there if you will take the time and pain to explore. The key is yours in return for patient understanding, sympathetic encouragement, and kindly wisdom. . . .

Oh, parents, parents everywhere, point out to us the ideals of truly glorious and upright living! Believe in us, that we may learn to believe in ourselves, in humanity, in God! Be the living examples of your teachings, that you may inspire us with hope and courage, understanding and truth, love and faith. Remember that we are the parents of the future. Help us to be worthy of the sacred trust that will be ours. Make your lives such an inspiration to us that we in our turn will strive to become an inspiration to our children and to the ages! Is it too much to ask?

Flappers Dancing (CORBIS-NY)

U.S. GOVERNMENT, *Survey of Employment Conditions: The Weaker Sex* **(1917)**

After women employees complained about discrimination, the U.S. government surveyed its employees. The survey revealed that sex-based discrimination did not exist. Clerical work in the U.S. government became increasingly available to women after the Civil War. Sex-segregated positions for government work reflected the same gendered occupational structures that prevailed in factories. In fact, the very idea of "woman's work" is a gender definition and is used in this survey to justify women's exclusion from most positions. How does the justification for exclusion relate to the *Muller v. Oregon* U.S. Supreme Court decision (see Chapter 13)?*

---

* From George Otis Smith to E. J. Ayers, January 31, 1917; in Record Group 48, "Records of the Department of the Interior," Office of the Secretary, Personnel Supervision and Management, 1907–1942, File 15–15–35, National Archives, Washington, D.C.

Office of the Director

January 31, 1917
Mr. E. J. Ayers,
Chief Clerk,
Department of the Interior
My dear Mr. Ayers:

In reply to your notation on the copy of the letter from Senator Jones, requesting information as to whether any discrimination against women based solely upon the grounds of their sex, was made by the Geological Survey:

As you are doubtless aware, much of the work carried on by the Survey requires field ability for which it is necessary to employ men rather than women. In the field branches, therefore, women necessarily are unable to meet the strain attendant upon constant exposure in all kinds of weather, and in the strenuous physical exertions that are required of the geologists, topographers, and hydrographic engineers. There are on the rolls of the Survey 417 men, distributed as follows among the different field branches: geologists, 188; topographers, 49; water resources engineers, 74; Alaskan geologists, 15.

In the Division of Engraving and Printing, the work is necessarily of a man's type, requiring the handling of machinery, heavy lifting, dirty work and various trades to which men are especially adapted. The conditions under which much of the engraving and printing work is done is such as to preclude the employment of women. There are 126 men employed in the various nonclerical jobs in the division of Engraving and Printing and no women.

The force of laborers, messengers, mechanics, etc., consists of 130 men and one woman. The character of the work performed is such as to practically preclude the possibility of employing women for the various duties.

From the above it will be seen that there are 646 positions in which, from the character of the work, the employment of men is necessitated.

Turning to the distinctly clerical jobs, the following table shows the distribution among the sexes of the different clerks:

Branches	Males	Females
Field	28	111
Engraving	3	0
Administrative	53	28
Total	84	139

It should be noted in the above table that the great number of males in the administrative branch is due to the including of all the various administrative officers not attached to the field service, as for instance, the Chief Clerk, the Chief Disbursing Officer, the Chief of the Accounts Division, the Chief of the Executive Division, the Chief of the Division of Distribution, etc. . . .

I think the above tables will clearly show that women are chosen for the clerical positions, in general, in preference to the men at a rate of about two to one, and that so far as the Geological Survey is concerned, the spirit, as well as the letter of the law, regarding equal chance to both sexes is lived up to.

Yours very truly,
Director.

[George Otis Smith]

MARY G. KILBRETH, *The New Anti-Feminist Campaign* (1921)

Even after the passage of the suffrage amendment, anti-suffragists remained relentless in their opposition to women voting. Opponents changed the name of their magazine from *Protest* to *The Woman Patriot: Dedicated to the Defense of Womanhood, Motherhood, the Family and the State AGAINST Suffragism, Feminism and Socialism.* The overly long title accurately spelled out their agenda. Calling themselves anti-feminists, they used their magazine to denounce both the equal rights objectives of the National Woman's Party as well as the pro-family, pro-motherhood objectives embodied in the Children's Bureau and newly passed Sheppard-Towner Maternity Act.

The following document expresses their campaign to roll back and prevent future women-centered reforms. Anti-feminists also hoped voting rights for women were temporary. What did the anti-feminists mean by the "Sex Revolution"? What aspects of women's post-suffrage power most upsets them?*

Suffragists and anti-suffragists have always agreed upon one point—that the importance of the issue is not in the ballot itself but in what follows woman suffrage.

To Feminists, the vote, as Mrs. Catt expressed it, "was only a symbol." They did not spend millions and work for years to mark a paper and drop it in a box. They worked for a **weapon** by which to achieve certain **results:** the "political, social and economic independence of women," as they called it.

Anti-suffragists, on the contrary, opposing the Feminist program root and branch, fought the grant of the ballot because they foresaw that it was the logical boundary line between the old institution-of-marriage ideal of the Family as the unit of society and the Feminist revolt against nature.

Mrs. Catt explicitly stated in the Woman's Journal:

> "What is Feminism? A world-wide revolt against all artificial barriers which laws and customs interpose between women and human freedom."

It is best to meet an enemy before he crosses your boundary line. The best way to have defeated Feminism would have been to have prevented woman suffrage.

But a nation worthy the name does not surrender to an enemy simply because it has been invaded. Neither do Anti-Feminists worthy the name submit to the Sex Revolution simply because suffrage forces have succeeded in crossing a boundary line.

All that suffragists have been able to secure thus far is a PROCLAMATION (of contested validity) and a showdown against themselves last November at the polls! The vast "paper" organizations of the League of Women Voters and the National Woman's Party did not make a dent at the last election. They could not defeat any one of the men they opposed, and they could not elect a single one of their 14 women candidates to Congress.

Suffragists themselves realize that the vote so far has only exposed their weakness at the polls. Their futile campaigns to defeat Senators Overman, Underwood, Moses, and Wadsworth were only equaled by their disastrous failure to protect Governor Roberts, of Tennessee, to whom they owed the Proclamation, against an outraged electorate of men and women.

Now their Proclamation itself is under fire. The legal battle against it is already docketed in the Supreme Court of the United States. (Fairchild vs. Colby, No. 572.) Since the vote itself has demonstrated the weakness of suffragists at the polls, they are relying upon a more powerful political weapon than the ballot to accomplish the Sex-Revolution.

The Secret Lobby and the Card-Index are the tools they now use to establish vast Feminist Bureaucracies. These, in turn, can be used as in the Russian Propaganda System, as channels of Revolution. Already publications of the Federal Children's Bureau have been used to spread the most extreme Socialist doctrines.

One hears no more of Feminist leaders trying to get "the women" to elect them Governors or Congressmen. Instead, they now put their money into a headquarters, close as they can get to the Capitol of the United States, "to watch Congress" and to

---

* From Mary G. Kilbreth, "The New Anti-Feminist Campaign," *The Woman Patriot*, June 15, 1921, 2–3.

lobby for bureaus and patronage and "offices for women"; hoping by appointments and the expansion of Federal bureaucracy to obtain a sinister propaganda power far more potent than any legitimate power they could exercise in the polling booth.

This new weapon which the Feminists have perfected, the permanent resident Lobby, working in connection with established Federal bureaus seeking their own expansion, is the solvent of all representative Government.

If they once obtain control of a Government-financed Propaganda System; operated by themselves, they can spread their revolutionary doctrines, through official agents on the Federal payroll, in every school and every home, and poison the Nation at its source. . . .

But had it not been for the determined resistance of Anti-Feminist men and women, over-burdened taxpayers might now be groaning under the bureaucratic burden of a Socialist "maternity benefit system," and nationalized "education," with "a woman in the Cabinet" and all the rest of it.

Suffragists have won a contested Proclamation and the temporary right to vote. But Anti-Suffragists have already checked the advance and are firmly resolved that the Feminist Revolution "shall not pass."

Anti-suffragists have nothing of which to be ashamed. They not only fought Feminism at the logical boundary line but have repulsed it on the open field ever since it crossed the boundary line, and regardless of what the future may hold, anti-suffragists will carry on "to the last quarter of an hour."

WOMEN STREETCAR CONDUCTORS FIGHT LAYOFFS (1921)

The involvement of the United States in World War I provided women with new employment opportunities, which were based solely on the scarcity of male labor. As this government document reveals, many women wished to retain their jobs after the end of the war. However, unions and management pressured them to leave. Workingwomen struggled against the effort to limit their work to their "appropriate" sphere. Why did the women want to keep their jobs? What role did the union play? Did women have the same right to work as men?*

Conspicuous among the occupations which were opened to women at the time of our entry into the war, was the work of conductor on street and elevated railways and subways. While women had been employed as ticket agents by various companies for many years, the woman streetcar conductor was a complete innovation, and about her employment in this capacity have centered much discussion and several bitter controversies. . . .

Having once been accepted as a successful participant in transportation work, there were two factors which were to influence the future employment of women in these occupations. First, Were the men employees going to accept women as fellow workers? Second, Was it going to prove possible such legal regulation as might be necessary for the protection of these women workers, and at the same time allow for the unusual difficulties with which a transportation company is faced in arranging the working hours of its employees?

The first question was soon answered in one way for the women conductors in Detroit and Cleveland, and in the opposite way in

---

* From "Controversies Regarding the Right of Women to Work as Conductors," *Women Streetcar Conductors and Ticket Agents* (Washington, D.C.: U.S. Government Printing Office, 1921).

Kansas City. The history of the situation in Detroit and Cleveland, as it affected the employment of women, is extremely significant. The issue was a clear-cut one, between the men on the one hand who wished to maintain the work of streetcar conductors as strictly men's work, and on the other hand the women who had proved that they could do the work well, and who were not ready to accept their exclusion from an occupation where the pay was good, and the hours and working conditions no more unsatisfactory than in many other occupations considered to come within the sphere of women's activities.

Women were put on as conductors during the after part of August, 1918, in Cleveland, when the street railway company of that city claimed that it could not secure a sufficient number of men for this work. The men objected to the employment of women and threatened to strike if it continued. But a compromise was finally effected and the matter submitted to Department of Labor investigators, who were to decide whether the women should be retained during the investigation, and whether there was a sufficient shortage of men to require the continued employment of women. The decision to retain the women during the investigation was made almost immediately, but after the investigation it was decided that while there was still a scarcity of male labor, it was not sufficient to justify the continued employment of women. This decision was rendered by the investigators in spite of their statement that "It is true the company will have to lower its standards somewhat, owing to the extraction of the best men from civil life into the military service of the county." It was recommended that the women be discharged from the service by November 1. The women protested against this and brought the matter before the War Labor Board. They claimed that it was illegal for the company and the men employees to make the original agreement to submit to arbitration the question of whether the women should be kept, as the

company had engaged the women to work during good behavior and to be discharged only for incompetency, insubordination, or other unsatisfactory service. The company expressed itself as completely satisfied with the work of the women, who claimed that the contracts between them and the company were still valid, and that they had not been consulted in any of the negotiations or investigations relative to their dismissal. They also claimed that the agreement to arbitrate was in disregard of their right to be employed and to hold employment as long as their work was satisfactory, and was an abridgment of their constitutional right to work.

The men claimed that the question of the employment of women was a matter between the company and the union. The union had an agreement with the company that no women should be employed, therefore the women had been engaged in disregard of this contract and were not parties to the discussion. . . . On December 2, the union formally demanded that the women be discharged, and threatened to go on strike immediately if this were not done. The strike began on December 3 and the War Labor Board was hurriedly appealed to by the Mayor of Cleveland, and immediately handed down the decision that the company should hereafter employ no more women, and that within the next 30 days all women should be replaced by competent men. This decision was not mandatory and the men refused to abide by it. The strike was finally settled by the following agreement between the union and the company:

It is hereby agreed by and between the undersigned that on and after this date there will be no more women employed as conductors; that the Cleveland Railway Co. will remove and displace the women that are now in its service as rapidly as possible.

This agreement was made by the officers of the union and the company without including the women at any stage of the negotiations. Vigorous protests by various women's organizations, as well by the women conductors themselves, followed this settlement, as it seemed to be a very dangerous precedent to deny women the right to work in any occupation, for no other reason than that their dismissal was demanded by the men, and without even giving the women a hearing so that they might present their case.

ANN MARTIN, *We Couldn't Afford a Doctor* (1920)

This excerpt from a magazine article written in support of the Sheppard-Towner Maternity Bill describes how poor women received inadequate prenatal care and gave birth to sickly babies. Women progressives advocated government funding for prenatal and maternity care. In an effort to appeal to newly enfranchised women, Congress passed the Maternity Bill in 1921. However, with the collapse of the mass-based women's movement, the effort to provide poor women with free medical services lost its political clout. Under increasing pressure from the male medical profession, Congress repealed the legislation in 1929. What evidence is offered that poor and rural women needed government-funded care?*

She went into the textile mills in Providence when she was twelve. She had worked there ever since, first to increase her father's and then her husband's insufficient wages. Her hours were from five in the afternoon till one in the morning. Her work was done standing at a machine during the whole eight hours, except for half an hour off for some food. She went home at one o'clock and slept till six, when she rose to cook breakfast and get her husband off to the mills and her children off to school.

"I always feel tired," she said. She looked it. Her hair was gray; she was thin and undersized and seemed fifty instead of thirty-five. She had borne six children, and another was coming very soon. With stoicism she told how she had always worked in the mill up to the last day, and had usually managed to return within a few days after the birth of her baby, so as to continue earning money. One baby was stillborn; three were too feeble at birth to live more than a few days; two had managed to survive. Owing to her rundown condition, she could not nurse any of them, she said, but could not have nursed them anyway, as she had to keep on at the mill.

She worked at night because it enabled her to "see the children some in the daytime," and to do the family washing, cooking, and sewing. She made over, for both the children and herself, old clothes which were sent by a relative. She had not had a new dress in eight years, or a vacation in twelve. The family earnings barely sufficed for the most meager supply of food and a place in which to live.

"I do not see how we can pay the doctor for coming for the next baby," she said. "He charges fifteen dollars and only comes once. The midwife will come eight times for eight dollars, but of course she doesn't know as much as the doctor. The housework always goes to pieces, though my husband cooks and does the best he can. But the children always get sick when I am sick, and everything in the house gets dirty, and we get in debt, so having babies is getting to be a horror to me."

The wife of a homesteader in Montana left the ranch with her husband in December, two weeks before confinement, and after a seventy-mile automobile drive to the railroad, traveled over one hundred miles by train to the nearest hospital. They started back before the baby was three weeks old, in bitter winter

---

* From Ann Martin, "We Couldn't Afford a Doctor," *Good Housekeeping,* April 1920, 19–20.

weather. They knew this was unwise, but the hospital expenses were heavy and the mother was worried about the other children, who had been left alone on the ranch. Owing to bad roads and a snowstorm, they were four days and nights driving the last seventy miles. One night they had to spend in the open.

"We intended to get to the hospital again for my next baby," said this Montana mother, "but the terrible expense of my last baby got us into debt, and then I couldn't get away in time because all the autos in the neighborhood were being used for sheepshearing."

She was attended only by a midwife in this next confinement, and suffered serious complications which caused the death of the baby.

These stories, as told to representatives of the Federal Children's Bureau, are typical of many thousands of others in the industrial cities and rural districts of the United States. Is it surprising that we have one of the highest infant death-rates in the world, that more babies die every year in the United States, under normal conditions and in proportion to the number born, than in almost any other county, great or small?

The facts are simple and tragic. Of the 2,500,000 babies born yearly in this country, at least a quarter of a million—one out of every ten babies born—die within the first twelve months of birth. Foreign countries long ago adopted government measures to save the lives of babies, and have thereby lowered the death rate. France loses only one out of thirteen babies born; Australia and Sweden one out of fourteen; Norway, one out of seventeen; New Zealand, which through its care for the mother before and after childbirth, has achieved the lowest baby death rate of any country in the world, loses only one out of twenty.

THE FARMER'S WIFE, *The Labor Savers I Use* **(1923)**

For housewives in general and farm women in particular, the technological developments that first made their appearance in rural areas during the 1920s revolutionized housework. In the following letters, farm wives applaud the way in which indoor plumbing, furnaces, and running water were not only laborsavers but "lifesavers." To what appliances and technological developments did women give the greatest praise? How did these lighten the burden of housework?*

Saving Every Minute

First comes my kitchen cabinet, standing five feet from and in front of the stove, and containing everything that is needed for baking. I can prepare anything for the oven without taking a step, till the cake, or pies or biscuits are ready to slip into the oven.

Next comes my built-in woodbox that can be filled from the shed and forms a nest in my kitchen beside the firebox end of the stove.

With my five babies all under five and one-third years of age, the bathroom on our first floor is a blessing. Two springs piped into a concrete reservoir supply the house and barn. The hot water tank is connected with my range.

And my laundry tubs! Such backache and time savers as they are. Mine are in the kitchen and covered as a table when not in use for washing. With no tubs to fill and empty, washing does not seem like washing. I had rather be without my hand-power washer than the tubs.

My husband had acetylene lights put in, so all the time I once used cleaning and filling

---

* From "The Labor Savers I Use" in *The Farmer's Wife,* February 1923, p. 301.

oil lamps is now used for other work. With the outfit is the hot plate, which makes summer cooking more comfortable.

I have an ironing board on a standard and a gasoline iron so I can iron when and where I choose.

One year I spent almost a day pitting cherries but never again! I bought a pitter and an apple parer. They not only do better and much quicker work, but my five-year-old boy can operate them as well as I. Doing every bit of my own work, sewing for all of us, even to the making of the children's coats, I must plan to save every minute I can so as to have a little time for reading and other things I enjoy.

By using my bread-mixer, it takes seven minutes to knead bread and have it set to rise.

I must also mention my mop wringer, dust mop and sweeper.

Winter used to mean spending a goodly share of each day carrying "chunks" from the woodshed to keep two heaters going. Now we have a pipeless furnace, all wood for it in the cellar and a much warmer house.—Mrs. L. L. S., N.Y.

Quartette of Life-Savers

When our laundry bill steadily mounted higher till we were paying two dollars every week for clothes not always well washed, we decided something had to be done. We had a gasoline engine but no washroom just a back porch too small for the engine and washing machine.

A washing machine with engine directly beneath the tub settled that problem, as it occupied no more space than an ordinary tub. Less than a year's laundry bill bought it. It not only took the drudgery out of washing but gave us *clean* clothes and saved money.

An old piano stool and a gasoline iron made the combination I thought-out, that saves so much time and energy and money on ironing days. I found that I could iron as well sitting as standing; the iron was always the right temperature; and no time was lost going to the stove for hot irons. One pint of gasoline

is sufficient for a big ironing; making the fuel cost almost nothing.

The Home Economics Clubs of this country have formed testing circles for trying out a number of laborsaving devices. I am using the wheeled table or kitchen jitney and have found it such an efficient maid that my boy is going to make me one at school.

The dishes and silver and all the food can be wheeled in at one trip, and at the close of the meal one load of used dishes goes back to the kitchen, instead of four or five as usual. Counting ten steps from kitchen to dining room (both are small) and at least five trips from one to the other, there is a saving of three hundred steps in one day in the preparation and clearing away of meals.

On ironing day this jitney is close at hand, and as the clothes are ironed they are piled on it, then wheeled to their proper places.

My kitchen is so small that there is not room for a drain board at the sink, but why should I worry? I have a large dish dryer with galvanized dripping pan underneath so I can use it on my kitchen cabinet. I wipe glasses and silver, but dishes and cooking utensils are scalded and dried by evaporation. Counting just one-half hour saved in a day in one week's time I am three and one half hours to the good.

These four articles constitute my much prized quartette of labor savers. Since the foremost women specialists of the American Medical Association agree that a large percent of the women who die are the unnecessary victims of the strain of housework, I think I may call them lifesavers, for they eliminate so much of the wasted energy that is expended in housekeeping.—Mrs. J.E.T., Wash.

Blessed Water

The running water in the house! What a constant cause of thankfulness! What a joy to use all I need and want! And I cannot bear to waste it unnecessarily even yet, for memory of former days has left scars so deep. It is foolish for me to say, "I *could* not keep house without it" for I have; and I'll not say. "I *would* not," for circumstances alter cases. One does so much for love and for necessity. But I will say, "I would much *rather* not keep house without it!"

Have you ever, in utter need, heard the clank of the dipper against the sides of an empty water pail? I remember hearing that dismal sound when my little girl, sick and feverish, was crying for a drink. Not a drop of cold water in the house for a craving child! The men from the hayfield had drunk the last drop and left the empty pail. The spring was downhill, a long, long way in the hot sun. I could not leave the child, so I took an umbrella for shade, a can for the water and carried her down to the spring.

How delicious it must have tasted on that feverish tongue. Then came the long, slow walk back up the hill, with the water and the child, who fortunately was quieted enough to manage the umbrella.

The water from that same spring is in our pressure-tank now, but to me *water* is the most necessary, the biggest item in the country household for saving the time and strength of the whole family. Other things shrink into insignificance beside that all-important one.

There is my washing machine. It doesn't *seem* as if I could put through by hand the big washes I have done in the machine. I think I have succeeded where my friends have been disappointed in theirs, because I have followed implicitly the directions accompanying it.

My mop wringer! I can remember my mother scrubbing floors on hands and knees with the old scrub brush, or later wringing the heavy, wet mop. My heart is truly thankful, I hope, for the things I do not have to do. I only wish I could share with so many of my neighbors who have not.

I must mention one other labor saver—the Little Maid In The House. She amuses the baby; she runs upstairs and down on errands for me; she sets the table; she is dishwasher and drier. She is indeed a constant joy and interest. Could I keep house without her? I would much rather not!—Mrs. H.W., Maine.

NATIONAL WOMAN'S PARTY, *Declaration of Principles* (1922)

During the 1920s, Alice Paul, president of the National Woman's Party (NWP), attempted to mobilize support for an Equal Rights Amendment (ERA). The amendment sought to nullify the reams of gender-based legislation that constrained women's equality. In pursuit of gender equity, the amendment would have negated protective legislation. The following document lists the objectives of the NWP. Although business and professional women joined the party, the goal of full-scale equal rights attracted relatively few women. Note the emphasis on independence and marital equality. The crusade for the ERA failed to win support of women's advocacy groups, including the League of Women Voters, settlement house leaders, and trade unionists. Major opposition sprang from the belief that women needed special legislative protection to safeguard their primary identification as wives and mothers. The ERA regained momentum in the 1970s but still failed to be ratified. How do these objectives relate to the 1848 Declaration of Sentiments discussed in Chapter 7? How would you relate these ERA objectives to contemporary women's issues?* What has or has not changed?

That women shall no longer be the governed half of society, but shall participate equally with men in the direction of life. . . .

That women shall no longer be barred from the priesthood or ministry, or any other position of authority in the church, but equally

---

* From National Woman's Party, "Declaration of Principles," *Equal Rights,* February 17, 1923.

with men shall participate in ecclesiastical offices and dignities.

That a double moral standard shall no longer exist, but one code shall obtain for both men and women.

That exploitation of the sex of women shall no longer exist, but women shall have the same right to the control of their persons as have men.

That women shall no longer be required by law or custom to assume the name of her husband upon marriage, but shall have the same right as a man to retain her own name after marriage.

That the wife shall no longer be considered as supported by the husband, but their mutual contribution to the family maintenance shall be recognized.

That the headship of the family shall no longer be in the husband alone, but shall be equally in the husband and wife. . . .

In short—that woman shall no longer be in any form of subjection to man in law or in custom, but shall in every way be on an equal plane in rights, as she has always been and will continue to be in responsibilities and obligations.

true partnership

CHARLOTTE HAWKINS BROWN, *Speech Given at the Women's Interracial Conference* (1920)

Jim Crow legislation, the law of the land since the *Plessy v. Ferguson* 1896 U.S. Supreme Court decision, further solidified white supremacy. By 1920, when Charlotte Hawkins Brown (1883–1961), a leader in the National Colored Woman's Club movement, gave this speech, little had changed. African Americans lived in a hostile racist environment. Ejecting black women from first-class train accommodations, the situation Brown describes in her speech, was only one of a host of degrading experiences that African American women confronted on a daily basis. This was the first time a white organization asked an African American woman to discuss racial problems. Brown's address initiated the interracial effort to end lynching.

As this document demonstrates, African American women experienced race and gender oppression in a manner very different from that of white women. Why does Brown appeal to white southern women for help? How does she refute the view that lynching protects white women?*

I came to Memphis crushed and humiliated. I have been very optimistic. My heart has sung within me. But on my way to this conference, I went into the station at Greensboro and I told the man I was coming to this conference and that I had to be on the train overnight. I had just opened school that day, had been working all day and I needed a night's sleep. I wasn't going into that sleeper because I wanted to be with white people. Nine times out of ten, in taking a sleeper, I don't go anywhere near the dressing room. And so I took a sleeper just as I had taken one before and I said to the agent, "Do you think it is all right to go on to Birmingham?" He said, "Yes." I stayed in the sleeper, until I thought we were perhaps a few hours away from Birmingham. I had a premonition of trouble and I got out of my berth. I saw a young colored girl sitting in the car and I said, "We won't occupy two seats, I am going to sit beside you," and so as I sat there as we rode into Anniston, Ala., and while backing out, three or four young men began to walk up and down the aisle and by and by they gathered more and they began to stand at one corner and then at another and my heart began to fill up with fear. I began to tremble

---

* From a speech by Charlotte Hawkins Brown, delivered to the Women's Interracial Conference, October 8, 1920.

and I began to pray. "Lord, thou knowest me on what errand I am bound, and I am asking you to take care of me now." Finally the group of three or four young men grew into eight or ten and then I counted twelve men. They represented in their forces the finest type of white men I have seen. One or two in the group were older men; they went first to the conductor and then to the porter. These twelve men came to look after two poor colored women. Will you just put yourself in my place. Just be colored for a few moments, and see yourself sitting down in a seat, helpless, with twelve young white men sitting around. A young man leaned forward and said, "We have wired ahead to have you taken off this train. Now, we give you your choice, to get off of this car right away and go into the day coach, or be taken off." I said, "I don't want any trouble." He said, "You must get up and go or we will take you." I said, "Let me see the conductor for a moment." They said, "No." So friends, not wishing to create a scene, wishing to get there, I said, "I want to get to that meeting. I want to tell those women that are gathered there that the women whom you had asked to come here and talk on race relations had to go through such an experience." The leader of the crowd said, "Let's march," and these young men got in front of us and two or three behind and we were ushered into the colored day coach. Friends,

I came here with a feeling of humiliation and I was so glad that Mrs. Johnson didn't call on me yesterday. Last night I prayed and poured out my soul to my God, and I want to tell you that it was a struggle, But finally I said, "God forgive those young men for I believe they were lacking in soul." . . .

Friends, what do you say about the cold-heartedness that we have felt? I told you to begin with, that we have become a little bit discouraged. We have begun to feel that you are not, after all, interested in us and I am going still further. The Negro women of the South lay everything that happens to the members of her race at the door of the Southern white woman. Just why I don't know, but we all feel that you can control your men. We feel that so far as lynching is concerned that, if the white woman would take hold of the situation that lynching would be stopped, mob violence stamped out and yet the guilty would have justice meted out by due course of law and would be punished accordingly. We do not condone criminality. We do not want our men to do anything that would make you feel that they were trying to destroy the chastity of our white women and, on the other hand, I want to say to you, when you read in the paper where a colored man has insulted a white woman, just multiply that by one thousand and you have some idea of the number of colored women insulted by white men.

ELEANOR WEMBRIDGE, *Petting and the College Campus* (1925)

Eleanor Wembridge (1882–1944) graduated from Radcliff College and was a writer of books, plays, and magazine articles for *McCall's* and *Mercury*. She was trained as a clinical psychologist and spent part of her career working as a psychologist for the juvenile court in Cleveland, Ohio. During the 1920s, she investigated the more permissive sexual standards that prevailed on college campuses. Shifting sexual norms were part of the development of a youth culture that rebelled against nineteenth-century Victorian constraints. Sex that was perceived as pleasurable and natural was replacing the feelings of shame and guilt instilled in young women during the previous century. Where once unmarried young women confronted social and cultural pressure to abstain from sex, Wembridge revealed the development of new codes of sexual behavior that combined a greater degree of intimacy but still protected female virginity. What evidence does Wembridge provide that sexual standards had changed from the time of the college students' parents and grandparents? Does the author identify with the new standards or does she seem judgmental? In terms of contemporary sexual standards, how would you evaluate these 1920s college norms?*

Last summer I was at a student conference of young women comprised of about eight hundred college girls from the middle western states. The subject of petting was very much on their minds, both as to what attitude they should take toward it with the younger girls (being upperclassmen themselves) and also how much renunciation of this pleasurable pastime was required of them. If I recall correctly, two entire mornings were devoted to discussing the matter, two evenings, and another overflow meeting. . . .

Before the conference I made it my business to talk to as many college girls as possible. I consulted as many, both in groups and privately, as I had time for at the conference. And since it is all to be repeated in another state this summer, I have been doing so, when opportunity offered, ever since . . . .

One fact is evident, that whether or not they pet, they hesitate to have anyone believe that they do not. It is distinctly the *mores* of the times to be considered as ardently sought after, and as not too priggish to respond. As one girl said—"I don't particularly care to be kissed by some of the fellows I know, but I'd let them do it any time rather than think I wouldn't dare. As a matter of fact, there are lots of fellows I don't kiss. It's the very young kids that never miss a chance."

That petting should lead to actual illicit relations between the petters was not advised nor countenanced among the girls with whom I discussed it. They drew the line quite sharply. That it often did so lead, they admitted, but they were not ready to allow that there were any more of such affairs than there had always been. School and college scandals, with their sudden departures and hasty marriages, have always existed to some extent, and they still do. But only accurate statistics hard to arrive at, can prove whether or not the sex carelessness of the present day extends to an increase of sex immorality. . . .

I sat with one pleasant college Amazon, a total stranger, beside a fountain in the park, when she asked if I saw any harm in her kissing a young man whom she liked, but whom she did not want to marry. "It's terribly exciting. We get such a thrill. I think it is natural to want nice men to kiss you, so why not do what is natural?" There was no embarrassment in her manner. Her eyes and her conscience were equally untroubled. I felt as if a girl from the Parthenon frieze had stepped down to ask if she might not sport in the glade with a handsome faun. Why not indeed? Only an equally direct forcing of twentieth-century science on primitive simplicity could bring us even to the same level in our conversation, and at that, the stigma of impropriety seemed to fall on me, rather than on her.

Letter to Margaret Sanger (1928)

Margaret Sanger (1879–1966) spent her life in a crusade for birth control. In 1916, she opened a birth control clinic in an immigrant, working-class neighborhood in Brooklyn, New York, in violation of state laws, which considered birth control to be a form of obscenity. She was soon arrested and the clinic closed. During the 1920s, middle-class women began to use contraception on a wide scale. However,

---

* From Eleanor Wembridge, "Petting and the Campus," *Survey* 54 (1 July 1925): 393–94.

many poor women still lacked access to modern contraception. As the nation's foremost advocate of birth control, Sanger received letters, such as the following, from women desperate for advice on how to avoid unwanted pregnancies. How do these letters support Sanger's belief that the ability to control pregnancy was women's most vital right?*

Please tell me what to do to keep from having any more babies. I am only twenty-six years old and the mother of five children the oldest eight years and the others six, four and two, and I have four living. The last time I had a six month's miscarriage and I have been weak ever since. It happened this past August. My husband is gone to try and find work and I have to support my children myself. I have to work so hard until I feel like it would kill me to give birth to another. I am nervous. My back and side give me a lot of trouble. I am not able to give my children the attention that I desire. I take in washing to support my children, I suffered this last time from the time I got that way until I lost it and am yet weak in my back. Please! for my sake tell me what to do to keep from having another. I don't want another child. Five is enough for me.

* * *

I don't care to bear any more children for the man I got he is most all the time drunk and not working and gone for days and nights and leave me alone most of the time. I'm sewing to support me and my baby that is two years old and one dead born so I know you don't blame me for not wanting any more children and he is always talking about leaving me he might as well for what he is doing but I am worried that I may get in wrong.

* * *

I was married when I was seventeen and seven months. After nine months married I had a miscarriage at eight months. After fourteen months I had a baby boy and he is living and is now seven years old. After three years I had another boy. He was born with consumption in the bones and would shake his head one side and another but doctors did not know what that was. Now I have them nervous spells myself. All through my married life I have been working in factories. I took my children to the day nursery. Two months before the birth of my last child my husband deserted me with my children. He had left home eleven time before that but always came back, but that night his mother gave him money to get out of town. I was then married five years to him. After four years I could not get no trace of him I got the divorce. I had to work hard to keep my furniture and pay the rent as I did not want to go boarding. Now as I was twenty-six and as I had no one to depend on I married again. He is good young man of twenty-five and he is not a lazy gambler like the other, but even with that I fear having any more children as they will not be healthy. We were married a few months ago and neither of us had any money and he is only a laborer and makes twenty-five dollars a week, so you see I have struggled with the first husband and I wish I will not struggle with this one, so please if you can help me.

---

* From Margaret Sanger, *Motherhood in Bondage* (New York: Brentano, 1928).

CHAPTER 15

The Great Depression and the New Deal:
Desperate Lives and Women Leaders

As a result of massive male unemployment, the right of married women to work came under attack during the Great Depression. Many married women lost their jobs. The government and private sector preferred to hire men. Gallup polls revealed that an overwhelming majority of Americans believed that married women should stay home, and that their employment took jobs away from men. Professional women, in particular, found diminished opportunity. Even women in traditionally female fields such as teaching were affected as school districts fired married women and hired men instead.

The popular perception that workingwomen deprived men of employment obscured the reality of the sex-segregated labor market. As reported by Ruth Shallcross, the issue of whether married women should remain in the workforce obscured the fact that in most cases, men and women did not compete for the same jobs. The Depression hit the male preserve of heavy industry with extreme force. Many married women scrambled to find work because their husbands faced chronic unemployment. In fact, the number of low-paying women's service and clerical positions continued to grow despite the Depression. Among employed women, the percentage of married women working rose. Given a belief system that equated employment with manhood, chronically unemployed husbands suffered a loss of status and masculinity.

As Meridel Le Sueur reported, millions of desperately poor white and African American women lived on the edge of disaster. Generally barred by race from factory work and other occupations, African American domestic workers experienced some of the most desperate economic conditions during the period. For at least some of these impoverished women, New Deal relief programs meant the difference between survival and starvation. However, class, race, and gender biases also pervaded New Deal policies. Employed mainly as farm and domestic laborers, neither African nor Mexican American workers would benefit from the old-age provisions of the Social Security Act, which failed to cover, as had the National Recovery Act, this type of work. African American women, including Pinkie Pilcher, wrote letters to President Franklin Roosevelt protesting the racist practices of white southerners that prevented impoverished African Americans from obtaining federal aid.

In contrast to the bleak conditions poor women faced, women social reformers found a welcome reception in the New Deal administration of Franklin Roosevelt. At the top level of government, a more significant female presence existed than in all previous administrations. New Deal federal programs provided career opportunities for a select number of women; many promoted legislation and programs that emphasized maternal concerns rather than widening employment opportunities for women. With ties to the Progressive-era social reform, these women clustered around Eleanor Roosevelt and Frances Perkins, who, as secretary of labor, became the first woman in U.S. history to receive a cabinet-level appointment. With their shared Hull House background and commitment to use government intervention on behalf of workplace safety, Frances Perkins and Dr. Alice Hamilton, the nation's leading advocate for removing toxic hazards from the workplace environment, joined forces to investigate the ill health of American miners exposed to silica dust.

Unemployment was the major priority of public works programs. When it came to these work programs, however, white women were treated as second-class citizens and black women suffered even more. Domestic labor, the major occupation for African American women was left out of Social Security guidelines. A woman's primary identity was still seen as that of a mother and not as a worker. New Deal employment policies pushed married women to give up their jobs so more men could be employed. The objective was to secure a family wage for the father so that mothers would not have to go to work. As a result of this maternal ideology, unemployed women did not receive government support commensurate with that of unemployed men.

Compassionate and responsive, Eleanor Roosevelt personified the administration's concern for the victims of economic disaster. She broke the rules for first ladies who usually remained behind the scenes and mainly served as White House hostesses. Eleanor successfully promoted the hiring of women within the Democratic National Committee and their appointment to positions in the New Deal administration. Active in the promotion of racial justice, she supported the anti-lynching effort of the NAACP and secured an administrative appointment for noted African American educator Mary McLeod Bethune, who helped widen employment opportunities for minority youth.

Although President Roosevelt refused to politically address the lynching issue, fearing it would result in loss of southern congressional support for New Deal legislation, white southerner Jesse Daniel Ames rallied other white southern women and organized an anti-lynching crusade.

The commitment of the New Deal administration to ameliorate suffering resulted in the Social Security Act's provision for aid to dependent women and their children as well as Social Security payments for widows. However, other provisions of the Social Security Act excluded many female workers from retirement benefits, particularly those clustered in the low-wage fields of waitress, domestics, and beauticians.

The exclusion of many women workers expressed the prevalent maternal belief system of New Deal policies that continued to devalue women's labor and see their work roles as supplemental to those of men. Democratic party activist and reformer Molly Dewson, who chaired the Women's Division of the Democratic National Committee, became the first woman to serve on the Social Security Board. Dewson, Perkins, and Eleanor Roosevelt supported maternal values and opposed the ERA. Perkins endorsed gendered assumptions about women's work that stereotyped women as supplemental workers and gave priority to male workers. Even in the case of federal emergency relief, women who were 25 percent of the unemployed received 13 percent of the jobs.

The federal government's commitment to welfare created new opportunities for educated women trained in the field of social work. In line with the earlier tradition of women's voluntary settlement house work, the female-designated area of social work widened employment opportunities without challenging a traditional male occupation. As in other women's fields, gender bias kept the status and pay scale in social work low.

Eleanor Roosevelt would later become a proponent of the ERA, and the Democratic Party adopted a commitment to it in 1941. During the thirties, Eleanor and the women in her circle of political leaders upheld protective legislation and maternal difference rather than gender equality. The National Woman's Party (NWP), during the twenties and thirties, served more as a political lobbying group for gender equality than a political party. During the thirties, the NWP achieved success in some states for legislation to allow women to serve on juries. Numerically weak, Alice Paul and other feminist supporters were continually in conflict with maternal and domestics ideals that molded mainstream attitudes and politics.

The Great Depression pushed to the brink communities of impoverished whites and African and Mexican Americans, who barely survived even during economic prosperity. Ann Low and her family stayed on their North Dakota farm despite the devastation of the Great Plains dust storms, but thousands of other Great Plains families, particularly those from the hardest hit area of Oklahoma, fled their dust-ravaged farms for California. Among the most vulnerable and hardest hit by the Depression were agricultural workers, sharecroppers, and migrant laborers, who suffered devastation as demand for agricultural produce declined and unemployment skyrocketed. Landless and jobless, thousands of African Americans left the South and migrated to northern cities in pursuit of work. Mexican Americans encountered massive unemployment, and many once viewed as a desirable source of cheap labor were now seen as an unnecessary surplus.

MERIDEL LE SUEUR, *The Despair of Unemployed Women* (1932)

Born in Iowa, Meridel Le Sueur (1900–1996) was a journalist, poet, and novelist. She was a leading writer during the thirties, compiling evidence and writing with empathy about the misery of impoverished women during the Depression. A socialist, her writing was blacklisted during the anti-Communism of the1950s. During the 1970s, her contributions and writings received renewed affirmation. This document is Le Sueur's eyewitness account of the desperation of unemployed women seeking domestic work. New Deal legislation addressed the needs of unemployed men, but unemployed women who were responsible for their own survival were a forgotten segment of the population. What life experiences do these women share? What evidence does Le Sueur offer that despite the women's efforts to find work, employment was unlikely?*

I am sitting in the city free employment bureau. It's the women's section. We have been sitting here now for four hours. We sit here every day, waiting for a job. There are no jobs. Most of us have had no breakfast. Some have had scant rations for over a year. Hunger makes a human being lapse into a state of lethargy, especially city hunger. Is there anyplace else in the world where a human being is supposed to go hungry amidst plenty

---

* From Meridel Le Sueur, "Women on the Breadlines." Originally published in *New Masses,* January 1932. Reprinted by permission.

without an outcry, without protest, where only the boldest steal or kill for bread, and the timid crawl the streets, hunger like the beak of a terrible bird at the vitals?

We sit looking at the floor. No one dares think of the coming winter. There are only a few more days of summer. Everyone is anxious to get work to lay up something for that long siege of bitter cold. But there is no work. Sitting in the room we all know it. That is why we don't talk much. We look at the floor dreading to see that knowledge in each other's eyes. There is a kind of humiliation in it. We look away from each other. We look at the floor. It's too terrible to see this animal terror in each other's eyes.

So we sit hour after hour, day after day, waiting for a job to come in. There are many women for a single job. A thin sharp woman sits inside a wire cage looking at a book. For four hours we have watched her looking at that book. She has a hard little eye. In the small bare room there are half a dozen women sitting on the benches waiting. Many come and go. Our faces are all familiar to each other, for we wait here every day.

This is a domestic employment bureau. Most of the women who come here are middle-aged, some have families, some have raised their families and are now alone, some have men who are out of work. Hard times and the man leaves to hunt for work. He doesn't find it. He drifts on. The woman probably doesn't hear from him for a long time. She expects it. She isn't surprised. She struggles alone to feed the many mouths. Sometimes she gets help from the charities. If she's clever she can get herself a good living from the charities, if she's naturally a lickspittle, naturally a little docile and cunning. If she's proud then she starves silently, leaving her children to find work, coming home after a day's searching to wrestle with her house, her children.

Some such story is written on the faces of all these women. There are young girls, too, fresh from the country. Some are made brazen too soon by the city. There is a great exodus of girls from the farms into the city now. Thousands of farms have been vacated completely in Minnesota. The girls are trying to get work. The prettier ones can get jobs in the stores when there are any, or waiting on table, but these jobs are only for the attractive and the adroit. The others, the real peasants, have a more difficult time.

Bernice sits next to me. She is a Polish woman of thirty-five. She has been working in people's kitchens for fifteen years or more. She is large, her great body in mounds, her face brightly scrubbed. She has a peasant mind and finds it hard even yet to understand the maze of the city, where trickery is worth more than brawn. Her blue eyes are not clever but slow and trusting. She suffers from loneliness and lack of talk. When you speak to her, her face lifts and brightens as if you had spoken through a great darkness, and she talks magically of little things as if the weather were magic, or tells some crazy tale of her adventures on the city streets, embellishing them in bright colors until they hang heavy and thick like embroidery. She loves the city anyhow. It's exciting to her, like a bazaar. She loves to go shopping and get a bargain, hunting out the places where stale bread and cakes can be had for a few cents. She likes walking the streets looking for men to take her to picture shows. Sometimes she goes to five picture shows in one day, or she sits through one the entire day until she knows all the dialogue by heart.

She came to the city a young girl from a Wisconsin farm. The first thing that happened to her, a charlatan dentist took out all her good shining teeth and the fifty dollars she had saved working in a canning factory. After that she met men in the park who told her how to look out for herself, corrupting her peasant mind, teaching her to mistrust everyone. Sometimes now she forgets to mistrust everyone and gets taken in. They taught her to get what she could for nothing, to count her change, to go back if she found herself cheated, to demand her rights.

She lives alone in little rooms. She bought seven dollars' worth of secondhand furniture eight years ago. She rents a room for perhaps three dollars a month in an attic, sometimes a cold house. Once the house where she stayed was condemned and everyone else moved out, and she lived there all winter alone on the top floor. She spent only twenty-five dollars all winter.

She wants to get married but she sees what happens to her married friends, left with children to support, worn out before their time. So she stays single. She is virtuous. She is slightly deaf from hanging out clothes in winter. She had done people's washings and cooking for fifteen years and in that time saved thirty dollars. Now she hasn't worked steady for a year and she has spent the thirty dollars. She had dreamed of having a little house or a houseboat perhaps with a spot of ground for a few chickens. This dream she will never realize.

She has lost all her furniture now along with the dream. A married friend whose husband is gone gives her a bed for which she pays by doing a great deal of work for the woman. She comes here every day now, sitting bewildered, her pudgy hands folded in her lap. She is hungry. Her great flesh has begun to hang in folds. She has been living on crackers. Sometimes a box of crackers lasts a week. She has a friend who's a baker and he sometimes steals the stale loaves and brings them to her.

A girl we have seen every day all summer went crazy yesterday at the Y.W. She went into hysterics, stamping her feet and screaming.

She hadn't had work for eight months. "You've got to give me something," she kept on saying. The woman in charge flew into a rage that probably came from days and days of suffering on her part, because she is unable to give jobs, having none. She flew into a rage at the girl and there they were facing each other in a rage, both helpless, helpless. This woman told me once that she could hardly bear the suffering she saw, hardly hear it, that she couldn't eat sometimes and had nightmares at night.

So they stood there, the two women in a rage, the girl weeping and the woman shouting at her.

RUTH SHALLCROSS, *Shall Married Women Work?* (1936)

As this document reveals, a majority of Americans believed that married women should not work. Both government and the private sector developed employment policies that excluded married female workers. In part, this discriminatory treatment expressed the traditional view that married women belonged at home taking care of their families. However, many married women sought work because their unemployed husbands could no longer provide for their families. In what fields did married women face the greatest discrimination?*

Legislative Action

Within the last few years, bills have been introduced in the legislatures of twenty-six states against married woman workers. Only one of these passed. This was in Louisiana, and it was later repealed. Six other states have either joint resolutions or governors' orders restricting married women's right to work.

---

* From Ruth Shallcross, "Shall Married Women Work?" National Federation of Business and Professional Women's Clubs, Public Affairs Pamphlet No. 40, New York, 1936. Reprinted by permission of Business Professional Women/USA, Washington, D.C.

Three other states have made a general practice of prohibiting married women from working in public employment. . . .

Extent of Discrimination

The National Federation of Business and Professional Women's Clubs made a survey early in 1940 of local employment policies. This was part of a general study which assembled all materials relating to the employment of married women. The survey shows that married women are most likely to find bars against them if they seek jobs as school teachers, or as office workers in public utilities or large manufacturing concerns. Only a very small number of department stores refuse jobs to married women. However, in 1939, the *Department Store Economist* reported that the sentiment against married women "is growing stronger." Opposition, it was found, came from customers, labor organizations, women's clubs, and miscellaneous groups of the unemployed. Despite this opposition, "nearly all stores are either doubtful whether it would be a wise plan to announce publicly a policy against hiring or retaining married women, or believe it would not be helpful to public relations." This attitude may reflect the fact that married women's employment has been advantageous to department stores because the necessary part-time arrangements suited both parties well. Single women usually want full-time employment, but many married women prefer to work only a few hours each day. . . .

Kinds of Bars

The bars against married women are of different kinds—all of which exist for some school teachers. They may take the form of refusal to hire married women (the most frequent), of dismissal upon marriage, delay in granting promotion, or actual demotion, and either permanent or temporary dismissal when pregnant. Discrimination is often difficult to detect; a married woman may assume that her marriage is the cause of her inability to hold a job, or to get a new one, when the real reason may lie in her lack of ability, personality, or training.

The National Education Association has from time to time made surveys of employment policies in local communities with respect to married women teachers. Its material is more complete than any other. Its survey, made in 1931, revealed that 77 percent of the cities reporting made a practice of not employing married women as new teachers, and 63 percent dismissed women teachers upon marriage. Tenure acts protect married teachers from being dismissed in some states. But although tenure acts may protect teachers who marry after being employed, they do not assure a new teacher that marriage will not be a bar to getting a job. The National Education Association reported in 1939 that teachers in at least thirteen states are legally protected by court decisions from being dismissed for being married. Kentucky seems to be the only state where the contract of marriage is deemed "the very basis of the whole fabric of society" and hence is not an obstacle to employment. . . .

Studies show that men have been affected by unemployment to a much greater extent than have women, because unemployment has been more acute in the heavy industries (steel, oil, mining, etc.) where men are mostly employed. . . . The administrative and clerical jobs connected with these industries, which are partially filled by women, have not been eliminated to anything like the same degree as production jobs.

Consumer and service industries (textile, food, beauty parlors, telephone service, to name only a few), where women are mostly to be found, were not affected as seriously as heavy industries by the Depression. The government's recovery measures, based on artificially increasing purchasing power, chiefly stimulated the consumer and service industries, thus opening up relatively more opportunities for women than men. As a result, women have fared better than men in getting new jobs. . . .

State and federal employment offices also give evidence of the relative ease with which women have obtained jobs compared with men, and indicate that men have been unemployed for longer periods of time than have women. One study of a community of 14,000 people in the West makes this point specific. Women's work in the town increased during the early years of the Depression in the needle trades and textiles, as well as in the service occupations, while men's work in glass declined sharply. Another study in a steel town showed much the same thing. Few of the people who oppose married women's employment seem to realize that a coal miner or steel worker cannot very well fill the jobs of nursemaids, cleaning women, or the factory and clerical occupations now filled by women. Unhappily, men accustomed to work in the heavy industries have not been able to fill the jobs in consumer and service industries. Retraining of these men has been practically negligible, and could not have been done in time to benefit them immediately. Expenditures for defense are now once more increasing opportunities in heavy industries, so we may expect to see a fundamental change in the situation in the coming months.

Pinkie Pilcher, *Letter to President Roosevelt* (1936)

During the Great Depression, local communities administered federal relief assistance. In the South, African Americans, representing some of the nations most desperate, found white administrators adopting a pro-white color line for distributing relief. Pinkie Pilcher, an impoverished black woman, wrote the following letter to President Franklin Roosevelt. Not only a plea for help, the letter also informs the federal government of the racist practices that added to the African American struggle for survival. What examples does Pilcher give of the unfair practices that made it impossible for her to get help? What role did white women play in the discriminatory practices? In what ways did poor whites benefit from federal aid?*

117 Ash St.
Greenwood, Miss.
Dec. 23, 1936
President Roosevelt

Dear Sir:

We are wondering what is going to become of this large number of widow women with and without children. These white women, at the head of the PWA is still letting we colored women when we go to the office to be certified for work to go hunt washings. . . .

I was in the office a few days ago. A woman was there she had five children and a husband not able to work. They told her to go hunt washings. . . . The white people dont pay anything for their washing. She cant do enough washing to feed her family. I was reading an article in the paper enquiring why colored men did not show up on WPA projects in some places. You all are not down here. So you has to take these white people word. . . .

I know we have had men here in Greenwood to walk [to the relief office] several weeks then white women and men would tell them come back tomorrow come back Monday. Finally they would say what are you Nigers [*sic*] keep on coming up here for. We cant take on any more go hunt you some work. Then they will write you all our men and women cant be found. Good many of our

---

* From Pinkie Pilcher, "Letter to President Roosevelt," December 23, 1936. From the WPA Collection of the Manuscript Division of the Moorland-Spingarn Research Center, Howard University. Reprinted by permission.

men have told me they would eat grass like a cow and drink water before they would go back to any of the relief offices, let them white people dog them again. We have old people cant get any help. If the old people go they will say go to your children if the children go to the relief they will tell them we cant take on any more. Like my father is old. Last week he came to me for help. He is on relief but cant get nothing. He lives in Carroll County.

. . . cant get work. I could not help him and he cant help me. I was at the coat house last week said to be colored people day to get cloth. They had about a dozen gowins at the coat house in a little draw they give the real old men and women one gown. I saw that with my own eyes if you all keep on sending cloth here these white people will have anough to last the next century. They are making themselves whole.

Now about a month ago they employed two white women, one to sit at the coat house then employed another under her to come visit the colored people. The money you all pay out for poor white women visiting the colored people you could throw it in the river or in the fire for what it do us. . . .

I visit my sick people because I feel like it is my duty. The white woman got mad with me because she thought I was taking note of how they was being treated. Come to my house to raise a fuss. Told me I better not take any note of the sick people she visit, if I did, what she was going to do. . . .

ANN MARIE LOW, *Dust Bowl Diary* (1934)

Excerpts from Ann Marie Low's diary show the contribution young unmarried women made to the family economy. Low and her family resided in North Dakota at a time when dust storms ravaged the Great Plains. Economic conditions of farmers hard hit by the Depression declined even further. Low's diary chronicled her coming of age amidst double disasters of unmitigated dust storm havoc and economic depression. The constant dust storms added to Low's despair and increased the burden of household tasks. What employment opportunities did Low have? How vital was her household labor to her family's well-being?*

April 25, 1934, Wednesday

Last weekend was the worst dust storm we ever had. We've been having quite a bit of blowing dirt every year since the drought started, not only here, but all over the Great Plains. Many days this spring the air is just full of dirt coming, literally, for hundreds of miles. It sifts into everything. After we wash the dishes and put them away, so much dust sifts into the cupboards we must wash them again before the next meal. Clothes in the closets are covered with dust.

Last weekend no one was taking an automobile out for fear of ruining the motor. I rode Roany to Frank's place to return a gear. To find my way I had to ride right beside the fence, scarcely able to see from one fence post to the next.

Newspapers say the deaths of many babies and old people are attributed to breathing in so much dirt.

May 7, 1934, Monday

The dirt is still blowing. Last weekend Bud [her brother] and I helped with the cattle and had fun gathering weeds. Weeds give us

---

* Reprinted from *Dust Bowl Diary* by Ann Marie Low by permission of the University of Nebraska Press. Copyright 1984 by the University of Nebraska Press.

greens for salad before anything in the garden is ready. We use dandelions, lamb's quarter, and sheep sorrel. I like sheep sorrel best. Also, the leaves of sheep sorrel, pounded and boiled down to a paste, make a good salve.

Still no job. I'm trying to persuade Dad I should apply for rural school #3 out here where we went to school. I don't see a chance of getting a job in a high school when so many experienced teachers are out of work.

He argues that the pay is only $60.00 a month out here, while even in a grade school in town I might get $75.00. Extra expenses in town would probably eat up that extra $15.00. Miss Eston, the practice teaching supervisor, told me her salary has been cut to $75.00 after all the years she has been teaching in Jamestown. She wants to get married. School boards will not hire married women teachers in these hard time because they have husbands to support them. Her fiancé is the sole support of his widowed mother and can't support a wife, too. So she is stuck in her job, hoping she won't get another salary cut because she can scarcely live on what she makes and dress the way she is expected to.

Dad argues the patrons always stir up so much trouble for a teacher at #3; some teachers

Migrant Mother (Courtesy of the Library of Congress)

have quit in mid-term. The teacher is also the janitor, so the hours are long.

I figure I can handle the work, kids, and patrons. My argument is that by teaching here I can work for my room and board at home, would not need new clothes, and so could send most of my pay to Ethel [her sister] and Bud.

MARY MCLEOD BETHUNE, *A Century of Progress of Negro Women* (1933)

In this speech, Mary McLeod Bethune (1875–1955) recounted the progress African American women had made since emancipation. In stark contrast to domestic workers, upwardly mobile African American women not only achieved middle-class status, but a few, despite enormous odds, even achieved national recognition. Bethune was one of those women. A child of freed slaves, Bethune established an elementary school for blacks that she later transformed into a college. An advisor to Franklin Roosevelt, she was the first African American woman to receive a high-level New Deal appointment. How did Bethune define the "character" of African American womanhood? Which specific groups of African American women are omitted from this account?*

---

* From Mary McLeod Bethune, "A Century of Progress of Negro Women." Speech delivered before the Chicago Women's Federation on June 30, 1933. The Mary McLeod Bethune Papers, Amistad Research Center at Tulane University.

To Frederick Douglass is credited the plea that, "the Negro be not judged by the heights to which he is risen, but by the depths from which he has climbed." Judged on that basis, the Negro woman embodies one of the modern miracles of the New World.

One hundred years ago she was the most pathetic figure on the American continent. She was not a person, in the opinion of many, but a thing—a thing whose personality had no claim to the respect of mankind. She was a household drudge—a means for getting distasteful work done; she was an animated agricultural implement to augment the service of mules and plows in cultivating and harvesting the cotton crop. Then she was an automatic incubator, a producer of human live stock, beneath whose heart and lungs more potential laborers could be bred and nurtured and brought to the light of toilsome day.

Today she stands side by side with the finest manhood the race has been able to produce. Whatever the achievement of the Negro man in letters, business, art, pulpit, civic progress and moral reform, he cannot but share them with his sister of darker hue. Whatever glory belongs to the race for a development unprecedented in history for the given length of time, a full share belongs to the womanhood of the race.

By the very force of circumstances, the part she has played in the progress of the race has been of necessity, to a certain extent, subtle and indirect. She has not always been permitted a place in the front ranks where she could show her face and make her voice heard with effect. But she has been quick to seize every opportunity which presented itself; to come more and more into the open and strive directly for the uplift of the race and nation. In that direction, her achievements have been amazing.

Negro women have made outstanding contributions in the arts. Meta V.W. Fuller and May Howard Jackson are significant figures in Fine Arts development. Angelina Grimké, Georgia Douglass Johnson and Alice Dunbar

Nelson are poets of note. Jessie Fausett has become famous as a novelist. In the field of Music; Anita Patti Brown, Lillian Evanti, Elizabeth Greenfield, Florence Cole-Talbert, Marian Anderson and Marie Selika stand out pre-eminently.

Very early in the post-emancipation period, women began to show signs of ability to contribute to the business progress of the Race. Maggie L. Walker, who is outstanding as the guiding spirit of the Order of Saint Luke, in 1902 went before her Grand Council with a plan for a Saint Luke Penny Savings Bank. This organization started with a deposit of about eight thousand dollars and twenty-five thousand in paid up capital, with Maggie L. Walker as the first Woman Bank President in America. For twenty-seven years she has held this place. Her bank has paid dividends to stockholders; has served as a depository for gas and water accounts of the city of Richmond, and has given employment to hundreds of Negro clerks, bookkeepers and office workers.

With America's great emphasis on the physical appearance, a Negro woman left her washtub and ventured into the world of facial beautification. From a humble beginning, Madame C. J. Walker built a substantial institution that is a credit to American business in every way.

Mrs. Annie M. Malone is another pioneer in this field of successful business. The C. J. Walker Manufacturing Company and the Poro College do not confine their activities in the field of beautification to race. They serve both races and give employment to both.

When the ballot was made available to the Womanhood of America, the sister of darker hue was not slow to seize the advantage. In sections where the Negro could gain access to the voting booth, the intelligent, forward-looking element of the Race's women have taken hold of political issues with an enthusiasm and mental acumen that might well set worthy examples for other groups. Of times she has led the struggle toward moral improvement and political record, and has compelled her reluctant brother to follow her determined lead.

In time of war as in time of peace, the Negro woman has ever been ready to serve for her people's and the nation's good. During the recent World War she pleaded to go in the uniform of the Red Cross nurse, and was denied the opportunity only on the basis of racial discrimination.

Addie W. Hunton and Kathryn M. Johnson gave yeoman service with the American Expeditionary Forces with the Y.M.C.A. group.

Negro women have thrown themselves whole-heartedly into the organization of groups to direct the social uplift of their fellow men, one of the greatest achievements of the race.

Perhaps the most outstanding individual social worker of our group today is Jane E. Hunter, founder and executive secretary of the Phillis Wheatley Association, Cleveland, Ohio.

In November, 1911, Miss Hunter, who had been a nurse in Cleveland for only a short time, recognizing the need for a Working Girls' Home, organized the Association and prepared to establish the work. Today the Association is housed in a magnificent structure of nine stories, containing one hundred thirty-five rooms, offices, parlours, a cafeteria and beautify parlour. It is not only a home for working girls but a recreational center and ideal hospice for the young Negro woman who is living away from home. It maintains an employment department and a fine, up-to-date camp. Branches of the activities of the main Phillis Wheatley are located in other sections of Cleveland, special emphasis being given to the recreational facilities for children and young women of the vicinities in which the branches are located.

In no field of modern social relationship has the hand of service and the influence of the Negro woman been felt more distinctly than in the Negro orthodox church. It may be safely said that the chief sustaining force in support of the pulpit and the various phases of missionary enterprise, has been the feminine element of the membership. The development of the Negro church since the Civil War has been another of the modern miracles. Throughout its growth the untiring effort, the unflagging enthusiasm, the sacrificial contribution of time, effort and cash earnings of the black woman have been the most significant factors, without which the modern Negro church would have no history worth the writing.

Both before and since emancipation, by some rare gift, she has been able to hold on to the fires of family unity and keep the home one unimpaired whole. In recent years it has become increasingly the case where in many instances the mother is the sole dependence of the home, and single-handed, fights the wolf from the door, while the father submits unwillingly to enforced idleness and unavoidable unemployment. Yet in myriads of instances she controls home discipline with a tight rein and exerts a unifying influence that is the miracle of the century.

The true worth of a race must be measured by the character of its womanhood.

As the years have gone on the Negro woman has touched the most vital fields in the civilization of today. Wherever she has contributed, she has left the mark of a strong character. The educational institutions she has established and directed have met the needs of her young people; her cultural development has concentrated itself into artistic presentation accepted and acclaimed by meritorious critics; she is successful as a poet and a novelist; she is shrewd in business and capable in politics; she recognizes the importance of uplifting her people through social, civic and religious activities; starting at the time when as a "mammy" she nursed the infants of the other race and taught him her meager store of truth, she has been a contributing factor of note to interracial relations. Finally, through the past century she has made and kept her home intact—humble though it may have been in many instances. She has made and is making history.

JESSIE DANIEL AMES, *Southern Women and Lynching* (1936)

Jessie Daniel Ames (1883–1972) organized and led the Association of Southern Women to Prevent Lynching. At its peak, the organization had forty thousand female members. The effort to eradicate lynching also represented the association's determination to eliminate the myth that white men lynched black men to uphold the purity of white southern women. Although by the standards of the South, an anti-lynching crusade led by white women was radical, the organization also upheld southern norms. It neither promoted federal anti-lynching legislation nor accepted black women as members. Instead, it sought to change public opinion, and in this respect enjoyed considerable success. In the following article, Ames records the organization's achievements. What accomplishments does she specifically acknowledge? How does she evaluate the role played by southern white women who supported lynching?*

Conference Called

The Association of Southern Women for the Prevention of Lynching grew out of a recognized need for some central committee to assume as its sole purpose the initiative for the eradication of lynching. Although some eight years before, small groups of women in each of the thirteen Southern states had issued statements condemning lynching among a dozen or more evils afflicting the South, they set in motion no special machinery by means of which public opinion would be changed toward this one special evil. When lynchings reached a new high level in 1930, it appeared imperative to some Southern women that something should be done by them to stop or abate this particularly revolting crime. Consequently, a conference was called for November 1, 1930, in Atlanta, Georgia, to discuss what Southern women could do to stop lynching.

Favorable response to this call to confer was inspired by an increasing awareness on the part of Southern women of the claim of lynchers and mobsters that their lawless acts were necessary to the protection of women.

Participation of Women in Lynchings

Before the day set for the conference statistics were carefully gathered on the two hundred and eleven lynchings during the eight preceding years (1922–1929). When the women convened the facts about these lynchings were laid before them. Though lynchings were not all committed in the South, very little encouragement was found for stating that lynching was not sectional. Out of the two hundred and eleven persons lynched, two hundred and four had met death at the hands of Southern mobs.

Consideration of the crimes of which the victims had been charged brought further enlightenment. Less than 29% of these two hundred and eleven persons were charged with crimes against white women. Then, what, asked the women, had the 79% [should read 71%] done? Offenses of some kind against white men, they were told.

Furthermore in every lynching investigated, some attention had been paid to the mobs as well as to the victims and the crimes. Women were present in some numbers at every lynching and not infrequently they participated.

Some of the women were mothers with young children. These children, members of a future generation of lynchers, were balanced precariously on parents' shoulders in order to have a better view. Young boys and girls were contributing their numbers to the mobs both as spectators and as leaders.

---

* From Document 16: Jessie Daniel Ames, "Southern Women and Lynching," October 1936, Association of Southern Women for the Prevention of Lynching Papers. Reprinted by permission of the Southern Regional Council, Atlanta, GA.

Repudiation of Lynching

Lynchings could no longer be considered objectively. Women everywhere must hear what happened when a mob seized control of local government. Some way must be found to arouse deep and abiding passion against lynching.

After many questions and some debate the conference came to the unanimous decision that the first and most necessary move on the part of white women was to repudiate lynching in unmistakable language as a protection to Southern women. Unless this idea of chivalry could be destroyed, lynchers would continue to use the name of women as an excuse for their crimes and a protection for themselves.

After adopting a resolution embodying their position on lynching, the conference of women voted to promote a movement of Southern white women through existing organizations, the chief purpose of which was to inform the public on the real nature of lynching. . . .

Three Points of Agreement

Three points formed the basis of a long time program of action and education:

First, all the resources of the Council of the Association were to be directed toward the development and promotion of educational programs against lynching, leaving the field of political action to other groups.

Second, emphasis at all times was to be placed on the repudiation of the claim that lynching is necessary to the protection of white women.

Third, The Association of Southern Women for the Prevention of Lynching would be limited in organization to a Central Council and a State Council in each of the thirteen Southern States. Members of these Councils would be key women, officers or chairmen of established organizations of women who would be expected to assist in formulating policies and directing methods of procedure. . . .

Between Outbursts of Mob Violence

The time to prevent lynchings is before a mob forms. Investigations have disclosed that no county in the South is free from the shadow of a possible lynching. Because the county is the important unit of Government, intensive activities are planned to be carried on by women in each county seat *before a mob ever threatens.*

The Association proposes to reach every county in the South by delegating to clubs and societies at the county seat the responsibility for:

1. Interesting every organization of men and women in the county in the campaign against lynching.
2. Securing signatures of officers and members of all organizations, religious, civic, and patriotic, in the town and county.
3. Securing signatures of county officials, preachers, teachers, and laymen.

ELEANOR ROOSEVELT, *Letter to Walter White* (1936)

Eleanor Roosevelt (1884–1962) wrote the following letter to Walter White, head of the National Association for the Advancement of Colored People. Roosevelt's own membership in the organization was just one of the many ways she promoted racial justice. She expanded the ceremonial first lady role from White House hostess to humanitarian activist. Whereas African Americans turned to her for support, many white southerners despised her. With reference to the horrific issue of lynching, discussed in her letter, Franklin Roosevelt remained unwilling to assume a leadership position. What reasons does Roosevelt give for the president's caution? Would President Roosevelt's states rights advocacy do anything to end lynching? In what ways were his suggestions similar to those of Jessie Daniel Ames?*

PERSONAL AND CONFIDENTIAL.
THE WHITE HOUSE
WASHINGTON
March 19, 1936

My dear Mr. White:

Before I received your letter today I had been in to the President, talking to him about your letter enclosing that of the Attorney General. I told him that it seemed rather terrible that one could get nothing done and that I did not blame you in the least for feeling there was no interest in this very serious question. I asked him if there were any possibility of getting even one step taken, and he said the difficulty is that it is unconstitutional apparently for the Federal Government to step in in the lynching situation. The Government has only been allowed to do anything about kidnapping because of its interstate aspect, and even that has not as yet been appealed so they are not sure that it will be declared constitutional.

The President feels that lynching is a question of education in the states, rallying good citizens, and creating public opinion so that the localities themselves will wipe it out. However, if it were done by a Northerner, it will have an antagonistic effect. I will talk to him again about the Van Nuys resolution and will try to talk also to Senator Byrnes and get his point of view. I am deeply troubled about the whole situation as it seems to be a terrible thing to stand by and let it continue and feel that one cannot speak out as to his feeling. I think your next step would be to talk to the more prominent members of the Senate.

Very sincerely yours,
Eleanor Roosevelt

FRANCES PERKINS AND ALICE HAMILTON, *Tri-State Conference on Silicosis, Missouri Testimony* (1940)

Premature aging, illness, and death stalked many industrial workers. Silicosis, a lung disease was a major health peril and led to a federal investigation in 1940. Alice Hamilton (1869–1970) offered evidence supporting workers' claims that inadequate safety precautions led to exposure to silica dust from clay, rock and sand. Frances Perkins (1882–1965), the first women appointed secretary of labor headed the investigation. Perkins and Hamilton (Public Health Service) had years of public service and supported government's role in the regulation of industrial health standards. Both women had resided at Hull House many years earlier. Progressive and New Deal reformers believed government intervention was necessary to protect worker safety and health. Such intervention contradicted the free market belief that workers assumed the risks of the workplace and were responsible for any illnesses they might develop. Until union organizing and government regulation, employers remained indifferent to occupational hazards and despite scientific evidence frequently refused to acknowledge workplace toxicity as a cause of illness. Hamilton played a key role in the development of industrial standards for occupational safety. What role did Perkins play in this investigation? How would you describe Hamilton's findings?**

---

* Eleanor Roosevelt, "Letter to Walter White," March 19, 1936.
** Tri-State Conference—Joplin, Missouri. Frances Perkins, Secretary of Labor, presiding. April 23, 1940, National Archives, Washington, D.C., Record Group 100 (Division of Labor Standards).

TRI-STATE CONFERENCE—JOPLIN, MISSOURI

Frances Perkins, Secretary of Labor, presiding
April 23, 1940

Frances Perkins, THE SECRETARY OF LABOR

First of all I want to say how glad I am that so many of you have shown interest in this problem, which we in the United States Department of Labor believe to be a part of one of the great problems of the United States—the prevention of industrial and occupational diseases. There is nothing unique about your situation, except that you have here at your gates one of the most difficult industrial diseases and one for which it is most difficult to find a cure.

We in the Department of Labor have a mandate which we received from the Congress of the United States in the basic act which creates the Department of Labor and the office of Secretary of Labor, in those words: "It shall be the duty of this Department and of the Secretary to foster, promote, and develop the welfare of the wage earners of the United States of America, to improve their working conditions, and to advance their opportunities for profitable employment." So it becomes the duty of the Department of Labor to inquire into anything that hinders the welfare of the wage earners of the United States, and to be as specific and practical as possible with regard to each situation.

One great problem is the exposure of workers to industrial and occupational diseases. Silicosis is not the only industrial disease; there are many others. Some of them take greater ravages in life and in continuing disability.

Silicosis is newly important to us because we have newly discovered it. Lead poisoning, chrome poisoning, nickel poisoning, these are some of the industrial diseases which everybody 25 and 30 years ago know something about. But it was only about 20 years ago that we in the United States began to realize what silicosis was, and to differentiate it from the old diseases that used to be called "grinder's rot" and "miner's consumption" and "miner's asthma."

The first basic medical literature on the subject came from South Africa. There they had long recognized this disease as one of the hazards of workers in the diamond mines.

In the past 25 years we have become conscious of silicosis, not only in mines and tunnels and open-cut foundations, but also in factories and mills where people work upon substances which generate a silica dust or have a silica basis. So, having become conscious of this disease and its extent, it is our duty in the Department of Labor of the United States to see if we can find ways to prevent it . . .

This morning I spoke with a group of women here in the mining area. They told me in their own simple words that they and their children and their husbands, many of them, had what they regarded as "the lung disease." Some of them spoke with bitterness, and some with question, and some with resignation. There was only one thing I could say for slight comfort to women who have lost their husbands, or whose little children are infected. It was that by cooperating with the doctor and the county health nurse and the State medical society and the State tuberculosis society, perhaps they could make it possible not only for their own children to be cured, but for others whom they did not know, whom they had never seen, who perhaps were yet to be born, to be protected from the ravages of this disease.

So I say to you that although some of you may not like the idea of this Tri-State area being used as a laboratory, can you not think of it perhaps as a great privilege? You may work out here the methods by which thousands of others, millions of others perhaps yet unborn, may be protected from the hazards which I know all of you—employers, taxpayers, labor people—regret as much as we in the Department of Labor do. Perhaps by the use of this area as a laboratory you may contribute more to the welfare of this community, and of the whole United States, than anyone has yet thought.

All of us here today have a social responsibility, a moral responsibility, and perhaps that lesser degree of responsibility which I call legal responsibility. For the latter is not as important as the social and moral responsibility which those who know of a problem have regard to it. The owners and operators of these properties have a great moral responsibility, and many of them have acknowledged it. That is one of the things that gives us courage to come here and ask them to cooperate in making a laboratory of their area, to find a way to prevent not only this but similar situations everywhere.

The people who work in those mines and those who represent the organized labor of the community generally, who take upon themselves the duty of speaking up for those who work in the mines, also have a moral responsibility to cooperate with every technical and economic effort to relieve the situation and to find the means of preventing silicosis and tuberculosis.

So too the community here, in Joplin and in all the towns down the line, have, as you have acknowledged by being here today, a moral and a social responsibility, because the problem is at your door. You didn't make it, but it is there.

The presence in this audience of a number of the ministers of religion reminds us, too, of the duty to bring about that kingdom of heaven on earth to which we all give lip service, to bring about better conditions for all the people of the United States.

Then we have here the representatives of government—of the local government, of county government, of State government, of the Federal Government. To me they are symbols of an order to which all of us in America have subscribed; an order and a pattern of society in which each individual, no matter how poor, still has tremendous worth and

value; and in which the disaster of one is the concern of all.

The officers of Government, be they State or county or Federal, came as the symbols of that great enterprise which we call government in a democracy. It is a government which does not rule, but expresses and gives reality to the desire of the people that everybody in America should have a chance. The men who are crushed by material burdens may still look to their government to find a way for them to contribute their moral worth to the building of our democratic society. . . .

There are a number of experts here who have come from long distances, who are very glad to be consulted while they are here, about all the details of these problems. Dr. [Alice] Hamilton has been for a long time one of the leading experts on the medical aspects of industrial hygiene. Dr. Sayers is here from the Public Health Service. There are engineers here. All of them are available for consultation in the next two days.

Dr. Hamilton, you have been here before, and perhaps you have a word you would like to say?

Dr. Alice Hamilton:

As has been said, I was here about 25 years ago. I am sorry to say that it seemed a very familiar landscape to me as I looked over it going through it today—the heaps of tailings (only they are bigger now), and the housing that I saw reminded me of 25 years ago. Of course, I did pass prosperous little villages that I don't remember from 25 years ago. One does not remember, after all, the worst things one sees more than better things. But the area is singularly unchanged in its outward appearance from when I was here.

At that time we knew very little about the silicosis hazard. And we never contemplated that there might be a danger to the community from the heaps of tailings. As has been said over and over again here, the problem does seem to resolve itself into three sub-problems—the control of the dust in the mining operation; the control of the surface dust; and the provision of better housing.

I noticed that one or two people said that this region is thoroughly "seeded" with tuberculosis. Why should it be? One can understand why an old neglected tenement, a slum area that has been standing in the city for a couple of generations, why those houses should be seeded with tuberculosis, but off here in the country there must be some real reason for it.

If that is true, then your housing problem really does become quite serious. Suppose you have only one case of open tuberculosis in the family; it is inevitably going to spread. I noticed another thing, that in the talk about the control of tuberculosis the stress was laid on the treatment and care of the incipient case. Of course that is very important. To leave a hopeless case in the bosom of his family because there is no use trying to do anything for him, is to neglect what is needed for the family. He must be removed in order to save the others in the family, especially the children, from that fate.

I should have supposed that wet drilling would solve this silicosis problem, and having all your mulch heaps wet would solve your dust problem. But if you have been doing that for 20 years and the cases of silicosis and tuberculosis haven't been prevented, even if they take 12 years to develop—why it is obvious that wet drilling isn't enough. So that there you have a problem that is still to be solved.

Then you have the main problem, which is only beginning to be worked on, of the surface dust. I understand that is being studied and that, although those of us who study it are not willing to make any statement yet, we shall really know whether that constitutes a danger to the families living in the region.

CHAPTER 16

World War II and Postwar Trends: Disruption, Conformity, and Counter Currents

During World War II, the number of women workers grew from 12 million to 16.5 million. The war enabled women to participate in male-designated fields such as munitions manufacture, shipbuilding, and the automobile and airplane industries. Women worked within steel mills and in coke plants and tended blast furnaces. The demand for labor made possible African American women's entry into positions previously denied them on the basis of race and gender. Even though women performed formerly forbidden work, gender-linked job classifications and lower pay perpetuated the customary bias against women's work. Women's assumption of nontraditional work was a response to wartime needs. At no time did the government, corporations, or unions intend to restructure gender roles or permanently alter workplace patterns. For those women who were mothers responsible for the care of young children, neither the U.S. government nor private industry made adequate provision for day care.

Approximately two hundred thousand women joined military auxiliaries. Of this group, around one thousand women pilots joined the air force. As members of the Women Airforce Service Pilots (WASPs), Ann Baumgartner Carl and other female pilots flew on noncombat military missions transporting and testing aircraft, including a bomber men feared to fly for safety reasons. Thirty-eight women died as a result of friendly fire or accidents while testing and transporting planes to military bases. None received a military funeral. The air force refused to acknowledge female pilots' service as anything other than civilian support and subordinate to that of male pilots. Until 1977, when Congress reclassified their service from civilian to military, the women pilots were denied all veterans' benefits and were never included in the G. I. Bill of Rights.

Identified as potential subversives, Japanese Americans were herded into internment camps during the war. They were denied civil liberties, and relocation entailed the loss of property and homes. Years later, Jeanne Wakatsuki Houston recalled the disruption of her childhood. She also noted that within the Manzanar prison camp, her parents' control weakened as she moved away from her Japanese cultural roots to a Christian and more Americanized identity.

At war's end, many women workers expressed their desire to remain in the postwar labor force. However, they confronted the determination of both the government and the private sector to return women, particularly married women, to full-time domestic roles. In fact, a complete reversal of propaganda occurred with regard to women workers. During the war, women were told it was selfish and unpatriotic to stay at home. After the war, the argument was reversed; even women who preferred to remain employed were told that their patriotic duty, unless they faced extreme economic hardship, was to leave the workforce. Emphasizing the duty of women to return to their domestic roles, Eleanor Roosevelt outlined the national message in 1944.

With the veterans' return, marriages proliferated and the birth rate soared. Subsequently labeled a baby boom, veterans and their families fueled the massive postwar suburban expansion. By the 1950s, the suburban lifestyle was the cultural norm. Women's magazines, educators, and psychologists popularized beliefs that female fulfillment depended on marriage, home, and family care. As Marynia Farnham and Ferdinand Lundberg defined women's discontent, the dissatisfied wife was both "unfeminine" and "unnatural," and in need of psychological help. Equally critical was the attack launched against the nation's mothers that first appeared in the early 1940s. Known as "momism," the role of mothers during World War II as well as in the postwar period came under intense scrutiny. Initiated by Philip Wylie, in his best selling book *Generation of Vipers* and popularized in magazines articles such as Amram Scheinfeld's 1946 "Are American Moms a Menace?" the nation's mothers appeared as manipulative, overly controlling, and responsible for emasculating their husbands and turning their sons into homosexuals.

Intensive mothering, now referred to as "smothering," presented a complete distortion of the earlier construction of the mother as moral guardian of the home. In the new construction, neurotic demon-like mothers paved the way for their son's homosexuality and support of Communism. In an era of extreme anxiety about Communist infiltration, as well as increasing numbers of married women working outside the home, the mother as enemy provided a convenient scapegoat. Between the 1940s and early 1960s, the "blame the mother" theme for family dysfunction and the nation's problems provided the focus of numerous magazine articles, books, and Hollywood films, including *Rebel Without a Cause* and the *Manchurian Candidate*.

Increasing tensions of the cold war and the pervasive belief that Communism menaced domestic security intensified support for traditional family values. In a postwar world of international tension and Senator Joseph McCarthy's hunt for Communists in the military and Hollywood film industry, anxieties about national security proliferated. An idealized version of the suburban home and family became the counterbalance. This sanitized depiction representing stability and the home as refuge from cold war tensions coexisted and contradicted the image of the manipulative "smother" mothers. Coexisting with "mom as menace" was the timeworn rhetoric about a mother's mission to her husband, sons, and nation. Adlai Stevenson, presidential hopeful and former governor of Illinois, addressed the 1955 Smith College graduating class. Stevenson outlined their future role as wives. He emphasized that they would use their education to promote their husbands' sense of purpose and provide the central influence in the "unfolding drama of our free society."

The postwar societal pressure to conform and the popularity of labeling alternative lifestyles as deviant further marginalized gays and lesbians from mainstream society. Despite oppression, a lesbian subculture continued to grow. The first organized lesbian rights organization, the Daughters of Bilitis, founded in San Francisco in

1955, expressed this crosscurrent of resistance to conformity. However, political and social hostility remained strong. Loretta Collier describes the harassment lesbians in the military encountered during the Korean War.

By the mid-1950s, undercurrents of deep dissatisfaction whirling beneath the images of domestic and political conformity came to the surface. Civil rights activism, in which African American women played a central role, shattered white complacency about the racist status quo. Jo Ann Gibson Robinson recounts how Rosa Parks's refusal to give her seat to a white passenger launched the Montgomery, Alabama, bus boycott and was the first of a series of mass-based civil rights demonstrations. Ann Moody describes her role in the effort to end segregated lunch counters. African American women's leadership role and participation in civil rights protests facilitated the development of the subsequent feminist movement.

As cold war tensions escalated, women organized peace demonstrations and protested nuclear proliferation and atomic testing. Women's Strike for Peace (WSP) advocates crusaded for an end to U.S. aboveground testing of nuclear bombs, as well as an international commitment to end nuclear proliferation. Rachel Carson, the mother of the modern environmental movement, exposed the lethal effects of pesticides on the environment, as well as their link to human health. Her book *Silent Spring* challenged the multi-billion-dollar chemical industry (see Chapter 17). In a flight from conventional roles, some young women joined the beatnik subculture only to find that sexism within the counterculture was pervasive. The 1963 publication of Betty Friedan's *The Feminine Mystique* added to the undermining of the increasingly fragile postwar restoration of domestic ideals. Her evidence demonstrated that for many white middle-class wives and mothers, all-enveloping domesticity produced more discontent than fulfillment. Equally compelling was Friedan's indictment of the "experts" who blamed women for social and political problems and created the image of failed "moms" who damaged their sons and weakened the nation.

ANN BAUMGARTNER CARL, Excerpt from *A Wasp Among Eagles: A Woman Military Test Pilot in World War 2* (1999)

A graduate of the Smith College class of 1940, Ann Baumgartner (1918–2008) joined the Women Airforce Service Pilots (WASPs) in 1943. In 1999, she published her recollections of her love of flying and her military service as a test pilot. The first woman to fly an army air force jet plane, she was stationed in Camp David, North Carolina. Carl and other WASPs tested airplanes and towed targets for male pilots to practice target shooting. The following excerpt recounts her experience as a pilot before she joined the WASPs. She also recalls the gender inequity and lack of validation that female air force pilots routinely encountered. How does Carl describe the qualifications for joining the WASPs? What examples does she provide of gender-based discrimination in the air force?*

In the United States "Rosie the Riveter" had become the national heroine. Women were replacing men in every facet of industry and performing excellently. Eleanor Roosevelt saw that this work could be a success only if there were planned daycare facilities for children. Henry Kaiser was first to provide this at his Swan Island Center in Oregon. Women were

---

* Smithsonian Institution, Folkways.

also enlisting in the WAVES (Women Accepted for Voluntary Emergency Service in the Navy) and WAAC (Women's Army Auxiliary Corps).

My mother and other housewives contributed by working at the Red Cross as contacts between soldiers and their families or simply as clerks (they all wore blue uniforms), or they grew and froze vegetables and meat, or saved grease or aluminum or rubber. My father was appointed by Civil Defense as an airplane spotter. Every night he served on the midnight to four watch, "spotting" and reporting any aircraft in the vicinity, and I went with him.

Our spotting post was in a tower of a large country house. After parking the car behind the big stone building, we entered a designated door. After passing through silent halls with closed doors, we climbed four stories to the dark tower. We relieved the former watch, signed in, and settled down to watch and listen. Our only light was a flashlight, when necessary. We had a telephone, a pad and pencil, and a pair of binoculars. Every once in a while, we heard the drone of a plane and reported its direction, probable altitude and speed, and guessed its type. It could be an enemy plane.

Otherwise, we spent the long cold hours looking out at the stars. My amateur-astronomer father introduced me to various constellations, to special stars like Sirius, brightest in the heavens, and to the North star, which over the ages has been different stars. Being a friend of Dr. Edwin Hubble, he knew the latest theories of the early universe and what its end might be. All this made celestial navigation, learned much later for the ocean-sailing my husband and I were to do, much more meaningful, and it was an introduction to the mysteries of space.

My particular project, now that I had my private pilot's license, was to build up the 200 hours of flying time required for a commercial license, the ticket to a job in aviation. I still had my eye on an assignment to an air ambulance. I bought half an airplane with another aspiring private pilot, Jasper Wright,

and we alternated in the use of our tired old Piper Cub (underpowered, no brakes, tears in the fabric) and flew, flew, flew.

It was certainly not an unpleasant task to have to go out and fly with a purpose in view, and even in one's own plane, though the plane was somewhat of a wreck. That added to the challenge. The last figures in its official number on the wing ended in "48," and it was known around the airport as "good old 48." Its engine popped and banged on the glide to land just like a P-51 fighter.

Some days I would simply go up and sightsee, enjoy the farmland below, and reach up to the scattered clouds above. Other times, I practiced flying maneuvers like lazy eights, wingovers, spins. I visited airports in the area. I flew in good weather and bad.

I did more serious flying for the national Civil Air Patrol. We not only practiced rescue missions and patrols but, as the war progressed, actually performed them. I introduced Boy Scouts and Girl Scouts to the joy of flying. I took my brother and my mother for rides, but my father never flew with me. He thought I would be nervous.

As I closed in on the magic number 200 in the summer of 1942, all private flying on the Eastern seaboard was prohibited because submarines had been seen offshore. Airplanes had to be dismantled, wings off, so they could not be flown at all.

Then I saw a news story explaining how the Air Force planned to use experienced women pilots for domestic military flying in order to release men for active duty overseas. Eleanor Roosevelt, in her "My Day" newspaper column on September 1, 1942, said that "women pilots are a weapon waiting to be used."

Back in July 1941, Jacqueline Cochran, already famous for her speed records and Harmon trophies, and, in fact, the leading woman pilot of the nation, had presented to Secretary of War for Air Robert Lovett (at the suggestion of President Roosevelt) a plan for using woman pilots to ferry new trainer-type aircraft to air bases, thus freeing men for more active roles. Lovett passed it on to Gen. H. H. "Hap" Arnold, Chief of the Air Force.

"How many experienced women pilots are there?" General Arnold asked.

Cochran and her staff laboriously checked through Civil Aeronautical Administration files and found that of 2,733 licensed women, 150 had over 200 hours flying time and between 72 and 100 had 300 hours and over. She sent questionnaires to these pilots asking whether they would be interested in serving with the Air Corps (the Air Corps became the Air Force after Pearl Harbor). "Yes," 130 answered enthusiastically. On July 30, Cochran presented a finished proposal to Col. Robert Olds, head of the Ferry Command of the Air Transport Command, for an "Organization of a Women Pilots' Division of the Army Air Corps Ferry Command." After all, she pointed out, women were successfully ferrying aircraft for the Royal Air Force in Britain, and in Russia women pilots were even flying combat missions (albeit with high losses) in tiny, old biplanes. . . .

The consolidation was called Women's Airforce Service Pilots, or WASPs, and all would wear the blue uniforms designed by Cochran.

Still, Cochran's hope for militarization of her pilots—and the rights that went with it—was not realized, nor would it be until the 1970s, long after the war. Eleanor Roosevelt, worrying

Recruitment Poster Celebrates Women's Wartime Work (U.S. Bureau of Engraving and Printing)

that men serving their country in World War II had lost years in which they could prepare for careers and families, had urged the president to pass the G.I. Bill of Rights. The bill provided that the government would underwrite education and training for returning veterans. The WASPs, as Civil Service, would not be eligible.

ELEANOR ROOSEVELT, *Women's Place After the War* (Aug. 1944)

Not surprisingly, Eleanor Roosevelt promoted the restoration of domestic norms after the war. Roosevelt and her New Deal female colleagues had previously sponsored maternal policies and disagreed with the equal rights agenda of the National Woman's Party. The war's extraordinary demands for female labor represented a response to a national emergency, not a restructuring of gender roles. With the conclusion of the war, a pivotal national priority was the return of mothers to full-time child care. Roosevelt's position on women's right to work and equitable pay changed over time. What exceptions did Roosevelt make that limited the full-time mothering role model? How did she deal with the issue of equitable pay for women? How does the link between working mothers and child care remain problematic in the contemporary era?*

---

* Originally published in *Click* 7 (August 1944): 17, 19.

1. "Will women want to keep their jobs after the war is over?" When I asked Miss Mary Anderson of the Bureau of Women in Industry, she told me it all boils down to economic necessity. Married women usually keep their jobs only when they have real need for money at home. This, of course, does not mean that women who take up some kind of work as a career will not stay in that work if they like it, whether they are married or single.

2. Let us analyze this whole question of women who work. Our attitude in this country has always been that any individual is more worthwhile if he pays his way in the world. We even have a little contempt for a woman who is nothing but an ornament.

3. Of late years since we have counted success so largely in the amount of money that people earned, it has become more and more natural for women to feel that if they actually were working to their full capacity, they must have recognition in the same coin as the male members of their families, or they would not be considered successful. An ever-growing number of young women in every walk of life are taking jobs as they finish school or college, but *the main job of the average woman in our country still is to marry and have a home and children.*

4. I surmise that the major occupation of a married woman in this country at the close of the war will be what it has always been—the care of the family as long as the family requires her care. There will always be exceptions, of course, as when a woman must take on the burden of work outside the home to supplement what the man earns, or, if the man cannot work, even must assume the place of the head of the family and earn a living for the household.

5. Many women, because of the urge to help their country and their own men during the war, will have acquired skills—skills which they will be able to use in the future. But I do not think they will use them if they have families and homes calling them back to a different kind of existence.

6. Recently, I saw women who drove long distances and worked long hours in a shipyard in New England. Most of them had made temporary arrangements for the care of their homes and children, and were working with their husbands if their husbands had not gone to war, so as to pay the mortgage on the farm, buy certain things long coveted which would make life easier in the future, or lay aside some money which would give the children some special advantages. They knew the work was temporary and feared they would never have the opportunity to achieve certain desires if they did not take advantage of the present need for workers.

Women's Work Prospects Depend Upon Job Availability

7. The first question that will be faced in the postwar period is simply to what extent jobs are available. *The first obligation of government and business is to see that every man who is employable has a job, and that every woman who needs work has it.* A woman does not need a job if she has a home and a family requiring her care and a member of the household is earning an adequate amount of money to maintain a decent standard of living. If, however, there is a margin of energy left in men or women and they want to put it into bettering their standard of living, it seems to me that they should have the opportunity. We should struggle to gear our economy to a place where we can give all people who desire to work,

whether full-time or part- time, a chance to work on something which gives them creative satisfaction.

8. From my point of view, there is no justification whatsoever for labor leaders to oppose the employment of women at the present time wherever they are needed. Foresight is valuable, but foresight that dreads to meet a present situation because there may be some difficulty in the future shows a lack of confidence in the intelligence and ability of human beings to cope with new situations.

9. There is one point, however, upon which I think labor leaders have a right to insist: *women should not come into any labor group and allow themselves to be used at present or in the future as a body for keeping down the wages of men, either because they can live on less or because they, being unorganized, have never understood the need to stand together with any group in order to help the group.*

10. A girl living at home and having few expenses may be able to accept, let us say, $10 a week for her work, using that money only for her own personal needs. Her employer will say to a man, "We can use girls in this job, therefore we do not need you; but if you want the job, you can have it at $10 a week." If the man can find no other job, he may be forced to take the one for $10 a week, which means that his family will live at a very low standard. And this will be the fault of the girl who did not understand that she was part of a big labor group and that she had to consider the good of the whole body.

11. So, I think labor leaders have a right to insist that women, as long as they are in the labor market, should be part of the organized labor movement and should not permit themselves to be used as competition for men to the advantage of unscrupulous employers.

Children of Working Mothers Must Have Adequate Care

12. A certain number of women, both in the professions and in skilled and unskilled trades, may not marry. But if they do, they must either subordinate their desires for work outside the home, or make arrangements which will be adequate for proper care of the home and children.

13. Rarely can anyone replace a mother, but there are some women who are not gifted with children and resent having to do the work of the home. In that case, it may sometimes be better to find someone who loves to do that job, and release the mother for a different kind of work. She will probably be a better mother and a better companion for her husband when she is home if she does work she enjoys. However, such cases are rare.

14. As I said in the beginning, whether women remain in the labor market or not will be, as it always has been, mainly a question of economic necessity.

POSTWAR PLANS OF WOMEN WORKERS (1946)

Government surveys provide explicit evidence that the majority of women employees wanted to continue working after the war. The following survey revealed that 75 percent of female workers planned to keep their wartime positions. Among this group, 84 percent alleged that they had no other means of support. Yet government and the private sector ignored the expressed needs of women, and many lost their jobs. What reasons did women give for wanting to keep their work? How does the post–World War II situation relate to the experience confronted by the women streetcar conductors after World War I? (see Chapter 14)*

That very large numbers of wartime women workers intend to work after the war is evidenced by their statements to interviewers. On the average, about 75 percent of the wartime-employed women in the 10 areas expected to be part of the postwar labor force. . . .

These prospective postwar women workers did not, for the most part, contemplate out-migration from their areas of wartime employment. Over 90 percent of them, in most areas, looked forward to continued employment after the war in the same areas where they had worked during the war period. . . .

In each area, the number of wartime-employed women who intended to work in the same area after the war, greatly exceeded the number of women employed in the area in 1940. In the Detroit area, for example, for every 100 women who were working in 1940, excluding household employees, 155 women will want postwar jobs. About two and one-half times as many women wanted to continue working in the Mobile area as were employed in 1940. . . .

The highest percentage of prospective postwar workers in most areas came from the group of women who had been employed before Pearl Harbor, rather than from those who had been in school or engaged in their own housework at that time. On average, over four-fifths of the women who had been employed both before Pearl Harbor and in the war period, intended to keep on working after the war. Among the war-employed women who had not been in the labor force the week before Pearl Harbor, over three-fourths of the former students expected to continue working, while over half of those

formerly engaged in their own housework had such plans. . . .

Very large proportions of the migrant women workers planned to continue work in the areas where they had been employed during the war. Although in comparison to resident women employed in the war period smaller proportions of the in-migrants planned to remain in the labor force, the bulk of the in-migrants who did expect to work wanted to do so in the same area where they had been employed during the war. Consequently, in the areas where in-migrants were important during the war, they also constituted a substantial proportion of the women who intended to work in the area after the war. In four of the seven areas where in-migrants were important, in-migrants constituted between 32 and 44 percent of the total group of women who planned to continue work; and in the other three areas where in-migrants were important, they represented between 10 and 26 percent of the women who planned to continue.

The nature of postwar employment problems is influenced not only by the number of wartime workers who expect to remain in the labor force, but also by their expressed desire for work in particular industries and occupations. Postwar job openings as cafeteria bus girls, for example, are not apt to prove attractive to women who are seeking work as screw-machine operators.

The bulk of the prospective postwar workers interviewed in this survey, or 86 percent, wanted their postwar jobs in the same industrial group as their wartime employment, and about the same proportion wanted to remain in the same occupational group. Postwar shifts to other industries were

---

* From *Women Workers in Ten War Production Areas and Their Postwar Employment Plans* (Washington, D.C.: U.S. Government Printing Office, 1946) (Women's Bureau, Bulletin 209).

contemplated on a somewhat larger scale, however, among the wartime employees in restaurants, cafeterias, and similar establishments, as well in the personal service industries in certain areas. In the Dayton area, for example, among the war-employed women who expected to remain in the labor force, fully 36 percent of those in eating and drinking places, and 30 percent of those in personal service industries said they wanted jobs in other industries after the war. . . .

In the Mobile area almost a third of the women employed in the war period were Negro. Four areas, between 10 and 19 percent inclusive, were non-white (including some non-white in San Francisco). In the remaining five areas less than 10 percent of the war-employed women were Negro or of other non-white races.

In each of the nine areas where there were enough non-white employed women to make comparison valid, a much higher proportion of the Negro women planned to continue work than of the white women. In six areas 94 percent or more of the Negro or other non-white women who were employed in the war period, planned to continue after the war. . . .

Responsibility for the support of themselves, or themselves and others, was the outstanding reason given by war-employed women for planning to continue work after the war. As already pointed out, about three-fourths of the wartime-employed women in the ten areas (excluding household employees) planned to keep on working after the war. Fully 84 percent of them had no other alternative, as this was the proportion among them who based their decision on their need to support themselves and often, other

persons as well. Eight percent offered special reasons for continuing at work, such as buying a home or sending children to school; and only eight percent reported they would remain in the labor force because they liked working, or liked having their own money.

Virtually all of the single women and those who were widowed or divorced (96 and 98 percent, respectively) who intended to remain in gainful employment after the war stated they would do so in order to support themselves, or themselves and others, whereas 57 percent of the married wartime workers who expected to remain at work gave this reason. The remaining married prospective postwar workers interviewed offered reasons of the special purpose type, such as buying a home, about as often as those of the "like-to-work" type. Because married women differed so much on this issue from women in other marital status groups, differences from area to area in the proportions of prospective postwar workers, who offered each of the three sets of reasons, reflect largely the relative concentration of married women in each area. . . .

That the need to work is just as pressing among some married women as among some single women was highlighted by the replies from the war-employed women on the number of wage earners in the family group. Out of every 100 married women who were living in family groups of two or more persons, 11 said they were the only wage earner supporting the family group. This was almost identical to the proportion of sole supporting wage earners among single women living with their families. The state of marriage, therefore, does not, in itself, always mean there is a male provider for the family.

JEANNE WAKATSUKI HOUSTON, *Farewell to Manzanar* (1973)

After the Japanese attack on Pearl Harbor, the U.S. government suspended civil liberties and ordered the internment of all Japanese, both foreign born and American born. The following autobiographical excerpt presents the recollections of a woman who lived through the traumatic disruption as a young child. Barbed wire and armed troops surrounded internment camps. The childhood memories recaptured in this excerpt refer not to the hostile physical environment but rather to the camp's effort to Americanize the children. What cultural collision course does Houston recall? How was the effort at her religious conversion resolved?*

Once we settled into Block 28 that ache I'd felt since soon after we arrived at Manzanar subsided. It didn't entirely disappear, but it gradually submerged, as semblances of order returned and our pattern of life assumed its new design.

For one thing, [my older brother] Kiyo and I and all the other children finally had *a school*. During the first year, teachers had been volunteers; equipment had been makeshift; classes were scattered all over camp, in mess halls, recreation rooms, wherever we could be squeezed in. Now a teaching staff had been hired. Two blocks were turned into Manzanar High, and a third block of fifteen barracks was set up to house the elementary grades. We had blackboards, new desks, reference books, lab supplies. . . .

In addition to the regular school sessions and the recreation program, classes of every kind were being offered all over camp: singing, acting, trumpet playing, tap-dancing, plus traditional Japanese arts like needlework, judo, and kendo. The first class I attended was in baton twirling, taught by a chubby girl about fourteen named Nancy. In the beginning I used a sawed-off broomstick with an old tennis ball stuck on one end. When it looked like I was going to keep at this, Mama ordered me one like Nancy's from the Sears, Roebuck catalogue. Nancy was a very good twirler and taught us younger kids all her tricks. For months I practiced, joined the baton club at school, and even entered contests. Since then I have often wondered what drew me to it at that age. I wonder, because of all the activities I tried out in camp, this was the one I stayed with, in fact returned to almost obsessively when I entered

high school in southern California a few years later. By that time I was desperate to be "accepted," and baton twirling was one trick I could perform that was thoroughly, unmistakably American—putting on the boots and a dress crisscrossed with braid, spinning the silver stick and tossing it high to the tune of a John Philip Sousa march.

Even at ten, before I really knew what waited outside, the Japanese in me could not compete with that. It tried—in camp, and many times later, in one form or another. My visit to the old geisha who lived across the firebreak was a typical example of how those attempts turned out. She was offering lessons in the traditional dancing called *odori*. A lot of young girls studied this in order to take part in the big *obon* festival held every August, a festival honoring dead ancestors, asking them to bring good crops in the fall. . . .

Among my explorations during these months, there was one more, final venture into Catholicism. The Maryknoll chapel was just up the street now and easy to get to. I resumed my catechism. Once again I was listening with rapt terror to the lives of the saints and the martyrs, although that wasn't really what attracted me this time. I had found another kind of inspiration, had seen another way the church might make me into something quite extraordinary.

I had watched a girl my own age shining at the center of one of their elaborate ceremonies. It appealed to me tremendously. She happened to be an orphan, and I figured that if this much could befall an orphan, imagine how impressive *I* would look in such a role. . . .

This girl had already been baptized. What I witnessed was her confirmation. She was dressed like a bride, in a white gown, white

* From *Farewell to Manzanar* by Jeanne W. Houston and James D. Houston. Copyright ©1973 by James D. Houston, renewed 2001 by Jeanne Wakatsuki Houston and James d. Houston. Reprinted by permission of Houghton Mifflin Harcourt Publishing Company. All rights reserved.

lace hood, and sheer veil, walking toward the altar, down the aisle of that converted barracks. Watching her from the pew I was pierced with envy for the position she had gained. At the same time I was filled with awe and with a startled wonder at the notion that this girl, this orphan, could become such a queen.

A few days later I let it be known that I was going to be baptized into the church and confirmed as soon as the nuns thought I was ready. I announced this to the Sisters and they rejoiced. I announced it at home, and Papa exploded.

"No," he roared. "Absolutely not!"

I just stood there, stunned, too scared to speak.

"You're too young!"

I started to cry.

"How are you going to get married?" he shouted. "If you get baptized a Catholic, you have to marry a Catholic. No Japanese boys are in the Catholic church. You get baptized now, how are you going to find a good Japanese boy to marry?"

I ran to Mama, but she knew better than to argue with him about this. I ran to the chapel and told Sister Bernadette, and she came hurrying to the barracks. She and Papa had become pretty good friends over the months. Once every week or so she would visit, and while he sipped his apricot brandy they would talk about religion. But this time, when she came to the door and called "*Wakatsuki-san?*" he met her there shouting, "No! No baptism!"

She raised her eyebrows, trying to stare him down.

He rose to his full height, as if she, about the size of Mama, were the general of some invading army, and said, "Too young!"

AMRAM SCHEINFELD, *"Are American Moms a Menace?"*
Ladies Home Journal (Nov. 1946)

During World War II, a new and discomforting image of mothers began to capture public attention. This highly negative view contradicted the war effort's portrayal of brave mothers who with unquestioned patriotic fervor made wartime sacrifices. It also contradicted the depiction of heroic women workers, shown in the images of Rosie the Riveter. Part of the alarm was growing concern with perceived homosexuality among American men that had resulted in their not being drafted. Moms were blamed for creating weak sons who were rejected for psychological reasons, as well as for causing the underlying reasons for veterans' later psychological trauma.

Four years after author Philip Wylie created the term *momism* to define neurotic mothers who emasculated their sons, Dr. Edward A. Strecker, a respected psychiatrist and university professor, added credibility to the issue, since Philip Wylie had no official psychological credentials. In the following article from the popular *Ladies' Home Journal,* journalist, Amram Scheinfeld (1897–1979) synthesized Strecker's views and offered advice to mothers on how to avoid their potential for lethal behavior. Why are "smother" mothers described as a national "peril"?*

"Mom" is sweet, doting and self-sacrificing. But she is not mothering her son—she is smothering him.

American mothers are so used to getting bouquets that it may come as a shock to hear that "mom" is often a dangerous influence on her sons and a threat to our national existence. "MOM DENOUNCED AS PERIL TO NATION" was the way the *New York Times* headlined it.

In brief, Prof. Edward A. Strecker, University of Pennsylvania psychiatrist and consultant to the Army and Navy surgeons

---

* Amram Scheinfeld, "Are American Moms a Menace?" *Ladies' Home Journal,* November 1945, 36.

general, has made this accusation: that the blame for many psychoneurotics in the armed forces, and for many neurotic rejectees, rests on their "moms," who either by overattention or stern domination during the formative years kept their sons from maturing emotionally. "Mother's boys" psychoneurotics are not to be confused with men who cracked up only under terrific battle pressures or after serious injuries, he adds. Nor are all American mothers to blame, for the majority of them are sensible, well-balanced and understanding.

Doctor Strecker is indicting the type of mother generally known as "mom." Usually she is sweet, doting and self-sacrificing, or she may be just the opposite—stern, capable and domineering. "Both these moms are busily engaged finding in their children ego satisfactions for life's thwartings and frustrations," believes Doctor Strecker. "The community applauds and fondly smiles on them. They are accorded praise and adulation for giving their lives to their children. Hidden from view is the hard and tragic fact that . . . they exact in payment the emotional lives of their children."

You may recall Sidney Howard's famous play, *The Silver Cord,* in which a domineering mother refuses to accept the fact that the umbilical cord was severed at her son's birth. Remember the lines, hurled by her daughter-in-law, *"You son-devouring tigress! You and your kind beat any cannibals I've ever heard of . . . . And what makes you doubly dangerous is that people admire you—you professional mother!"*

If most American mothers were this domineering, says Doctor Strecker, so many young men would have been ruined for military service that instead of being victorious in the war "we might now be facing the prospect of defeat."

All of this involves a pretty serious charge, and must make every mother wonder about her influence on her sons. However, it is not fair to place sole responsibility for the development of a boy's character on his mother. A lot depends on the boy himself, the presence of other children (a brother or two can help a lot!) and, above all, the character and role of the father. In the majority of American homes there is a balanced situation, with a sensible mother in her proper place. But danger looms when the father's influence is weakened or missing, and the mother becomes a "mom," either of the overbearing type, who squashes her son, or the indulgent kind, who pampers and spoils him with saccharine over-attention. . . .

The "mother's boy" reveals himself by these traits: He is apt to be hypersensitive, worrisome, fussy, vain and somewhat of an exhibitionist. He basks in attention and sulks if he doesn't get it. Although he strongly desires affection and is very eager to make friends, he may not hold on to them. Being sensitive and intuitive to a high degree, he may be very understanding, sympathetic and anxious to help others, which often leads him into public life, charitable work or social service. On the other hand, if he is ambitious and calculating, the same faculty of sensing people enables him to exploit them to his personal advantage.

The victim of maternal overprotection may be impelled toward great heights of achievement or toward depths of failure, depending upon the mother's character and the boy's inherent capabilities. History is full of notable "mother's boys." We could start with our late President Franklin D. Roosevelt, whose lifelong attachment to his mother and her profound influence on him are well known. He was an only son, whose father died when he was eighteen, and up until her death a few years before his, his mother was one of his closest confidants. Another great president, Abraham Lincoln, said, "All that I am or hope to be, I owe to my angel mother." President Harry Truman also appears to have been greatly influenced by his mother. She was an active campaigner for her son when he first ran for the Senate, and at ninety-two is still much in the foreground. "The resemblance between mother and son is deeper than a physical likeness," wrote one reporter recently. . . .

It is worth nothing that although some mom-coddled boys achieve great success, many are nonetheless socially maladjusted and personally unhappy. . . .

In their relationships with women, many mother's boys continue the trend toward extremes. If successful in amours, they may become Don Juans and Lotharios, going from one romance to another in search of emotional satisfaction which the ever-present mother fixation keeps them from attaining. To quote Dr. Otto Fenichel, "The Don Juan seeks his mother in all women and cannot find her." However, if the mother's boy is not appealing to women or fears he won't be, or has an "incest" feeling regarding opposite-sex relations because of identification with his mother, he may shun women altogether and frequently turns to homosexuality.

Reporting on the background of many male homosexuals, Professors Lewis M. Terman and Catharine C. Miles say in their study, *Sex and Personality,* "The psychosocial formula for developing homosexuality in boys would seem to run somewhat as follows: too demonstrative affection from an excessively emotional mother, especially in the case of a first, last or only child; a father who is unsympathetic, autocratic, brutal, much away from home, or deceased; treatment of the child as a girl, coupled with lack of encouragement or opportunity to associate with boys and to take part in the rougher masculine activities; overemphasis of neatness, niceness and spirituality; lack of vigilance against the danger of seduction by older homosexual males."

The formula need not always work, of course, for even from the environment described many boys grow up to make normal sexual adjustments. But in any event, the mother's boy may remain a bachelor for a long time or permanently. An Army psychologist told me, "We're afraid that a lot of unmarried G.I. Joe's who put their moms on pedestals may have developed mother fixations while overseas, and, now that they are coming back, they may have difficulty in finding wives who will measure up to their overidealized notions of womanhood."

In recent years, many factors have contributed to the overbalance of maternal influence in the American home. Where fathers have been away in service for prolonged periods, little boys are started off with a one-sided mother attachment, and if the father fails to return, the mother may seek to make up for the loss through her sons' affections. Apart from this, the trend toward more mother's boys has gained impetus from the decrease in family size, resulting in more only sons. Moreover, various changes in American life are tending to keep more fathers away from their homes and to leave young sons largely to the mothers, with nurses, domestics and women schoolteachers adding to the feminine atmosphere. Another factor has been the ever-higher survival rate of wives compared with husbands. This has led to an increasing number of widows, and hence to more control by mothers over the family purse strings and business interests, increasing their sons' dependence on them economically as well as emotionally. . . .

If we have indeed gone too far in the direction of maternal conditioning, we must see that the psychological diet of our boys is supplemented by more "masculine vitamins." American fathers must be impressed with the need of greater participation in the rearing of their sons. Every mother can agitate for more male teachers in our elementary and high schools, and she can encourage manly activity for her boy through the Boy Scouts, other boys' groups and young men's organizations. Compulsory military service at the age of eighteen would also help, some authorities feel.

Strangely enough, it is in the more privileged and enlightened groups that the situation needs most attention, for it is among these that only sons are most common, that psychological tension is apt to be greatest, that fathers are the most neglectful and mothers most inclined to be domineering.

Prof. Arthur T. Jersild, child psychologist of Columbia University, told me, "Where the more ordinary women take the rearing of their sons in stride, many so-called 'sophisticated' mothers are so eager to do a thorough job of mothering that they wear themselves and their boys to frazzles." Or, as a highly neurotic man patient told one of my psychoanalyst friends, "My trouble is my mother didn't mother me—she *smothered me.*"

MARYNIA FARNHAM AND FERDINAND LUNDBERG, *Modern Women: The Lost Sex* (1947)

Despite the restoration of domestic norms after the end of World War II, growing numbers of women entered the workforce between 1947 and 1960. Statistics cite the upward trend in the number of working mothers with young children: 11.9 percent in 1950 and 16.2 percent in 1955. To counteract this emerging trend, pro-family advocates promoted women's domestic identity.*

The following excerpt from the popular *Modern Women: The Lost Sex* captures the postwar doomsday pronouncements about career-oriented women and working mothers. The book exemplifies the conservative effort to return women to a total and selfless immersion in home and family life. What strategies do the writers employ to make working mothers feel unnatural? Why do they refer to women as the "lost sex"? On what do they base their claim that women employed outside their homes will experience sexual malfunctions in their marriages? Does this document in any way offer parallels with Edward Clarke's (see Chapter 9) and Grover Cleveland's (see Chapter 10) advice to women not to go to college and not to join clubs?**

The woman arriving at maturity today does so with certain fixed attitudes derived from her background and training. Her home life, very often, has been distorted. She has enjoyed an education identical with that of her brother. She expects to be allowed to select any kind of work for which she has inclination and training. She also, generally, expects to marry. At any rate, she usually intends to have "a go" at it. Some women expect to stop working when they marry; many others do not. She expects to find sexual gratification and believes in her inalienable right so to do. She is legally free to live and move as she chooses. She may seek divorce if her marriage fails to gratify her. She has access to contraceptive information so that, theoretically, she may control the size and spacing of her family. In very many instances, she owns and disposes of her own property. She has, it appears, her destiny entirely in her own hands.

All of this serves less to clarify and simplify her life than to complicate it with conflict piled on conflict. These conflicts are between her basic needs as a woman and the destiny she has carved out for herself—conflicts between the head and the heart, if you will. . . .

Thus she finds herself squarely in the middle of the most serious kind of divided purpose. If she is to undertake occupation outside her home with any kind of success, it is almost certain in the present day to be time-consuming and energy-demanding. So it is also with the problems she faces in her home. Certainly the tasks of a woman in bearing and educating children as well as maintaining, as best she may, the inner integrity of her home are capable of demanding all her time and

---

* For statistical information, see Sandra Opdycke, *The Routledge Historical Atlas of Women in America* (New York: Routledge, 2000), p. 132.

** Excerpt from *Modern Woman: The Lost Sex* by Ferdinand Lundberg. Copyright 1947 by Ferdinand Lundberg and Marynia F. Farnham. Copyright renewed. Reprinted by permission of HarperCollins Publishers Inc.

best attention. However, she cannot obtain from them, so attenuated are these tasks now, the same sort of community approval and ego-satisfaction that she can from seemingly more challenging occupations which take her outside the home. Inevitably the dilemma has led to one compromise after another which we see exemplified on every hand in the modern woman's adaptation—an uneasy patchwork. . . .

It is becoming unquestionably more and more common for the woman to attempt to combine both home and child care and an outside activity, which is either work or career. Increasing numbers train for professional careers. When these two spheres are combined it is inevitable that one or the other will become of secondary concern and, this being the case, it is certain that the home will take that position. This is true, if only for the practical reason that no one can find and hold remunerative employment where the job itself doesn't take precedence over all other concerns. All sorts of agencies and instrumentalities have therefore been established to make possible the playing of this dual role. These are all in the direction of substitutes for the attention of the mother in the home and they vary from ordinary, untrained domestic service through the more highly trained grades of such service, to the public and private agencies now designed for the care, supervision and emotional untanglement of the children. The day nursery and its more elegant counterpart, the nursery school, are outstanding as the major agencies which make it possible for women to relinquish the care of children still in their infancy. . . .

Work that entices women out of their homes and provides them with prestige only at the price of feminine relinquishment, involves a response to masculine strivings. The more importance outside work assumes, the more are the masculine components of the woman's nature enhanced and encouraged. In her home and in her relationship to her children, it is imperative that these strivings be at a minimum

and that her femininity be available both for her own satisfaction and for the satisfaction of her children and husband. She is, therefore, in the dangerous position of having to live one part of her life on the masculine level, another on the feminine. It is hardly astonishing that few can do so with success. One of these tendencies must of necessity achieve dominance over the other. The plain fact is that increasingly we are observing the masculinization of women and with it enormously dangerous consequences to the home, the children (if any) dependent on it, and to the ability of the woman, as well as her husband, to obtain sexual gratification. . . .

The dominant direction of feminine training and development today . . . discourages just those traits necessary to the attainment of sexual pleasure: receptivity and passiveness, a willingness to accept dependence without fear or resentment, with a deep inwardness and readiness for the final goal of sexual life—impregnation. It doesn't admit of wishes to control or master, to rival or dominate. The woman who is to find true gratification must love and accept her own womanhood as she loves and accepts her husband's manhood. Women's rivalry with men today, and the need to "equal" their accomplishments, engenders all too often anger and resentfulness toward men. Men, challenged, frequently respond in kind. So it is that women envy and feel hostile to men for just the attributes which women themselves require for "success" in the world. The woman's unconscious wish herself to possess the organ upon which she must thus depend militates greatly against her ability to accept its vast power to satisfy her when proffered to her in love.

Many women can find no solution to their dilemma and are defeated in attempts at adaptation. These constitute the array of the sick, unhappy, neurotic, wholly or partly incapable of dealing with life. . . .

It is not only the masculine woman who has met with an unhappy fate in the present situation. There are still many women who succeed in achieving adult life with largely unimpaired feminine strivings, for which home, a husband's love and children are to them the entirely adequate answers. It is their misfortune that they must enter a society in which such attitudes are little appreciated and are attended by many concrete, external penalties. Such women cannot fail to be affected by finding that their traditional activities are held in low esteem and that the woman who voluntarily undertakes them is often deprecated by her more aggressive contemporaries. . . .

So it is that society today makes it difficult for a woman to avoid the path leading to discontent and frustration and resultant hostility and destructiveness. Such destructiveness is, unfortunately, not confined in its effects to the woman alone. It reaches into all her relationships and all her functions. As a wife she is not only often ungratified but ungratifying and has, as we have noted, a profoundly disturbing effect upon her husband. Not only does he find himself without the satisfactions of a home directed and cared for by a woman

happy in providing affection and devotion, but he is often confronted by circumstances of even more serious import for his own emotional integrity. His wife may be his covert rival, striving to match him in every aspect of their joint undertaking. Instead of supporting and encouraging his manliness and wishes for domination and power, she may thus impose upon him feelings of insufficiency and weakness. Still worse is the effect upon his sexual satisfactions. Where the woman is unable to admit and accept dependence upon her husband as the source of gratification and must carry her rivalry even into the act of love, she will seriously damage his sexual capacity. To be unable to gratify in the sexual act is for a man an intensely humiliating experience; here it is that mastery and domination, the central capacity of the man's sexual nature, must meet acceptance or fail. So it is that by their own character disturbances these women succeed ultimately in depriving themselves of the devotion and power of their husbands and become the instruments of bringing about their own psychic catastrophe.

LORETTA COLLIER, *A Lesbian Recounts Her Korean War Military Experience* (1990)

In the following excerpt from an interview, Loretta "Ret" Collier bitterly recalls her military experience during the Korean War. Although she describes her total commitment and identification with military life, her lesbian relationship with a civilian ultimately led to an "undesirable" discharge. During an era of anti-Communist investigations and heightened cultural and social conformity, public opinion increasingly labeled homosexual behavior as deviant. For gays and lesbians, successful military careers depended on secrecy and suppression of sexual orientation. What factors drew Collier to military service? What strategies did the military pursue in the effort to terminate her service? How would you evaluate the actions of the military?*

You know, I never entered the military with the idea of finding other lesbians or having any sort of affairs or anything. I entered the military *knowing* that I was a lesbian, but

also knowing that I wanted to do what was right by military standards and stay there! But, by God, when I got into basic, I thought I had been transferred to hog heaven! No damn

* Excerpt from *My Country, My Right to Serve* by MaryAnn Humphrey. Copyright (c) 1990 by MaryAnn Humphrey. Reprinted by permission of HarperCollins Publishers, Inc.

kidding! Lordy! But I was smart enough to know that doing anything would be my downfall. And like I said, I really wanted to stay in. There was no doubt in my mind, from the time I raised my hand and was sworn in until the day I was discharged, that that's where I wanted to be. I liked everything about it. I loved the parades, I loved the uniform, I loved . . . even liked taking orders. I liked standing at attention. I liked getting out there on the field, standing there at parade rest for an hour and a half waiting for a parade. I liked everything about it. I even *liked* KP. I liked everything about it. You would have thought they would have been smarter than to have kicked someone out who liked KP!

I did very well. I did *very* well. I was up at two o'clock ironing my uniforms, and when the whistle blew at 4:30 to get up, man, I was out there and loved it. The challenge was great, and I went for it with gusto. Yeah, I was made squad leader. I remember our trainer was a corporal by the name of Tater, and everybody called her Spud. I have pictures of her and her lover, Powers, who was also there, and Corporal Nichols, who was a dyke, just like they were. They were all affiliated with our flight. Even though there was never anything mentioned, you know, there was that bond that exists that is never acted upon or never mentioned. But the rapport—that was there, and I had that. Actually, once we recognized the bond, believe it or not, we pretty much *stayed away* from each other. In retrospect, I'm sure, it was the survival instinct. I guess we all seem to have it. . . .

I would stay with this gal over the weekend, and I figured, now, when I put on my civilian clothes and go into Sacramento, that's my weekend and what I do has no bearing on what's going on at the base. So I had this relationship with Marie and there were never any problems, until right around the spring of 1953, when basketball season had ended . . . and the OSI started stalking me. My theory is that periodically they'd go through the bases and go on these purges. They would start first with all the women who were involved in athletics and then move from there with any info they had gotten, to snare other women.

They opened my mail. They'd get me up in the middle of the night and take me over to the OSI office for questioning. They'd look under my mattress for anything that I might have hidden, any material, letters, notes, valentines, just anything that I might have hidden that could be incriminating. They'd call me from work or they'd come down and personally escort me back to the OSI office. I was embarrassed being called away from work. I'd just say, "I have to see the OSI," and off I'd go and come back whenever I was released. Sometimes I'd be there ten minutes. Sometimes I'd be there two hours. Most of the time, I would say if I had to make an average, probably forty to forty-five minutes, but their short times were in the middle of the night, just enough time to get me up, awake, out of bed, and disturb my whole night. . . .

The next time they called me in, I said, "Well, what do I have to sign?" They surprised me by saying, "Tell us about your relationship with Marie." I wasn't sure what that had to do with my own discharge, particularly since she was a civilian, but I did. I told them all about my relationship with Marie. A day or two passed and they never bothered me. Then they called me in again and said, "Okay, now we need to hear this story again," so I had to tell them again. I left, and the very next day, the major called me in again and said, "I've been contacted by the OSI, and you're going to have a hearing in about a week." I was shocked, and said, "A hearing, what for?" "Well, yes, in order for them to do the paperwork on this and get your discharge, you have to go through a hearing." And I said, "Is that the same as a court-martial?" And she said, "Yes." To protect herself, she was quite detached and official-acting. It was a pretty sad scenario as I recall.

Once the "court-martial" was in session, nobody read me any rights, told me I could have a defense counsel, or that it was my right to have somebody on that board representing me. I was like a lamb to slaughter. They asked me things like: Did I think that my homosexuality had an adverse effect on my Air Force performance and my military performance? Did I think that being a homosexual in the AF influenced other people? Did I realize that I was a security risk being a homosexual? Those were the kinds of questions, but never anything at all as far as "Is there anything you want to say?" until the end, the very end.

The entire process took about fifteen minutes, including my comments. And when I was allowed to speak, I said, "Well, about the only thing I want to say in my defense is that I don't think I deserve this, to be released, to be discharged from the service, because I feel that my record speaks for itself, that I have never done anything injurious or harmful to anybody else." You know, I was totally career-oriented, and I reiterated to them the fact that I had planned on being a thirty-year Waf and was exceptionally gung ho as far as the AF was concerned. Obviously, all my words fell on deaf ears. . . .

I was pretty devastated. I was pretty numb, but, honestly, I think what I felt was relief that I wasn't going to go through that anymore. However, the down side was that the impact of an undesirable discharge had never occurred to me, *never* occurred to me. I knew it wasn't an honorable, I knew it wasn't the general that I was promised, but the force of it never dawned on me. But I was grateful to be out from under all that pressure and all that investigation. It wasn't until two weeks or so after I was discharged that I realized the impact of *this* discharge. Two pieces of paper arrived in this envelope telling me all the things that I couldn't do because of my undesirable discharge. I could no longer vote. I didn't have any benefits. I could never work for any government-affiliated agency or company. I could not do anything with any state-run organization or state supported agencies like education or any civil service that had to do with prisons. I couldn't be involved in anything that had to do with security because I could never get a security clearance. I couldn't even work for the post office! You know, all these places where I could never work, the list went on and on.

JO ANN GIBSON ROBINSON, *The Montgomery Bus Boycott* (1955)

African American women such as Rosa Parks and Jo Ann Gibson Robinson (1912–1992) played major roles in the initiation of the civil rights movement. In the following document, Robinson, a college professor and community activist, recounts the unfolding of the Montgomery, Alabama, bus boycott. In addition to being a seamstress, Rosa Parks also was secretary of the Montgomery NAACP. What role did these women play in launching the boycott?*

In the afternoon of Thursday, December 1, [1955] a prominent black woman named Mrs. Rosa Parks was arrested for refusing to vacate her seat for a white man. Mrs. Parks was a medium-sized, cultured mulatto woman; a civic and religious worker; quiet unassuming, and pleasant in manner and appearance; dignified and reserved; of high morals and a strong character. She was—and still is, for she lives to tell the story—respected in all black circles. By trade she was a seamstress, adept and competent in her work.

---

* From Jo Ann Gibson Robinson, *The Montgomery Bus Boycott and the Women Who Started It: The Memoir of Jo Ann Gibson Robinson,* edited by David J. Garrow (Knoxville: University of Tennessee Press, 1987), 43-45. Reprinted by permission of the University of Tennessee Press.

Tired from work, Mrs. Parks boarded a bus. The "reserved seats" were partially filled, but the seats just behind the reserved section were vacant, and Mrs. Parks sat down in one. It was during the busy evening rush hour. More black and white passengers boarded the bus, and soon all the reserved seats were occupied. The driver demanded that Mrs. Parks get up and surrender her seat to a white man, but she was tired from her work. She remained seated. In a few minutes, police summoned by the driver appeared, placed Mrs. Parks under arrest and took her to jail.

It was the first time the soft-spoken, middle-aged woman had been arrested. She maintained her decorum and poise, and the word of her arrest spread. Mr. E.D. Nixson, a longtime stalwart of our NAACP branch, along with liberal white attorney Clifford Durr and his wife Virginia, went to the jail and obtained Mrs. Parks's release on bond. Her trial was scheduled for Monday, December 5, 1955.

The news traveled like wildfire into every black home. Telephones jangled; people congregated on street corners and in homes and talked. But nothing was done. A numbing helplessness seemed to paralyze everyone. Very few stayed off the buses the rest of that day or the next. There was fear, discontent, and uncertainty. Everyone seemed to wait for someone to *do* something, but nobody made a move. For that day and a half, black Americans rode the buses as before, as if nothing had happened. They were sullen and uncommunicative, but they rode the buses. There was a silent, tension-filled waiting. For blacks were not talking loudly in public places—they were quiet, sullen, waiting. Just waiting!

Thursday evening came and went. Thursday night was far spent, when, at about 11:30 P.M., I sat in my peaceful, single-family dwelling on a side street. I was thinking about the situation. Lost in thought, I was startled by the telephone's ring. Black attorney Fred Gray, who had been out of town all day, had just gotten back and was returning the phone message I had left him about Mrs. Parks's arrest. Attorney Gray, though a very young man, had been one of my most active colleagues in our previous meetings with bus company officials and Commissioner Birmingham. A Montgomery native who had attended Alabama State and been one of my students, Fred Gray had gone on to law school in Ohio before returning to his hometown to open a practice with the only

Rosa Parks Arrested (Gene Herrick/AP Wide World Photos)

other black lawyer in Montgomery, Charles Langford.

Fred Gray and his wife Bernice were good friends of mine, and we talked often. In addition to being a lawyer, Gray was a trained, ordained minister of the gospel, actively serving as assistant pastor of Holt Street Church of Christ.

Tonight his voice on the phone was very short and to the point. Fred was shocked by the news of Mrs. Parks's arrest. I informed him that I already was thinking that the WPC [Women's Political Council] should distribute

thousands of notices calling for all bus riders to stay off the buses on Monday, the day of Mrs. Parks's trial. "Are you ready?" he asked. Without hesitation, I assured him that we were. With that he hung up, and I went to work.

I made some notes on the back of an envelope: "The Women's Political Council will not wait for Mrs. Parks's consent to call for a boycott of city buses. On Friday, December 2, 1955, the women of Montgomery will call for a boycott to take place on Monday, December 5."

ANNE MOODY, *The Movement* (1963)

African American women actively participated in the mass-based civil rights movement of the 1960s. In the following source, Anne Moody (b. 1940), a Mississippi college student, provides an eyewitness account of the effort to end segregated lunch counters at Woolworth's. What role did Moody and other women play in this event?*

I had counted on graduating in the spring of 1963, but as it turned out, I couldn't, because some of my credits still had to be cleared with Natchez College. A year before, this would have seemed like a terrible disaster, but now I hardly even felt disappointed. I had a good excuse to stay on campus for the summer and work with the Movement, and this was what I really wanted to do. I couldn't go home again anyway, and I couldn't go to New Orleans—I didn't have money enough for bus fare.

During my senior year at Tougaloo, my family hadn't sent me one penny. I had only the small amount of money I had earned at Maple Hill. I couldn't afford to eat at school or live in the dorms, so I had gotten permission to move off campus. I had to prove that I could finish school, even if I had to go hungry every day. I knew Raymond and Miss Pearl were just waiting to see me drop out. But something happened to me as I got more and more involved with the Movement. It no

longer seemed important to prove anything. I had found something outside myself that gave meaning to my life.

I had become very friendly with my social science professor, John Salter, who was in charge of NAACP activities on campus. All during the year, while the NAACP conducted a boycott of the downtown stores in Jackson, I had been one of Salter's most faithful canvassers and church speakers. During the last week of school, he told me that sit-in demonstrations were about to start in Jackson and that he wanted me to be the spokesman for a team that would sit-in at Woolworth's lunch counter. The two other demonstrators would be classmates of mine, Memphis and Pearlena. Pearlena was a dedicated NAACP worker, but Memphis had not been very involved in the Movement on campus. It seemed that the organization had had a rough time finding students who were in a position to go to jail. I had nothing to lose one way or the other. Around ten o'clock the

---

* From *Coming of Age in Mississippi* by Anne Moody. Copyright © 1968 by Anne Moody. Used by permission of Doubleday, a division of Random House, Inc.

morning of the demonstrations, NAACP head-quarters alerted the news services. As a result, the police department was also informed, but neither the policemen nor the newsmen knew exactly where or when the demonstrations would start. They stationed themselves along Capitol Street and waited.

To divert attention from the sit-in at Woolworth's, the picketing started at J.C. Penney's a good fifteen minutes before. The pickets were allowed to walk up and down in front of the store three or four times before they were arrested. At exactly 11 a.m., Pearlena, Memphis, and I entered Woolworth's from the rear entrance. We separated as soon as we stepped into the store, and made small purchases from various counters. Pearlena had given Memphis her watch. He was to let us know when it was 11:14. At 11:14 we were to join him near the lunch counter and at exactly 11:15 we were to take seats at it.

Seconds before 11:15 we were occupying three seats at the previously segregated Woolworth's lunch counter. In the beginning the waitresses seemed to ignore us, as if they really didn't know what was going on. Our waitress walked past us a couple of times before she noticed we had started to write our orders down and realized we wanted service. She asked us what we wanted. We began to read to her from our order slips. She told us that we would be served at the back counter, which was for Negroes.

"We would like to be served here," I said.

The waitress started to repeat what she had said, then stopped in the middle of the sentence. She turned the lights out behind the counter, and she and the other waitresses almost ran to the back of the store, deserting all their white customers. I guess they thought that the violence would start imme-diately after the whites at the counter realized what was going on. There were five or six other people at the counter. A couple of them just got up and walked away. A girl sitting next to me finished her banana split

before leaving. A middle-aged white woman who had not yet been served rose from her seat and came over to us. "I'd like to stay here with you," she said, "but my husband is waiting."

The newsmen came in just as she was leaving. They must have discovered what was going on shortly after some of the people began to leave the store. One of the newsmen ran behind the woman who spoke to us and asked her to identify herself. She refused to give her name, but said she was a native of Vicksburg and a former resident of California. When asked why she had said what she said to us, she replied, "I am in sympathy with the Negro movement." By this time a crowd of cameramen and reporters had gathered around us taking pictures and asking ques-tions, such as Where were we from? Why did we sit-in? What organization sponsored it? Were we students? From what school? How were we classified?

I told them that we were all students at Tougaloo College, that we were represented by no particular organization, and that we planned to stay there even after the store closed. "All we want is service," was my reply to one of them. After they had finished probing for about twenty minutes, they were almost ready to leave.

At noon, students from a nearby white high school started pouring in to Woolworth's. When they first saw us they were sort of surprised. They didn't know how to react. A few started to heckle and the newsmen became interested again. Then the white students started chanting all kinds of anti-Negro slogans. We were called a little bit of everything. The rest of the seats, except the three we were occupying, had been roped off to prevent others from sitting down. A couple of the boys took one end of the rope and made it into a hangman's noose. Several attempts were made to put it around our necks. The crowds grew as more students and adults came in for lunch.

We kept our eyes straight forward and did not look at the crowd except for occasional glances to see what was going on. All of a sudden I saw a face I remembered—the drunkard from the bus station sit-in. My eyes lingered on him just long enough for us to recognize each other. Today he was drunk too, so I don't think he remembered where he had seen me before. He took out a knife, opened it, put it in his pocket, and then began to pace the floor. At this point, I told Memphis and Pearlena what was going on. Memphis suggested that we pray. We bowed our heads, and all hell broke loose. A man rushed forward, threw Memphis from his seat, and slapped my face. Then another man who worked in the store threw me against an adjoining counter.

Down on my knees on the floor, I saw Memphis lying near the lunch counter with blood running out of the corners of his mouth. As he tried to protect his face, the man who'd thrown him down kept kicking him against the head. If he had worn hard-soled shoes instead of sneakers, the first kick probably would have killed Memphis. Finally a man dressed in plain clothes identified himself as a police officer, and arrested Memphis and his attacker. Pearlena had been thrown to the floor. She and I got back on our stools after Memphis was arrested. There were some white Tougaloo teachers in the crowd. They asked Pearlena and me if we wanted to leave. They said that things were getting too rough. We didn't know what to do. While

we were trying to make up our minds, we were joined by Joan Trumpauer. Now there were three of us and we were integrated. The crowd began to chant, "Communists, Communists, Communists." Some old man in the crowd ordered the students to take us off the stools.

"Which one should I get first?" a big husky boy said.

"That white nigger," the old man said.

The boy lifted Joan from the counter by her waist and carried her out of the store. Simultaneously, I was snatched from my stool by two high school students. I was dragged about thirty feet toward the door by my hair when someone made them turn me loose. As I was getting up off the floor, I saw Joan coming back inside. We started back to the center of the counter to join Pearlena. Lois Chaffee, a white Tougaloo faculty member, was now sitting next to her. So Joan and I just climbed across the rope at the front end of the counter and sat down. There were now four of us, two white and two Negroes, all women. The mob started smearing us with ketchup, mustard, sugar, pies, and everything on the counter. Soon Joan and I were joined by John Salter, but the moment he sat down he was hit on the jaw with what appeared to be brass knuckles. Blood gushed from his face and someone threw salt into the open wound. Ed King, Tougaloo's chaplain, rushed to him.

GOVERNOR ADLAI STEVENSON, *"A Purpose for Modern Women," Smith College Commencement Speech* (1955)

Adlai Stevenson (1900–1965), two-time failed Democratic presidential candidate (1952 and 1956) and former governor of Illinois, addressed the Smith College graduation class of 1955. This commencement speech followed gender prescriptions. Statistically many women did marry in their early twenties and the focus on home and child care was culturally pervasive. Still, the speaker addressed only the wife/mother role and emphasized the private realm of the home as separate from the husband's public realm of business activity. As was the case in the 1850s, Stevenson depicted the home as the refuge for the husband, and it was the wife's responsibility to make his well-being her primary objective in life. Stevenson linked the "humble role of housewife" to the salvation of the western world. He noted that by helping her husband create a purposeful existence, she was also helping freedom to survive. He endowed the wife's role with awesome responsibility reminiscent of the Republican motherhood construct of the 1800's. (Stevenson used the term *the West* to refer to the western nations of free world in contrast to Communist nations.)

From the perspective of Elizabeth Cady Stanton or the Grimké sisters or other advocates of women's rights, how would Stevenson's advice sound? Contrast this depiction of women's role in marriage with Amram Scheinfeld's discussion of "momism"? How would you evaluate Stevenson's speech?*

I think there is much you can do about our crisis in the humble role of housewife.

The peoples of the West are still struggling with the problems of a free society and just now are in dire trouble. For to create a free society is at all times a precarious and audacious experiment. Its bedrock is the concept of man as an end in himself. But violent pressures are constantly battering away at this concept, reducing man once again to subordinate status, limiting his range of choice, abrogating his responsibility and returning him to his primitive status of anonymity in the social group. I think you can be more helpful in identifying, isolating and combatting these pressures, this virus, than you perhaps realize.

Let me put it this way: individualism has promoted technological advance, technology promoted increased specialization, and specialization promoted an ever closer economic interdependence between specialties.

As the old order disintegrated into this confederation of narrow specialties, each pulling in the direction of its particular interest, the individual person tended to become absorbed literally by his particular function in society. Having sacrificed wholeness of mind and breadth of outlook to the demands of their specialties, individuals no longer responded to social stimuli as total human beings; rather they reacted in partial ways as members of an economic class or industry or profession whose concern was with some limited self-interest.

Thus this typical Western man, or typical Western husband, operates well in the realm of means, as the Romans did before him. But outside his specialty, in the realm of ends, he is apt to operate poorly or not at all. And this neglect of the cultivation of more mature values can only mean that his life, and the life of the society he determines, will lack valid purpose, however busy and even profitable it may be.

And here's where you come in: to restore valid, meaningful purpose to life in your home; to beware of instinctive group reaction to the forces which play upon you and yours, to watch for and arrest the constant gravitational pulls to which we are all exposed—your workaday husband especially—in our specialized, fragmented society, that tend to widen the breach between reason and emotion, between means and ends.

And let me also remind you that you will live, most of you, in an environment in which "facts," the data of the senses, are glorified, and values—judgments—are assigned inferior status as mere "matters of opinion." It is an environment in which art is often regarded as an adornment of civilization rather than a vital element of it, while philosophy is not only neglected but deemed faintly disreputable because "it never gets you anywhere." Even religion, you will find, commands a lot of earnest allegiance that is more verbal than real, more formal than felt.

You may be hitched to one of these creatures we call "Western man" and I think part of your job is to keep him Western, to keep him truly purposeful, to keep him whole. In short—while I have had very little experience as a wife or mother—I think one of the biggest jobs for many of you will be to

---

* Adlai Stevenson, "A Purpose for Modern Woman," excerpted from a Commencement Address, Smith College, 1955, in *Women's Home Companion* (September 1955).

frustrate the crushing and corrupting effects of specialization, to integrate means and ends, to develop that balanced tension of mind and spirit which can be properly called "integrity."

This assignment for you, as wives and mothers, has great advantages.

In the first place, it is home work—you can do it in the living-room with a baby in your lap or in the kitchen with a can opener in your hand. If you're really clever, maybe you can even practice your saving arts on that unsuspecting man while he's watching television!

And, secondly, it is important work worthy of you, whoever you are, or your education, whatever it is, because we will defeat totalitarian, authoritarian ideas only by better ideas; we will frustrate the evils of vocational specialization only by the virtues of intellectual generalization. Since Western rationalism and Eastern spiritualism met in Athens and that mighty creative fire broke out, collectivism in various forms has collided with individualism time and again. This twentieth-century collision, this "crisis" we are forever talking about, will be won at last not on the battlefield but in the head and heart.

So you see, I have some rather large notions about you and what you have to do to rescue us wretched slaves of specialization and group thinking from further shrinkage and contraction of mind and spirit. But you will have to be alert or you may get caught yourself—even in the kitchen or the nursery—by the steady pressures with which you will be surrounded. . . .

Women, especially educated women, have a unique opportunity to influence us, man and boy, and to play a direct part in the unfolding drama of our free society. But I am told that nowadays the young wife or mother is short of time for such subtle arts, that things are not what they used to be; that once immersed in the very pressing and particular problems of domesticity, many women feel

frustrated and far apart from the great issues and stirring debates for which their education has given them understanding and relish. Once they read Baudelaire. Now it is the Consumers' Guide. Once they wrote poetry. Now it's the laundry list. Once they discussed art and philosophy until late in the night. Now they are so tired they fall asleep as soon as the dishes are finished. There is, often, a sense of contraction, of closing horizons and lost opportunities. They had hoped to play their part in the crisis of the age. But what they do is wash the diapers. (Or do they any longer?)

Now I hope I have not painted too depressing a view of your future, for the fact is that Western marriage and motherhood are yet another instance of the emergence of individual freedom in our Western society. Their basis is the recognition in women as well as men of the primacy of personality and individuality. I have just returned from sub-Sahara Africa where the illiteracy of the African mother is a formidable obstacle to the education and advancement of her child and where polygamy and female labor are still the dominant system.

The point is that whether we talk of Africa, Islam or Asia, women "never had it so good" as you do. And in spite of the difficulties of domesticity, you have a way to participate actively in the crisis in addition to keeping yourself and those about you straight on the difference between means and ends, mind and spirit, reason and emotion— not to mention keeping your man straight on the differences between Botticelli and Chianti. . . .

In modern America the home is not the boundary of a woman's life. There are outside activities aplenty. But even more important is the fact, surely, that what you have learned and can learn will, fit you for the primary task of making homes and whole human beings in whom the rational values of freedom, tolerance, charity and free inquiry can take root.

BETTY FRIEDAN, *The Problem That Has No Name* (1963)

Betty Friedan's (1921–2006) *The Feminine Mystique* described the cultural context and collective significance of why many women felt their lives lacked meaning. Although Friedan based her critique on surveys of Smith College graduates and the voices of suburban women who mainly came from privileged backgrounds, the book was widely read. Women identified with the message that their despair was not a personal psychological problem but rather the result of a "feminine mystique" that pushed women into full-time domestic roles and disregarded their other needs. How does Friedan describe the "mystique of feminine fulfillment"? What is "the problem that has no name"?*

The problem lay buried, unspoken, for many years in the minds of American women. It was a strange stirring, a sense of dissatisfaction, a yearning that women suffered in the middle of the twentieth century in the United States. Each suburban wife struggled with it alone. As she made the beds, shopped for groceries, matched slipcover material, ate peanut butter sandwiches with her children, chauffeured Cub Scouts and Brownies, lay beside her husband at night—she was afraid to ask even of herself the silent question—"Is this all?"

For over fifteen years there was no word of this yearning in the millions of words written about women and for women, in all the columns, books and articles by experts telling women their role was to seek fulfillment as wives and mothers. Over and over women heard in voices of tradition and Freudian sophistication, that they could desire no greater destiny than to glory in their own femininity. Experts told them how to catch a man and how to keep him, how to breastfeed children and handle their toilet training, how to cope with sibling rivalry and adolescent rebellion; how to buy a dishwasher, bake bread, cook gourmet snails, and build a swimming pool with their own hands; how to dress, look, and act more feminine and make marriage more exciting; how to keep their husbands from dying young and their sons from growing into delinquents. They were

taught to pity the neurotic, unfeminine, unhappy women who wanted to be poets or physicists or presidents. They learned that truly feminine women do not want careers, higher education, political rights—the independence and the opportunities that the old-fashioned feminists fought for. Some women, in their forties and fifties, still remembered painfully giving up those dreams, but most of the younger women no longer even thought about them. A thousand expert voices applauded their femininity, their adjustment, their new maturity. All they had to do was devote their lives from earliest girlhood to finding a husband and bearing children. . . .

The suburban housewife—she was the dream image of the young American women and the envy, it was said, of women all over the world. The American housewife—freed by science and labor-saving appliances from the drudgery, the dangers of childbirth and the illnesses of her grandmother. She was healthy, beautiful, educated, concerned only about her husband, her children, her home. She had found true feminine fulfillment. As a housewife and mother, she was respected as a full and equal partner to man in his world. She was free to choose automobiles, clothes, appliances, supermarkets: she had everything that women ever dreamed of.

In the fifteen years after World War II, this mystique of feminine fulfillment became the cherished and self-perpetuating core of

---

* Betty Friedan, "The Problem that has no name" from The Feminine Mystique. Copyright © 1983, 1974, 1973, 1963 by Betty Friedan. Used by permission of W.W. Norton & Company, Inc.

contemporary American culture. Millions of women lived their lives in the image of those pretty pictures of the American suburban housewife, kissing their husband goodbye in front of the picture window, depositing their station wagonsful of children at school, and smiling as they ran the new electric waxer over the spotless kitchen floor. They baked their own bread, sewed their own and their children's clothes, kept their new washing machines and dryers running all day. They changed the sheets on the beds twice a week instead of once, took the rug-hooking classes in adult education, and pitied their poor frustrated mothers, who had dreamed of having a career. Their only dream was to be perfect wives and mothers; their highest ambition to have five children and a beautiful house, their only fight to get and keep their husbands. They had no thought for the unfeminine problems of the world outside the home; they wanted the men to make the major decisions. They gloried in their role as women, and wrote proudly on the census blank: "Occupation: housewife."

For over fifteen years, the words written for women, and the words women used when they talked to each other, while their husbands sat on the other side of the room and talked shop or politics or septic tanks, were about problems with their children, or how to keep their husband happy, or improve their children's school, or cook chicken or make slipcovers. Nobody argued whether women were inferior or superior to men; they were simply different. Words like "emancipation" and "career" sounded strange and embarrassing; no one had used them for years. When a Frenchwoman named Simone de Beauvoir wrote a book called *The Second Sex,* an American critic commented that she obviously "didn't know what life was all about," and besides, she was talking about French women. The "woman problem" in America no longer existed.

Gradually I came to realize that the problem that has no name was shared by countless women in America. As a magazine writer I often interviewed women about problems with their children, or their marriages, or their houses, or their communities. But after a while I began to recognize the telltale signs of this other problem. I saw the same signs in suburban ranch houses and split-levels on Long Island and in New Jersey and Westchester County; in colonial houses in a small Massachusetts town; on patios in Memphis; in suburban and city apartments; in living rooms in the Midwest. Sometimes I sensed the problem, not as a reporter, but as a suburban housewife, for during this time I was also bringing up my own three children in Rockland County, New York. I heard echoes of the problem in college dormitories and semi-private maternity wards, at PTA meetings and luncheons of the League of Women Voters, at suburban cocktail parties, in station wagons waiting for trains, and in snatches of conversation overheard at Schrafft's. The groping words I heard from other women on quiet afternoons when the children were at school, or on quiet evenings when husbands worked late, I think I understood first as a woman long before I understood their larger social and psychological implications.

Just what was this problem that has no name? What were the words women used when they tried to express it? Sometimes a woman would say "I feel empty somehow . . . incomplete." Or she would say, "I feel as if I don't exist.". . .

It is no longer possible to ignore that voice, to dismiss the desperation of so many American women. This is not what being a woman means, no matter what the experts say. For human suffering there is a reason: perhaps the reason has not been found because the right questions have not been asked, or pressed far enough. I do not accept the answer that there is no problem because American women have luxuries that women in other times and lands never dreamed of; part of the strange newness of the problem is that it cannot be understood in terms of the age-old material problems of man: poverty, sickness, hunger, cold. The women who suffer this problem have a hunger that food cannot fill. It persists in women whose husbands are struggling interns and law clerks, or prosperous doctors and lawyers; in wives of workers and executives who make $5,000 a year or $50,000. It is not caused by lack of material advantages; it may not even be felt by women preoccupied with desperate problems of hunger, poverty or illness. And women who think it will be solved by more money, a bigger house, a second car, moving to a better suburb, often discover it gets worse.

It is no longer possible today to blame the problem on loss of femininity; to say that education and independence and equality with men have made American women unfeminine. I have heard so many women try to deny this dissatisfied voice within themselves because it does not fit the pretty picture of femininity the experts have given them. I think, in fact, that this is the first clue to the mystery; the problem cannot be understood in the generally accepted terms by which scientists have studied women, doctors have treated them, counselors have advised them, and writers have written about them. Women who suffer this problem, in whom this voice is stirring, have lived their whole lives in the pursuit of feminine fulfillment. They are not career women (although career women may have other problems); they are women whose greatest ambition has been marriage and children. For the oldest of these women, these daughters of the American middle-class, no other dream was possible. The ones in their forties and fifties who once had other dreams gave them up and threw themselves joyously into life as housewives. For the youngest, the new wives and mothers, this was the only dream. They are the ones who quit high school and college to marry, or marked time in some job in which they had no real interest until they married. These women are very "feminine" in the usual sense, and yet they still suffer the problem. . . .

If I am right, the problem that has no name stirring in the minds of so many American women today, is not a matter of loss of femininity or too much education, or the demands of domesticity. It is far more important than anyone recognizes. It is the key to these other new and old problems that have been torturing women and their husbands and children, and puzzling their doctors and educators for years. It may well be the key to our future as a nation and a culture. We can no longer ignore that voice within women that says: "I want something more than my husband and my children and my home."

CHAPTER 17

From Municipal House Keeping to Environmental Justice

The intersection of environmental activism and women's history is at the cutting edge of contemporary historical research. Women's words testify to the lines of continuity and the wide range of interlocking objectives that have shaped women's environmental roles. From the Progressive era to the present, women have played activist roles in all aspects of environmental reform, from ridding the workplace of hazardous chemicals to addressing clean water, municipal sanitation, and wilderness preservation. One of the first women to sound an environmental alarm against the impact of industrial pollution on habitat and human lives was the nineteenth-century novelist Rebecca Harding Davis. In recent years, women's environmental activism has included a global component expressing both concern for female empowerment and an end to environmental degradation. This chapter provides an overview of primary sources and the centrality of women such as Ellen Swallow Richards, Alice Hamilton, Rachel Carson, Margie Richard, and Winona LaDuke to environmental reform.

Although Richards, Hamilton, and Carson had careers that spanned the post–Civil War period through the post–World War II era, they all faced the formidable barrier of male claims to the ownership of science. Richards was a pioneer environmental scientist who graduated from MIT in 1873 and became a junior faculty member, an entry-level rank she held throughout her career. Despite her national prominence in the scientific investigation of toxins in the industrial workplace and her evidence linking workplace contaminants to worker's ill heath, Hamilton encountered similar sexist institutional discrimination at Harvard. The first woman hired as a faculty member in Harvard's Medical School in 1919, she also remained at a permanent entry-level position, and because of gender bias she was barred from faculty attendance at Harvard's graduation ceremonies. Carson trained and worked as a marine biologist in an overwhelmingly male field. Author of *Silent Spring*, published in 1962, she warned the nation that chemical pesticides caused peril to wildlife and humans. Male critics lashed out with sexist stereotypes accusing her of overly emotional, even hysterical reactions.

The early-twentieth-century connection between female environmental reformers and areas such as *municipal housekeeping* and *domestic science* confined women to a gendered niche that obscured the complexity and significance of their achievements. Female municipal reformers in New York City took pride in their achievement of cleaner streets that they alleged included combating the ignorance, incompetency, and apathy of male political leaders. Municipal housekeepers in cities and towns throughout the nation embraced a wide range of objectives including efforts for safe drinking water, cleaner streets, and better sanitation and public health (see Chapter 13).

Progressive-era women helped carve their own environmental reform space, much of which reinforced gender norms. They were comfortable with the domestic terminology that expressed the gendered constraints of their era and justified their increasing public involvement and political participation. Richards applied science to the home environment and pioneered the study of the way domestic technology and household appliances could pose environmental hazards. She developed the construct of ecology and the interdependence of the natural and domestic realms.

Women also played a central role in the nation's preservation and conservation movements. In fact, preservation of nature was initially perceived as a sentimental female concern. Male preservationists, eager to avoid identification with such an allegedly feminine pursuit, distanced themselves from their female counterparts through exclusive organizations that barred women from membership and the establishment of professional standards that undercut women's voluntary work. Men such as John Muir overshadowed the nationwide participation of women in conservation movements. Nevertheless, the General Federation of Women's Clubs (GFWC) organized and mobilized women's Progressive-era environmental activism. Club members mobilized the collective effort of women to create the national park system. Women supported John Muir's effort to save Yosemite's Hetch Hetchy in California from construction of a massive dam. Unsuccessful there, women succeeded in saving the forest in Franconia Notch, in New Hampshire's White Mountains, from the lumber industry. Mary Hunter Austin's passionate plea for preservation of the Southern California desert in her 1903 book *Land of Little Rain* paralleled that of John Muir for preservation of Yosemite. Yet, until recently, her environmental message received limited acknowledgment. In the mid-twentieth century, Marjorie Stoneman Douglas's investigation and subsequent publication of her book on the Florida Everglades, *River of Grass*, led to government effort to rescue of a national resource. Yet, her work has received little attention in environmental texts that remain male-centric in their coverage.

After World War II, women engaged in political protests against the proliferation of nuclear bombs and aboveground atomic testing. Their protest organization and demonstrations occurred at the height of cold war tensions and challenged the conventional stereotypes of housewives' conformity. With viewpoints that diverged from the cold war nuclear arms race and McCarthy-era politics that exploited the fear of Communist infiltration in the United States, the women's strategies employed maternal concerns that emphasized their anti-nuclear positions. Women's fears concerning the impact on health of aboveground nuclear testing may have been well founded. Fallout from U.S. nuclear testing brought death not only to livestock but also may have caused, as Terry Tempest Williams relates in *The Clan of One-Breasted Women,* an increase in breast cancer for female residents in the direct radiation fallout zones of communities in Utah, Idaho, and Nevada that were downwind of the nuclear test sites. In the contemporary era, Theo Colborn has investigated what she believes to be the disastrous impact of synthetic hormones on animal and human life.

Concern for the health of her own children transformed Lois Gibbs in the late 1970s from a stay-at-home mom into a politically engaged activist who led her upstate New York, Love Canal community in a fight for justice against Hooker Chemical's toxic dumping. Gibbs lived with the nightmare of approximately 21,000 tons of toxic chemicals leaching into the soil and water of her community. Her children and those of her neighbors were growing up in toxic homes and attending a school built on a chemical dumping ground. Gibbs mobilized her community to have the government relocate families. In 1984, Mexican American women organized the Mothers of East Los Angeles (MELA). MELA has led a series of community battles for environmental justice, including prevention of a hazard waste treatment plant near a neighborhood high school.

Beginning at the grassroots level and gaining national recognition, an environmental crusade for racial justice has gained momentum over the past quarter of a century. Women of color and white women have led their poor and working-class communities in a fight against corporate polluters and the environmental degradation of their neighborhoods. African American women such as Margie Eugene Richard and Dollie Burwell assumed leadership roles in the fight against environmental racism and the chemical contamination of communities of color. Richard led a grassroots struggle in Louisiana against contamination caused by Shell Oil. Burwell helped mobilize her community against the intentional dumping of toxic PCBs not far from their homes in Warren County, North Carolina.

Communities of color and poorer communities in general have disproportionately served as dumping grounds for industrial waste, chemical contamination, and environmental degradation. It is estimated that 90 percent of the membership in grassroots environmental movements, across racial and ethnic lines, are women who also comprise the majority of community leaders. In Boone County, West Virginia, women helped form Coal River Mountain Watch (CRMW) in 1998, in an effort to end Massey Coal from continued blasting, which removed mountaintops and resulted in toxic sludge run-off and contaminated water. American Indian advocate and environmental activist Winona LaDuke challenged the federal government's choice of tribal reservations for the dumping of chemical and nuclear waste. LaDuke was Ralph Nader's running mate on the Green Party ticket in 1996 and 2000.

Proponents use the term *eco-feminism* to portray women as worldwide caretakers of the environment who apply their maternal love to the earth's protection. From this perspective, women worldwide defend environmental protection. Critics claim the term is imprecise, simplifies the female experience, and places too much emphasis on women's essential difference from men without consideration of historical context. Regardless of the acceptance or rejection of the construct, activist women in grassroots and global organizations, have led and continue to lead a movement for environmental justice.

REBECCA HARDING DAVIS, Excerpt from *Life in the Iron Mills* (1861)

Rebecca Harding Davis (1831–1910) grew up surrounded by the iron mills of Wheeling, West Virginia, that had already begun to crowd out daylight. The iron mills spewed smoke, and an unremitting soot and grime polluted the environment and warped the natural landscape and in Davis's perception took a heavy toll on workers' lives. Smoke abatement would provide a major issue for early Progressive-era women reformers. The opening paragraphs from Davis's short story dramatically portray the conditions of early industrial pollution. Industrial pollution obliterated the natural environment and combined with low wages, hazardous conditions, and long hours created the unhealthy, toxic conditions that Ellen Swallow Richards and Alice Hamilton would subsequently investigate. Davis's work won recognition for its realistic, gritty portrayal of industrial workers' lives warped by economic injustice and environmental pollution. What aspects of this vividly depicted toxic environment did Davis find most distressing?*

"Is this the end?
O Life, as futile, then, as frail!
What hope of answer or redress?"

A cloudy day: do you know what that is in a town of iron-works? The sky sank down before dawn, muddy, flat, immovable. The air is thick, clammy with the breath of crowded human beings. It stifles me. I open the window, and, looking out, can scarcely see through the rain the grocer's shop opposite, where a crowd of drunken Irishmen are puffing Lynchburg tobacco in their pipes. I can detect the scent through all the foul smells ranging loose in the air.

The idiosyncrasy of this town is smoke. It rolls sullenly in slow folds from the great chimneys of the iron-foundries, and settles down in black, slimy pools on the muddy streets. Smoke on the wharves, smoke on the dingy boats, on the yellow river,—clinging in a coating of greasy soot to the house-front, the two faded poplars, the faces of the passers-by. The long train of mules, dragging masses of pig-iron through the narrow street, have a foul vapor hanging to their reeking sides. Here, inside, is a little broken figure of an angel pointing upward from the mantel-shelf; but even its wings are covered with smoke, clotted and black. Smoke everywhere! A dirty canary chirps desolately in a cage beside me. Its dream of green fields and sunshine is a very old dream,—almost worn out, I think.

From the back-window I can see a narrow brick-yard sloping down to the river-side, strewed with rain-butts and tubs. The river, dull and tawny-colored, (la belle riviere!) drags itself sluggishly along, tired of the heavy weight of boats and coalbarges. What wonder? When I was a child, I used to fancy a look of weary, dumb appeal upon the face of the negro-like river slavishly bearing its burden day after day. Something of the same idle notion comes to me to-day, when from the street-window I look on the slow stream of human life creeping past, night and morning, to the great mills. Masses of men, with dull, besotted faces bent to the ground, sharpened here and there by pain or cunning; skin and muscle and flesh begrimed with smoke and ashes; stooping all night over boiling caldrons of metal, laired by day in dens of drunkenness and infamy; breathing from infancy to death an air saturated with fog and grease and soot, vileness for soul and body. What do you make of a case like that, amateur psychologist? You call it an altogether serious thing to be alive: to these men it is a drunken jest, a joke,—horrible to angels perhaps, to them commonplace enough. My fancy about the river was an idle one: it is no type of such a life. What if it be stagnant and slimy here? It knows that beyond there waits for it odorous sunlight, quaint old gardens, dusky with soft, green foliage of apple-trees, and flushing crimson with roses,—air, and fields, and mountains. The future of the Welsh puddler passing just now is not so pleasant. To be stowed away, after his grimy work is done, in a hole in the muddy graveyard, and after that, not air, nor green fields, nor curious roses.

Can you see how foggy the day is? As I stand here, idly tapping the windowpane, and looking out through the rain at the dirty

---

* In the public domain.

back-yard and the coalboats below, fragments of an old story float up before me,—a story of this house into which I happened to come to-day. You may think it a tiresome story enough, as foggy as the day, sharpened by no sudden flashes of pain or pleasure.—I know: only the outline of a dull life, that long since, with thousands of dull lives like its own, was vainly lived and lost: thousands of them, massed, vile, slimy lives, like those of the torpid lizards in yonder stagnant water-butt.–Lost? There is a curious point for you to settle, my friend, who study psychology in a lazy, dilettante way. Stop a moment. I am going to be honest. This is what I want you to do. I want you to hide your disgust, take no heed to your clean clothes, and come right down with me,—here, into the thickest of the fog and mud and foul effluvia. I want you to hear this story. There is a secret down here, in this nightmare fog, that has lain dumb for centuries: I want to make it a real thing to you. You, Egoist, or Pantheist, or Arminian, busy in making straight paths for your feet on the hills, do not see it clearly,—this terrible question which men here have gone mad and died trying to answer. I dare not put this secret into words. I told you it was dumb. These men, going by with drunken faces and brains full of unawakened power, do not ask it of Society or of God. Their lives ask it; their deaths ask it. There is no reply. I will tell you plainly that I have a great hope; and I bring it to you to be tested. It is this: that this terrible dumb question is its own reply; that it is not the sentence of death we think it, but, from the very extremity of its darkness, the most solemn prophecy which the world has known of the Hope to come. I dare make my meaning no clearer, but will only tell my story. It will, perhaps, seem to you as foul and dark as this thick vapor about us, and as pregnant with death; but if your eyes are free as mine are to look deeper, no perfume-tinted dawn will be so fair with promise of the day that shall surely come.

ELLEN SWALLOW RICHARDS, *Transcript to Women's Education Association* (1877)

MIT was opened for only five years when Ellen Swallow Richards (1842–1911) applied for admission to further her studies in chemistry. She graduated in 1873 and was admitted to the faculty in what would be a permanent second-class status, an entry-level rank of junior faculty, despite her outstanding scientific achievement. At a time when male academics such as Dr. Edward Clarke of Harvard expressed doubts that women were capable of intellectual achievement, Richards defied gender norms and entered the male preserve of chemical investigation. She conducted scientific experiments and worked for a decade investigating water quality in Massachusetts. She applied her chemical training to the emerging field of public health. Her interest in the interdependence of the natural and built environments and the impact of the environment on heath led to her development of the construct of ecology. She also applied science to domesticity, which expressed her own acceptance of the era's gendered notions of women's appropriate home-centered concerns. Among multiple achievements, she warned housewives about health hazards in the home environment introduced by new laborsaving technology.

In the following document, Richards discusses her role in promoting scientific education for women. MIT reluctantly allowed a separate women's chemistry lab. MIT provided space, but the Women's Education Association provided the financing for the research equipment. Although not part of the women's rights movement, Richards believed that scientific education for women was a key to female empowerment. What specific arguments did she make in her support for women's scientific advancement?*

---

* In the public domain.

Massachusetts Institute of Technology, Women's Laboratory, 1876–1883

Transcription of the first report by Ellen S. Richards to the Women's Education Association, 1877

It is always pleasant to us to have our prophecies fulfilled and especially pleasant when some doubt has been expressed as to the probability of fulfillment. I hope to be pardoned therefore if I seem to boast of the fulfillment of my own predictions. I recall so clearly a conversation with two officers of the association on the morning on which we paid over the last installment of money collected for the Laboratory and while both of the ladies were very much interested in the plan and delighted with the hearty response given to their appeal they both expressed their doubts as to the result. One said to me: I wish I could feel as sure as you do that there are women who do really want this kind of opportunity. When I said that I felt perfectly sure of 15 students during the first year; both exclaimed oh if there are 8 or 10 I shall be quite happy and think the money well spent.

The rooms were not open until the last of October and were not advertised outside of the Association except by a few circulars sent to friends of the members and to contributors. At this date we have had 23 students in the Chemical Laboratory, 10 or 12 other applicants failed to come by reason of sickness, inability to pay, or insufficient preparation. Some 15 are already enrolled for next year.

Doubt as to the success of the enterprise was also expressed in another way. Those who have had experience with the free science classes said that we should find the number of those who were willing to pay for their instruction very small. This statement was not far from the truth if we substitute "able" for "willing". Of the 23 only 5 (as far as I am able to judge) have been in a condition to pay the fee without sacrifice and self denial. This makes the number who spend much time in Laboratory quite small. They study as much as possible outside and gain as much as they can in an afternoon. While this increases the *usefulness* of the Laboratory it materially lessens its income, the receipts from the 23 students will hardly be equal to the amount received from 5 regular students.

Some statement as to the class of work done may interest us. First in importance we may place that of aid rendered to the teachers. During Nov. and Dec. the Laboratory had the honor to number among its students our friend from Smith College later her successor at Wellesley and that lady's successor at Framingham Normal. The teacher of sciences at Bradford Academy spent a month with us. 3 teachers of chemistry at the Girls High School have given Saturdays to practical work. 7 others are looking forward to becoming teachers of science. These students have been given work which would illustrate principles and merely facts. All their instruction has had for its end the broadening of their ideas of science and fitting them thus to impress on their pupils the depths of the channel and not merely its surface breadth as is so apt to be the result of popular scientific teaching. Of the remaining number—2 are engaged in original research. 3 are studying for the use they may put it to in the future but with no definite aim for the immediate future. Their work is more strictly educational and had a more direct bearing on their own minds. We have 4 married women—3 of them with families of children from 5 to 18 years old. The aid that the Laboratory has been able to give them has been to me its pleasured feature, the proof of its truly broad and liberal character.

I have felt the greatest satisfaction in opening the treasures of our store-house to two of theses ladies in particular. One is studying in order to become a physician. Her husband is a doctor of long practice and I presume a very intelligent man—but he sees the defects in the education of his early days and wishes her to have the best of modern times. In the two months that she stayed with us we gave her an insight into microscopical work as well as some practice in the theoretical and medical chemistry and taught her to read scientific German with the aid of a dictionary. We feel that superficial and slight as was the actual amount of knowledge she gained it will nevertheless make her a far more intelligent and thoughtful pupil of the medical school to which she is going.

The other lady has been studying mineralogy only but this case deserves notice because of the possibility of many others taking courage to carry out even at a late day their early longings. . . .

I have been over the ground thus minutely in order to show you the variety of work made possible in this one little room with earnest workers therein. Even if the belief of people in general that woman's mind is not capable of deep scientific thought is proved true—yet we must acknowledge that the valleys and foot-hills of science are very attractive to the feminine mind even if they can never hope to scale the heights snow capped above them.

I will hazard the statement that when the opportunities are equal $\frac{4}{5}$ of the intelligent girls will choose science and will become industrious workers in the field of observation, gathering together heaps of facts from which their superiors may build generalizations.

The other more expensive room, the Optical Laboratory has not yet been perfected. The other room required so much more time than we anticipated by reason of the number and variety of pupils that we have made slow progress.

Nevertheless the Institute class in Vegetable Physiology numbering 8 or 9—the Boston University class in Botany and 3 gentlemen have been accommodated there in a far better manner than would have been possible in any other place in Boston. 6 or 8 of the students in chemistry have also availed themselves of its privileges by employing 2 to 4 hours a week in this way.

As to the future prospects, this Optical Laboratory promises the widest field when it becomes known. It proposes to occupy an entirely new field, looking toward Biology from the Chemical side—not supplanting the work of Biological Laboratories but sending to them for better prepared pupils—

The old adage well begun is half done has much truth in it—We can certainly call this new enterprise well begun and as one of the Trustees said last—it will be easier to let it go on than to stop it.

"In Behalf of Clean Streets" Transactions of the National Council of Women of the United States, (1891)

This report focuses on women's urban reform objectives to create a sanitary and safe environment in New York City. The women's words illuminate not only the fundamental objectives of municipal housekeeping but also attitudes about the need to "combat the ignorance, incompetency, and apathy of men in official positions." How do the women evaluate their role? What does this article tell us about the women's roles in the public sphere? What accomplishments gave the reformers particular pride?*

---

* In the public domain.

No earnest reformer can avoid "having a shy" at the condition of the streets of New York. The women put better street-cleaning in the forefront of their endeavors for 1887. The chairman of the committee on this subject investigated the whole matter in foreign and American cities, and proposed a plan of cleaning which Mr. Coleman, then the Commissioner of Street-Cleaning, several physicians, and various sanitary experts approved as practical, economical, and efficient. The plan was then submitted in a memorial to Mayor Hewitt, who expressed himself as much pleased with many of the suggestions, and advised Mr. Coleman to act upon them. As long as Mr. Coleman did so there was a marked improvement in the condition of the streets, and especially of the sidewalks, where the ash-barrel and garbage nuisance was reduced to a minimum.

In 1888 the women organized a public meeting at Chickering Hall in furtherance of this reform, Judge C. P. Daly presiding. In 1889 the women importuned Mayor Grant and his street-cleaning commissioners to do something for the city's dirty thoroughfares, but only "received polite attention, with promises for the future, which"—the women pathetically say in their last report— "we are still looking forward to have fulfilled." Following the policy of gathering information and massing scientific authorities when unable to do anything else, the women engaged General Egbert L. Viele to inspect and report on the Merz crematory at Buffalo. There all the garbage and kitchens' refuse of the city is, instead of being dumped, at once destroyed by fire or converted into whatever economic elements it may possess. General Viele's report was wholly in favor of the adoption of this method in this city,—garbage, he said, being the most offensive and deadly of all the kinds of refuse which accumulate in large cities.

The forces that the Association has constantly to combat are chiefly the ignorance, incompetency, and apathy of men in official positions. A bare enumeration of the remaining directions in which the women have exerted their reforming zeal must suffice. They have successfully striven to improve the hygiene of the public schools. They anticipated the Board of Health in recognizing the contamination of the Croton watersheds at Brewsters as the probable cause of diseases prevalent in the city in 1888. They have, with other organizations, persistently pressed the matter of the appointment of women as factory inspectors and as matrons at police-stations. They have brought to the attention of the Board of Health and caused the abolition of nuisances arising from the sewers of the city. They suppressed a bone-boiling establishment which had long been a source of intolerable annoyance to surrounding residents. In fact, wherever they have found an evil in any way detrimental to health they have lent their aid in suppressing it. Among the enlightened part of the community they have met with encouragement and assistance, and they say in their last report, "we thank the Board of Health for their prompt attention to all of our complaints." From eleven members at organization, the Association has grown in five years to a membership of seven hundred.

We propose to go on with our work until we force the men, whose large salaries we are taxed to pay, to do their work and give a clean city, or turn over the whole matter to us, who will see that the coming generations have at least pure air, clean streets, healthful food, and in God's good time bring about the millennium. . . .

After the benediction the National Council of Women of the United States adjourned.

ALICE HAMILTON, *Autobiography, Exploring the Dangerous Trades* (1943)

Born into an affluent family, Alice Hamilton (1869–1970) attended college and pursued medical studies in the United States and Europe. She was the first woman faculty member hired by Harvard Medical School. Her acceptance was contingent on her assignment to a permanent subordinate status. Gender bias held greater significance for Harvard than for Hamilton, despite her record of public service and national recognition in the field of industrial medicine. As the only female faculty member, she was banned from marching in graduation processions and remained in the entry-level position of assistant professor from the time she was hired at age fifty until her retirement sixteen years later.

Although Hamilton developed the fields of industrial medicine and the scientific investigation of workplace toxicity, the first female factory workers in the Lowell Mills had previously associated work-related illnesses to unsafe factory conditions, including the lack of ventilation, fibers in the air, and hazardous machinery. Hamilton devoted most of her long career in a struggle to have management acknowledge responsibility and reduce toxicity from the industrial workplace. How did she assess her own contributions? What role did her Hull House residency play in her subsequent career? According to Hamilton's evidence, why did it take so long to protect industrial workers from poisonous substances?*

It was also my experience at Hull-House that aroused my interest in industrial diseases. Living in a working-class quarter, coming in contact with laborers and their wives, I could not fail to hear tales of the dangers that workingmen faced, of cases of carbon-monoxide gassing in the great steel mills, of painters disabled by lead palsy, of pneumonia and rheumatism among the men in the stockyards. Illinois then had no legislation providing compensation for accident or disease caused by occupation. (There is something strange in speaking of "accident and sickness compensation." What could "compensate" anyone for an amputated leg or a paralyzed arm, or even an attack of lead colic, to say nothing of the loss of a husband or son?) There was a striking occurrence about this time in Chicago which brought vividly before me the unprotected, helpless state of workingmen who were held responsible for their own safety.

A group of men were sent out in a tug to one of Chicago's pumping stations in Lake Michigan and left there while the tug returned to shore. A fire broke out on the tiny island

and could not be controlled, the men had the choice between burning to death and drowning, and before rescue could arrive most of them were drowned. The contracting company, which employed them, generously paid the funeral expenses, and nobody expected them to do more. Widows and orphans must turn to the County Agent or private charity—that was the accepted way, back in the dark ages of the early twentieth century. William Hard, then a young college graduate living at Northwestern Settlement, wrote of this incident with a fiery pen, contrasting the treatment of the wives and children of these men whose death was caused by negligence with the treatment they would have received in Germany. His article and a copy of Sir Thomas Oliver's Dangerous Trades, which came into my hands just then, sent me to the Crerar Library to read everything I could find on the dangers to industrial workers, and what could be done to protect them. But it was all German, or British, Austrian, Dutch, Swiss, even Italian or Spanish—everything but American. In those countries industrial

---

* In the public domain.

medicine was a recognized branch of the medical sciences; in my own country it did not exist. When I talked to my medical friends about the strange silence on this subject in American medical magazines and textbooks, I gained the impression that here was a subject tainted with Socialism or with feminine sentimentality for the poor. The American Medical Association had never had a meeting devoted to this subject, and except for a few surgeons attached to large companies operating steel mills, or railways, or coal mines, there were no medical men in Illinois who specialized in the field of industrial medicine.

Everyone with whom I talked assured me that the foreign writings could not apply to American conditions, for our workmen were so much better paid, their standard of living was so much higher, and the factories they worked in so much finer in every way than the European, that they did not suffer from the evils to which the poor foreigner was subject. That sort of talk always left me skeptical. It was impossible for me to believe that conditions in Europe could be worse than they were in the Polish section of Chicago, and in many Italian and Irish tenements, or that any workshops could be worse than some of those I had seen in our foreign quarters. And presently I had factual confirmation of my disbelief in the happy lot of the American worker through the reading of John Andrews's manuscript on "phossy jaw" in the match industry in the United States.

Phossy jaw is a very distressing form of industrial disease. It comes from breathing the fumes of white or yellow phosphorus, which gives off fumes at room temperature, or from putting into the mouth food or gum or fingers smeared with phosphorus. Even drinking from a glass which has stood on the workbench is dangerous. The phosphorus penetrates into a defective tooth and down through the roots to the jawbone, killing the tissue cells which then become the prey of suppurative germs from the mouth, and abscesses form. The jaw swells and the pain is intense, for the suppuration is held in by the tight covering of the bone and cannot escape, except through a surgical operation or through a fistula boring to the surface. Sometimes the abscess forms in the upper jaw and works up into the orbit, causing the loss of an eye. In severe cases one lower jawbone may have to be removed, or an upper jawbone—perhaps both. There are cases on record of men and women who had to live all the rest of their days on liquid food. The scars and contractures left after recovery were terribly disfiguring, and led some women to commit suicide. Here was an industrial disease which could be clearly demonstrated to the most skeptical. Miss Addams told me that when she was in London in the 1880s she went to a mass meeting of protest against phossy jaw and on the platform were a number of pitiful cases, showing their scars and deformities.

All this I had learned, but I had been assured by medical men, who claimed to know, that there was no phossy jaw in the United States because American match factories were so scrupulously clean. Then in 1908 John Andrews came to Hull House and showed me the report of his investigation of American match factories and his discovery of more than 150 cases of phossy jaw. It seems that in the course of a study of wages of women and children made by the Bureau of Labor, under Carroll Wright, investigators came across cases of phossy jaw in women match workers in the South. This impelled Wright to institute an investigation in other match centers. Andrews was asked to carry it out and did so, with a result most disconcerting to American optimism. Some of the cases he discovered were quite as severe as the worst reported in European literature—the loss of jawbones, of an eye, sometimes death from blood poisoning.

This episode in the history of industrial disease is very characteristic of our American way of dealing with such matters. We learned about phossy jaw almost as soon as Europe did. The first recognized case was described by

Lorinser of Vienna in 1845; the first American case was treated in the Massachusetts General Hospital only six years later, in 1851. Bust while all over continental Europe and England there was eager discussion of this new disease, many cases were reported and all sorts of preventive measures proposed, practically nothing was published in American medical journals from 1851 to 1909, both laymen and public health authorities contenting themselves with the assurance that all was well in our match industry. When, however, the facts were at last made public in 1909, action was prompt. A safe substitute for white phosphorus had been discovered by a French chemist, the sesquisulphide, the American patent rights for which had been bought by the Diamond Match Company. This company with rare generosity, waived its patent rights and allowed the free use of sesquisulphide to the whole industry, and this made it possible for Congress to pass the Esch law, which imposed a tax on white-hosphorus matches high enough to cover the difference in cost between them and sesquisulphide matches. So phossy jaw disappeared from American match factories. . . .

We were staggered by the complexity of the problem we faced and we soon decided to limit our field almost entirely to the occupational poisons, for at least we knew what their action was, while the action of the various kinds of dust, and of temperature extremes and heavy exertion, was only vaguely known at that time. Then we looked for an expert to guide and supervise the study, but none was to be found and so I was asked to do what I could as managing director of the survey, with the help of twenty young assistants, doctors, medical students, and social workers. As I look back on it now, our task was simple compared with the one that a state nowadays faces when it undertakes a similar study. The only poisons we had to cover were lead, arsenic, brass, carbon monoxide, the cyanides, and turpentine. Nowadays, the list involved in a survey of the painters' trade alone is many times as long as that.

But to us it seemed far from a simple task. We could not even discover what were the poisonous occupations in Illinois. The Factory Inspector's office was blissfully ignorant, yet that was the only governmental body concerned with working conditions. There was nothing to do but begin with trades we knew were dangerous and hope that, as we studied them, we would discover others less well known.

MARY HUNTER AUSTIN, *The Land of Little Rain* (1903)

Mary Hunter Austin (1868–1934) moved with her family from Illinois to California when she was still a child. She lived for most of her adult life in desert environment of Southern California. Her deep love and abiding respect for the natural desert environment matched that of John Muir for Yosemite. Her wilderness sensibility was not filtered through the screen of the era's conventional maternal rhetoric. She possessed a deep appreciation for the desert environment and the American Indian way of life in which humans interacted with the natural environment without dominating it. Austin expressed views that contradicted the deeply rooted values of progress based on the mastery of nature. She portrayed the negative role of human interference and the toll taken from extracting wealth and creating commercially profitable enterprise regardless of the resulting environmental degradation.

What example does Austin provide of environmental interdependence and the relationship between Indians and the desert environment?*

---

* In the public domain.

Shoshone Land

It is true I have been in Shoshone Land, but before that, long before, I had seen it through the eyes of Winnenap' in a rosy mist of reminiscence, and must always see it with a sense of intimacy in the light that never was. Sitting on the golden slope at the campoodie, looking across the Bitter Lake to the purple tops of Mutarango, the medicine-man drew up its happy places one by one, like little blessed islands in a sea of talk. For he was born a Shoshone, was Winnenap'; and though his name, his wife, his children, and his tribal relations were of the Paiutes, his thoughts turned homesickly toward Shoshone Land. Once a Shoshone always a Shoshone. Winnenap' lived gingerly among the Paiutes and in his heart despised them. But he could speak a tolerable English when he would, and he always would if it were of Shoshone Land.

He had come into the keeping of the Paiutes as a hostage for the long peace which the authority of the whites made interminable, and, though there was now no order in the tribe, nor any power that could have lawfully restrained him, kept on in the old usage, to save his honor and the word of his vanished kin. He had seen his children's children in the borders of the Paiutes, but loved best his own miles of sand and rainbow-painted hills. Professedly he had not seen them since the beginning of his hostage; but every year about the end of the rains and before the strength of the sun had come upon us from the south, the medicine-man went apart on the mountains to gather herbs, and when he came again I knew by the new fortitude of his countenance and the new color of his reminiscences that he had been alone and unspied upon in Shoshone Land.

To reach that country from the campoodie, one goes south and south, within hearing of the lip-lip-lapping of the great tideless lake, and south by east over a high rolling district, miles and miles of sage and nothing else. So one comes to the country of the painted hills,—old red cones of craters, wasteful beds of mineral earths, hot, acrid springs, and steam jets issuing from a leprous soil. After the hills the black rock, after the craters the spewed lava, ash strewn, of incredible thickness, and full of sharp, winding rifts. There are picture writings carved deep in the face of the cliffs to mark the way for those who do not know it. On the very edge of the black rock the earth falls away in a wide sweeping hollow, which is Shoshone Land.

South the land rises in very blue hills, blue because thickly wooded with ceanothus and manzanita, the haunt of deer and the border of the Shoshones. Eastward the land goes very far by broken ranges, narrow valleys of pure desertness, and huge mesas uplifted to the sky-line, east and east, and no man knows the end of it.

It is the country of the bighorn, the wapiti, and the wolf, nesting place of buzzards, land of cloud-nourished trees and wild things that live without drink. Above all, it is the land of the creosote and the mesquite. The mesquite is God's best thought in all this desertness. It grows in the open, is thorny, stocky, close grown, and iron-rooted. Long winds move in the draughty valleys, blown sand fills and fills about the lower branches, piling pyramidal dunes, from the top of which the mesquite twigs flourish greenly. Fifteen or twenty feet under the drift, where it seems no rain could penetrate, the main trunk grows, attaining often a yard's thickness, resistant as oak. In Shoshone Land one digs for large timber; that is in the southerly, sandy exposures. Higher on the tabletopped ranges low trees of juniper and piñon stand each apart, rounded and spreading heaps of greenness. Between them, but each to itself in smooth clear spaces, tufts of tall feathered grass.

This is the sense of the desert hills, that there is room enough and time enough. Trees grow to consummate domes; every plant has its perfect work. Noxious weeds such as come up thickly in crowded fields do not flourish in the free spaces. Live long enough with an Indian, and he or the wild things will show you a use for everything that grows in these borders.

The manner of the country makes the usage of life there, and the land will not be lived in except in its own fashion. The Shoshones live like their trees, with great spaces between, and in pairs and in family groups they set up wattled huts by the infrequent springs. More wickiups than two make a very great number. Their shelters are lightly built, for they travel much and far, following where deer feed and seeds ripen, but they are not more lonely than other creatures that inhabit there.

The year's round is somewhat in this fashion. After the piñon harvest the clans foregather on a warm southward slope for the annual adjustment of tribal difficulties and the medicine dance, for marriage and mourning and vengeance, and the exchange of serviceable information; if, for example, the deer have shifted their feeding ground, if the wild sheep have come back to Waban, or certain springs run full or dry. Here the Shoshones winter flockwise, weaving baskets and hunting big game driven down from the country of the deep snow. And this brief intercourse is all the use they have of their kind, for now there are no wars, and many of their ancient crafts have fallen into disuse. The solitariness of the life breeds in the men, as in the plants, a certain well-roundedness and sufficiency to its own ends. Any Shoshone family has in itself the man-seed, power to multiply and replenish, potentialities for food and clothing and shelter, for healing and beautifying.

When the rain is over and gone they are stirred by the instinct of those that journeyed eastward from Eden, and go up each with his mate and young brood, like birds to old nesting places. The beginning of spring in Shoshone Land—oh the soft wonder of it!—is a mistiness as of incense smoke, a veil of greenness over the whitish stubby shrubs, a web of color on the silver sanded soil. No counting covers the multitude of rayed blossoms that break suddenly underfoot in the brief season of the winter rains, with silky furred or prickly viscid foliage, or no foliage at all. They are morning and evening bloomers chiefly, and strong seeders. Years of scant rains they lie shut and safe in the winnowed sands, so that some species appear to be extinct. Years of long storms they break so thickly into bloom that no horse treads without crushing them. These years the gullies of the hills are rank with fern and a great tangle of climbing vines.

Just as the mesa twilights have their vocal note in the love call of the burrowing owl, so the desert spring is voiced by the mourning doves. Welcome and sweet they sound in the smoky mornings before breeding time, and where they frequent in any great numbers water is confidently looked for. Still by the springs one finds the cunning brush shelters from which the Shoshones shot arrows at them when the doves came to drink.

Rachel Carson, Excerpt from *Silent Spring* (1962)

The following document contains an excerpt from Rachel Carson's (1907–1964) compelling and controversial book *Silent Spring*, published in 1962. Carson trained as a marine biologist and was one of two women who worked for the U.S. Government Bureau of Fisheries. Written from the perspective of a concerned scientist with an accessible message for the general reader, she alerted the American public to the dangers of chemical contamination to human health, the natural habitat, and animals. Her book ignited fierce controversy in the pre-protest era of the early sixties. Stressing ecological interdependence, her message was a dire warning about impending planetary disaster. Defenders of pesticide usage and the chemical industry attacked her findings, wrapping their critique in sexist clichés and misogyny in their effort to depict her as a hysterical woman. In actuality, she applied her scientific training to warn the nation about environmental hazards and successfully challenged the post–World War II power of the chemical pesticide industry.

How would you summarize Carson's major concerns? What aspect of this excerpt from *Silent Spring* do you find most compelling? What did Carson mean by her comment that insecticides should more accurately be called "biocides"?*

There was once a town in the heart of America where all life seemed to live in harmony with its surroundings. The town lay in the midst of a checkerboard of prosperous farms, with fields of grain and hillsides of orchards where, in spring, white clouds of bloom drifted above the green fields. In autumn, oak and maple and birch set up a blaze of color that flamed and flickered across a backdrop of pines. Then foxes barked in the hills and deer silently crossed the fields, half hidden in the mists of the fall mornings. Along the roads, laurel, viburnum and alder, great ferns and wildflowers delighted the traveler's eye through much of the year. Even in winter the roadsides were places of beauty, where countless birds came to feed on the berries and on the seed heads of the dried weeds rising above the snow. The countryside was, in fact, famous for the abundance and variety of its bird life, and when the flood of migrants was pouring through in spring and fall people traveled from great distances to observe them. Others came to fish the streams, which flowed clear and cold out of the hills and contained shady pools where trout lay. So it had been from the days many years ago when the first settlers raised their houses, sank their wells, and built their barns.

Then a strange blight crept over the area and everything began to change. Some evil spell had settled on the community: mysterious maladies swept the flocks of chickens; the cattle and sheep sickened and died. Everywhere was a shadow of death. The farmers spoke of much illness among their families. In the town the doctors had become more and more puzzled by new kinds of sickness appearing among their patients. There had been several sudden and unexplained deaths, not only among adults but even among children, who would be stricken suddenly while at play and die within a few hours.

There was a strange stillness. The birds, for example—where had they gone? Many people spoke of them, puzzled and disturbed. The feeding stations in the backyards were deserted. The few birds seen anywhere were moribund; they trembled violently and could not fly. It was a spring without voices. On the mornings that had once throbbed with the dawn chorus of robins, catbirds, doves, jays, wrens, and scores of other bird voices there was now no sound; only silence lay over the fields and woods and marsh. . . .

It took hundreds of millions of years to produce the life that now inhabits the earth—eons of time in which that developing and evolving and diversifying life reached a state of adjustment and balance with its surroundings. The environment, rigorously shaping and directing the life it supported, contained elements that were hostile as well as supporting. Certain rocks gave out dangerous radiation; even within the light of the sun, from which all life draws its energy, there were short-wave radiations with power to injure. Given time—time not in years but in millennia—life adjusts, and a balance has been reached. For time is the essential ingredient; but in the modern world there is no time.

The rapidity of change and the speed with which new situations are created follow the impetuous and heedless pace of man

* From SILENT SPRING by Rachel Carson. Copyright © 1962 by Rachel L. Carson, renewed 1990 by Roger Christie. Reprinted by permission of Houghton Mifflin Harcourt Publishing Company. All rights reserved.

rather than the deliberate pace of nature. Radiation is no longer merely the background radiation of rocks, the bombardment of cosmic rays, the ultraviolet of the sun that have existed before there was any life on earth; radiation is now the unnatural creation of man's tampering with the atom. The chemicals to which life is asked to make its adjustment are no longer merely the calcium and silica and copper and all the rest of the minerals washed out of the rocks and carried in rivers to the sea; they are the synthetic creations of man's inventive mind, brewed in his laboratories, and having no counterparts in nature.

To adjust to these chemicals would require time on the scale that is nature's; it would require not merely the years of a man's life but the life of generations. And even this, were it by some miracle possible, would be futile, for the new chemicals come from our laboratories in an endless stream; almost five hundred annually find their way into actual use in the United States alone. The figure is staggering and its implications are not easily grasped—500 new chemicals to which the bodies of men and animals are required somehow to adapt each year, chemicals totally outside the limits of biologic experience.

Among them are many that are used in man's war against nature. Since the mid-1940's over 200 basic chemicals have been created for use in killing insects, weeds, rodents, and other organisms described in the modern vernacular as "pests"; and they are sold under several thousand different brand names.

These sprays, dusts, and aerosols are now applied almost universally to farms, gardens, forests, and homes—nonselective chemicals that have the power to kill every insect, the "good" and the "bad," to still the song of birds and the leaping of fish in the streams, to coat the leaves with a deadly film, and to linger on in soil—all this though the intended target may be only a few weeds or insects. Can anyone believe it is possible to lay down such a barrage of poisons on the surface of the earth without making it unfit for all life?

They should not be called "insecticides," but "biocides."

The whole process of spraying seems caught up in an endless spiral. Since DDT was released for civilian use, a process of escalation has been going on in which ever more toxic materials must be found. This has happened because insects, in a triumphant vindication of Darwin's principle of the survival of the fittest, have evolved super races immune to the particular insecticide used, hence a deadlier one has always to be developed—and then a deadlier one than that. It has happened also because . . . destructive insects often undergo a "flareback," or resurgence, after spraying, in numbers greater than before. Thus the chemical war is never won, and all life is caught in its violent crossfire.

Along with the possibility of the extinction of mankind by nuclear war, the central problem of our age has therefore become the contamination of man's total environment with such substances of incredible potential for harm—substances that accumulate in the tissues of plants and animals and even penetrate the germ cells to shatter or alter the very material of heredity upon which the shape of the future depends.

Rachel Carson (Erich Hartmann/Magnum Photos, Inc.)

TERRY TEMPEST WILLIAMS, *Clan of One-Breasted Women* (1991)

Terry Tempest Williams (b. 1955) is an author, conservationist, and environmental activist. The following document is an excerpt from her book, *An Unnatural History of Family and Place*. One of the unnatural occurrences that Williams recounts is the environmental calamity the U.S. government created by testing aboveground atomic bombs seemingly without regard for the consequences to human health. Williams describes how her Mormon background stressed obedience combined with trust in government. Her family remained unaware of nuclear testing and the hazards of radiation poisoning. The epilogue to her book is titled "Clan of One-Breasted Women" in recognition of the high incidence of breast cancer in her family that Tempest attributes to radiation contamination. Above ground testing occurred from 1951 to 1962; underground testing continued until 1992.

How does Williams describe the acceptance of nuclear testing? In what ways does her testimony express defiance of her community norms? How does she assess the government's responsibility to the residents of communities that were downwind of the test sites?*

I belong to a Clan of One-Breasted Women. My mother, my grandmothers, and six aunts have all had mastectomies. Seven are dead. The two who survive have just completed rounds of chemotherapy and radiation.

I've had my own problems: two biopsies for breast cancer and a small tumor between my ribs diagnosed as a "borderline malignancy."

This is my family history.

Most statistics tell us breast cancer is genetic, hereditary, with rising percentages attached to fatty diets, childlessness, or becoming pregnant after thirty. What they don't say is living in Utah may be the greatest hazard of all.

We are a Mormon family with roots in Utah since 1847. The "word of wisdom" in my family aligned us with good foods—no coffee, no tea, tobacco, or alcohol. For the most part, our women were finished having their babies by the time they were thirty. And only one faced breast cancer prior to 1960. Traditionally, as a group of people, Mormons have a low rate of cancer.

Is our family a cultural anomaly? The truth is, we didn't think about it. Those who did, usually the men, simply said, "bad genes."

The women's attitude was stoic. Cancer was part of life. On February 16, 1971, the eve of my mother's surgery, I accidently picked up the telephone and overheard her ask my grandmother what she could expect.

"Diane, it is one of the most spiritual experiences you will ever encounter."

I quietly put down the receiver.

Two days later, my father took my brothers and me to the hospital to visit her. She met us in the lobby in a wheelchair. No bandages were visible. I'll never forget her radiance, the way she held herself in a purple velvet robe, and how she gathered us around her.

"Children, I am fine. I want you to know I felt the arms of God around me."

We believed her. My father cried. Our mother, his wife, was thirty-eight years old.

A little over a year after Mother's death, Dad and I were having dinner together. He had just returned from St. George, where the Tempest Company was completing the gas lines that would service southern Utah. He spoke of his love for the country, the sandstoned landscape, bare-boned and beautiful. He had just finished hiking the Kolob trail in Zion National Park. We got caught up in reminiscing, recalling with fondness our

---

* "The Clan of One-Breasted Women" from *Refuge: An Unnatural History of Family and Place* by Terry Tempest Williams. Copyright © 2001 Vintage Books. Reprinted by permission.

walk up Angel's Landing on his fiftieth birthday and the years our family had vacationed there.

Over dessert, I shared a recurring dream of mine. I told my father that for years, as long as I could remember, I saw this flash of light in the night in the desert—that this image had so permeated my being that I could not venture south without seeing it again, on the horizon, illuminating buttes and mesas.

"You did see it," he said.

"Saw what?"

"The bomb. The cloud. We were driving home from Riverside, California. You were sitting on Diane's lap. She was pregnant. In fact, I remember the day, September 7, 1957. We had just gotten out of the Service. We were driving north, past Las Vegas. It was an hour or so before dawn, when this explosion went off. We not only heard it, but felt it. I thought the oil tanker in front of us had blown up. We pulled over and suddenly, rising from the desert floor, we saw it, clearly, this golden-stemmed cloud, the mushroom. The sky seemed to vibrate with an eerie pink glow. Within a few minutes, a light ash was raining on the car."

I stared at my father.

"I thought you knew that," he said. "It was a common occurrence in the fifties."

It was at this moment that I realized the deceit I had been living under. Children growing up in the American Southwest, drinking contaminated milk from contaminated cows, even from the contaminated breasts of their mothers, my mother—members, years later, of the Clan of One-Breasted Women.

It is a well-known story in the Desert West, "The Day We Bombed Utah," or more accurately, the years we bombed Utah: above ground atomic testing in Nevada took place from January 27, 1951 through July 11, 1962. Not only were the winds blowing north covering "low-use segments of the population" with fallout and leaving sheep dead in their tracks, but the climate was right. The United States of the 1950s was red, white, and blue.

The Korean War was raging. McCarthyism was rampant. Ike was it, and the cold war was hot. If you were against nuclear testing, you were for a communist regime.

Much has been written about this "American nuclear tragedy." Public health was secondary to national security. The Atomic Energy Commissioner, Thomas Murray, said, "Gentlemen, we must not let anything interfere with this series of tests, nothing."

Again and again, the American public was told by its government, in spite of burns, blisters, and nausea, "It has been found that the tests may be conducted with adequate assurance of safety under conditions prevailing at the bombing reservations." Assuaging public fears was simply a matter of public relations. "Your best action," an Atomic Energy Commission booklet read, "is not to be worried about fallout." A news release typical of the times stated, "We find no basis for concluding that harm to any individual has resulted from radioactive fallout."

On August 30, 1979, during Jimmy Carter's presidency, a suit was filed, *Irene Allen v. The United States of America*. Mrs. Allen's case was the first on an alphabetical list of twenty-four test cases, representative of nearly twelve hundred plaintiffs seeking compensation from the United States government for cancers caused by nuclear testing in Nevada.

Irene Allen lived in Hurricane, Utah. She was the mother of five children and had been widowed twice. Her first husband, with their two oldest boys, had watched the tests from the roof of the local high school. He died of leukemia in 1956. Her second husband died of pancreatic cancer in 1978.

In a town meeting conducted by Utah Senator Orrin Hatch, shortly before the suit was filed, Mrs. Allen said, "I am not blaming the government, I want you to know that, Senator Hatch. But I thought if my testimony could help in any way so this wouldn't happen again to any of the generations coming up after us . . . I am happy to be here this day to bear testimony of this." . . .

In Mormon culture, authority is respected, obedience is revered, and independent thinking is not. I was taught as a young girl not to "make waves" or "rock the boat."

"Just let it go," Mother would say. "You know how you feel, that's what counts."

For many years, I have done just that—listened, observed, and quietly formed my own opinions, in a culture that rarely asks questions because it has all the answers. But one by one, I have watched the women in my family die common, heroic deaths. We sat in waiting rooms hoping for good news, but always receiving the bad. I cared for them, bathed their scarred bodies, and kept their secrets. I watched beautiful women become bald as Cytoxan, cisplatin, and Adriamycin were injected into their veins. I held their foreheads as they vomited green-black bile, and I shot them with morphine when the pain became inhuman. In the end, I witnessed their last peaceful breaths, becoming a midwife to the rebirth of their souls.

The price of obedience has become too high.

The fear and inability to question authority that ultimately killed rural communities in Utah during atmospheric testing of atomic weapons is the same fear I saw in my mother's body. Sheep. Dead sheep. The evidence is buried.

I cannot prove that my mother, Diane Dixon Tempest, or my grandmothers, Lettie Romney Dixon and Kathryn Blackett Tempest, along with my aunts developed cancer from nuclear fallout in Utah. But I can't prove they didn't.

My father's memory was correct. The September blast we drove through in 1957 was part of Operation Plumbbob, one of the most intensive series of bomb tests to be initiated. The flash of light in the night in the desert, which 1 had always thought was a dream, developed into a family nightmare. It took fourteen years, from 1957 to 1971, for cancer to manifest in my mother—the same time, Howard L. Andrews, an authority in radioactive fallout at the National Institute of Health, says radiation cancer requires to become evident. The more I learn about what it means to be a "downwinder," the more questions I drown in.

What I do know, however, is that as a Mormon woman of the fifth generation of Latter-day Saints, I must question everything, even if it means losing my faith, even if it means becoming a member of a border tribe among my own people. Tolerating blind obedience in the name of patriotism or religion ultimately takes our lives.

When the Atomic Energy Commission described the country north of the Nevada Test Site as "virtually uninhabited desert terrain," my family and the birds at Great Salt Lake were some of the "virtual uninhabitants."

LOIS GIBBS, *Learning From Love Canal: 20th Anniversary Retrospective* (1998)

Lois Gibbs's (b. 1946) life followed the predictable pattern of the American dream of home ownership and suburban living, albeit on a modest scale. What propelled her into activism was the issue of toxic contamination of the neighborhood school and homes in Love Canal, in Niagara, New York—a suburban development with more than twenty thousand tons of toxic chemicals leaching into the water, soil, basements of homes, and the neighborhood school. Hooker Chemical, a subsidiary of Occidental Petroleum, had dumped and buried the chemical waste in the unfinished Love Canal and donated a toxic landfill for a neighborhood school. Hooker Chemical had left the area, and issues of accountability and restitution to homeowners remained uncertain.

Lois Gibbs played a key role in the mobilization of homeowners. Community mothers moved from victims to politically engaged activists and eventually achieved government-funded relocation of families nearest the contamination. In the process, they also learned that government officials might not have community health needs on their agendas. Gibbs's commitment to environmentalism became a full-time career, and she is the founder and director of the Center for Health, Environment and Justice.

What specific maternal issues served as the catalyst for Gibbs's activism? What according to Gibbs are the lessons of Love Canal contamination regarding government's responsibility to communities faced with environmental peril? In what ways is Gibbs's assessment of government similar to that of Williams?*

Twenty years ago the nation was jolted awake when a blue-collar community uncovered a serious public health crisis resulting from the burial of chemical wastes in their small suburban neighborhood. As the events unfolded, network television, radio, and print media covered the David and Goliath struggle in Love Canal, New York. The country watched as mothers with children in their arms and tears in their eyes cried out for help.

The words "Love Canal" are now burned in our country's history and in the memory of the public as being synonymous with chemical exposures and their adverse human health effects. The events at Love Canal brought about a new understanding among the American people of the correlation between low-level chemical exposures and birth defects, miscarriages, and incidences of cancer. The citizens of Love Canal provided an example of how a blue-collar community with few resources can win against great odds (a multi-billion-dollar international corporation and an unresponsive government), using the power of the people in our democratic system.

Now, 20 years later, science has shown that some of the same chemicals found at Love Canal are present in our food, water, and air. As important now as ever, the main lesson to be learned from the Love Canal crisis is that in order to protect public health from chemical contamination, there

needs to be a massive outcry . . . a choir of voices by the American people demanding change. . . .

In October cleanup began on the dump site. A drainage trench was installed around the perimeter of the canal to catch waste that was permeating into the surrounding neighborhood. A clay cap was placed on top of the site to reduce water infiltration from rain or melting snow. Sewer lines and the creek to the north of the canal were also cleaned up. However, the waste that had migrated throughout the neighborhood and into the homes remained.

At that time, there were approximately 660 families living in the community who were not given the option to relocate. They continued to pressure the governor and federal authorities, including President Carter, to expand the evacuation area. A health study was conducted by volunteer scientists and community members, revealing that 56 percent of children born between 1974 and 1978 suffered birth defects. The miscarriage rate increased 300 percent among women who had moved to Love Canal. And urinary-tract disease had also increased 300 percent, with a great number of children being affected. . . .

It is unfortunate that every action at Love Canal, from the first health study to the final evacuation, was taken for political reasons. Members of LCHA [Love Canal Homeowners Association] truly believe that

---

* Lois Gibbs, "Learning from Love Canal: 20th Anniversary Retrospective," *Orion Afield,* spring 1998. Copyright © 1998 Lois Gibbs. Published by The Orion Society.

if we hadn't assembled this large, strong citizen organization, we would still be living at Love Canal, with authorities still maintaining that there are no health problems. There are many reasons why the various levels of government did not want to evacuate the people in this community. These reasons include:

- The expense incurred. Together, state and federal governments spent over $60 million on Love Canal, which was later repaid by Occidental Chemical through a government lawsuit.
- The precedent that would be set by evacuating a neighborhood because of chemical exposures. At the time, there were an estimated 30–50,000 similar sites scattered across the nation.
- The lack of peer-reviewed scientific studies. The scientific understanding of human health effects resulting from exposure to low-level chemicals had been based on adult workers exposed over a 40-hour work-week, while at Love Canal the threat was residential, involving pregnant women and children exposed to multiple chemicals 24 hours a day.

Eventually, the 239 homes closest to the canal were demolished and the southern sections of the neighborhood declared unsuitable for residential use. But in September 1988, the 200 homes in the northern section of Love Canal were declared "habitable," which should not be confused with "safe." This decision to move people back into Love Canal is an appalling idea that cannot be justified by legitimate scientific or technical data. These homes are still contaminated, as are the yards around the adjacent evacuated homes. The only separation between them and those still considered uninhabitable is a suburban street. Anyone can freely cross the street and walk through the abandoned sections of the neighborhood. In fact, children ride their bikes and play frequently among the abandoned homes. And 20,000 tons of waste still remain in the dump.

The world is a very different place now for families who lived through the Love Canal crisis. What was once taken for granted is no longer—that if you work hard, pay your taxes, vote on election days, and teach your children right from wrong, you can achieve the American Dream. Eyes were opened to the way our democracy works—and doesn't work. Former residents of this blue-collar community have come to see that corporate power and influence are what dictated the actions at Love Canal, not the health and welfare of citizens.

Each step in the events as they unfolded shocked and stunned the public. It was not conceivable to families that their government would lie or manipulate data and studies to protect corporate interests. It was difficult to grasp the reality—obvious, in retrospect—that corporations have more influence and rights than taxpaying citizens. This realization left us feeling alone, abandoned, and empty inside. Love Canal taught us that government will protect you from such poisoning only when you force it to.

If you think you're safe, think again. And, if you're ever in doubt about what a company is doing, or what government is telling you, talk with your neighbors, seek out the truth beyond the bland reassurances of the authorities, and don't be afraid to dig your heels in to protect your community. The number of children with cancer is increasing, as are the incidences of breast and prostate cancer in adults. Children suffer more today than ever before from birth defects, learning disabilities, attention-deficit disorders, and asthma. These diseases and adverse health problems are no longer located in someone else's backyard; they're in everyone's backyard, and in our food, water, and the air we breathe.

THEO COLBORN, Our Stolen Future, *"Theo Colborn Reflects on Working Toward Peace"* (1995)

Theo Colborn (b. 1927) has been compared to Rachel Carson in continuing the whistle-blower tradition of creating public awareness of the damage to all forms of life from chemical contamination. Colborn's specific focus of concern is synthetic hormones, which she believes are endocrine disrupters, a cause of cancer, and damaging to prenatal cognitive development. Her endocrine disruption hypothesis provides evidence that hormones pervade the environment from conception to birth and throughout life. Her scientific research began with the impact of pollution on wildlife in the Great Lakes area. Like Rachel Carson, she studied environmental interdependence and links between animals and humans.

Why does Colborn depict the womb as an environmental site? In what way are Colborn's core values similar to those of Rachel Carson?*

Of all nature's masterpieces, the newborn, whether fish, bird, mammal, or human, is surely the most exquisite. This wondrous creature is testimony to the peace and harmony that existed in the womb, or the egg, prior to its entering the world. For centuries, humankind considered the womb environment sacred, free of violence and trespass. In that prenatal environment, with unbelievable precision, cells replicate, move about, and form buds and limbs and brains and sensory and reproductive organs, contributing to the most miraculous phenomenon on earth. From the moment the sperm enters the egg, embryonic development is orchestrated by the endocrine system using chemical messengers called hormones. With symphonic precision and harmony, constantly shifting hormonal blends instruct cells when to divide and where to move. Like the music from a grand organ, the tunes of these hormonal chords direct the formation of tissues and flesh, and even tell tissues when to die back after the tissue is no longer needed.

And now, within the past decade, chemists have been able to measure the infinitesimally small concentrations of hormones that conduct development from conception through birth. The endocrine system is so fine-tuned that it depends upon hormones in concentrations as little as a tenth of a trillionth of a gram to control the womb environment, as inconspicuous as one second in 3,169 centuries. The endocrine system also controls reproduction and thus assured the integrity and survival of species since life first evolved on earth—until humankind unwittingly produced synthetic chemicals that invade the security of the womb and create dissonance rather than harmony.

Peace begins in the womb. The newborn reflects this truth. Order is transferred from cell to tissue, to organs, to organisms, to families, communities, and nations. Unfortunately, when development is violated in the womb by man-made chemicals, the newborn is compromised. For animals in the wild, their survival is threatened. They can disappear without our ever knowing why. For humans, such exposure can lead to reduced intelligence, discontent, failure, and the inability to socially integrate. Man-made chemicals deprive societies of responsible leaders and thinkers. The social and economic impacts are incalculable. Widespread loss of security in the womb can lead to loss of stability at the national and international level.

Humans in their race to space have diverted attention and limited resources

---

* "Theo Colburn reflects on working toward peace." Copyright Theo Colburn. Published by Markkula Center for Applied Ethics.

away from learning about the workings of the inner world from which life evolves. As we have searched in outer space, we seem to have forgotten the inner space, from which all humankind emerges. The thirst to learn more about the solar system than the system in which we all resided prior to birth has left humankind vulnerable. The same technology that made space exploration possible and created modern society has led to production of chemicals that invade the womb. In our ignorance we assumed that the womb was inviolable, while at the same time we produced more and more synthetic chemicals to improve the quality of our lives. We also assumed that since these man-made products did not rapidly induce cancer, they were safe. We also thought that the lakes, oceans, soil, and atmosphere would assimilate infinite amounts of waste from the new technologies.

Disregard for the environment has been rampant on a global scale. Now, as we begin the twenty-first century, we are suddenly faced with the realization that wherever we have destroyed the environment, we have left behind desperation, hunger, fear, and strife. To this we must add another legacy of the chemical industry: the invasion of the inner environment of all animals on earth, including humans. From the Arctic to the Antarctic, man-made chemicals are found in all animal tissue. No longer is the offspring secure in the womb. No child born today is free of man-made chemicals. Mothers share these chemicals through their blood with the babies developing in their wombs. There are no cures for a child whose vital physiological, immunological, and neurological systems did not develop normally. When society takes heed and spends more on infrastructures for prevention than on remediation and healing, stability and integrity can be restored in the womb. Nations of the world must unite with a single purpose to restore peace in the inner world, assuring every newborn the opportunity to reach his or her fullest potential.

MARGIE EUGENE RICHARD, *Taking Our Human Rights Struggle to Geneva*

Margie Eugene Richard (b. 1942) was born and raised in Norco, Louisiana, in an African American neighborhood called Old Diamond, but popularly known as "Cancer Alley" because of the unusually high incidence of cancer. In southeastern Louisiana, near the Mississippi River, a conglomeration of oil refineries released toxic fumes into the air and poisoned nearby communities of color for decades. Richard was propelled into activism as a result of a lifetime in a contaminated environment that grew more toxic and damaging to health as Shell Oil increased the size of its plant. Many of the families that continued to live in the area were too poor to move away to a safer environment.

In 1989, Richard organized Concerned Citizens of Norco with the objective of holding the Shell Oil Company accountable for pollution and lack of worker safety. The grassroots activism of women of color is currently nationwide. In this case, the search for environmental justice involved a global giant corporation, Royal Dutch Shell Company Oil, which over the years created a toxic environment that poisoned the air, releasing two million pounds of toxic fumes annually. Chronic damage to the environment and human health escalated with refinery explosions and hazardous chemical spills. In recognition of her environmental leadership, Richard won the Goldman prize for environmental achievement in 2004.

Why does Richard consider the community crusade against Shell Oil a human rights issue? What evidence does she offer that there is an explicit racial component?*

---

* Margie Eugene Richard, "Taking our human rights struggle to Geneva." Copyright © Sierra Club Books.

I am the president of Concerned Citizens of Norco. My hometown is located in the southeastern section of Louisiana along the Mississippi River. In 1926 the Royal Dutch/Shell Group purchased 460 acres of the town called Sellers and began building its oil refinery. When Shell purchased the town of Sellers, which is now Norco, they displaced African American families from one section to another.

We are now surrounded by twenty-seven petrochemical and oil refineries, refineries like the one from which Norco received its name: Norco is an acronym for New Orleans Refinery Company. Our town is approximately one mile in diameter and is home to five thousand residents. The four streets near the Shell plants are occupied by African Americans; these streets are Washington, Cathy, Diamond, and East. My house is located on Washington Street and is only twenty-five feet away from the fence line of the fifteen-acre Shell chemical plant that expanded in 1955. Norco is situated between Shell's refinery on the east and Shell's chemical plant on the west. The entire town of Norco is only half the size of the oil refinery and chemical plant combined.

Nearly everyone in the community suffers from health problems caused by industry pollution. The air is contaminated with bad odors from carcinogens, and toxic chemicals such as benzene, toluene, sulfuric acid, ammonia, xylene, and propylene.

My sister died at the age of forty-three from an allergenic disease called sarcoidosis. This disease affects one in one thousand people in the United States, yet in Norco there are at least five known cases in fewer than five hundred people of color. My youngest daughter and her son suffer from severe asthma; my mother has breathing problems and must use a breathing machine daily. Many of the residents suffer from chronically sore muscles and cardiovascular, liver, and kidney diseases. Many die prematurely from poor health caused by pollution from toxic chemicals.

Please indulge me while I share with you a few stories that express some of our

fears, because these tragedies can happen at any moment, without notice. In 1973, a Shell pipeline exploded, killing Helen Washington and Joseph Jones. Washington was inside her home asleep and her neighbor, Jones, was cutting grass in his backyard; they both died from burns sustained from the explosion.

In 1988, an explosion at the Shell oil refinery created a nightmare. Houses collapsed. Afterward, people suffered from numerous health problems. The Shell explosion affected people up to thirty-seven miles away. In 1994, the oil refinery had a major acid spill. On May 10, 1998, a lime truck inside the company's chemical plant exploded and spilled the lime into the community. And on December 8, 1998, the chemical plant spilled methyl ethyl ketone into the community. Over the past decade, Shell has released over 2 million pounds of toxic chemicals each year.

Daily, we smell foul odors, hear loud noises, and see blazing flares and black smoke that emanates from those foul flares. The ongoing noisy operations and the endless traffic of huge trucks contribute to the discomfort of Norco citizens. We know that Shell and the U.S. government are responsible for the environmental racism in our community and other communities in the United States and many communities throughout this world. There must be an end to industrial pollution and environmental racism.

Even though we are U.S. citizens, our government does not protect us from environmental racism in the United States. I would like to see justice in action and an end to this struggle. Norco and many other communities of color across our nation suffer the same ills. We are not treated as citizens with equal rights according to U.S. law and international human rights law, especially the United Nations' International Convention on the Elimination of All Forms of Racial Discrimination, which our government ratified as the law of the land in 1994. I bring these issues before you to end support for these human rights violations by the United States. I propose that we take action to protect communities of color from being dumping places for industrial waste, because these deadly toxic substances cause poor health and a degraded environment. I also propose that we change the way human beings are mistreated by multinational corporations worldwide.

On July 5, 2002, Concerned Citizens of Norco celebrated the buyout of our community by Shell. Thirty years of intense community struggle culminated in sit-down meetings with Shell, in which the company finally built trust with local residents and produced a buyout plan for all families who wanted to move away from the company's plant in Norco. The plan is a model of respect for human dignity and community choice that Shell can and should replicate in all other troubled areas where it does business.

The environmental justice movement is made up largely of small, democratically run grassroots groups. It is important to note that women of color lead the vast majority of the grassroots environmental justice groups—a significant deviation from the leadership of national environmental and conservation organizations. Most women activists were pressed into duty because of environmental threats to their families, homes, communities, and workplaces. With meager financial resources, these women warriors have defied all odds. They have stayed focused, they have persevered, and, in many instances, they have won their battles. Their leadership emerged despite the racism and sexism that permeate the larger society and the environmental movement.

WINONA LADUKE, *UN Address, Beijing China, "The Indigenous Women's Network, Our Future, Our Responsibility* (1995)

Winona LaDuke (b. 1959) is Harvard educated and has a national reputation as an activist for Native American and environmental justice. The following document is an excerpt from her 1995 UN speech. LaDuke ran on the Green Party ticket in 1996 and 2000 as the running mate of Ralph Nader. She is the nation's best-known advocate for Native American environmental justice, fighting against corporate power as well as the American government's efforts to use tribal lands as storage for nuclear waste. In her UN address, LaDuke speaks on behalf of the indigenous heritage of living within the environment, taking only what is necessary for sustainable development. She repudiates the American historical and contemporary domination over the natural world for individual and corporate profit.

What are the major points in LaDuke's appeal for environmental justice? Which specific arguments are gender based? How does her concern for environmental contamination and health relate to Terry Williams's and Theo Colborn's arguments?*

I am from the Mississippi Band of Anishinabeg of the White Earth reservation in northern Minnesota, one of approximately 250,000 Anishinabeg people who inhabit the great lakes region of the North American continent. Aniin indinawaymugnitok. Me gweich Chi-iwewag, Megwetch Ogitchi taikwewag. Nindizhinikaz, Beenaysayikwe, Makwa nin dodaem. Megwetch indinawaymugunitok.

I am greeting you in my language and thanking you, my sisters for the honor of speaking with you today about the challenges facing women as we approach the 21st century.

A primary and central challenge impacting women as we approach the 21st century will be the distance we collectively as women and societies have artificially placed ourselves from our Mother the Earth, and the inherent environmental, social, health and psychological

---

* Winona LaDuke, UN Address, Beijing China, "The Indigenous Women's Network, Our Future, Our Responsibility."
Copyright © Winona LaDuke.

consequences of colonialism, and subsequently rapid industrialization on our bodies, and our nations. As a centerpiece of this problem is the increasing lack of control we have over ourselves, and our long term security. This situation must be rectified through the laws of international institutions, such as the United Nations, but as well, the policies, laws and practices of our nations, our communities, our states, and ourselves.

The situation of Indigenous women, as a part of Indigenous peoples, we believe is a magnified version of the critical juncture we find ourselves in as peoples, and the problems facing all women and our future generations as we struggle for a better world. Security, militarism, the globalization of the economy, the further marginalization of women, increasing intolerance and the forced commodification and homogenization of culture through the media.

The Earth is our Mother. From her we get our life, and our ability to live. It is our responsibility to care for our mother, and in caring for our Mother, we care for ourselves. Women, all females, are the manifestation of Mother Earth in human form. We are her daughters and in my cultural instructions: Minobimaatisiiwin. We are to care for her. I am taught to live in respect for Mother Earth. In Indigenous societies, we are told that Natural Law is the highest law, higher than the law made by nations, states, municipalities and the World Bank. That one would do well to live in accordance with Natural Law. With those of our Mother. And in respect for our Mother Earth of our relation— indinawaymuguni took.

One hundred years ago, one of our Great Leaders—Chief Seattle stated, "What befalls the Earth, befalls the People of the Earth." And that is the reality of today, and the situation of the status of women, and the status of Indigenous women and Indigenous peoples.

While I am from one nation of Indigenous peoples, there are millions of Indigenous people worldwide. An estimated 500 million people are in the world today. We are in the Cordillera, the Maori of New Zealand, we are in East Timor, we are the Wara Wara of Australia, the Lakota, the Tibetans, the peoples of Hawai'i, New Caledonia and many other nations of Indigenous peoples. Indigenous peoples. We are not populations, not minority groups, we are peoples. We are nations of peoples. Under international law we meet the criteria of nation states, having a common economic system, language, territory, history, culture and governing institutions. Despite this fact, Indigenous Nations are not allowed to participate at the United Nations.

Nations of Indigenous people are not, by and large, represented at the United Nations. Most decisions today are made by the 180 or so member states to the United Nations. Those states, by and large, have been in existence for only 200 years or less, while most Nations of Indigenous peoples, with few exceptions, have been in existence for thousands of years. Ironically, there would likely be little argument in this room, that most decisions made in the world today are actually made by some of the 47 transnational corporations and their international financiers whose annual income is larger than the gross national product for many countries of the world.

This is a centerpiece of the problem. Decision-making is not made by those who are affected by those decisions, people who live on the land, but corporations, with an interest which is entirely different than that of the land, and the people, or the women of the land. This brings forth a fundamental question: What gives these corporations like CONOCO, SHELL, EXXON, DIASHAWA, ITT, RIO TINTO ZINC, and the WORLD BANK, a right which supersedes or is superior to my human right to live on my land, or that of my family, my community, my nation, our nations, and to us as women? What law gives that right to them? Not any law of the Creator, or of Mother Earth. Is that right contained within their wealth? Is that right contained within their wealth, that which is historically acquired immorally, unethically, through colonialism, imperialism, and paid for with the lives of millions of people, or species of plants and entire ecosystems? They should have no such right, that right of self-determination, and to determine our destiny, and that of our future generations.

The origins of this problem lie with the predator-prey relationship industrial society has developed with the Earth, and subsequently, the people of the Earth. This same relationship exists *vis a vis* women. We, collectively find that we are often in the role of the prey, to a predator society, whether for sexual discrimination, exploitation, sterilization, absence of control over our bodies, or being the subjects of repressive laws and legislation in which we have no voice. This occurs not only on an individual level, but, equally, and more significantly on a societal level. It is also critical to point out at this time that most matrilineal societies, societies in which governance and decision-making are largely controlled by women, have been obliterated from the face of the Earth by colonialism, and subsequently industrialism. The only matrilineal societies which exist in the world today are those of Indigenous nations. We are the remaining matriineal societies. Yet we also face obliteration.

On a worldwide scale and in North America, Indigenous societies historically, and today, remain in a predator-prey relationship with industrial society, and prior to that colonialism and imperialism. We are the peoples with the land—land and natural resources required for someone else's development program and the amassing of wealth. The wealth of the United States, that nation which today determines much of world policy, easily expropriated from our lands. Similarly the wealth of Indigenous peoples of South Africa, Central, South American countries, and Asia was taken for the industrial development of Europe, and later for settler states which came to occupy those lands. That relationship between development and underdevelopment adversely affected the status of our Indigenous societies, and the status of Indigenous women.

Eduardo Galeano, the Latin American writer and scholar has said.

In the colonial to neocolonial alchemy, gold changes to scrap metal and food to poison, we have become painfully aware of the mortality of wealth which nature bestows and imperialism appropriates.

Today, on a worldwide scale, we remain in the same situation as one hundred years ago, only with less land, and fewer people. Today, on a worldwide scale, 50 million indigenous peoples live in the world's rainforests, a million indigenous peoples are slated for relocation for dam projects in the next decade (thanks to the World Bank, from the Narmada Project in India, to the Three Gorges Dam Project, here in China, to the Jasmes Bay Hydro Electric Project in northern Canada).

Almost all atomic weapons which have been detonated in the world are also detonated on the lands or waters of Indigenous people. This situation is mimicked in the North American context. Today, over 50% of our remaining lands are forested, and both Canada and the United States continue aggressive clearcutting policies on our land. Over two thirds of the uranium resources in the United States, and similar figures for Canada are on Indigenous lands, as is one third of all low-sulphur coal resources. We have huge oil reserves on our reservations, and we have the dubious honor of being the most highly bombed nation in the world, in this case, the Western Shoshone Nation, on which over 650 atomic weapons have been detonated. We also have two separate accelerated proposals to dump nuclear waste in our reservation lands, and similarly over 100 separate proposals to dump toxic waste on our reservation lands.

We understand clearly the relationship between development for someone else, and our own underdevelopment. We also understand clearly the relationship between the environmental impacts of types of development on our lands, and the environmental and subsequent health impacts in our bodies as women. That is the cause of the problems.

CHAPTER 18

Feminist Revival and Women's Liberation

Despite the resurgence of the cult of domesticity during the 1950s, married women with children were entering the workforce in ever-greater numbers. Women in the workplace undermined one-dimensional domestic roles even as popular culture emphasized them. The introduction of the birth control pill and increasing societal acceptance of contraception furthered the separation between sex and motherhood. Developed by Dr. Gregory Pincus, the pill was a team effort promoted by longtime birth control advocate Margaret Sanger (see Chapter 14) and funded by Katherine McCormick, Sanger's associate, whose women's rights advocacy stretched back to the early twentieth century. The 1965 U.S. Supreme Court decision *Griswold v. Connecticut* severed the remaining legal prohibition against the dissemination of contraceptives. The post–World War II baby boom peaked in 1957. Climbing birth rates began to level off. Lengthening life spans and fewer children combined to produce an "empty nest" syndrome among middle-aged women after their last child left home. Growing numbers of older women entered the workforce and joined younger married women who also sought employment to supplement family incomes and to achieve personal fulfillment.

By 1960, signs of government interest in women's issues appeared within the administration of John F. Kennedy, Eleanor Roosevelt and other prominent women active in Democratic politics pressured the administration to express a greater commitment to women's issues. Of particular concern were employment opportunities and equitable pay for the growing numbers of women now in the workforce. The result was the appointment of a Presidential Commission on the Status of Women that successfully promoted the congressional passage of an Equal Pay Act (1963). Although the legislation promised women pay scale equity with men, it was difficult, if not impossible, to determine whether male and female jobs actually were equal because of the concept of women's work that resulted in jobs classified by female and male designations that created a gender-structured workplace with the majority of jobs reserved for men.

Title VII of the 1964 Civil Rights Act was a far more significant advance for gender equity. The Civil Rights Act prohibited discrimination in employment on the basis of sex as well as race, color, religion, or national origin. The inclusion of sexual discrimination in the act was a result of the efforts of Alice Paul and a small group of politically active feminists, who had unsuccessfully promoted the Equal Rights Amendment. Now they effectively linked sexual discrimination to civil rights legislation. To deal with discrimination, Title VII established the Equal Employment Opportunity Commission (EEOC); however, the EEOC's sluggish efforts to address women's grievances about employment discrimination helped spark the revival of women's rights activism.

The women's rights or feminist movement that developed in the mid-1960s expressed the concerns of two diverse groups of women. Educated, mainly white middle-class women who had reached maturity during the postwar period formed the National Organization for Women (NOW) in 1966. Demanding a massive reconstruction of gender roles, they stressed the need for women to have equal employment opportunities with men, and for married couples to create a truly equal partnership in home and family care. Under the leadership of Betty Friedan, the founder and first president of NOW, women also used the organization as a forum to express their discontent with their restrictive domestic roles and home bound life styles.

Although they did not establish one official organization, younger women who had been active in antiwar and civil rights protest spoke on behalf of women's liberation and directly confronted the issue of sexism that they maintained caused as much harm to women as racism did to African Americans. They alleged that sexism pervaded language as well as institutional structures, creating male privilege and preferential treatment in all areas of life. Red Stockings and other women's liberation groups blamed male control or patriarchy for the constraints and oppression that limited women's lives. Calling for an end to patriarchy and a united sisterhood, liberation advocates met in small "consciousness-raising" groups dedicated to helping women view their personal problems in a political context. Creating women's health clinics, liberationists sought to give women greater control over their own bodies and also created an alternative style of medical care that was more sensitive to women's emotional needs.

Liberationists also called for collective action to deal with issues concerning patriarchal power and also its abuse: male violence toward women. Liberation feminists redefined rape as act of terror and oppression. They vehemently disagreed with the prevailing perception that women encouraged rape by wearing provocative clothing or being on the wrong street at the wrong time. Feminists noted that legal restrictions made it difficult for women to testify at rape trials. Law enforcement officials also dismissed domestic battering of women, even after repeated attacks. Because of the feminist campaign to increase public awareness about violence against women, spousal abuse, workplace harassment, and rape—that had either remained unacknowledged or was blamed on the victim—began to receive national attention.

Women's liberation groups also promoted greater sexual freedom and the end to the double standard that still held females to a higher standard of sexual behavior than males. Whereas moral reformers of the nineteenth century had proposed a single standard of purity, liberationists were more in accord with Victoria Woodhull's advocacy of free love, a belief in a single standard of sexual pleasure, with women as well as men entitled to that pleasure (see Chapter 4). Demands for greater sexual freedom also developed on college campuses within the context of student protest. Under increasing pressure from student demands, colleges removed curfews and dormitory restrictions that had attempted to restrict sexual activity. A new era of permissive sexuality reshaped the older one of constraint. To college student Joyce Maynard, the new norms of sexual permissiveness promoted peer group pressure for women to become sexually active.

Despite their greater militancy, liberationist groups shared major objectives with NOW. Both upheld a commitment to the dynamic expansion of female opportunity and gender equity. Both campaigned for the right of women to obtain medically safe abortions and the passage of the ERA. NOW also adopted the liberationist perspective on the destructive impact of sexism and supported consciousness-raising groups. Educated, white women from middle-class and professional backgrounds played the dominant role in the resurgence of feminism. Gloria Steinem, a graduate of Smith College, founded *Ms.* magazine. The title expressed the objective of finding a feminine counterpart to the designation of "Mr." *Ms.* expressed an independent identity for women who were married and also avoided the explicit recognition of a woman's marital status. Some married women, in the manner of Lucy Stone more than a century earlier, also kept their maiden names (see Chapter 7). In their fundamental concern to promote gender equity and end sexism and the widespread societal and cultural acceptance of male privilege, women's liberationists believed that they spoke in a universal voice for all American women. In many ways, their effort at social transformation echoed the call for action of the women's rights advocates or pioneer feminists who had assembled in Seneca Falls in 1848. As was the case in the first women's movement, the second women's movement or second wave as it is also became known, shared a feminist analysis that exposed patriarchal control and sexism and gender-based inequality, but critics alleged it did not encompass multiple definitions of womanhood or the complexities of the female experience.

During the early 1970s, white feminists increasingly came under attack from other change-oriented women who believed that the feminist movement needed to be more inclusive. African American, Chicana, working-class women, and lesbians denounced white feminists for indifference to issues of oppression that sprang more from race, class, and sexual orientation than from gender bias. Allegations from women of color and lesbians that NOW was too white, too privileged, and too heterosexual led to the creation of separate feminist, identity based-organizations. African American women organized the National Black Feminist Organization and issued a manifesto alleging that gender discrimination intersected with race and class and could be addressed only in the context of what it meant to be black in white America. They asserted that gender discrimination was just one and not necessarily the most abusive oppression women faced. They also alleged that white women joined the ranks of the oppressors when they exercised their own racial and class privileges.

Criticism and theoretical contributions of women of color were absolutely fundamental to an expanded definition of feminism and diverse definitions of what it meant to be a woman. Feminism proved a dynamic belief system that changed over time and responded to diverse women's needs. Lesbians looked to heterosexual feminists to help combat homophobia and to include lesbian rights in the feminist agenda. In the interest of promoting their lesbian liberation, they formed their own identity group, the Lesbian Feminist Organization. Working-class women prodded NOW to move to address the problems of single, working-class mothers and the limited options of poor women in general and women of color in particular.

The proliferation of organizations sharing feminist objectives but distinct from the mainstream feminist movement also included Chicana women who promoted sisterhood for

Chicanas as their organizing principle. The splintering of the concept of universal sisterhood into separate identity groups also included those representing Native American women the elderly, and the disabled. At the same time, NOW was still trying to serve as an umbrella organization; widen its objectives; and address cultural, sexual, and racial diversity.

From NOW's inception, conservative women had rejected the feminist effort to strip away their primary identity as wives and mothers. As NOW became more inclusive, officially adding lesbian rights to its agenda, conservatives found the organization's validation of lesbian and single mother lifestyles an even more extreme example of the feminist determination to destroy the primary definition of women as wives and mothers. Concerned Women for America, founded in 1979, was one attempt by conservative Christian women to promote biblical values and provide a collective Christian opposition to the feminist agenda and NOW (see Chapter 21).

Aimed directly at ending sex discrimination in education, Title IX mandated that schools provide equal resources for all aspects of the educational experience, including women's sports. Sports equity for professional women also received national attention with the media coverage of the 1973 tennis match between Bobby Riggs and Billie Jean King. With decisive scores in King's favor, the match illuminated the significance of the recently passed federal funding for providing girls with athletic opportunities equal to those of boys. Billie Jean King symbolized the potential of women athletes. Her victory was more than a spectacular media event.

Women's liberation also expressed defiance against the fashion and beauty standards that caused pain or discomfort, such as the wearing of high-heeled shoes and constricting girdles. Clothing liberation was reminiscent of the nineteenth-century dress reform objectives that sought comfort and health in preference to the decrees of fashion. The lack of feminist attention to the demands of fashion challenged the fashion and cosmetics industries. Wearing pants and informal attire became a new norm and clothing for women became less feminine. The second women's rights movement as an organized protest and social reform movement flourished at a time of collective protest ranging from civil rights to anti–Vietnam War demonstrations. Despite lack of recognition, American women had served in the Vietnam War. By 1980, gender equality remained a work in progress, one that was bitterly contested. The era of organized protest and reform had lost momentum. Women's rights encountered a major political and cultural backlash and increasing internal divisions further weakened collective action.

NATIONAL ORGANIZATION FOR WOMEN, *Statement of Purpose* (1966)

The National Organization for Women (NOW) envisioned that a transformation of gender roles would enable men and women to share domestic and child care tasks. NOW also proposed child care institutions that would enable women to combine full-time motherhood and a career. In what ways did NOW follow in the path of the Declaration of Sentiments (see Chapter 7)? In what ways did their objectives differ? In terms of the present, how would you evaluate the NOW agenda?*

---

* Reprinted from the National Organization for Women "Statement of Purpose." It should be noted that this is a historical document and does not reflect all current NOW policies and priorities.

We, men and women who hereby constitute ourselves as the National Organization for Women, believe that the time has come for a new movement toward true equality for all women in America, and toward a fully equal partnership of the sexes, as part of the worldwide revolution of human rights now taking place within and beyond our national borders.

The purpose of NOW is to take action to bring women into full participation in the mainstream of American society now, exercising all the privileges and responsibilities thereof in truly equal partnership with men.

We believe the time has come to move beyond the abstract argument, discussion and symposia over the status and special nature of women, which has raged in America in recent years; the time has come to confront, with concrete action, the conditions that now prevent women from enjoying the equality of opportunity and freedom of choice which is their right as individual Americans, and as human beings.

NOW is dedicated to the proposition that women first and foremost are human beings, who, like all other people in our society, must have the chance to develop their fullest human potential. We believe that women can achieve such equality only by accepting to the full the challenges and responsibilities they share with all other people in our society, as part of the decision-making mainstream of American political, economic and social life.

We organize to initiate or support action, nationally or in any part of this nation, by individuals or organizations, to break through the silken curtain of prejudice and discrimination against women in government, industry, the professions, the churches, the political parties, the judiciary, the labor unions; in education, science, medicine, law, religion and every other field of importance in American society. . . .

There is no civil rights movement to speak for women, as there has been for Negroes and other victims of discrimination. The National Organization for Women must therefore begin to speak.

WE BELIEVE that the power of American law, and the protection guaranteed by the U.S. Constitution to the civil rights of all individuals, must be effectively applied and enforced to isolate and remove patterns of sex discrimination, to ensure equality of opportunity in employment and education, and equality of civil and political rights and responsibilities on behalf of women, as well as for Negroes and other deprived groups.

We realize that women's problems are linked to many broader questions of social justice; their solution will require concerted action by many groups. Therefore, convinced that human rights for all are indivisible, we expect to give active support to the common cause of equal rights for all those who suffer discrimination and deprivation, and we call upon together organizations committed to such goals to support our efforts toward equality for women.

WE DO NOT ACCEPT the token appointment of a few women to high-level positions in government and industry as a substitute for a serious continuing effort to recruit and advance women according to their individual abilities. To this end, we urge American government and industry to mobilize the same resources of ingenuity and command with which they have solved problems of far greater difficulty than those now impeding the progress of women. . . .

WE REJECT the current assumptions that a man must carry the sole burden of supporting himself, his wife, and a family, and that a woman is automatically entitled to lifelong support by a man upon her marriage; or that marriage, home and family are primarily a woman's world and responsibility—hers, to dominate, his to support. We believe that a true partnership between the sexes demands a different concept of marriage, an equitable sharing of the responsibilities of home and children, and of the economic burdens of their support. We believe that proper recognition should be given to the economic and social value of homemaking and child care. To these ends, we will seek to open a reexamination of laws and mores governing marriage and divorce, for we believe that the current state of "half-equality" between the sexes discriminates against both men and women, and is the cause of much unnecessary hostility between the sexes.

WE BELIEVE that women must now exercise their political rights and responsibilities as American citizens. They must refuse to be segregated on the basis of sex into separate-and-not-equal ladies' auxiliaries in the political parties, and they must demand representation according to their numbers in the regularly constituted party committees—at local, state, and national levels—and in the informal power structure, participating fully in the selection of candidates and political decision-making, and running for office themselves.

IN THE INTERESTS OF THE HUMAN DIGNITY OF WOMEN, we will protest and endeavor to change the false image of women now prevalent in the mass media, and in the texts, ceremonies, laws and practices of our social institutions. Such images perpetuate contempt for women by society and by women for themselves. We are similarly opposed to all policies and practices—in church, state, college, factory or office—which, in the guise of protectiveness, not only deny opportunities but also foster in women self-denigration, dependence, and evasion of responsibility, undermine their confidence in their own abilities and foster contempt for women.

Excerpt from *GRISWOLD V. CONNECTICUT* (March 1965)

Strange as it might sound in the present era, as late as 1965 the state of Connecticut held those who were involved in the sale and distribution of contraceptives guilty of committing a criminal offense. Estelle Griswold, the executive director of the Planned Parenthood League in Connecticut, as well as the male medical director of the organization, a licensed physician, were found guilty of violating the law and providing contraceptives to women. Although Margaret Sanger, the pioneer birth control advocate had been imprisoned in Brooklyn, New York, for a similar violation, the Griswold conviction occurred more than a half century later at a time when contraception was widely used. After a Connecticut court upheld the guilty conviction, the case made its way to the Supreme Court. *Griswold* v. *Connecticut* is a pivotal Supreme Court decision, establishing the constitutionality of married couples to have the right of privacy to make their own decisions regarding birth control, free from any government interference. The right of privacy also became the basis in the better-known *Roe v. Wade* Supreme Court decision of 1973 that legalized abortion.

The *Griswold* decision wiped out the last vestiges of the effort of states to ban contraception. Although many women applauded the decision, the Catholic Church was deeply opposed and continued its advocacy against married couples using contraception. How would you evaluate this Supreme Court decision and the issue of privacy?*

Appeal from the Supreme Court of Errors of Connecticut.

No. 496.

Argued March 29–30, 1965.

Decided June 7, 1965.

Appellants, the Executive Director of the Planned Parenthood League of Connecticut, and its medical director, a licensed physician, were convicted as accessories for giving married persons information and medical advice on how to prevent conception and, following examination, prescribing a contraceptive device or material for the wife's use. A Connecticut statute makes it a crime for any

---

* *Griswold v. Connecticut,* Supreme Court of the United States, 1965, 381 U.S. 479.

person to use any drug or article to prevent conception. Appellants claimed that the accessory statute as applied violated the Fourteenth Amendment. An intermediate appellate court and the State's highest court affirmed the judgment. Held:

1. Appellants have standing to assert the constitutional rights of the married people. Tileston v. Ullman, 318 U.S. 44, distinguished. p. 481.
2. The Connecticut statute forbidding use of contraceptives violates the right of marital privacy which is within the penumbra of specific guarantees of the Bill of Rights. pp. 481–486.

151 Conn. 544, 200 A. 2d 479, reversed.

Thomas I. Emerson argued the cause for appellants. With him on the briefs was Catherine G. Roraback.

Joseph B. Clark argued the cause for appellee. With him on the brief was Julius Maretz.

Briefs of amici curiae, urging reversal, were filed by Whitney North Seymour and Eleanor M. Fox for Dr. John M. Adams et al.; by Morris L. Ernst, Harriet F. Pilpel and Nancy F. Wechsler for the Planned Parenthood Federation of America, Inc.; by Alfred L. Scanlon for the Catholic Council on Civil Liberties, and by Rhoda H. Karpatkin, Melvin L. Wulf and Jerome E. Caplan for the American Civil Liberties Union et al. [381 U.S. 479, 480]

MR. JUSTICE DOUGLAS delivered the opinion of the Court.

Appellant Griswold is Executive Director of the Planned Parenthood League of Connecticut. Appellant Buxton is a licensed physician and a professor at the Yale Medical School who served as Medical Director for the League at its Center in New Haven—a center open and operating from November 1 to November 10, 1961, when appellants were arrested.

United States, 360 U.S. 109, 112 ; Baggett v. Bullitt, 377 U.S. 360, 369. Without [381 U.S.

479, 483] those peripheral rights the specific rights would be less secure. And so we reaffirm the principle of the Pierce and the Meyer cases. . . .

The present case, then, concerns a relationship lying within the zone of privacy created by several fundamental constitutional guarantees. And it concerns a law which, in forbidding the use of contraceptives rather than regulating their manufacture or sale, seeks to achieve its goals by means having a maximum destructive impact upon that relationship. Such a law cannot stand in light of the familiar principle, so often applied by this Court, that a "governmental purpose to control or prevent activities constitutionally subject to state regulation may not be achieved by means which sweep unnecessarily broadly and thereby invade the area of protected freedoms." NAACP v. Alabama, 377 U.S. 288, 307. Would we allow the police to search the sacred precincts of marital bedrooms for telltale signs of the use of contraceptives? The [381 U.S. 479, 486] very idea is repulsive to the notions of privacy surrounding the marriage relationship.

We deal with a right of privacy older than the Bill of Rights—older than our political parties, older than our school system. Marriage is a coming together for better or for worse, hopefully enduring, and intimate to the degree of being sacred. It is an association that promotes a way of life, not causes; a harmony in living, not political faiths; a bilateral loyalty, not commercial or social projects. Yet it is an association for as noble a purpose as any involved in our prior decisions.

Reversed.

MR. JUSTICE GOLDBERG, whom THE CHIEF JUSTICE and MR. JUSTICE BRENNAN join, concurring. I agree with the Court that Connecticut's birth-control law unconstitutionally intrudes upon the right of marital privacy, and I join in its opinion and judgment. Although I have not accepted the view that "due process" as used in the Fourteenth

Amendment incorporates all of the first eight Amendments (see my concurring opinion in Pointer v. Texas, 380 U.S. 400, 410, and the dissenting opinion of MR. JUSTICE BRENNAN in Cohen v. Hurley, 366 U.S. 117, 154), I do agree that the concept of liberty protects those personal rights that are fundamental, and is not confined to the specific terms of the Bill of Rights. My conclusion that the concept of liberty is not so restricted and that it embraces the right of marital privacy though that right is not mentioned explicitly

in the Constitution it is supported both by numerous [381 U.S. 479,487 decisions of this Court, referred to in the Court's opinion, and by the language and history of the Ninth Amendment. In reaching the conclusion that the right of marital privacy is protected, as being within the protected penumbra of specific guarantees of the Bill of Rights, the Court refers to the Ninth Amendment, ante, at 484.I add these words to emphasize the relevance of that Amendment to the Court's holding.

REDSTOCKINGS MANIFESTO (1969)

Women's liberation groups such as Redstockings shared the view that male oppression represented society's major form of control over women. To oppose oppression, they called for a united sisterhood that crossed class, race, and ethnic lines. Groups such as Redstockings emphasized that a woman's personal experience could be understood only in the context of unequal power relationships between men and women and sexist institutions. How did Redstockings support their allegation that men are the agents of women's oppression? What similarities exist between this manifesto and the official agenda of NOW as stated in 1966? What are the differences?*

I. After centuries of individual and preliminary political struggle, women are uniting to achieve their final liberation from male supremacy. Redstockings is dedicated to building this unity and winning our freedom.

II. Women are an oppressed class. Our oppression is total, affecting every facet of our lives. We are exploited as sex objects, breeders, domestic servants, and cheap labor. We are considered inferior beings, whose only purpose is to enhance men's lives. Our humanity is denied. Our prescribed behavior is enforced by the threat of physical violence.

Because we have lived so intimately with our oppressors, in isolation from each other, we have been kept from seeing our personal suffering as a political condition. This creates the illusion that a woman's relationship with her man is a matter of interplay between two unique personalities, and can be worked out individually. In reality, every such relationship is a *class* relationship, and the conflicts between individual men and women are *political* conflicts that can only be solved collectively.

III. We identify the agents of our oppression as men. Male supremacy is the oldest, most basic form of domination. All other forms of

---

* From "The Redstockings Manifesto," July 7, 1969. Women's Liberation materials from the 1960s and from current-day organizing are available from Redstockings Women Liberation Archives for Action Distribution Project, P.O. Box 2625, Gainesville, FL 32602. Redstockings can be reached at P.O. Box 744, Stuyvesant Station, New York, NY 10009. Web: www.redstockings.org.

exploitation and oppression (racism, capitalism, imperialism, etc.) are extensions of male supremacy: men dominate women, a few men dominate the rest. All power structures throughout history have been male-dominated and male-oriented. Men have controlled all political, economic and cultural institutions, and backed up this control with physical force. They have used their power to keep women in an inferior position. *All men* receive economic, sexual and psychological benefits from male supremacy. *All men* have oppressed women.

IV. Attempts have been made to shift the burden of responsibility from men to institutions or to women themselves. We condemn these arguments as evasions. Institutions alone do not oppress; they are merely tools of the oppressor. To blame institutions implies that men and women are equally victimized, obscures the fact that men benefit from the subordination of women, and gives men the excuse that they are forced to be oppressors. On the contrary, any man is free to renounce his superior position, provided that he is willing to be treated like a woman by other men.

We also reject the idea that women consent to or are to blame for their own oppression. Women's submission is not the result of brainwashing, stupidity, or mental illness, but of continual, daily pressure from men. We do not need to change ourselves, but to change men.

The most slanderous evasion of all is that women can oppress men. The basis for this illusion is the isolation of individual relationships from their political context, and the tendency of men to see any legitimate challenge to their privileges as persecution.

V. We regard our personal experience, and our feelings about that experience, as the basis for an analysis of our common situation. We cannot rely on existing ideologies as they are all products of male supremacy culture. We question every generalization and accept none that are not confirmed by our experience.

Our chief task at present is to develop female class consciousness through sharing experiences and publicly exposing the sexist foundation of all our institutions. Consciousness-raising is not "therapy," which implies the existence of individual solutions and falsely assumes that the male-female relationship is purely personal, but the only method by which we can ensure that our program for liberation is based on the concrete realities of our lives.

The first requirement for raising class consciousness is honesty, in private and in public, with ourselves and other women.

VI. We identify with all women. We define our best interest as that of the poorest, most brutally exploited woman.

We repudiate all economic, racial, educational or status privileges that divide us from other women. We are determined to recognize and eliminate any prejudices we may hold against other women.

We are committed to achieving internal democracy. We will do whatever is necessary to ensure that every woman in our movement has an equal chance to participate, assume responsibilities, and develop her political potential.

VII. We call on all our sisters to unite with us in struggle.

We call on all men to give up their male privileges and support women's liberation in the interest of our humanity and their own.

In fighting for our liberation we will always take the side of women against their oppressors. We will not ask what is "revolutionary" or "reformist," only what is good for women.

The time for individual skirmishes has passed. This time we are going all the way.

July 7, 1969

GLORIA STEINEM, *Statement to Congress* (1970)

Gloria Steinem (b. 1934), a graduate of Smith college, an activist for women's rights and the founder of *Ms.* magazine, defended the ERA by minimizing the biological differences between men and women. She urged all women, regardless of class and racial background, to fight "outdated myths" that enforced both race and gender inequities. In the effort to achieve complete gender equity, advocates of the ERA advanced a legal identity for women that was not dependent on their roles as wives and mothers. Although the amendment received congressional approval, conservatives successfully mobilized to prevent states from ratifying it. What are the "outdated myths" that Steinem discusses?*

My name is Gloria Steinem. I am a writer and editor, and I am currently a member of the policy council of the Democratic committee. And I work regularly with the lowest-paid workers in the country, the migrant workers, men, women and children both in California and in my own State of New York. . . .

During twelve years of working for a living, I have experienced much of the legal and social discrimination reserved for women in this country. I have been refused service in public restaurants, ordered out of public gathering places, and turned away from apartment rentals; all for the clearly stated, sole reason that I was a woman. And all without the legal remedies available to blacks and other minorities. I have been excluded from professional groups, writing assignments on so-called "unfeminine" subjects such as politics, full participation in the Democratic party, jury duty, and even from such small male privileges as discounts on airline fares. Most important to me, I have been denied a society in which women are encouraged, or even allowed, to think of themselves as first-class citizens and responsible human beings.

However, after two years of researching the status of American women, I have discovered that in reality, I am very, very lucky. Most women, both wage-earners and housewives, routinely suffer more humiliation and injustice than I do.

As a freelance writer, I don't work in the male-dominated hierarchy of an office. (Women, like blacks and other visibly different minorities, do better in individual professions such as the arts, sports, or domestic work; anything in which they don't have authority over white males.) I am not one of the millions of women who must support a family. Therefore, I haven't had to go on welfare because there are no day-care centers for my children while I work, and I haven't had to submit to the humiliating welfare inquiries about my private and sexual life, inquiries from which men are exempt. I haven't had to brave the sex bias of labor unions and employers, only to see my family subsist on a median salary 40 percent less than the male median salary.

I hope this committee will hear the personal, daily injustices suffered by many women—professionals and day laborers, women housebound by welfare as well as by suburbia. We have all been silent for too long. But we won't be silent anymore.

The truth is that all our problems stem from the same sex based myths. We may appear before you as white radicals or the middle-aged middle-class or black soul

---

* From "The Equal Rights Amendment: Hearings Before the Subcommittee on Constitutional Amendments of the Committee on Judiciary of the United States Senate," 91st Congress, May 5, 6, 7, 1970 (Washington, D.C.: U.S. Government Printing Office, 1970), 331–35, 38–41, 575–78.

sisters, but we are all sisters in and against these outdated myths. Like racial myths, they have been reflected in our laws. Let me list a few.

[That women are biologically inferior to men. In fact, an equally good case can be made for the reverse.] Women live longer than men, even when the men are not subject to business pressures. Women survived Nazi concentration camps better, keep cooler heads in emergencies currently studied by disaster-researchers, are protected against heart attacks by their female sex hormones, and are so much more durable at every stage of life that nature must conceive 20 to 50 percent more males in order to keep the balance going.

Man's hunting activities are forever being pointed to as tribal proof of superiority. But [while he was hunting, women built houses, tilled the fields, developed animal husbandry, and perfected language.] Men, being all alone in the bush, often developed into a creature as strong as women, fleeter of foot, but not very bright.

However, I don't want to prove the superiority of one sex to another. That would only be repeating the male mistake. English scientists once definitely proved, after all, that the English were descended from the angels, while the Irish were descended from the apes; it was the rationale for England's domination of Ireland for more than a century. The point is that science is used to support current myth and economics almost as much as the church was.

What we do know is that the difference between two races or two sexes is much smaller than the difference to be found within each group. Therefore, in spite of the slide show on female inferiorities that I understand was shown to you yesterday, the law makes much more sense when it treats individuals, not groups bundled together by some condition of birth. . . .

Another myth, that women are already treated equally in this society: I am sure there has been ample testimony to prove that equal pay for equal work, equal chance for advancement and equal training or encouragement is obscenely scarce in every field, even those—like food and fashion industries—that are supposedly "feminine."

A deeper result of social and legal injustice, however, is what sociobiologists refer to as "Internalized Aggression." Victims of aggression absorb the myth of their own inferiority, and come to believe that their group is in fact second class. Even when they themselves realize they are not second class, they may still think their group is, thus the tendency to be the only Jew in the club, the only black woman on the block, the only woman in the office.

Gloria Steinem (Scott Applewhite/AP Wide World Photos)

Joyce Maynard, *An Eighteen Year Old Looks Back at Life* (1972)

Joyce Maynard (b. 1953), a contemporary author, was a first-year student at Yale when she wrote this *New York Times Magazine* article. Student protests during the sixties toppled the nationwide social controls used to limit sexual behavior on campus. Prior to the permissive sexual environment of the seventies, dorm room visiting restrictions and strict curfews imposed constraints. The sexual revolution coincided with a renewed affirmation of female sexuality. Yet women such as Maynard found that sexual liberation created a new set of problems. What issues does she confront? How do Maynard's observations relate to those described in the Wembridge article in Chapter 14?*

The freshman women's dorm at Yale has no house mother. We have no check-in hours or drinking rules or punishments for having boys in our rooms past midnight. A guard sits by the door to offer, as they assured us at the beginning of the year, physical—not moral—protection. All of which makes it easy for many girls who feel, after high-school curfews and dating regulations, suddenly liberated. (The first week of school last fall, many girls stayed out all night, every night, displaying next morning the circles under their eyes the way some girls show off engagement rings.)

We all received the "Sex at Yale" book, a thick, black pamphlet filled with charts and diagrams and a lengthy discussion of contraceptive methods. And at the first women's assembly, the discussion moved quickly from course-signing-up procedures to gynecology, where it stayed for much of the evening.

Somebody raised her hand to ask where she could fill her pill prescription, someone else wanted to know about abortions. There was no standing in the middle any more—you had to either take out a pen and paper and write down the phone numbers they gave out or stare stonily ahead, implying that those were numbers *you* certainly wouldn't be needing. From then on it seemed the line had been drawn.

But of course the problem is that no lines, no barriers, exist. Where, five years ago a girl's decisions were made for her (she had to be in at 12 and, if she was found—in—with her boyfriend. . . .); today the decision rests with her alone. She is surrounded by knowledgeable, sexually experienced girls and if *she* isn't willing to sleep with her boyfriend, somebody else will. It's peer-group pressure, 1972 style—the embarrassment of virginity.

RAPE, AN ACT OF TERROR (1971)

Women's liberation groups emphasized that a woman's individual encounter with male abuse was more than the random behavior of a violent man. As can be seen from this document, these groups viewed rape as a form of terrorism, the most extreme manifestation of male abuse of women. Liberationists also alleged that cultural norms and laws regarding rape were biased in favor of the rapist. The rape victim needed to prove her innocence by obtaining corroborating evidence, establishing prior virtue, and proving non-provocative behavior. Why did liberationists argue that rape is "a political act of *oppression*"? What does the reference to "Sexist Ideology" mean?**

---

* From Joyce Maynard, "An Eighteen Year Old Looks Back at Life." Originally published in *The New York Times Magazine*, April 23, 1972. Reprinted by permission of the author.

** From "Rape: An Act of Terror" by Barbara Mehrhof and Pamela Kearon in *Women's Liberation: Notes from the Third Year* (1971). Originally published by New York Radical Women. Reprinted by permission.

[Terror is an integral part of the oppression of women. Its purpose is to ensure, as a final measure, the acceptance by women of the inevitability of male domination.] . . . The most important aspect of terrorism is its indiscriminateness with respect to members of the terrorized class. There are no actions or forms of behavior sufficient to avoid this danger. There is no sign that designates a rapist since each male is potentially one. While simple fear is utilitarian, providing the impetus to act for one's safety, the effect of terror is to make all action impossible. . . .

Rape is a punishment without crime or guilt—at least not subjective guilt. It is punishment for the *objective* crime of femaleness. That is why it is indiscriminate. It is primarily a lesson for the whole class of women—a strange lesson, in that it does not teach a form of behavior which will save women from it. *Rape teaches instead the objective, innate, and unchanging subordination of women relative to men.*

Rape supports the male class by projecting its power and aggressiveness on the world. For the individual male, the possibility of rape remains a prerogative of his in-group; its perpetration rekindles his faith in maleness and his own personal worth.

Rape is only slightly forbidden fruit. . . . In New York State, for instance, the law stipulates that the woman must prove she was raped by force, that "penetration" occurred, and that someone witnessed the rapist in the area of the attack. Although the past convictions of the defendant are not admissible evidence in a rape trial, the "reputation" of the rape victim is. The police will refuse to accept charges in many cases, especially if the victim is alone when she comes in to file them. In New York City only certain hospitals will accept rape cases and they are not bound to release their findings to the courts. Finally, the courts consistently refuse to indict men for rape.

It is clear that women do not come under the law on anything like an equal footing with men—or rather, that women as women do not enjoy the protection of law at all. Women as victims of rape, unlike the general victims of assault, are not assumed to be independent, indistinguishable, and equal citizens. They are viewed by the law as subordinate, dependent, and an always potential hindrance to male action and male prerogative. Rape laws are designed to protect males against the charge of rape. The word of a peer has a special force; the word of a dependent is always suspicious, presumed to be motivated by envy, revenge, or rebellion.

Rape . . . is not an arbitrary act of violence by one individual on another; it is a political act of *oppression* (never rebellion) exercised by members of a powerful class on members of the powerless class. Rape is supported by a consensus in the male class. It is preached by a male-controlled and all-pervasive media with only a minimum of disguise and restraint. It is communicated to the male population as an act of freedom and strength and a male right never to be denied. . . .

Many women believe that rape is an act of sick men or is provoked by the female. Thus women as a class do not yet have a consensus on a counter-reality which defines the true meaning of rape for us. . . .

The first step toward breaking the debilitating hold on us of the Sexist Ideology is the creation of a counter-reality, a mutually guaranteed support of female experience undistorted by male interpretation. . . . We *must* understand rape as essentially an act of terror against women—whether committed by white men or minority group males. This is the only means of freeing our imagination so that we can act together—or alone if it comes to it—against this most perfect of political crimes.

CHICANA DEMANDS (1972)

A Chicana feminist protest movement developed in the 1960s with a range of demands calling for an end to multiple forms of oppression. Chicanas' demands were rooted in their experience as women of color and as non-Anglo-speaking and working-class women. By the 1970s, Chicana-founded newspapers provided a key vehicle for communication. Both Ana Nieto-Gomez and Bernice Rincon joined other Chicanas to bring an end to interlocking systems of oppression including "inhumane" sweatshop labor. In what ways do these Chicana demands express the intersection of class, ethnic, and feminist issues? Which specific issues differ from NOW's official agenda?*

We, as *Chicanas,* are a vital part of the *Chicano* community. (We are workers, unemployed women, welfare recipients, housewives, students.) Therefore, we demand that we be heard and that the following resolutions be accepted.

Be it resolved that we, as *Chicanas,* will promote *la hermanidad* [sisterhood] concept in organizing *Chicanas.* As *hermanas,* we have a responsibility to help each other in problems that are common to all of us. . . .

Be it also resolved, that we as *Raza* must not condemn, accept, or transfer the oppression of *La Chicana.*

That all *La Raza* literature should include *Chicana* written articles, poems, and other writings to relate the *Chicana* perspective in the *Chicano* movement.

That *Chicanas* be represented in all levels of *La Raza Unida* party and be run as candidates in all general, primary and local elections.

Jobs

Whereas the *Chicana* on the job is subjected to unbearable inhumane conditions, be it resolved that:

Chicanas receive equal pay for equal work; working conditions, particularly in the garment-factory sweatshops, be improved; *Chicanas* join unions and hold leadership positions within these unions; *Chicanas* be given the opportunity for promotions and be given free training to improve skills; there be maternity leaves with pay.

Prostitution

Whereas prostitution is used by a corrupt few to reap profits for themselves with no human consideration of the needs of *mujeres,* and *whereas* prostitutes are victims of an exploitative economic system and are not criminals, and *whereas* legalized prostitution is used as a means of employing poor women who are on welfare, be it resolved that:

1. those who reap profits from prostitution be given heavy prison sentences and be made to pay large fines;
2. that *mujeres* who are forced to prostitution not be condemned to serve prison sentences;
3. that prostitution not be legalized.

Abortions

Whereas we, as *Chicanas,* have been subjected to illegal, dehumanizing, and unsafe abortions, let it be resolved that we endorse legalized medical abortions in order to protect the human right of self-determination. . . .

Community-Controlled Clinics

We resolve that more *Chicano* clinics (self-supporting) be implemented to service the *Chicano* community. . . .

---

* From "Chicana Demands" in *Ms.,* December 1972, 128.

Child-Care Centers

In order that women may leave their children in the hands of someone they trust and know will understand the cultural ways of their children, be it resolved that *Raza* child-care programs be established in *nuestros barrios*.

NATIONAL BLACK FEMINIST ORGANIZATION, *Manifesto* (1974)

African American feminists developed their own agenda and separated themselves from white women's groups. Unlike white women, African American women found themselves oppressed by both racism and sexism. At the core of African American feminist protest is recognition of this dual and simultaneous oppression that also has resulted in keeping most African American women poor. What are the "distorted images" of black women referred to in the document? What does the organization mean by the remark that black women are the "almost cast-aside half of the black race"?*

The distorted male-dominated media image of the Women's Liberation Movement has clouded the vital and revolutionary importance of this movement to Third World women, especially black women. The Movement has been characterized as the exclusive property of so-called white middle-class women and any black women seen involved in this Movement have been seen as "selling out," "dividing the race," and an assortment of nonsensical epithets. Black feminists resent these charges and have therefore established The National Black Feminist Organization, in order to address ourselves to the particular and specific needs of the larger, but almost cast-aside half of the black race in Amerikka, the black woman.

[Black women have suffered cruelly in this society from living the phenomenon of being black and female, in a country that is *both* racist and sexist. There has been very little real examination of the damage it has caused in the lives and on the minds of black women. Because we live in a patriarchy, we have allowed a premium to be put on black male suffering. No one of us would minimize the pain or hardship, or the cruel and inhumane treatment experienced by the black man. But history, past or present, rarely deals with the malicious abuse put upon the black woman. We were seen as breeders by the master; despised and historically polarized from/by the master's wife, and looked upon as castrators by our lovers and husbands. The black woman has had to be strong, yet we are persecuted for having survived. We have been called "matriarchs" by white racists and black nationalists; we have virtually no positive self-images to validate our existence. Black women want to be proud, dignified, and free from all those false definitions of beauty and womanhood that are unrealistic and unnatural. We, not white men or black men, must define our own self-image as black women, and not fall into the mistake of being placed upon the pedestal, which is even being rejected by white women. It has been hard for black women to emerge from the myriad of distorted images that have portrayed us as grinning Beulahs, castrating Sapphires and pancake-box Jemimas. As black feminists, we realized the need to establish ourselves as an independent black

---

* From "National Black Feminist Organization Manifesto," in *Ms.,* May 1974, 99.

feminist organization. Our aboveground presence will lend enormous credibility to the current Women's Liberation Movement, which unfortunately is not seen as the serious political and economic revolutionary force that it is. We will strengthen the current efforts of the Black Liberation struggle in this country, by encouraging *all* of the talents and creativities of black women to emerge, strong and beautiful, not to feel guilty or divisive, and assume positions of leadership and honor in the black community.

We will encourage the black community to stop falling into the trap of the white male left, utilizing women only in terms of domestic or servile needs. We will continue to remind the Black Liberation Movement that there can't be liberation for half the race. We must together, as a people, work to eliminate racism, from without the black community, which is trying to destroy us as an entire people; but we must remember that sexism is destroying and crippling us from within.

LESBIAN FEMINIST LIBERATION, *Constitution* (1973)

Lesbians looked to the feminist movement to address the inequities they faced as women and as lesbians. In this manifesto, lesbian women alleged that even the liberation of gays would still leave them oppressed as women. Aside from the controversy surrounding homosexuality, lesbian lifestyles raised the issue of female independence from men in its most extreme form. What is meant by the term "heterosexual chauvinism"?*

We, Lesbian Feminist Liberation, dedicate ourselves to promoting our identities as Lesbians and combating sexism as it manifests itself in heterosexual chauvinism and male supremacy.

We as Lesbian-feminists assert the right of every woman to be a self-defined individual. We declare the necessity for all women to discover and use the potentials and resources which exist in themselves and each other. We assert the right of every woman to express herself with her body, intellect and emotions as the complete human being that society has discouraged her from being. We assert the right of every woman to express her sexuality in any way she chooses as an affirmation of her individuality. We declare our intention to confront and disarm the attitudes and institutions that attempt to limit these rights.

We foresee the day when all individuals are free to define themselves in a non-sexist society. However, our present oppression as Lesbians and as women makes it imperative that we not content ourselves with this utopian vision. Because the achievement of our liberation as gay people would leave us still oppressed as women, we recognize that our primary strength is in feminism. Feminism is not so much a given set of specific issues, as it is a way of life which considers as primary our identities as women. As Lesbian-feminists the focus of all our thoughts and actions centers on our identities as Lesbian women. Now we must dedicate our energies primarily to discovering ourselves and our special causes, and, acting as our own spokeswomen, to promoting ourselves everywhere, at all times, as Lesbian women. To this end, it is crucial that we function as an organization distinct from both

---

* From "Lesbian Feminist Liberation Constitution," 1973.

the gay and feminist movements, unique unto ourselves, yet making coalitions with groups on gay and feminist issues, specifically as they relate to our Lesbian identities.

Our feminism and our Lesbianism fuse in our love and respect for women. We are determined to live as we see fit, with other women, in pride and dignity.

NATIONAL ORGANIZATION FOR WOMEN, *General Resolution Lesbian/Gay Rights* (1973)

Initially, NOW's leadership attempted to distance itself from the enormously controversial issue of same sex orientation or preference. However, as the following resolution states, lesbian civil rights issues became a part of NOW's agenda. Has civil rights legislation successfully reduced discrimination against lesbians?*

Whereas, women have the basic right to develop to the maximum their full human sexual potential, and

Whereas, diversity is richly human, and all women must be able to freely define and to express their own sexuality and to choose their own life style, and

Whereas, NOW's public relations and communications have omitted references to the unified efforts of women of tradition and diverse sexual experience, and

Whereas, Lesbians have formed a caucus in NOW to communicate openly, without fear and hostility, and

Whereas, the threat traditionally felt from Lesbianism must no longer be a barrier to open communication between all people, and

Whereas, we recognize that women are all oppressed by one common oppression, and therefore, surely we must not oppress one another for any reason;

Therefore be it resolved that a statement adopting the sense of this resolution be included in all appropriate NOW publications and policy statements; and,

Be it further resolved that NOW actively introduce and support civil rights legislation designed to end discrimination based on sexual orientation, and to introduce with legislation to end discrimination based on sex, the phrase "sexual orientation" in areas such as, but not limited to, housing, unemployment, credit, finance, child custody and public accommodations.

KATHY CAMPBELL, TERRY DALSEMER, AND JUDY WALDMAN, *Women's Night at the Free Clinic* (1972)

Giving women more control over their bodies was an important objective of the second women's movement. Feminists criticized male-centered medical information and male doctors who frequently lacked understanding of women's specific medical problems. They advocated an alternative medical approach that would be woman centered and responsive to the patient rather than just the medical problem. The following document demonstrates what a woman-centered medical approach was like.

---

* From the National Organization for Women's Resolutions of the 1973 National Conference. Reprinted by permission.

What evidence do the writers supply that male doctors were insensitive to women? What specific female support structures do the writers advocate?*

The People's Free Medical Clinic in Baltimore had been in operation for about nine months when the push for a Women's Night began in response to these concerns. Prior to this time, our commitment to women was most clearly seen in the Women's Counseling section of the Clinic, which was then open three nights a week. The women's counselors run early pregnancy detection tests, arrange abortion referrals, and rap with women about birth control methods, VD, female sexuality, etc. The women's counselors emphasize preventive medicine (i.e., birth control). For many reasons, including the fact that we were overcrowded, the medical staff of the Clinic was more concerned with infectious diseases. Healthy women coming in for birth control were given low priority and could be seen only after people who had more immediate problems.

Women's problems, medical and otherwise, are complex, and up to then no conventional institutions had dealt with them comprehensively or adequately. In spite of our commitment to meeting women's needs, problems of space, time, and medical priorities made it increasingly apparent that another clinic night devoted only to women was necessary. Women's Night was to become a night of women sharing with women: rapping about themselves—their medical problems, family situations, personal problems. We wanted to change some of the ideas about the staff and its relationship to women coming in. We wanted to place more emphasis on relating to individuals and groups about all our mutual concerns. We hoped to further break down artificial relationships between "staff" and "patients." Certain role divisions

were eliminated, allowing a freer interaction between all women who were involved in Women's Night, be they staff or patients. We wanted to continue to provide comprehensive primary medical care, along with a gynecological consult, with increased emphasis on birth control information and all kinds of counseling. We had hoped that most of our professional staff, like the general staff, would be women.

The planning meetings for Women's Night convened once a week for about six weeks. We asked ourselves what we wanted to do and how we wanted to do it. Did we want to follow the Clinic procedures we were used to or did we want to start from scratch? What were the things we wanted changed? Did we want only women doctors? Impossible.

There is an indefinable difference between Women's Night and any other Clinic night. Women sit and talk with each other. There is a calm, unhurried air, even on the most frantic nights when there are two doctors and forty patients. Women bring food or fruit to share. Someone leaves loaves of homemade bread and a sign apologizing for the price, fifty cents a loaf. There is formal counseling, but there is also informal advice, help, and support from staff members and other patients who may be sitting in a group rapping and sharing problems and solutions. The waiting room crowd on Women's Night tends to be, not little islands of one or two people, sitting reading or starting at the wall, but clusters of three to five women, talking, eating, laughing. Women leave to see the doctor, or to assist in a pelvic exam. The groups change and grow. Women talk about

---

* From "Women's Night at the Free Clinic" by Kathy Campbell, Terry Dalsemer and Judy Waldman, 1972. Reprinted by permission.

children, marriage, divorce, housing hassles, their successes or failures with various birth control methods. What will cure vaginitis and what won't. The state of the women's move-ment. The date of the next women's dance. There's a feeling of warmth, shelter, of "yes, you've come to the right place; what can we share with you?"

We wanted to stress that women are not simply "pelvics," but people, and should be treated as such. In case one of the clinic doctors should forget this, we as a group are there to confront him and talk it out.

One night we experienced a good example of how little control we have over our bodies and how Women's Night hopes to change this. A woman, complaining of cramps related to her I.U.D. was examined by a male gynecologist, new to our staff. The woman was extremely nervous and uncomfortable during the exam, and needed constant reassurance from the advocate who was there assisting both the patient and the doctor with the exam. Although he found nothing wrong, there was something he wanted another doctor to see, so that he insisted she have another examination. The advocate strongly questioned the necessity for this, and although the woman reluctantly agreed to be reexamined, the issue was brought up again at our evaluation session at the end of the evening. (This session includes everyone—patients and staff.) We then talked with this doctor and others about their using our bodies for teaching (especially without being open about this and asking our permission) and how we wanted to be sure that we control what is being done to us and our bodies. We felt good—we were speaking together as women; we were being heard and making some changes.

CHAPTER 19

Contested Terrain:
Change and Resistance

Feminism played a major role in the transformation of gender norms and the empowerment of women. In response to the resurgence of feminist collective action during the 1970s, Congress passed a variety of gender equity acts. Women entered nontraditional fields as police and fire *persons*. Even language changed and became, as the preceding job titles illustrate, gender neutral. Gender-designated advertising for employment ended. Women's studies and women's history joined the college curriculum. Textbooks displayed a new sensitivity to the issues of gender bias. New employment opportunities led to an upsurge in the numbers of women in law, medicine, and college teaching. Women entered the formerly male preserve of news and even sports broadcasting. In *Roe v. Wade* (1973), the U.S. Supreme Court upheld the right of women to choose to have an abortion.

Yet, even as the women's movement gained momentum, victories met with increasing opposition. Right-to-life groups mobilized to repeal *Roe v. Wade*. Although Congress passed the Equal Rights Amendment (ERA) in 1972, the requisite number of states did not ratify it. Anti-amendment groups rallied around conservative activist Phyllis Schlafly in a highly effective Stop ERA campaign. In *The Positive Woman,* Schlafly continued to promote the views of nineteenth-century authors such as Amelia Barr and Catharine Beecher, namely that the difference between men and women was profound, enduring, and God ordained. Schlafly alleged that women fighting for rights were deeply confused, fighting nonexistent wrongs; public policy and employment did not discriminate but merely reflected females' differences from men. From this perspective, ERA was a contradiction of normal and innate male and female differences. Among its multiple meanings, the 1980 election of Ronald Reagan for president expressed a societal retreat from widespread social and cultural change. Despite the political shift, President Reagan appointed Sandra Day O'Connor to the U.S. Supreme Court, the first woman to serve since the founding of the Court. The Republican Party withdrew its support from the ERA, and its political leaders spoke out against abortion rights and in favor of Christian family values. Increasingly, conservative critics blamed the women's movement with causing the increased divorce rate and the destabilization of families. During the 1980s, feminist objectives also fostered hostility from men. Caught in the spiral of the national transformation to a postindustrial and global economy that caused the loss of jobs and downward mobility, some white men lashed out at the women's movement as the cause of their economic and social distress. An electoral gender gap emerged: Compared with white women, white men voted in higher numbers for conservative Republican candidates.

Advocates of women's rights also confronted a generation gap. Many younger women did not identify with women's issues, or the need for women as a group to resolve remaining gender inequities. In a manner reminiscent of young women of the 1920s they focus on individual achievement. Benefiting from greater educational and employment opportunities and increasing acceptance of liberated lifestyles, they distanced themselves from the older generation of feminists. Some joined the backlash described by Susan Faludi. Despite the decline of organized momentum and the growing conservative backlash, the feminist agenda still responded to the needs of millions of women. The feminist philosophy that the "personal is political" continued to resonate. Issues such as spousal abuse, sexual harassment, and abortion rights received grassroots support and national attention. Battered women were no longer silent victims but sought community understanding and professional support. Activist women continued to campaign for the resolution of persistent workplace inequities and the provision of adequate and affordable child care. Even before the organized women's movement, growing numbers of married women with children had been entering the workforce. For many, the difficulties involved in combining work and motherhood remained enormous. Single mothers generally faced the greatest hardship. The media publicized their plight as the growing "feminization of poverty." By the mid-1990s, welfare mothers faced the prospect of a rollback of the entitlements in place since the 1930s.

As the backlash gained momentum, internal conflicts also tore at the fabric of second wave feminism. During the 1980s, a major rift developed among women who identified as feminists over the issue of pornography and whether pornography exploited women and violated their rights. In what became known as the "sex wars," two rival feminist factions debated whether pornography was an act of violence against women or conversely an expression of sexuality based on choice. Anti-pornography advocates repudiated pornography as sexually abusive and a violation of women's civil rights. In her memoir, Susan Brownmiller recalled the polarizing impact of the conflict. A member of Women against Pornography (WAP), she and her associates battled against the saturation of the pornography industry in the Times Square section of New York City. Reformers such as Brownmiller encountered the criticism of so-called pro-sex feminists who alleged that efforts at suppression and censorship harked back to the outdated moral reform objectives of the nineteenth century.

An outpouring of writing and lesbian activism also characterized the closing decades of the twentieth century. Mab Segrest struggled to dismantle all forms of sexism, racism, and homophobia. African American Audre Lorde stressed the need for women of color and lesbians to develop their own agendas for overturning systems of oppression. Lesbian women such as Segrest and Lorde exemplified the multiple dimensions of the female experience as well as the existence of interlocking oppressions.

Anita Hill's allegations of sexual harassment at the confirmation hearings for Supreme Court nominee Clarence Thomas riveted the nation's attention and also brought the issue of sexual harassment into national prominence. Galvanized by the hearings, young women developed a revised feminism suitable for the changing conditions of their era, which they defined as the third wave. The quest of young women for new forms of feminist identification contrasted with the dominant trend of many women who took feminists' gains for granted and accepted the complacency of an allegedly post-feminist age. The aggressive behavior of the senators who sought to discredit Hill helped ignite the senatorial bids of several women. In a precedent-breaking election, four women, all Democrats, were elected to the senate and 1992 became known as "the year of the women." President Bill Clinton's nomination of Ruth Bader Ginsburg to the Supreme Court won the support of change-oriented women's groups. A graduate of Columbia Law School with impeccable academic credentials, Ginsburg had gained recognition for her successful advocacy of gender equity in the workplace. Her judicial philosophy included the right to privacy, the foundational basis of the *Roe v. Wade* decision.

In significant ways, the formation of the nation's domestic policy during the 1980s and early 1990s expressed the cultural battles being waged between groups demanding the restoration of traditional family values and those protecting women's changing gender roles. The contest over women's rights has remained pivotal to the policy debate. It has influenced U.S. Supreme Court appointments and helped determine election results. Although the election of a Democratic president in 1992 resulted in the greater affirmation of women's rights, the 1994 congressional victories of conservative Republicans signified the potential for retreat. This contested terrain of women's rights remained central to the nation's cultural and political experience.

Excerpt from *Roe v. Wade* (1973)

The *Roe v. Wade* U.S. Supreme Court decision upheld the right of women to obtain medically safe abortions. The class action lawsuit argued before the Supreme Court challenged the right of the state of Texas to criminalize abortion except in the case of saving the mother's life. To feminists, abortion rights were essential to women's freedom. For abortion opponents, fetal rights took precedence over women's rights. Moreover, the ability of a woman to terminate a pregnancy represented the ultimate challenge to what many religious and conservative groups still considered women's God-given maternal function. The most divisive of all women's issues, the controversy between the right to abortion and the right to life continues to divide not only women, but the nation in general. Essentially the Court upheld the right to privacy, a position taken in the *Griswold* decision some years earlier (see Chapter 18). How did the Court define the right to privacy? What limits did the Court place on the right to choose an abortion?*

Mr. Justice Blackmun delivered the opinion of the Court

It perhaps is not generally appreciated that the restrictive criminal abortion laws in effect in a majority of States today are of relatively recent vintage. Those laws, generally proscribing abortion or its attempt at any time during pregnancy except when necessary to preserve the pregnant woman's life, are not of ancient or even of common-law origin. Instead, they derive from statutory changes effected, for the most part, in the latter half of the 19th century.

Three reasons have been advanced to explain historically the enactment of criminal abortion laws in the 19th century and to justify their continued existence.

It has been argued occasionally that these laws were the product of a Victorian social concern to discourage illicit sexual conduct. Texas, however, does not advance this justification in the present case, and it appears that no court or commentator has taken the argument seriously. . . .

A second reason is concerned with abortion as a medical procedure. When most criminal abortion laws were first enacted, the procedure was a hazardous one for the woman. . . . Thus, it has been argued that a State's real concern in enacting a criminal abortion law was to protect the pregnant woman, that is, to restrain her from submitting to a procedure that placed her life in serious jeopardy.

Modern medical techniques have altered this situation. Appellants and various amici refer to medical data indicating the abortion in early pregnancy, that is, prior to the end of the first trimester, although not without its risk, is now relatively safe. Mortality rates for women undergoing early abortions, where the procedure is legal, appear to be as low or lower than the rates for normal childbirth. Consequently, any interest of the State in protecting the woman from an inherently hazardous procedure, except when it would be equally dangerous for her to undergo it, has largely disappeared. Of course, important state interests in the area of health and medical standards do remain. . . .

The third reason is the State's interest— some phrase it in terms of duty—in protecting prenatal life. Some of the argument for its justification rests on the theory that a new human life is present from the moment of conception. The State's interest and general obligation to protect life then extends, it is argued, to prenatal life. Only when the life of the pregnant mother herself is at stake, balanced against the life she carries within her, should the interest of the embryo or fetus not prevail. Logically, of course, a legitimate state interest in this area need not stand or fall

on acceptance of the belief that life begins at conception or at some other point prior to live birth. In assessing the State's interest, recognition may be given to the less rigid claim that as long as at least *potential* life is involved, the State may assert interests beyond the protection of the pregnancy woman alone. . . .

The Constitution does not explicitly mention any right of privacy. In a line of decisions, however, the Court has recognized that a right of personal privacy, or a guarantee of certain areas or zones of privacy, does exist under the Constitution. . . .

This right of privacy, whether it be founded in the Fourteenth Amendment's concept of personal liberty and restrictions upon state action, as we feel it is, or, as the District Court determined, in the Ninth Amendment's reservation of right to the people, is broad enough to encompass a woman's decision whether or not to terminate her pregnancy. The detriment that the State would impose upon the pregnant women by denying this choice altogether is apparent. Specific and direct harm medically diagnosable even in early pregnancy may be involved. Maternity, or additional offspring, may force upon the woman a distressful life and future. Psychological harm may be imminent. Mental and physical health may be taxed by child care. There is also the distress, for all concerned, associated with the unwanted child, and there is the problem of bringing a child into a family already unable, psychologically and otherwise, to care for it. In other cases, as in this one, the additional difficulties and continuing stigma of unwed motherhood may be involved. All these are factors the woman and her responsible physician necessarily will consider in consultation.

On the basis of elements such as these, appellant and some amici argue that the woman's right: is absolute, that she is entitled to terminate her pregnancy at whatever time, in whatever way, and for whatever reason she alone chooses. With this we do not agree. Appellant's arguments that Texas either has no valid interest at all in regulating the abortion decision, or no interest strong enough to support any limitation upon the woman's sole determination, is unpersuasive. The Court's decisions recognizing a right of privacy, also acknowledge that some state regulation in areas protected by that right is appropriate. As noted above, a State may properly assert important interests in safeguarding health, in maintaining medical standards, and in protecting potential life. At some point in pregnancy, these respective interests become sufficiently compelling to sustain regulation of the factors that govern the abortion decision. The privacy right involved, therefore, cannot be said to be absolute. . . .

We, therefore, conclude that the right of personal privacy includes the abortion decision, but that this right is not unqualified and must be considered against important state interests in regulation. . . .

With respect to the State's important and legitimate interest in the health of the mother, the "compelling" point, in the light of present medical knowledge, is at approximately the end of the first trimester. This is so because of the now-established medical fact that until the end of the first trimester mortality in abortion may be less than mortality in normal childbirth. It follows that, from and after this point, a State may regulate the abortion procedure to the extent that the regulation reasonably relates to the preservation and protection of maternal health. . . .

With respect to the State's important and legitimate interest in potential life, the "compelling" point is viability. This is so because the fetus then presumably has the capability of meaningful life outside the mother's womb. State regulation protective of fetal life after viability thus has both logical and biological justifications. If the State is interested in protecting fetal life after viability, it may go so far as to proscribe abortion during that period, except when it is necessary to preserve the life or health of the mother.

PHYLLIS SCHLAFLY, *The Positive Woman* (1977)

Politically active in conservative causes since the 1950s, Phyllis Schlafly (b.1924) became well known for her successful mobilization of opposition to the ERA. In this excerpt from her book *The Power of the Positive Woman,* Schlafly argues that female attributes are God given and part of the fixed order of nature and the universe. For Schlafly, "positive women" accept their inborn nature, and feminists are unnatural. Gender as a cultural and social construction that changes over time has no meaning to critics such as Schlafly. What does Schlafly mean by women's "kind of superior strength"? What does she mean by the statement "men are philosophers, women are practical and, twas ever thus"? How are her views similar to those of Amelia Barr (see Chapter 9)?*

The first requirement for the acquisition of power by the Positive Woman is to understand the differences between men and women. Your outlook on life, your faith, your behavior, your potential for fulfillment, all are determined by the parameters of your original premise. The Positive Woman starts with the assumption that the world is her oyster. She rejoices in the creative capability within her body and the power potential of her mind

* From *The Power of the Positive Woman* by Phyllis Schlafly. Copyright © 1977 by Phyllis Schlafly. Used by permission of Arlington House, a division of Random House, Inc.

and spirit. She understands that men and women are different, and that those very differences provide the key to her success as a person and fulfillment as a woman. The women's liberationist, on the other hand, is imprisoned by her own negative view of herself and of her place in the world around her. This view of women was most succinctly expressed in an advertisement designed by the principal women's liberationist organization, the National Organization for Women (NOW), and run in many magazines and newspapers, and as spot announcements on many television stations. The advertisement showed a darling curlyheaded girl with the caption: "This healthy, normal baby has a handicap. She was born female."

This is the self-articulated dog-in-the-manger, chip-on-the-shoulder, fundamental dogma of the women's liberation movement. Someone—it is not clear who, perhaps God, perhaps the "Establishment," perhaps a conspiracy of male chauvinist pigs—dealt women a foul blow by making them female. It becomes necessary, therefore, for women to agitate and demonstrate and hurl demands on society, in order to wrest from an oppressive male-dominated social structure the status that has been wrongfully denied to women through the centuries.

By its very name, therefore, the women's liberation movement precipitates a series of conflict situations—in the legislatures, in the courts, in the schools, in industry—with man targeted as the enemy. Confrontation replaces cooperation as the watchwords of all relationships. Women and men become adversaries instead of partners.

The second dogma of the women's liberationists is that, of all the injustices perpetuated upon women through the centuries, the most oppressive is the cruel fact that women have babies and men do not. Within the confines of the women's liberationist ideology, therefore, the abolition of this overriding inequality of women becomes the primary goal. This goal must be achieved at any and all costs—to the woman herself, to the baby, to the family, and to society. Women must be made equal to men in their ability *not* to become pregnant and *not* be expected to care for babies they may bring into the world. . . .

The Positive Woman will never travel that dead-end road. It is self-evident to the Positive Woman that the female body with its baby-producing organs was not designed by a conspiracy of men, but by the Divine Architect of the human race. Those who think it is unfair that women have babies, whereas men cannot, will have to take up their complaint with God because no other power is capable of changing that fundamental fact. . . .

The third basic dogma of the women's liberation movement is that there is no difference between male and female, except the sex organs, and that all those physical, cognitive, and emotional differences you *think* there are, are merely the results of centuries of restraints imposed by male-dominated society and sex-stereotyped schooling. The role imposed on women is, by definition, inferior, according to the women's liberationists.

The Positive Woman knows that, while there are some physical competitions in which women are better (and can command more money) than men, including those that put a premium on grace and beauty, such as figure skating, the superior physical strength of males over females in competitions of strength, speed, and short-term endurance is beyond rational dispute. . . .

Does the physical advantage of men doom women to a life of servility and subservience? The Positive Woman knows that she has a complementary advantage which is at least as great—and, in the hands of a skillful woman, far greater. The Divine Architect who gave men a superior strength to lift weights also gave women a different kind of superior strength.

The women's liberationists and their dupes who try and tell each other that the sexual drive of men and women is really the same, and that it is only societal restraints that inhibit women from an equal desire, and equal enjoyment, and an equal freedom from the consequences, are doomed to frustration forever. It just isn't so, and pretending cannot make it so. The differences are not a woman's weakness but her strength. . . .

The new generation can brag all it wants about the new liberation of the new morality, but it is still the woman who is hurt the most. The new morality isn't just a "fad"—it is a cheat and a thief. It robs the woman of her virtue, her youth, her beauty, and her love— for nothing, just nothing. It has produced a generation of young women searching for their identity, bored with sexual freedom, and despondent from the loneliness of living a life without commitment. They have abandoned the old commandments, but they can't find any new rules that work. . . .

The differences between men and women are also emotional and psychological. Without woman's innate maternal instinct, the human race would have died out centuries ago. There is nothing so helpless in all earthly life as the newborn infant. It will die within hours if not cared for. Even in the most primitive, uneducated societies, women have always cared for their newborn babies. They didn't need any schooling to teach them how. They didn't need any welfare workers to tell them it is their social obligation. Even in societies to whom such concepts as "ought,"

"social responsibility," and "compassion for the helpless" were unknown, mothers cared for their new babies.

Why? Because caring for a baby serves the natural maternal need of a woman. Although not nearly so total as the baby's need, the woman's need is nonetheless real. The overriding psychological need of a woman is to love something alive. A baby fulfills this need in the lives of most women. If a baby is not available to fill this need, women search for a baby-substitute. This is the reason why women have traditionally gone into teaching and nursing careers. They are doing what comes naturally to the female psyche. The schoolchild or the patient of any age provides an outlet for a woman to express her natural maternal need. . . .

Finally, women are different from men in dealing with the fundamentals of life itself. Men are philosophers, women are practical, and 'twas ever thus. Men may philosophize about how life began and where we are heading; women are concerned about feeding the kids today. No woman would ever, as Karl Marx did, spend years reading political philosophy in the British Museum while her child starved to death. Women don't take naturally to a search for the intangible and the abstract. The Positive Woman knows who she is and where she is going, and she will reach her goal because the longest journey starts with a very practical first step.

A Letter from a Battered Wife (1983)

Feminists made women's private concerns public and connected the personal to the political. They argued that male violence stemmed from inequitable power relationships and society's permissive attitude toward abuse of women. What evidence does the abused wife offer of her relative helplessness? This letter was written in 1983; what gains, if any, have women made in combating male violence?*

---

* From *Battered Wives* by Del Martin. Reprinted by permission of Volcano Press, P.O. Box 270, Volcano, CA 95689.

I am in my thirties and so is my husband. I have a high school diploma and am presently attending a local college, trying to obtain the additional education I need. My husband is a college graduate and a professional in his field. We are both attractive and, for the most part, respected and well-liked. We have four children and live in a middle-class home with all the comforts we could possibly want.

I have everything, except a life without fear.

For most of my married life I have been periodically beaten by my husband. What do I mean by "beaten"? I mean that parts of my body have been hit violently and repeatedly, and that painful bruises, swelling, bleeding wounds, unconsciousness, and combinations of these things have resulted.

Beating should be distinguished from all other kinds of physical abuse—including being hit and shoved around. When I say my husband threatens me with abuse I do not mean he warns me that he may lose control. I mean he shakes his fist against my face or nose, makes punching-bag jabs at my shoulder, or makes similar gestures which may quickly turn into a full-fledged beating.

I have had glasses thrown at me. I have been kicked in the abdomen when I was visibly pregnant. I have been kicked off the bed and hit while I was lying on the floor—again, while I was pregnant. I have been whipped, kicked and thrown, picked up again and thrown down again. I have been punched and kicked in the head, chest, face, and abdomen more times than I can count. . . .

Now the first response to this story, which I myself think of, will be "Why didn't you seek help?"

I did. Early on in our marriage I went to a clergyman who, after a few visits, told me that my husband meant no real harm, and he was just confused and felt insecure. I was encouraged to be more tolerant and understanding. Most important, I was told to forgive him the beatings just as Christ had forgiven me from the cross. I did that, too. . . .

I turned to a professional family guidance agency. I was told there that my husband needed help and that I should find a way to control the incidents. I couldn't control the beatings—that was the whole point of my seeking help. At the agency I found I had to defend myself against that suspicion that I wanted to be hit, that I invited the beatings. Good God! Did the Jews invite themselves to be slaughtered in Germany?

I called the police one time. They not only did not respond to the call, they called several hours later to ask if things had "settled down." I could have been dead by then!

I have nowhere to go if it happens again. No one wants to take in a woman with four children. Even if there were someone kind enough to care, no one wants to become involved in what is commonly referred to as a "domestic situation."

As a married woman I have no recourse but to remain in the situation which is causing me to be painfully abused. I have suffered physical and emotional battering and spiritual rape because the social structure of my world says I cannot do anything about a man who wants to beat me. . . . But staying with my husband means that my children must be subjected to the emotional battering caused when they see their mother's beaten face or hear her screams in the middle of the night.

I know that I have to get out. But when you have nowhere to go, you know that you must go on your own, and expect no support. I have to be ready for that. I have to be ready to support myself and the children completely, and still provide a decent environment for them. I pray that I can do that before I am murdered in my own home.

I have learned that no one believes me and that I cannot depend upon any outside help. All I have left is the hope that I can get away before it is too late.

I have learned also that the doctors, the police, the clergy, and my friends will excuse my husband for distorting my face, but won't forgive me for looking bruised and broken.

The greatest tragedy is that I am still praying, and there is not a human person to listen.

Being beaten is a terrible thing; it is most terrible of all if you are not equipped to fight back. I recall an occasion when I tried to defend myself and actually tore my husband's shirt. Later, he showed it to a relative as proof that I had done something terribly wrong. The fact that at that moment I had several raised spots on my head hidden by my hair, a swollen lip that was bleeding, and a severely damaged cheek with a blood clot that caused a permanent dimple didn't matter to him. What mattered was that I tore his shirt! That I tore it in self-defense didn't mean anything to him.

My situation is so untenable I would guess that anyone who has not experienced one like it would find it incomprehensible. I find it difficult to believe myself.

AUDRE LORDE, *The Master's Tools Will Never Dismantle the Master's House* (1984)

Although Andre Lorde (1934–1992) particularly notes the deficiencies of papers presented at an academic conference, her concerns were wider. An outspoken poet, essayist, black radical, and feminist lesbian, Lorde did not advocate tolerance but empowerment for groups the power structure, including white women, marginalized. In the following essay, she raised issues that she maintained white, heterosexual feminists ignored. Lorde's criticism had much in common with Third World feminists who also rejected white feminists' efforts to speak for women of color and to present their own agenda in universal terms. How would you explain the meaning of Lorde's title? Why is she critical of white women?*

I agreed to take part in a New York University Institute for the Humanities conference a year ago, with the understanding that I would be commenting upon papers dealing with the role of difference within the lives of American women: difference of race, sexuality, class, and age. The absence of these considerations weakens any feminist discussion of the personal and the political.

It is a particular academic arrogance to assume any discussion of feminist theory without examining our many differences, and without a significant input from poor women, Black and Third World women, and lesbians. And yet, I stand here as a Black lesbian feminist, having been invited to comment within the only panel at this conference where the input of Black feminists and lesbians is represented. What this says about the vision of this conference is sad, in a country where racism, sexism, and homophobia are inseparable. To read this program is to assume that lesbian and Black women have nothing to say about existentialism, the erotic, women's culture and silence, developing feminist theory, or heterosexuality and power. And what does it mean in personal and political terms when even the two Black women who did present here were literally found at the last hour? What does it mean when the tools of a racist patriarchy are used to examine the fruits of that same patriarchy? It means that only the most narrow perimeters of change are possible and allowable.

The absence of any consideration of lesbian consciousness or the consciousness of Third World women leaves a serious gap within this conference and within the papers presented here. For example, in a paper on material relationships between women, I was conscious of an either/or model of nurturing which totally dismissed my knowledge as a Black lesbian. In this paper there was no examination of

---

* From *Sister Outsider*, The Crossing Press Feminist Series (1984).

mutuality between women, no systems of shared support, no interdependence as exists between lesbians and women-identified women. Yet it is only in the patriarchal model of nurturance that women "who attempt to emancipate themselves pay perhaps too nigh a price for the results," as this paper states.

For women, the need and desire to nurture each other is not pathological but redemptive, and it is within that knowledge that our real power is rediscovered. It is this real connection which is so feared by a patriarchal world. Only within a patriarchal structure is maternity the only social power open to women.

Interdependency between women is the way to a freedom which allows the I to be, not in order to be used, but in order to be creative. This is a difference between the passive be and the active being.

Advocating the mere tolerance of difference between women is the grossest reformism. It is a total denial of the creative function of difference in our lives. Difference must be not merely tolerated, but seen as a fund of necessary polarities between which our creativity can spark like a dialectic. Only then does the necessity for interdependency become unthreatening. Only within that interdependency of different strengths, acknowledged and equal, can the power to seek new ways of being in the world generate, as well as the courage and sustenance to act where there are no charters.

Within the interdependence of mutual (nondominant) differences lies that security which enables us to descend into the chaos of knowledge and return with true visions of our future, along with the concomitant power to effect those changes which can bring that future into being. Difference is that raw and powerful connection from which our personal power is forged.

As women, we have been taught either to ignore our differences, or to view them as causes for separation and suspicion rather than as forces for change. Without community there is no liberation, only the most vulnerable and temporary armistice between an individual and

her oppression. But community must not mean a shedding of our differences, nor the pathetic pretense that these differences do not exist.

Those of us who stand outside the circle of this society's definition of acceptable women; those of us who have been forged in the crucibles of difference—those of us who are poor, who are lesbians, who are Black, who are older—know that survival is not an academic skill. It is learning how to stand alone, unpopular and sometimes reviled, and how to make common cause with those others identified as outside the structures in order to define and seek a world in which we can all flourish. It is learning how to take our differences and make them strengths. For the master's tools will never dismantle the master's house. They may allow us temporarily to beat him at his own game, but they will never enable us to bring about genuine change. And this fact is only threatening to those women who still define the master's house as their only source of support.

Poor women and women of Color know there is a difference between the daily manifestations of marital slavery and prostitution because it is our daughters who line 42nd Street. If white American feminist theory need not deal with the differences between us, and the resulting difference in our oppressions, then how do you deal with the fact that the women who clean your houses and tend your children while you attend conferences on feminist theory are, for the most part, poor women and women of Color? What is the theory behind racist feminism? In a world of possibility for us all, our personal visions help lay the groundwork for political action. The failure of academic feminists to recognize difference as a crucial strength is a failure to reach beyond the first patriarchal lesson. In our world, divide and conquer must become define and empower.

Why weren't other women of Color found to participate in this conference? Why were two phone calls to me considered a consultation? Am I the only possible source of names of Black feminists? And although the Black panelist's paper ends on an important and powerful connection of love between women, what about interracial cooperation between feminists who don't love each other?

In academic feminist circles, the answer to these questions is often, "We did not know who to ask." But that is the same evasion of responsibility, the same cop-out, that keeps Black women's art out of women's exhibitions, Black women's work out of most feminist publications except for the occasional "Special Third World Women's Issue," and Black women's texts off your reading lists. But as Adrienne Rich pointed out in a recent talk, white feminists have educated themselves about such an enormous amount over the past ten years, how come you haven't also educated yourselves about Black women and the differences between us—white and Black—when it is key to our survival as a movement?

Women of today are still being called upon to stretch across the gap of male ignorance and to educate men as to our existence and our needs. This is an old and primary tool of all oppressors to keep the oppressed occupied with the master's concerns. Now we hear that it is the task of women of Color to educate white women—in the face of tremendous resistance—as to our existence, our differences, our relative roles in our joint survival. This is a diversion of energies and a tragic repetition of racist patriarchal thought.

Simone de Beauvoir once said: "It is in the knowledge of the genuine conditions of our lives that we must draw our strength to live and our reasons for acting."

Racism and homophobia are real conditions of all our lives in this place and time. I urge each one of us here to reach down into that deep place of knowledge inside herself and touch that terror and loathing of any difference that lives there. See whose face it wears. Then the personal as the political can begin to illuminate all our choices.

MAB SEGREST, Excerpt from *"Confessions of a Closet Baptist"* (1985)

As a college professor and social activist, Mab Segrest's (b.1949) life has represented a struggle to repudiate and combat racism, homophobia, and anti-Semitism. During the eighties and nineties, Segrest played a key role combating the Ku Klux Klan and neo-Nazi groups in North Carolina. In the following document, she notes that overcoming her inability to accept her own lesbian identity proved liberating and facilitated her leadership in fighting not only homophobia but also other forms of hatred. Segrest's feminist activism demonstrated her recognition that sexism and misogyny were only one form of oppression that confronted women.

Today it is widely recognized among feminists that women do not have a single set of experiences stemming from a one-dimensional female identity. Intersections of gender with race, class, religion, and so on prevail. Women oppressed by gender constraints may exercise privileges of race, class, or sexual orientation to oppress others. How did Segrest's understanding of her own oppression as a lesbian serve as a catalyst for her activism against other forms of oppression? What does her term *closet Baptist* refer to in terms of her experience as a lesbian?*

I lead a double life. By day I'm a relatively mild-mannered English teacher at a Southern Baptist college. By night—and on Tuesdays and Thursdays and weekends—I am a lesbian writer and editor, a collective member of *Feminary,* a lesbian-feminist journal for the South. My

---

* Reprinted from *My Mama's Dead Squirrel: Lesbian Essays On Southern Culture,* by Mab Segrest. Copyright © 1985 by Mab Segrest. Reprinted by permission of Firebrand Books, Ithaca, New York. Material excerpted from pages 72–77.

employers do not know about my other life. When they find out, I assume I will be fired, maybe prayed to death. For the past four years my life has moved rapidly in opposite directions.

When I started teaching English at my present school five years ago, I knew I was a lesbian. I was living with P, my first woman lover. I wasn't out politically. I had not yet discovered the lesbian culture and lesbian community that is now such an important part of my life. The first time I had let myself realize I was in love with P, I sat under a willow tree by the lake at the Girl Scout camp where we both worked and said aloud to myself in the New York darkness: "I am a lesbian." I had to see how it sounded, and after I'd said that, gradually, I felt I could say anything. When, three years ago, P left to live with a man, I knew my life had changed. I read lesbian books and journals with great excitement. I joined the collective of *Feminary,* then a local feminist journal, and helped turn it into a journal for Southern lesbians. I started writing. I did all this while working for the Baptists, feeling myself making decisions that were somehow as frightening as they were inevitable. Early issues of *Feminary* record the process. First there is a poem by "Mabel." Then an article by "Mab." Then the whole leap: "Mab Segrest." I knew if I could not write my name, I couldn't write anything. I also knew: if I can't be myself and teach, I won't teach. . . .

Teaching is the work I love best. I can bring much of myself to it and much of it to myself. But as a lesbian teacher in a society that hates homosexuals—especially homosexual teachers—I have learned a caution towards my students and my school that saddens me. The things my life has taught me best I cannot teach directly. I do not believe that I am the only one that suffers.

The first time homosexuality came up in my classroom it was a shock to my system. It was in freshman composition, and I was letting a class choose debate topics. They picked gay rights, but nobody wanted to argue the gay side. Finally, three of my more vociferous students volunteered. I went home shaken.

I dreamed that night I was in class, my back to my students, writing on the board (I always feel most vulnerable then), and students were taunting me from the desks—"lesbian! queer!"

The day of the debate I took a seat in the back row, afraid that if I stood up in front *IT* would show. I would give myself away: develop a tic, tremble, stutter, throw up, then faint dead away. I kept quiet as my three pro-gay students held off the Bible with the Bill of Rights, to everyone's amazement, including my own. (I certainly knew it could be done; I just didn't expect them to do it. No one else in the class had figured any legitimate arguments were possible.) Then the anti-gay side rallied and hit on a winning tactic. They implied that if the opponents really believed their own arguments, they were pretty "funny." I called an end to the debate, and the pro-gay side quickly explained how they didn't mean anything they had said. Then one of my female students wanted to discuss how Christians should love people even when they were sick and sinful. I said the discussion was over and dismissed the class. The only time I had spoken during the entire debate was in response to a male student behind me who had reacted defensively to a mention of homosexuality in the army with, "Yes, and where *my* father works, they castrate people like that." I turned to him with quiet fury. "Are you advocating it?" All in all I survived the day, but without much self-respect.

The next year, on a theme, a freshman explained to me how you could tell gay people "by the bandannas they wear in their pockets and around their necks." She concluded, "I think homosexuals are a menace to society. *What do you think?"* A pregnant question, indeed. I pondered for awhile, then wrote back in the margin, "I think society is a menace to homosexuals." I resisted wearing a red bandanna the day 1 handed back the papers. . . .

I see the unease of most college students over sexuality—whether they express it swaggering and hollow laughter over queer jokes, or in timidity, or in the half-proud confession of a preacher at how he knocked his wife's teeth out—and how it is part of a larger disease with sexuality and the definitions of *men* and *women* in this society. I see how they, and most of us, have been taught to fear all of our feelings. And I understand all too well when I realize I am afraid to write—to even know—what I think and feel for fear of losing my job; how money buys conformity; how subtly we are terrorized into staying in line.

The closest I ever came to saying what I wanted to was in an American literature class last year. Gay rights came up again—I think I may have even steered the discussion in that direction. And a student finally said to me, "But what about teachers? We can't have homosexuals teaching students!" I resisted leaping up on the podium and flashing the big *L* emblazoned on a leotard beneath my blouse. Instead, I took a deep breath and began slowly. "Well, in my opinion, you don't learn sexual preference in the classroom. I mean that's not what we are doing here. *If you* had a gay or lesbian teacher, he or she would not teach you about preference." I paused to catch my breath. They were all listening. "What he or she would say, *if you had* a gay teacher, is this . . ." (by now I was lightly beating on the podium) "'. . . don't let them make you afraid to be who you are. To know who you are.' She would tell you, 'Don't let them get you. Don't let them make you afraid.'" I stopped abruptly and in the silence turned to think of something to write on the board.

If they ever *do* have a lesbian teacher, that is exactly what she will say.

Susan Brownmiller, *In Our Time: Memoir of a Revolution* (1999)

One of the leaders of the second wave of feminist reform, Susan Brownmiller (b. 1935) wrote a controversial book *Against Our Will* (1975) that helped overturn conventional social and legal views about rape. In the following excerpt from her memoir, *In Our Time,* she recounts the history of and traces her role in the major events of the feminist movement. Direct action characterized much of second-wave feminist protest. Brownmiller describes how, in an effort to close down New York City's Times Square pornography centers in the late 1970s, she organized Women Against Pornography (WAP). WAP members considered pornography a form of violence against women and were outraged by its sadomasochistic elements. They believed porn helped promote a rape culture. The feminist anti-pornography crusade ultimately failed to achieve consensus. What issues caused WAP to splinter into warring factions? Which side of this debate would you support? Why?*

In what became our most popular tactic, Women Against Pornography opened up the hidden life of Times Square for a suggested five-dollar donation. I plotted the itinerary and wrote a script based on information, supplied by Carl Weisbrod and Maggie Smith, about which mobster reputedly owned what X-rated theater or coin arcade, and what sort of wages the employees at Show World, the Dating Room, the Mardi Gras, or the Pussycat received of an evening. A WAP tour was never without spontaneous encounters—getting tossed out bodily by hysterical managers; watching the customers, often white men in business suits, slink away in confusion; engaging in short, frank dialogues with the amused, blasé, embarrassed, or furious Live! Nude! Topless! Bottomless! performers when they emerged from their circular cages to take their hourly breaks. The unexpected appearance of women in clothes, to observe

---

* From *In Our Time: Memoir of a Revolution* by Susan Brownmiller. Copyright © 1999 by Susan Brownmiller. Used by permission of The Dial Press.

men in clothes watching naked women writhe in mock sexual pleasure for the men's entertainment, dramatically altered the atmosphere of the live sex shows' self-contained world. We had not thought this out very clearly beforehand, but our intrusion was shattering to the careful construct of denial the performers relied on to get them through the night. . . .

We already had an inkling that some feminists were not happy about what we were doing, although the opposition hadn't yet solidified into an organized campaign. The slide show was hitting raw nerves. Dolores Alexander, a whiz at raising money through the lesbian social network, had encountered a negative reaction at

one of her presentations. When she projected a slide of women in bondage, a guest screamed, "You're attacking my sexuality! I find that picture very sexy!" We began to get agitated responses from straight women as well. Sometimes they were emotional defenses of free speech, but to our bewilderment, we also saw that some women identified their sexuality with the s/m pictures we found degrading. Porn turned them on, and they didn't want to hear any political raps about how women were conditioned to find their sexual pleasure within the misogynistic scenarios created by men. They claimed we were condemning their minds and behavior, and I guess we were.

ANITA HILL, *Statement to the Senate Judiciary Committee* (1991)

Anita Hill's (b. 1956) allegation that U.S. Supreme Court nominee Clarence Thomas, the former head of the Equal Employment Opportunity Commission (EEOC), was guilty of sexual harassment propelled the issue to national attention. As a result of Hill's testimony, many other women filed sexual harassment complaints. Over the centuries, African American women have struggled against the simultaneous oppression of race and gender. The testimony of Hill, an African American female, against Thomas, an African American male, raised both race and gender issues. What would some of these issues be?*

Mr. Chairman, Senator Thurmond, members of the committee:

My name is Anita F. Hill, and I am a professor of law at the University of Oklahoma. I was born on a farm in Okmulgee County, Oklahoma, in 1956. I am the youngest of thirteen children. . . .

For my undergraduate work, I went to Oklahoma State University and graduated from there in 1977. I am attaching to this statement a copy of my resume for further details of my education. . . .

I graduated from the university with academic honors, and proceeded to the Yale Law School, where I received my J.D. degree in 1980.

Upon graduation from law school, I became a practicing lawyer with the Washington, D.C., firm of Wald, Wakrader & Ross. In 1981 I was introduced to now Judge Thomas by a mutual friend.

Judge Thomas told me that he was anticipating a political appointment, and asked if I would be interested in working with him.

He was in fact appointed as assistant secretary of education for civil rights. After he had taken that post, he asked if I would become his assistant, and I accepted that position.

In my early period, there, I had two major projects. First was an article I wrote for Judge Thomas's signature on the education of

---

* From Anita Hill, "Statement to the Senate Judiciary Committee in Hearings before the Committee on the Judiciary," U.S. Senate, 102nd Congress, 1st Session; nomination of Judge Clarence Thomas to be Associate Justice of the Supreme Court of the United States (Washington, D.C.: U.S. Government Printing Office, 1993), part 4, 36–40.

minority students. The second was the organization of a seminar on high-risk students, which was abandoned because Judge Thomas transferred to the EEOC, where he became the chairman of that office.

During this period at the Department of Education my working relationship with Judge Thomas was positive. I had a good deal of responsibility and independence. I thought he respected my work, and that he trusted my judgment.

After approximately three months of working there, he asked me to go out socially with him. What happened next, and telling the world about it, are the two most difficult things—experiences of my life.

It is only after a great deal of agonizing consideration, and a number of sleepless nights, that I am able to talk of these unpleasant matters to anyone but my closest friends.

I declined the invitation to go out socially with him, and explained to him that I thought it would jeopardize what at the time I considered to be a very good working relationship. I had a normal social life with men outside the office. I believed then, as now, that having a social relationship with a person who was supervising my work would be ill-advised. I was very uncomfortable with the idea and told him so.

I thought that by saying no and explaining my reasons, my employer would abandon his social suggestions. However, to my regret, in the following few weeks, he continued to ask me out on several occasions.

He pressed me to justify reasons for saying no to him. These incidents took place in his office, or mine. They were in the form of private conversation, which would not have been overheard by anyone else.

My working relationship became even more strained when Judge Thomas began to use work situations to discuss sex. On these occasions he would call me into his office for a course on education issues and projects, or he might suggest that because of the time pressures of his schedule, we go to lunch to a government cafeteria.

After a brief discussion of work, he would turn the conversation to a discussion of sexual matters. His conversations were very vivid. He spoke about acts that he had seen in pornographic films involving such matters as women having sex with animals, and films showing group sex or rape scenes.

He talked about pornographic materials depicting individuals with large penises or large breasts, involving various sex acts. . . .

Throughout the period of these conversations, he also from time to time asked me for social engagements. My reaction to these conversations was to avoid them by limiting opportunities for us to engage in extended conversations.

This was difficult because, at the time, I was his only assistant at the office of education—or the office for civil rights. During the latter part of my time at the Department of Education, the social pressures, and any conversation of his offensive behavior, ended. I began both to believe and hope that our relationship could be a proper, cordial, and professional one.

When Judge Thomas was made chair of the EEOC, I needed to face the question of whether to go with him. I was asked to do so, and I did.

The work itself was interesting, and at the time it appeared that the sexual overtures which had so troubled me had ended.

I also faced the realistic fact that I had no alternative job. While I might have gone back to private practice, perhaps in my old firm or another, I was dedicated to civil rights work and my first choice was to be in that field. Moreover, at that time, the Department of Education itself was a dubious venture. President Reagan was seeking to abolish the entire department.

For my first months at the EEOC, where I continued to be an assistant to Judge Thomas, there were no sexual conversations or overtures. However, during the fall and winter of 1982, these began again. The comments were random and ranged from pressing me about why I didn't go out with him, to remarks about my personal appearance. I remember his saying that some day I would have to tell him the real reason that I wouldn't go out with him.

He began to show displeasure in his tone and voice, and his demeanor and his continued pressure for an explanation. He commented on what I was wearing in terms of whether it made me more or less sexually attractive. The incidents occurred in his inner office at the EEOC.

One of the oddest episodes I remember was an occasion in which Thomas was drinking a Coke in his office. He got up from the table at which we were working, went over to his desk, looked at the can, and asked, "Who has put pubic hair on my Coke?"

On other occasions, he referred to the size of his own penis as being larger than normal, and he also spoke on some occasions of the pleasures he had given to women with oral sex. At this point, late in 1982, I began to be concerned that Clarence Thomas might take out his anger with me by degrading me, or not giving me important assignments. I also thought that he might find an excuse for dismissing me.

In January of 1983, I began looking for another job. I was handicapped because I feared that if he found out, he might make it difficult for me to find other employment and I might be dismissed from the job I had. Another factor that made my search more difficult was that this was during a period of a hiring freeze in the government. . . .

On, as I recall, the last day of my employment at the EEOC in the summer of 1983, I did have dinner with Clarence Thomas. We went directly from work to a restaurant near the office. We talked about the work I had done, both at Education and at the EEOC. He told me that he was pleased with all of it, except for an article and speech that I had done for him while we were at the Office for Civil Rights. Finally he made a comment that I will vividly remember. He said that if I ever told anyone of his behavior it would ruin his career. This was not an apology; nor was it an explanation. That was his last remark about the possibility of our going out or reference to his behavior.

In July of 1983 I left the Washington, D.C., area and I've had minimal contacts with Judge Clarence Thomas since. . . .

It would have been more comfortable to remain silent. I took no initiative to inform anyone. But when I was asked by a representative of this committee to report my experience, I felt that I had to tell the truth. I could not keep silent.

RUTH BADER GINSBURG, *On Being Nominated to the Supreme Court* (1993)

Judge Ruth Bader Ginsburg's (b. 1933) nomination to the U.S. Supreme Court expressed the Clinton administration's decision to appoint women to the highest-level national positions. A nationally known advocate for gender equity, Ginsburg who graduated from Cornell and Columbia School of Law, joined Sandra Day O'Connor, the first woman appointed to the Supreme Court. Contrast Ginsburg's experiences with those of Myra Bradwell (See Chapter 9). What changes have occurred for women in the law profession between the late 1950s and the present?*

The announcement the President just made is significant, I believe, because it contributes to the end of the days when women, at least half the talent pool in our society, appear in high places only as one-at-a-time performers. Recall that when President

---

* From Ruth Bader Ginsburg, "On Being Nominated to the Supreme Court," in White House Press Release, June 14, 1993.

Carter took office in 1976, no woman had ever served on the Supreme Court, and only one woman . . . then served at the next Federal court level, the United States Court of Appeals.

Today Justice Sandra Day O'Connor graces the Supreme Court bench, and close to twenty-five women serve at the Federal Court of Appeals level, two as chief judges. I am confident that more will soon join them. That seems to me inevitable, given the change in law school enrollment.

My law school class in the late 1950s numbered over 500. That class included less than 10 women. . . . Not a law firm in the entire city of New York bid for my employment as a lawyer when I earned my degree. Today few law schools have female enrollment under 40 percent, and several have passed the 50 percent mark. And thanks to Title VII, no entry doors are barred. . . .

I am indebted to so many for this extraordinary chance and challenge: to a revived women's movement in the 1970s that opened doors for people like me, to the Civil Rights movement of the 1960s from which the women's movement drew inspiration. . . .

I have a last thank you. It is to my mother, Celia Amster Bader, the bravest and strongest person I have ever known, who was taken from me much too soon. I pray that I may be all that she would have been had she lived in an age when women could aspire and achieve, and daughters are cherished as much as sons. I look forward to stimulating weeks this summer and, if I am confirmed, to working at a neighboring court to the best of my ability for the advancement of the law in the service of society. Thank you.

SUSAN FALUDI, *Backlash* (1992)

Journalist Susan Faludi (b. 1959) wrote that the "backlash" against women involved media distortions of feminism, as well as governmental denial of vital support necessary to sustain working mothers. In this excerpt from her book, *Backlash,* she describes the 1980 election in terms of a gender gap over women's rights. Why does Faludi believe that some white men "feared and reviled feminism"?*

But what exactly is it about women's equality that even its slightest shadow threatens to erase male identity? What is it about the way we frame manhood that, even today, it still depends so on "feminine" dependence for its survival? A little-noted finding by the Yankelovich Monitor survey, a large nationwide poll that has tracked social attitudes for the last two decades, takes us a good way toward a possible answer. For twenty years, the Monitor's pollsters have asked its subjects to define masculinity. And for twenty years, the leading definition, ahead by a huge margin, has never changed. It isn't being a leader, athlete, lothario, decision maker, or even just being "born male." It is simply this: being a "good provider for his family."

If establishing masculinity depends most of all on succeeding as the prime breadwinner, then it is hard to imagine a force more directly threatening to fragile American manhood than the feminist drive for economic equality. And if supporting a family epitomizes what it means to be a man, then it is little wonder that the backlash erupted when it did—against the backdrop of the '80s

* From *Backlash* by Susan Faludi. Copyright © 1991 by Susan Faludi. Used by permission of Crown Publishers, a division of Random House, Inc.

economy. In this period, the "traditional" man's real wage shrank dramatically (a 22 percent free-fall in households where white men were the sole breadwinners), and the traditional male breadwinner himself became an endangered species (representing less than 8 percent of all households). That the ruling definition of masculinity remains so economically based helps to explain, too, why the backlash has been voiced most bitterly by two groups of men: blue-collar workers, devastated by the shift to a service economy, and younger baby boomers, denied the comparative riches their fathers and elder brothers enjoyed. The '80s was the decade in which plant closings put blue-collar men out of work by the millions, and only 60 percent found new jobs—about half at lower pay. It was a time when, of all men losing earning power, the younger baby boom men were losing the most. The average man under thirty was earning 25 to 30 percent less than his counterpart in the early '70s. Worst off was the average young man with only a high-school education: he was making only $18,000, half the earnings of his counterpart a decade earlier. As pollster Louis Harris observed, economic polarization spawned the most dramatic attitudinal change recorded in the last decade and a half: a spectacular doubling in the proportion of Americans who describe themselves as feeling "powerless."

When analysts at Yankelovich reviewed the Monitor survey's annual attitudinal data in 1986, they had to create a new category to describe a large segment of the population that had suddenly emerged, espousing a distinct set of values. This segment, now representing a remarkable one-fifth of the study's national sample, was dominated by young men, median age thirty-three, disproportionately single, who were slipping down the income ladder—and furious about it. They were the younger, poorer brothers of the baby boomers, the ones who weren't so celebrated in '80s media and advertising tributes to that

generation. The Yankelovich report assigned the angry young men the euphemistic label of "the Contenders."

The men who belonged to this group had one other distinguishing trait: they feared and reviled feminism. ["It's these downscale men, the ones who can't earn as much as their fathers, who we find are the most threatened by the women's movement," Susan Hayward, senior vice president at Yankelovich, observes.] They represent 20 percent of the population that cannot handle the changes in women's roles. They were not well employed, they were the first ones laid off, they had no savings and not very much in the way of prospects for the future. By the late '80s, the American Male Opinion Index found that the *largest* of its seven demographic groups was now the "Change Resisters," a 24-percent segment of the population that was disproportionately under-employed, "resentful," convinced that they were "being left behind" by a changing society, and most hostile to feminism.

To single out these men alone for blame, however, would be unfair. The backlash's public agenda has been framed and promoted by men of far more affluence and influence than the Contenders, men at the helm in the media, business, and politics. Poorer or less-educated men have not so much been the creators of the antifeminist thesis as its receptors. Most vulnerable to its message, they have picked up and played back the backlash at distortingly high volume. The Contenders have dominated the ranks of the militant wing of the '80s antiabortion movement, the list of plaintiffs filing reverse-discrimination and "men's rights" lawsuits, the steadily mounting police rolls of rapists and sexual assailants. They are men like the notorious Charles Stuart, the struggling fur salesman in Boston who murdered his pregnant wife, a lawyer, because he feared that she—better educated, more successful—was gaining the "upper hand."

CHAPTER 20

Entering the Twenty-First Century:
Elusive Equality

A s the new century approached, women's issues and the national experience remained deeply intertwined. The diametrically opposed abortion rights positions that Al Gore and George W. Bush advocated during the 2000 presidential campaign reflected the deep divisions that polarized the nation. With the likelihood of U.S. Supreme Court appointments during the coming administration, Bush pledged during the campaign to select candidates who would uphold the strict construction of the Constitution. Once elected, Bush wasted no time in reversing the Clinton administration's pro–reproductive rights policies. In blocking U.S. funding for international family planning groups that offered abortion counseling, he reinstated the two previous Republican administrations' anti-choice position. With his nomination of John Ashcroft for attorney general and Tommy Thompson to head Health and Human Services, Bush again demonstrated his pro-life convictions. Both men were high-profile right-to-life advocates known for their outspoken anti-choice positions. While reproductive rights groups unsuccessfully contested the nominations, pro-life women's groups celebrated.

The presidential election results of 1996 and 2000 dramatically demonstrated gender gap voting patterns. In 1996, women preferred Bill Clinton, and their choice revealed not only candidate preference but also the continued loyalty of white women to the Democratic Party. In contrast, white men in increasing numbers over a more than thirty-year period have shifted their support to the Republican Party. In the 2000 presidential election, the white male preference for Bush manifested itself early in the campaign and never faltered. Exit poll interviews revealed that among white men, approximately 60 percent voted for Bush and only 36 percent voted for Gore. White women split their vote almost evenly between the two candidates. The overall male vote was 54 percent for Bush and only 42 percent for Gore. The overall female vote displayed similar percentages—only in reverse.* Minority voters overwhelmingly identify with

---

* Exit poll gender gap figures showed only minor variations. See, for example, Center for American Women and Politics, "Gender Gap in the 2000 Elections." http://www.rci.rutgers.edu/~cawp/facts/elections/gg2000.html.

Democratic candidates, and the women's vote demonstrated the significance of the intersection of race and gender. Analysts also believe that part of male/female voting divide expresses women's preference for the Democratic Party's greater attention to women's issues and more compassionate social policies.

Throughout the decade, gender-gap workplace and career inequities showed both persistence and change. Dramatically narrowing the White House gender gap during his administration, Clinton selected an unprecedented number of women for cabinet appointments. With Janet Reno as attorney general and Madeleine Albright as secretary of state, women held the highest-ranking cabinet positions in the U.S. government. The appointment of Ruth Bader Ginsburg added a second woman to the U.S. Supreme Court. Several women also received a number of cabinet appointments in the Bush administration. President Bush named New Jersey's former governor Christy Todd Whitman to head the Environmental Protection Agency and appointed Dr. Condoleezza Rice, an African American, as national security advisor. Rice was appointed secretary of state in 2005, a position she held until 2009.

Although the "glass ceiling" limited opportunity at top management and administrative levels in the private sector, women continued to make gains in corporate and professional fields. By the early twenty first century, a trend was clearly in progress; more women than men received bachelor's and master's degrees, and the number of women receiving doctoral degrees increased. However, women still lagged seriously behind in physical sciences, computer science, engineering, and math. Despite the expansion of workplace and educational opportunity, women's salaries still lagged behind those of men. The wage gap had narrowed from women receiving 60.2 percent of what men made in 1980 to 73.8 percent in 1996. The majority of women remained clustered in traditional, lower-paid women's fields of office and factory work, health, and child care. The American Association of University Women expressed its concern that the burgeoning high-tech computer field also displayed a gender gap. Girls were less interested than boys in computer technology and once in the workplace were overrepresented in low-paying word-processing positions. Even more poorly paid and among the nation's most exploited workers were immigrant women, such as Petra Mata, who work in the sweatshop labor conditions of an increasingly global economy.

Whether they choose or are compelled by financial need, mothers with children under the age of six have continued to enter the workforce since the 1950s. The difficulty of combining work and motherhood makes the pursuit of economic equality elusive. Women who have inadequate resources for quality child care frequently sacrifice workplace advancement for more flexible hours. Concerns about child care tend to limit middle-class women's career choices or pursuit of career advancement. Impoverished women have fewer options. The Welfare to Workforce Bill, signed by Clinton in 1996, exposed the nation's poorest women to the dilemma of combining low-paying jobs necessary for survival with limited child care options.

During the nineties, feminist groups continued their crusade to end violence against women. With the active support of the Clinton administration, they struggled to make zero tolerance for male violence against women a national priority. The National Organization for Women and other women's rights groups successfully lobbied Congress for the Violence Against Women Act (VAWA), passed in 1994 and reauthorized in 2000. Activists on college campuses publicized the usually hushed-up issue of acquaintance or date rape. The campaign to end the multiple forms of violence against women provoked a backlash alleging that feminists exploited the issue of male abuse of women to keep the public focused on the feminist agenda. Paula Kamen compiled the evidence and analysis to refute the backlash allegations of women such as Katie Roiphe that date rape was a feminist exaggeration and an overblown issue exploited by women who had agreed to sex and later regretted it. Naomi Wolf, who recently had written *The Beauty Myth* depicting the exploitation of women by the cosmetic and fashion industries, shifted her emphasis from women as victims to female power and agency. Wolf joined other critics who labeled the orientation of the second-wave feminists as "victim feminism." The emphasis on female power and agency challenged the discourse on victimization and patriarchal oppression. Third-wave younger feminists published their *Manifesta*. Their agenda aligned more with power feminism and embraced individuality and fluid gender identities and diverse sexualities. They emphasized that feminism encompassed multiple definitions and was based on individual choice rather than collective action or identity.

Second-wave feminists' gender-based equality objectives and collective activism receded but did not disappear. Undeterred by arguments that they overemphasized women's victimization, feminist organizations continued their struggle to end violence against women, a struggle that did not portray women as passive victims but rather as agents of resistance in pursuit of expanded rights, including the right of protection against sexual abuse. In the formation of non governmental organizations (NGOs), activists for women's rights on a global level, such as Robin Morgan, gave their support to the United Nations' effort to expand women's rights and end global violence against women.

The unprecedented calamity of September 11, 2001, eclipsed all other issues. National security and homeland defense became the nation's foremost priorities. The U.S. war against the Taliban regime in Afghanistan, with its exposure of the Taliban's reign of terror against women, reinvigorated feminist advocacy groups. They have responded to the oppression of Afghani women with sympathy and support and increased their resolve to end violence against women on a worldwide level. The war in Afghanistan and subsequent 2003 invasion of Iraq also have involved unprecedented numbers of American women serving in combat zones. The line between male and female combat roles has continued to erode.

Women's rights advocates have reshaped gender norms and the way most Americans think about fundamental issues of equality and gender equity. The construct of gender and gender gap analysis have become topics of media interest and entered the national discourse. Voices from non-Western and Islamic women such as Leila Ahmed have added insights about the intersection of Islam, culture, and gender and the need for cross-cultural nuanced understanding.

Although unexpected developments are always possible, it is not likely that women who have benefited from unprecedented opportunity and increased empowerment will retreat to the confines of domesticity or female subordination. Nonetheless, from right-wing religious groups unremitting effort to block the U.N. adoption of women's rights as human rights to the Bush administration's anti-choice policies, opposition abounds. At the opening of a new century, the agenda to constrain women's rights serves as an ever-present reminder of their vulnerability.

ROBIN MORGAN, *Sisterhood Is Global* (1984)

Robin Morgan (b. 1941) is a major feminist activist and writer, closely identified with the second-wave construct of transnational, global sisterhood. In the preface to the revised edition of her book *Sisterhood Is Global*, Morgan expresses her conviction that women share a community of concerns across cultural and national borders, including the necessity of ending rape, domestic battering, honor killings, and sexual exploitation. Critics from the Third World allege that the term *sisterhood* has no universal meaning and serves mainly to justify U.S. imperialist and feminist intrusion in Third World women's issues. In the following excerpt from *Sisterhood Is Global*, Morgan rejects this negative assessment. She also emphasizes the need to incorporate difference but urges culturally diverse women to recognize areas of shared concern. What role does she assign to the global construct of sisterhood? How does she counter arguments from non-Western cultures that feminists are "outside agitators"?*

A growing awareness of the vast resources of womanpower is becoming evident in a proliferation of plans of action, resolutions, legislative reforms, and other blueprints for change being put forward by national governments, international congresses and agencies, and multinational corporations. Women have served or are serving as heads of states and governments in more nations than ever before, including Belize, Bolivia, Dominica, Iceland, India, Israel, Norway, Portugal, Sri Lanka, the United Kingdom, and Yugoslavia. Yet these women still must function within systems devised and controlled by men and imbued with androcentric values. What resonates with even greater potential is what "ordinary" women all over the globe are beginning to whisper, say, and shout, to ourselves and one another, *autonomously*—and what we are proceeding to *do,* in our own countries and across their borders. . . .

The Inside Agitator

No matter where she was born, no matter where she turns, a stereotype awaits her. She is a hot Latin or a cold WASP, a wholesome Dutch matron, a docile Asian or a Dragon Lady, a spoiled American, a seductive Scheherazade, a hip-swaying Pacific Island hula maiden, a Caribbean matriarch, a merry Irish colleen, a promiscuous Scandinavian, a noble-savage Native Indian, a hero-worker mother. . . .

But stereotypes become ineffectual unless constantly enforced. This necessitates the patriarchy's vast and varied set of rules that define not only a woman's physical appearance but her physical reality itself, from her forced enclosure in *purdah* to her forced exposure in beauty contests and pornography, from female genital mutilation to cosmetic plastic surgery, from facial scarification to carcinogenic hair dye, from the veil to the dictates of fashion. . . .

Still, a forced physical reality, however hideous, is not sufficient. For the power holders to be secure, it is necessary to constrain women's minds as well as our bodies. Organized religion, custom, tradition, and all the abstract patriarchal "isms" (nationalism, capitalism, communism, socialism, patriotism, etc.) are called into play, doubtless in the hope that women will not notice just *who* has dogmatized the religions, corrupted the customs, defined the traditions, and created, perpetuated, and profited by the various other "isms." The most pernicious of all patriarchal tactics to keep women a divided and subhuman world caste is the lie that "feminism is an 'outside' or alien phenomenon, not needed or desired by 'our' [local] women."

---

* Robin Morgan, *Sisterhood is Global.* Copyright © 1996 by The Feminist Press at CUNY.

This argument is wondrously chameleonic. In many Third World countries, feminists are warned that the "imported thought" of feminism is a neocolonialist plot. In Western industrialized countries, on the other hand, feminists frequently are regarded as being radical agents of communism. In the USSR and some other Eastern European nations, feminists are attacked as bourgeois agents of imperialism. (Truly, it is quite amazing how the male Right and the male Left can forge such a literal Big Brotherhood in response to the threat posed by women merely insisting on being recognized as part of humanity.) . . .

This is hardly a new tactic. It has been used by colonists about native populations, by slaveholders in the early American South, by management about workers trying to unionize, etc. Discontent and rebellion among the oppressed, according to those in power, is always the work of "outside agitators."

The strongest argument to the "feminists as outside agitators" attack is the simple truth: *an indigenous feminism has been present in every culture in the world and in every period of history since the suppression of women began*. Indeed, that has emerged as the predominant theme of *Sisterhood Is Global*. It will be difficult, I think, for anyone to finish this book and ever again believe that feminism is a geographically narrow, imported, or even for that matter recent phenomenon, anywhere.

NAOMI WOLF, *The Beauty Myth* (1992)

Written by a young feminist, Naomi Wolf's (b. 1962) *The Beauty Myth* continues the second-wave feminist theme of how unrealistic standards of beauty control major aspects of women's lives. Second-wave white feminists protested Miss America beauty pageants and advocated that women abandon fashion slavery and dependence on cosmetics. African American women faced with beauty norms based on white, largely Anglo ideals of blue eyes and straight blond hair advocated an "Afro" natural look.

Although dress codes have relaxed and beauty norms respond to multiculturalism, millions of women remain seemingly addicted to fashion's latest trends and literally unattainable beauty norms. Wolf argues that a cult of ultra thinness and the desire to be forever young dominate women's lives. What evidence does Wolf present about the way the media and advertising industry purposefully present beauty standards as a way to diminish female empowerment? Could other explanations also be correct? Discuss whether women are victims of beauty myths or agents of their own pursuit of beauty.*

During the past decade, women breached the power structure; meanwhile, eating disorders rose exponentially and cosmetic surgery became the fastest-growing medical specialty. During the past five years, consumer spending doubled, pornography became the main media category, ahead of legitimate films and records combined, and thirty-three thousand American women told researchers that they would rather lose ten to fifteen pounds than achieve any other goal. More women have more money and power and scope and legal recognition than we have ever had before; but in terms of how we feel about ourselves *physically,* we may actually be worse off than our unliberated grandmothers. Recent research consistently shows that inside the majority of the West's controlled, attractive, successful working women, there is a secret "underlife" poisoning our freedom; infused with notions of beauty, it is a dark vein of self-hatred, physical obsessions, terror of aging, and dread of lost control.

---

* From *The Beauty Myth* by Naomi Wolf. Copyright © 1991 by Naomi Wolf. Reprinted by permission of HarperCollins Publishers Inc.

It is no accident that so many potentially powerful women feel this way. We are in the midst of a violent backlash against feminism that uses images of female beauty as a political weapon against women's advancement: the beauty myth. It is the modern version of a social reflex that has been in force since the Industrial Revolution. As women released themselves from the feminine mystique of domesticity, the beauty myth took over its lost ground, expanding as it waned to carry on its work of social control.

The contemporary backlash is so violent because the ideology of beauty is the last one remaining of the old feminine ideologies that still has the power to control those women whom second wave feminism would have otherwise made relatively uncontrollable: It has grown stronger to take over the work of social coercion that myths about motherhood, domesticity, chastity, and passivity, no longer can manage. It is seeking right now to undo psychologically and covertly all the good things that feminism did for women materially and overtly.

This counterforce is operating to checkmate the inheritance of feminism on every level in the lives of Western women. Feminism gave us laws against job discrimination based on gender; immediately case law evolved in Britain and the United States that institutionalized job discrimination based on women's appearances. Patriarchal religion declined; new religious dogma, using some of the mind-altering techniques of older cults and sects, arose around age and weight to functionally supplant traditional ritual. Feminists, inspired by Friedan, broke the stranglehold on the women's popular press of advertisers for household products, who were promoting the feminine mystique; at once, the diet and skin care industries became the new cultural censors of women's intellectual space, and because of their pressure, the gaunt, youthful model supplanted the happy housewife as the arbiter of successful womanhood. The sexual revolution promoted the discovery of female sexuality; "beauty pornography"—which for the first time in women's history artificially links a commodified "beauty" directly and explicitly to sexuality—invaded the mainstream to undermine women's new and vulnerable sense of sexual self-worth. Reproductive rights gave Western women control over our own bodies; the weight of fashion models plummeted to 23 percent below that of ordinary women, eating disorders rose exponentially, and a mass neurosis was promoted that used food and weight to strip women of that sense of control. Women insisted on politicizing health; new technologies of invasive, potentially deadly "cosmetic" surgeries developed apace to re-exert old forms of medical control of women. . . .

Since middle-class Western women can best be weakened psychologically now that we are stronger materially, the beauty myth, as it has resurfaced in the last generation, has had to draw on more technological sophistication and reactionary fervor than ever before. The modern arsenal of the myth is a dissemination of millions of images of the current ideal; although this barrage is generally seen as a collective sexual fantasy, there is in fact little that is sexual about it. It is summoned out of political fear on the part of male-dominated institutions threatened by women's freedom, and it exploits female guilt and apprehension about our own liberation—latent fears that we might be going too far. This frantic aggregation of imagery is a collective reactionary hallucination willed into being by both men and women stunned and disoriented by the rapidity with which gender relations have been transformed: a bulwark of reassurance against the flood of change. The mass depiction of the modern woman as a "beauty" is a contradiction: Where modern women are growing, moving, and expressing their individuality, as the myth has it, "beauty" is by definition inert, timeless, and generic. That this hallucination is necessary and deliberate is evident in the way "beauty" so directly contradicts women's real situation.

And the unconscious hallucination grows ever more influential and pervasive because of what is now conscious market manipulation: powerful industries—the $33-billion-a-year diet industry, the $20-billion cosmetics industry, the $300-million cosmetic surgery industry, and the $7-billion pornography industry—have arisen from the capital made out of unconscious anxieties, and are in turn able, through their influence on mass culture, to use, stimulate, and reinforce the hallucination in a rising economic spiral.

PAULA KAMEN, *Acquaintance Rape: Revolution and Reaction* (1996)

In *Feminist Fatale,* published in 1991, Paula Kamen, a 1989 college graduate with a degree in journalism, brought the insights of a young feminist to her analysis of why so many women of her generation distanced themselves from feminist identity. In this 1996 article, she responds to backlash allegations that feminists on college campuses have exaggerated date rape statistics and created date rape hysteria. The date rape controversy Kamen addresses is part of a larger backlash movement that claims feminist overemphasis has led many women to claim an unwarranted victim status. What evidence does Kamen give to refute these backlash allegations? How are college advisors better preparing young women to understand the dynamics of date rape? What do "Take Back the Night" marches signify?*

I have seen this movement to examine men's behavior evolve slowly. In 1985, when I was a freshman at the Big Ten giant, the University of Illinois in Urbana–Champaign, about the only rape prevention education offered throughout the country was directed exclusively toward women, warning them about strangers. But in the next few years I witnessed the university develop a model program for prevention and education that targets men. More and more university programs across the country have also evolved to look at acquaintance rape, and many schools are including a component to examine men's attitudes and responsibilities. This focus is radical because it takes the exclusive and historical burden of responsibility off women's shoulders. "It's acknowledging that men are the ones committing rape," said Barb Gilbert, an architect of my campus program, in a 1989 interview. "And the only role that women have is to the extent that we can prevent opportunity and prevent the effectiveness [protect ourselves]."

Men's antirape activism is part of a broad, hardly recognized, slowly developing sexual revolution of this generation. While the sexual revolution of the 1970s was largely about women saying yes (to really prove themselves liberated), a new movement is empowering them to also say no, along with when, where, and how. As a result, women are more closely examining what turns them off—and also what turns them on. They are daring to study and even critique what happens to them in bed. Young women are not content with the rules of the old 1970s sexual revolution, which have collapsed under the weight of their own rigidity—and stupidity. That movement, which was liberating mostly for men, has saddled women with too much old patriarchal baggage, including a continuing double standard for women, which discourages communication and honesty from

---

* From "Acquaintance Rape: Revolution and Reaction" by Paula Kamen in *Bad Girls/Good Girls: Women, Sex and Power in the Nineties,* edited by Nan Bauer Maglin and Donna Perry, 1996, 139–144. Reprinted by permission of the author. (For Kamen's sources, see her essay in its original publication.)

both sexes. Activists are striving for a new model and new freedoms that offer pleasure and freedom from absolute rules, as well as self-respect, autonomy, and responsibility. Their movement is parallel to others I have seen become increasingly visible on college campuses, including efforts to gain reproductive freedom, fight sexual harassment, and secure rights for gays and lesbians.

Antifeminist Backlash

Yet, in the past few years, I have also seen the antifeminist skeptics eclipse all others in the popular press and in slick upscale magazines. While feminists come in all ideological shapes and sizes, the most "wacky" ones have always made the best copy. Most magazine articles addressing acquaintance rape in 1993 and 1994 take the angle that date rape is mostly hype, and seriously question the extent and even the existence of the problem.

A variety of critics, from lofty newspaper columnists to the writers of *Saturday Night Live,* have taken easy aim at "feminist antisex hysteria" by making fun of the extreme Antioch College guidelines, first widely publicized in 1993. The sexual offense policy from this small Ohio liberal arts college has come to represent feminists' supposedly overpowering rhetorical invasion of the minds of college students. The eight-page policy states that students must give and get verbal consent before "each new level of physical and/or sexual contact/conduct." "Sexual contact" includes the touching of thighs, genitals, buttocks, the pubic region, or the breast/chest area. The policy spells out six categories of offenses: rape, sexual assault, sexual imposition, insistent and/or persistent sexual harassment, nondisclosure of sexually transmitted diseases (STDs), and nondisclosure of positive HIV status. Complaints against violators can be brought before the campus judicial board. . . .

A major leader of the date-rape hysteria charge was twenty-five-year-old Katie Roiphe, author of *The Morning After: Sex, Fear, and Feminism on Campus* (1993). She says such feminist discussion confuses young women into mislabeling a wide array of normal, often unpleasant, sexual experiences as rape. Her thesis is that the battle against date rape is a symptom of young women's general anxiety about sex. They allegedly displace their fear of sex onto a fear of rape. Roiphe reasons that since some cases are false, all claims of acquaintance rape are unfounded; if one is against rape, one must also be against sex. Those that speak out against rape are nothing but malleable dupes of feminists or hysterics, liars, or prudes.

A major gripe of Roiphe and others is that educators are putting an undue burden on men by advising them to obtain articulated mutual consent. "With their advice, their scenarios, their sample aggressive male, the message projects a clear comment on the nature of sexuality: women are often unwilling participants," Roiphe writes in her book (p. 61). Indeed, rape educators do admit that women have been forced to have sex against their will by people they know. In contrast, Roiphe portrays an idealized, "post-feminist" reality that places men and women in a vacuum, untouched by social attitudes and pressures.

The greatest threat of Roiphe's distortions is that they push acquaintance rape back in the closet. Roiphe is characteristically narrow in her definition of what constitutes a "real" rape—incidents of violence that can never be confused with "bad sex." In her *New York Times Magazine* article, she gives as examples of rape brutal assaults by strangers, such as those of Bosnian girls and "a suburban teen-ager raped and beaten while walking home from a shopping mall" (p. 28). To back up her argument, Roiphe takes liberties with data. Her "findings" that discredit date-rape prevention work are often based on out-of-context second-hand false examples of radical feminist rhetoric and flimsy "evidence" that questions the validity of professionally scrutinized scientific studies.

A central target of Roiphe and others is a major, influential 1985 survey by a University of Arizona medical school professor, Mary Koss, sponsored by the Ms. Foundation and financed by the National Institute of Mental Health. One of the study's major findings was that 27.9 percent—or, as most often quoted, "one in four"—of the college women surveyed reported being a victim of rape or attempted rape since the age of fourteen, with a majority having known the assailants.

Roiphe, Sommers, and other critics cited here have condemned Koss's findings as invalid without ever contacting Koss to get her side of the story or further information. Roiphe repeats the most commonly waged criticism of Koss: "Seventy-three percent of the women categorized as rape victims did not initially define their experience as rape: it was Mary Koss, the psychologist conducting a study, who did." According to Roiphe, "Today's definition has stretched beyond bruises and knives, threats of death or violence to include emotional pressure and the influence of alcohol."

However, as all of these critics failed to report, Koss makes clear that she used a standard legal definition of rape similar to that used in the majority of states. Also, contrary to Roiphe's allegations, Koss did not make emotional pressure a variable in her 15.8 percent completed rape statistic. She does ask questions about "sexual coercion," but she does not include this group in the 27.9 percent statistic of rape or attempted rape.

Koss explained to me that she included in her figures women who did not label their experiences as rape because of the prevailing public misconception that the law does not cover such cases of date rape. Also, at the time of the 1985 survey public awareness about the possibility that an attack between acquaintances was legally rape was much lower than it is today.

Koss points out in her writings that the majority of her respondents who reported experiences legally defined as rape still indicated, themselves, that they felt victimized; she did not project this onto them. According to the study, as all these critics fail to mention, of respondents who reported an incident of forced sex (whether or not they called it rape), 30 percent considered suicide afterward, 31 percent sought psychotherapy, and 82 percent said the experience had changed them. . . .

But, the most convincing evidence of the accuracy of Koss's study comes from the most accurate and comprehensive sex survey in America: the National Health and Social Life Survey (NHSLS) conducted by the National Opinion Research Center. In 1994, it was released in two books, one for a popular and another for an academic audience. The NHSLS found that, since puberty, 22 percent of women were forced by a man to do something sexually, and 30 percent of them were forced by more than one man. And even these numbers underestimate the true level of sexual violence in our society, as researchers point out: "Because forced sex is undoubtedly underreported in surveys because of the socially stigmatized nature of the event, we believe that our estimates are probably conservative 'lower-bound' estimates of forced sex within the population."

In more than three-quarters of the cases, the perpetrator was someone the woman knew well (22 percent), was in love with (46 percent), or married to (9 percent)—only 4 percent were attacked by a stranger. These forced sexual experiences had an impact on women's lives. Fifty-seven percent of the forced women (versus 42 percent of the rest) had emotional problems in the past year which interfered with sex, and 34 percent (versus 18 percent of those not forced) said sex in the past year was not pleasurable. Twenty percent (versus 12 percent of those not forced) generally said they were sometimes fairly unhappy or unhappy most of the time.

The NHSLS data strongly confirm Koss's findings. It found that 25 percent of women eighteen to twenty-four had been forced to do something sexually. The survey also revealed that most of these attacks probably occurred when women were relatively young, since women eighteen to twenty-four had virtually identical rates of forced sex—about 25 percent.

The slightly lower number of responses from older women can probably be accounted for by a greater reluctance to admit to being forced sexually and by a smaller number of sex partners.

JENNIFER BAUMGARDNER AND AMY RICHARDS, *ManifestA: Young Women, Feminism, and the Future* (2000)

Third-wave feminists Jennifer Baumgardner and Amy Richards wrote *ManifestA* in an effort to mobilize young women to move beyond the personal benefits gained from second-wave feminist reforms. Richards is a co-founder of the Third Wave Foundation. Both women have either past or present editorial ties to *Ms.* magazine. Although they acknowledge their generation's debt to second-wave feminism, they argue that young women must develop and lead their own third-wave movement. Third-wave objectives emphasize inclusion and welcome young women across lines of sexual orientation, class, ethnicity, race, and disparate values.

At present the Third Wave exists more as a series of collected writings and websites than an organized movement. *ManifestA* calls for collective action, but the authors describe their generation's interest in mobilization as still undeveloped. The following excerpt documents the thirteen-point agenda for a third-wave feminist movement. In what ways do these objectives express the concerns of younger women? What aspects express continuity with second-wave feminist reform?*

Third Wave MANIFESTA: A Thirteen-Point Agenda

1. To out unacknowledged feminists, specifically those who are younger, so that Generation X can become a visible movement and, further, a voting block of eighteen- to forty-year-olds.

2. To safeguard a woman's right to bear or not to bear a child, regardless of circumstances, including women who are younger than eighteen or impoverished. To preserve this right throughout her life and support the choice to be childless.

3. To make explicit that the fight for reproductive rights must include birth control; the right for poor women and lesbians to have children; partner adoption for gay couples; subsidized fertility treatments for all women who choose them; and freedom from sterilization abuse. Furthermore, to support the idea that sex can be—and usually is—for pleasure, not procreation.

4. To bring down the double standard in sex and sexual health, and foster male responsibility and assertiveness in the following areas: achieving freedom from STDs; more fairly dividing the burden of family planning as well as responsibilities such as child care; and eliminating violence against women.

5. To tap into and raise awareness of our revolutionary history, and the fact that almost all movements began as youth movements. To have access to our

* "Third Wave ManifestA: A Thirteen-Point Agenda" from *ManifestA: Young Women, Feminism, and the Future* by Jennifer Baumgardner and Amy Richards. Copyright © 2000 by Jennifer Baumgardner and Amy Richards. Reprinted by permission of Farrar, Straus and Giroux, LLC.

intellectual feminist legacy and women's history; for the classics of radical feminism, womanism, *mujeristas,* women's liberation, and all our roots to remain in print; and to have women's history taught to men as well as women as a part of all curricula.

6. To support and increase the visibility and power of lesbians and bisexual women in the feminist movement, in high schools, colleges, and the workplace. To recognize that queer women have always been at the forefront of the feminist movement, and that there is nothing to be gained—and much to be lost—by downplaying their history, whether inadvertently or actively.

7. To practice "autokeonony" ("self in community"): to see activism not as a choice between self and community but as a link between them that creates balance.

8. To have equal access to health care, regardless of income, which includes coverage equivalent to men's and keeping in mind that women use the system more often than men do because of our reproductive capacity.

9. For women who so desire to participate in all reaches of the military, including combat, and to enjoy all the benefits (loans, health care, pensions) offered to its members for as long as we continue to have an active military. The largest expenditure of our national budget goes toward maintaining this welfare system, and feminists have a duty to make sure women have access to every echelon.

10. To liberate adolescents from slut-bashing, listless educators, sexual harassment, and bullying at school, as well as violence in all walks of life, and the silence that hangs over adolescents' heads, often keeping them isolated, lonely, and indifferent to the world.

11. To make the workplace responsive to an individual's wants, needs, and talents. This includes valuing (monetarily) stay-at-home parents, aiding employees who want to spend more time with family and continue to work, equalizing pay for jobs of comparable worth, enacting a minimum wage that would bring a full-time worker with two children over the poverty line, and providing employee benefits for freelance and part-time workers.

12. To acknowledge that, although feminists may have disparate values, we share the same goal of equality, and of supporting one another in our efforts to gain the power to make our own choices.

13. To pass the Equal Rights Amendment so that we can have a constitutional foundation of righteousness and equality upon which future women's rights conventions will stand.

LEILA AHMED, *A Border Passage: From Cairo to America— A Woman's Journey* (2000)

Professor of women's studies in religion at Harvard's Divinity School, Leila Ahmed (b. 1940) wrote a memoir, *A Border Passage,* that recounts her journey from an Islamic Egyptian childhood to professor of women's studies in the United States. In the following excerpt, she differentiates between the separate worlds of male and female Islam. What connection does Ahmed make between gender studies and "medieval men's Islam"? Why does she believe Western academics are contributing to this rigid, textual interpretation? In what ways does her critique of Islamic patriarchy relate to Elizabeth Cady Stanton's interpretation of Christian teachings and female subordination (see

Chapter 10)? What does she mean by the statement "throughout history official Islam has been our enemy and our oppressor"?*

We seem to be living through an era of the progressive, seemingly inexorable erasure of the oral and ethical traditions of lived Islam and, simultaneously, of the ever-greater dissemination of written Islam, textual, "men's" Islam (an Islam essentially not of the Book but of the Texts, the medieval texts) as *the* authoritative Islam. Worse still, this seems to be an era of the unstoppable spread of fundamentalist Islam, textual Islam's more narrow and more poorly informed modern descendant. It is a more ill-informed version of old-style official Islam in that the practitioners of that older Islam usually studied many texts and thus at least knew that even in these medieval texts there were disagreements among scholars and many possible interpretations of this or that verse. But today's fundamentalists, literate but often having read just a single text, take it to be definitive and the one and only "truth.". . .

Ironically, therefore, literacy has played a baneful part both in spreading a particular form of Islam and in working to erase oral and living forms of the religion. For one thing, we all automatically assume that those who write and who put their knowledge down in texts have something more valuable to offer than those who simply live their knowledge and use it to inform their lives. And we assume that those who write and interpret texts in writing—in the Muslim context, the sheikhs and ayatollahs, who are the guardians and perpetuators (perpetrators) of this written version of Islam—must have a better, truer, deeper understanding of Islam than non–specially trained Muslim. Whereas the fact is that the only Islam that they have a deeper understanding of is their own gloomy, medieval version of it.

Even the Western academic world is contributing to the greater visibility and legitimacy of textual Islam and to the gradual silencing and erasure of alternative oral forms of lived Islam. For we too in the West, and particularly in universities, honor, and give pride of place to, texts. Academic studies of Islam commonly focus on its textual heritage or on visible, official institutions such as mosques. Consequently it is this Islam—the Islam of texts and of mosques—that becomes visible and that is presented as in some sense legitimate, whereas most of the Muslims whom I know personally, both in the Middle East and in Europe and America, would never go near a mosque or willingly associate themselves with any form of official Islam. Throughout history, official Islam has been our enemy and our oppressor. We have learned to live with it and to survive it and have developed dictums such as "There is no priesthood in Islam" to protect ourselves from it; we're not now suddenly and even in these new lands going to easily befriend it. It is also a particular and bitter irony to me that the very fashionableness of gender studies is serving to disseminate and promote medieval men's Islam as the "true" and "authentic" Islam. (It is "true" and "authentic" because it is based on old texts and represents what the Muslim male powers have considered to be true for centuries.) Professors, for example, including a number who have no sympathy whatever for feminism, are now jumping on the bandwagon of gender studies and directing a plethora of dissertations on this or that medieval text with titles like "Islam and Menstruation." But such dissertations should more aptly have titles along the lines of "A Study of Medieval Male Beliefs about Menstruation." For what, after all, do these men's beliefs, and the rules that they laid down on the basis of their beliefs, have to do with Islam?

---

* Excerpt from *A Border Passage: Cairo to America—A Woman's Journey* by Leila Ahmed. Copyright © 1999 by Leila Ahmed. Reprinted by permission of Farrar, Straus and Giroux, LLC.

KATHLEEN SLAYTON, *Gender Equity Gap in High Tech* (2001)

The following document is Kathleen Slayton's summary of a report compiled by the American Association of University Women (AAUW). The organization promotes women's rights and emphasizes the need for educational and workplace gender equity. The AAUW report expresses concern that at the beginning of the twenty-first century, a high-tech gender gap exists. Because of inadequate preparation at school, women cluster in the low-paid, low-end field of computerized clerical work. The lack of advanced technological skills locks women out of challenging, well-paid careers. What reasons does the report cite for girls more limited involvement with computers? Why do female students avoid high-level computing classes? What solutions are offered?*

The AAUW Educational Foundation has conducted a research program and produced a report, "Gender Gaps," which found cause for serious concern in the area of information technology. The report indicated alarming disparities in girls and boys enrollments in advanced computer courses. Girls were less likely to take high-level computing classes in high school, and comprised just 17 percent of those taking Advanced Placement computer science exams. Girls outnumbered boys only in their enrollment in word processing classes, arguably the 1990 version of typing classes.

While high school girls and boys take similar numbers of science courses, boys are more likely than girls to take all three core science courses—biology, chemistry, and physics—by graduation.

This year, AAUW Educational Foundation's publication, "Tech-Savvy," found that while girls are innately more verbal than boys, they do not necessarily have a working knowledge of computer language. As a result, girls are more likely to express bewilderment and confusion about technology. They differ in their attitudes and abilities more than boys. Girls enjoy the computer for the connections and friendships they make via e-mail. Boys prefer the shoot 'em up games.

Interestingly, girls take the moral high ground, positioning themselves as morally or socially more evolved than boys who, they tell us, enjoy taking things apart and interacting with machines. They tend to present the Internet as a vice in the hands of boys, but a virtue in the hands of girls, because boys use it to play games and fool around while girls use it as a source of information. In addition, girls have specific criticisms of the violence in current games as well as the general sense that they would be more interested in games that allowed them to create rather than destroy.

It is encouraging to see that K-Mart and WalMart are limiting the sale of violent videogames to those above 18, but this doesn't limit the access to minors once the game is in the home.

Consequently, girls' more limited involvement with computers has more to do with disenchantment than with anxiety or intellectual deficiency.

Science, Math, and Computer Technology are the springboard to the moneyed jobs our nation offers. The more young women enter these fields, the more we break the cycle of the feminization of poverty. The failure to include and encourage girls in advanced-level computer science courses threatens to make women bystanders in the technological 21st century. Instead of dividing our society into the haves and have-nots, it will be divided into those who can do, and those who cannot.

---

* From "Gender Equity Gap in High Tech" by Kathleen M. Slayton. Originally presented in an October 2000 report to the American Association of University Women. Reprinted by permission of the author.

Recommendations

- **We need to "change the public face of computing."** Girls complain that they do not see women in the media who are actively involved in computing. . . .
- **We need to increase the visibility of women who have taken the lead in designing and using computer technology.** Girls express an interest in seeing such women, who have often not become public figures.
- **We need to continue the conversation about issues of gender in the computer culture.** This conversation

must take seriously girls' and women's valid critiques of computer design, use, and applications. . . .

- **We need to highlight the human, social and cultural dimensions of computers rather than technical advances, or the speed of the machines.**
- **Parents and educators need to encourage girls to "tinker" with computers.** These activities are crucially important for empowering women as designers and builders, not just consumers and end users.

MIRIAM CHING YOON LOUIE, *Sweatshop Warriors* (2001)

Mexican-born Petra Mata, an immigrant women worker, was interviewed by Miriam Ching Yoon Louie in her book *Sweatshop Warriors*. Like many other immigrant women, Mata worked for minimum wages in the volatile labor market of the global economy. Levi's decision to close its San Antonio, Texas, plant left her without a job. Rather than passively accept the closing, Mata became a labor activist and union organizer. How does Mata describe her role as Levi employee and her subsequent activist transformation?*

[Petra Mata Interview (1997)]

When Levi's closed, it was a disaster for most of the families. My husband has had to work at two jobs since they shut us down. In the evening he's a cook at the Marriott Hotel and in the morning he's working with vegetables in a lot of grocery stores. Before I lost my job I sent one of my kids to college. My two older kids had everything that they needed, not what they wanted, but at least what they needed. The ones who suffered most were the small ones. They remember that we could buy five pairs of pants, one for each day. When I lost my job my small boy said, "Mom, how come we can only buy two pants, one to use today and the other one tomorrow?" He asked, "Why did Junior have this and I cannot?" It was hard for them to understand.

About two months before they shut us down, they started reducing personnel. They paid us whatever they wanted. Workers didn't know how to calculate their pay. So we started comparing. "How much do you have?" "How much did you get?" And they said, "Well, look I got less than you and I was working more years." That's when we started to get together, decided to form Fuerza Unida, and declared the boycott against Levi's.

At first we didn't have any office. We did all of the work from Rubén's house. Rubén [Solís of the Southwest Public Workers Union] was the one who helped us start to put together Fuerza Unida. The first day they made the shut down announcement, Rubén was there protesting in front of the plant. We got a lawyer right away. We had meetings and

---

* Miriam Ching Yoon Louie, Sweatshop Warrior. Copyright © 2001 South End Press. Used with permission.

formed the *Concilio* [Board of Directors]. The workers got involved, and we decided to put together our demands. Then we got a very little place at the Esperanza Peace and Justice Center on South Flores Street.

For six months we got unemployment benefits, $200 every two weeks. After that ran out, we felt very bad. We put more and more attention and time into Fuerza Unida. We put aside our personal and family problems. We used to cry *noches* [nights] to see the people with no food. We started having trainings and participating in conferences—locally, nationally, internationally. We moved again to 3946 South Zarzamora and stayed for almost two years until we moved over here [to 710 New Laredo Highway] where the rent is cheaper. We're low on income. The owner is a very good, cooperative man. . . .

Every several weeks, we went to San Francisco to organize the campaign at Levi's corporate headquarters. We had to leave our families. It was good but hard. We needed to walk so far and learn to be good leaders to head the campaign. We have learned that if we want to do something, we just need to develop our own goals. I have a lot of friends who do not know what they can do. They see themselves as a wife and mother, washing dishes, cooking dinner, or making clothes only for their own families. A lot of women are heads of households; not enough attention is paid to the problems they face. San Antonio is very poor. Sometimes women fall deep down into that depression they must learn to cross so they can get to the other side. We also need to be motivated by other issues and aware of other people's problems to make changes. We tell women that if someone is trying to abuse you, you must speak up.

Of course, we learned these things. When we started picketing and going to protests, I held the poster up to cover my face. I was afraid. Now if people don't call me, I call them. If you are denied opportunities, you have to look for and create opportunities.

CHAPTER 21

Women's Rights:
National and Global Perspectives

Complementing contemporary globalization, American women's scholarship is moving in a transnational and global direction. This field of inquiry also expresses the identification of women's rights as human rights on a worldwide scale. Focusing on the relationship between national and global women's rights, this chapter spans the closing decade of the twentieth century through the opening decade of the twenty-first century. The Clinton administration (1992–2000) crafted affirmative policies on global gender equity, including reproductive choice perceived as both a right and a vital aspect of women's health. In terms of policies women's rights as human rights gained strength within the United Nations. Hillary Clinton's address to the Fourth UN Conference on Women in Beijing in 1995 epitomized the growing concern to end violations against women's rights. Sisterhood rhetoric was displaced by a universal rights discourse that included ending violence against women and the expansion of rights as a gender-based category in need of worldwide attention. UN declarations proclaimed that non-discriminatory treatment of women was to replace gender-based, culturally defined and defended forms of oppression. As secretary of state in the Obama administration, Hillary Clinton has reaffirmed her allegiance to women's rights as human rights.

During George W. Bush's administration, different priorities prevailed. Within the United States, women promoting conservative family values played a role in the redirection of national and global policies. Evangelical Protestant women organized the nongovernmental Concerned Women for America (CWA) and supported the Bush administration's policies. At the United Nations, they joined the Vatican and Saudi Arabia in opposing pivotal aspects of women's rights, namely reproductive rights and family planning services. Although the political discourse of conservative family and religious groups revolved around contested issues of reproductive rights for women versus those of the unborn, divergent positions also related to fundamental questions: Who controls the female body, defines female sexuality, and determines female identity and social roles? The anti-choice movement gained momentum, and the contested terrain of women's reproductive rights became a pivotal political issue. The Bush administration supported the rolling back of *Roe v. Wade*, restrictions on the use of contraception, and abstinence counseling instead of sex education. The crusade against access to abortion had multiple dimensions, including federal and state funding of Pregnancy Crisis Centers as part of abstinence-only programs and also providing counseling against the termination of pregnancy.

The 2008 presidential election further demonstrated the oppositional positions of the two major parties. Democratic primary contenders Hillary Clinton and Barack Obama shared a women's rights agenda at wide variance from that of their Republican opponents. Clinton's positions on women's rights were well known from both her time as First Lady (1992–2000) and later as U.S. senator from New York. As the first African American presidential candidate, Barack Obama's Democratic primary contest with Hillary Clinton brought issues of race and gender to the foreground. John McCain's choice of Sarah Palin, governor of Alaska, for his running mate on the Republican Party ticket was also precedent breaking. Palin was the first female Republican vice presidential candidate and second woman vice presidential candidate chosen since 1984 when Geraldine Ferraro was selected as the Democratic running mate of Walter Mondale. Despite some faltering interviews with the mainstream media, Palin remained popular with the Republican base; her positions on creationism and abstinence education and her repudiation of abortion resonated with right-wing Republicans. Some supporters depicted her as a pro-life icon who successfully merged motherhood and career goals. Hillary Clinton's and Sarah Palin's diametrically opposite positions on women's issues and disparate female constituencies served as a timely reminder that women do not represent a homogeneous voting bloc. The ideological division between Clinton and Palin trumped gender identification. In fact, the discordant views on women's rights expressed during the 2008 campaign reflected the polarized national debate that continues to unfold.

Obama campaigned on a message of "change." During the first months of his presidency, change did indeed occur on the issue of women's reproductive rights and his support for strengthening equal pay legislation. Once in office, Obama lost little time in the reversal of Bush's policies on the national and global levels. The new president lifted the "global gag rule" that the Bush administration used to prevent U.S. funding of UN programs that provided family planning and certain forms of contraception and supported reproductive rights. Reproductive choice also remained a central issue in the health care debates of 2009.

In addition to the dramatic contrast on issues of reproductive rights, Bush and Obama also held divergent positions on the Supreme Court decision dealing with Lilly Ledbetter and pay equity. A proponent of gender equality in the workplace, Obama signed the Lilly Ledbetter Fair Pay Act in 2009 that guaranteed greater flexibility for workers filing sex discrimination lawsuits. Ledbetter had filed a lawsuit against her employer Goodyear Tire and Rubber Company for gender-based discrimination with reference to unequal pay over many years of employment. Men in the same managerial rank had received greater raises and pension benefits. The case ultimately came before the Supreme Court, whose decision negated Ledbetter's lawsuit on the ground that she had exceeded the statute of limitations for legal redress. Ledbetter was unaware of the pay inequity until she was about to retire. Since the nineteenth century, pay equity has been an objective of women's rights advocates and a cornerstone of the second-wave women's movement of the 1960s and 1970s. Reaffirming support for gender equity in the workplace, Feminist Historians for a New, New Deal urged the newly elected president to promote gender equity in government's economic stimulus plans. Conservative groups and Republicans in Congress generally opposed the government's promoting workplace gender-based equity, The conservative Independent Women's Forum argued against the Fair Pay Act and government intervention alleging that the workplace regulates itself. Pay inequities reflect women's choices, not accepting challenges or working late for example, rather than gender discrimination.

When Alice Walker's documentary *Warrior Marks* was produced in 1994, Third World critics of American feminism denounced the film for its intrusive and insensitive depiction of the rite of female genital cutting practiced in many African countries and upheld as a requirement for marriage. Although the UN declared the practice a violation of women's bodily integrity and human rights, opponents continued to accuse American women's rights activists of exporting their own biased rescue agenda, reminiscent of nineteenth-century missionaries. Critics deny that American women have the authority to speak for women of different cultural, religious, and historical backgrounds. They allege that women in the Middle East, Asia, and Africa are not the victims portrayed in American stereotypes, but women who possess their own identity and agency. Not too long after the publicity surrounding *Warrior Marks* and a CNN documentary on the same subject, an asylum seeker brought the controversy of universal women's rights versus culturally based practices such as female genital cutting to the United States.

The Fauziya Kasinga immigration asylum case ultimately resulted in changing U.S. immigration policy to include gender abuse as a legitimate appeal for asylum. From the perspective of universal women's rights, asylum extends agency to those who lack the power within their own countries for autonomous choice. The Obama administration also has extended gender-based asylum for severely battered women. In 2009, Equality Now, a major international women's rights organization, in conjunction with grassroots feminist activists from diverse African countries produced a documentary film, *Africa Rising*, focusing on the struggle of activist African women to eradicate this practice. The documentary also promotes public awareness in the United States that female genital cutting follows immigrant communities across national borders and persists in the United States despite restrictive legislation.

Sex trafficking in a global environment also has become a women's human rights issue as well as a highly profitable transnational enterprise. Although trafficking is widely seen as a violation of human rights, enmeshed in the wider issue is a long-standing debate on female prostitution as choice or coercion. Defenders of prostitution as sex work struggle to separate voluntary prostitution from trafficking. They endorse a sex workers' rights perspective and note that many sex workers cross national borders in search of economic opportunity. In complete disagreement are organizations such as the international Coalition Against Trafficking in Women (CATW) that advocate the complete abolition of prostitution as inherently inseparable from trafficking. These advocates formed coalitions with Evangelical groups. The Bush administration supported their objectives.

A connection between women's rights within the United States and the issue of whether the United States speaks for women's rights in Afghanistan emerged after September 11. Supplementing the U.S. war effort to overthrow the Taliban and destroy Bin Laden, a women's rights component to military objectives quickly emerged. Feminist organizations in the United States agreed with Laura Bush, who since the beginning of the U.S. war in Afghanistan repeatedly addressed the role of the United States in ending the

Taliban's abuse of Afghan women. Eleanor Smeal, president of The Feminist Majority, a long-term proponent of Afghan women's rights, joined the American-based Women for Afghanistan Women (WAW) to pressure the Obama administration not to abandon Afghan women and girls. Despite support for continued intervention, critics challenged U.S. policy. In terms of women's issues, they questioned whether the protracted war, loss of life, and unremitting violence helped or hindered women's rights. They noted the replacement of the Taliban with ruling Islamic fundamentalist warlords, as well as the tolerant attitude toward women's oppression demonstrated by the U.S.-backed Hamid Karzai government. President Obama's speech outlining the need for troop escalation did not link continued military intervention to women's rights issues. The American war in Iraq produced a similar controversy about the relationship between U.S. military intervention and U.S. coalition building with Islamic fundamentalists opposed to women's rights.

The intersection of American women's rights and women's human rights on a global level resulted in the creation of a new position, Ambassador-at-Large for Global Women's Issues, and the appointment of Melanne Verveer, who had previously worked with Hillary Clinton when she was First Lady. Affirmation of global women's rights has converged with movements to end environmental degradation and promote women's empowerment.

Whereas some women within the Protestant Evangelical community argue for a Biblical restoration of a wife's submission to her husband's authority, within the Catholic Church defiant nuns promote ordination of women to the priesthood. Efforts to counter this resistance to male authority on the part of the Catholic priesthood and the Vatican appear to have grown. One result is the effort to silence Sister Louise Akers of the Cincinnati Sisters of Charity, who has campaigned for years to have the Church ordain women. Significant numbers of nuns are also protesting aspects of the Vatican's investigation of their religious communities. In July 2010, the Vatican decreed the ordination of women to the priesthood a "grave crime."

The development of new waves of feminism has led to a more pronounced generational division within the wider women's rights movement. After years of bashing and backlash, *feminism* as a term referring to the women's movement of the sixties and seventies became bent out of shape. Stereotypes replaced complexity and many younger women who benefited from feminist social transformation distanced themselves from the feminist label. In contrast to this detachment, from the 1990s to the present, a new generation of women refashioned feminism for an era of greater gender equality and less concern with oppression and patriarchal privilege. Claiming an inclusive feminist identity, third- and what has recently been called fourth-wave feminists support a plurality of lifestyles, including "girly" or feminine consumption of beauty products and fashion as well as pop cultural values. Second-wave feminists focused on political and social transformation and rejected consumerism and pop culture as lifestyle guides.

The Internet is currently the primary forum for communication for younger feminists and might even be the defining aspect of a new wave of feminism. Whether the proliferations of feminist blogs that currently exist have transformative potential in the real world of politics and decision making remains uncertain. At present they serve more as discussion boards—interactive voices rather than collective political activism. Despite generational differences, conflict between different "waves" of women's rights activists, as well as conservative opposition, women's voices continue to resonate with the core values of gender equality and expansion of rights.

HILLARY CLINTON, *Speech, Beijing U.N. Fourth World Conference on Women* (1995)

Working within the guidelines of the Clinton administration's China policy, First Lady Hillary Clinton's (b. 1946) Beijing speech is widely recognized as a definitive statement in support of women's rights as human rights. Right-wing organizations and subsequent Bush administration supporters objected to the equation of women's rights as human rights, alleging it implied the inclusion of a woman's right to reproductive choice and contraceptive devices, as well as workplace gender equity. They also remained opposed to any international standard of rights for women. As President Obama's secretary of state, Clinton has made women's human rights an integral aspect of foreign policy. How does Clinton support the equation of women's rights and human rights?*

Thank you very much, Gertrude Monqella, for your dedicated work that has brought us to this point, distinguished delegates, and guests:

I would like to thank the Secretary General for inviting me to be part of this important United Nations Fourth World Conference on Women. This is truly a celebration, a celebration of the contributions women make in every aspect of life: in the home, on the job, in the community, as mothers, wives, sisters, daughters, learners, workers, citizens, and leaders.

It is also a coming together, much the way women come together every day in every country. We come together in fields and factories, in village markets and supermarkets, in living rooms and board rooms. Whether it is while playing with our children in the park, or washing clothes in a river, or taking a break at the office water cooler, we come together and talk about our aspirations and concern. And time and again, our talk turns to our children and our families. However different we may appear, there is far more that unites us than divides us. We share a common future, and we are here to find common ground so that we may help bring new dignity and respect to women and girls all over the world, and in so doing bring new strength and stability to families as well.

By gathering in Beijing, we are focusing world attention on issues that matter most in our lives—the lives of women and their families: access to education, health care, jobs and credit, the chance to enjoy basic legal and human rights and to participate fully in the political life of our countries.

There are some who question the reason for this conference. Let them listen to the voices of women in their homes, neighborhoods, and workplaces. There are some who wonder whether the lives of women and girls matter to economic and political progress around the globe. Let them look at the women gathered here and at *Huairou*—the homemakers and nurses, the teachers and lawyers, the policymakers and women who run their own businesses. It is conferences like this that compel governments and peoples everywhere to listen, look, and face the world's most pressing problems. Wasn't it after all—after the women's conference in Nairobi ten years ago that the world focused for the first time on the crisis of domestic violence? . . .

What we are learning around the world is that if women are healthy and educated, their families will flourish. If women are free from violence, their families will flourish. If women have a chance to work and earn as full and equal partners in society, their families will

---

* In the public domain.

flourish. And when families flourish, communities and nations do as well. That is why every woman, every man, every child, every family, and every nation on this planet does have a stake in the discussion that takes place here.

Over the past 25 years, I have worked persistently on issues relating to women, children, and families. Over the past two-and-a half years, I've had the opportunity to learn more about the challenges facing women in my own country and around the world.

I have met new mothers in Indonesia, who come together regularly in their village to discuss nutrition, family planning, and baby care. I have met working parents in Denmark who talk about the comfort they feel in knowing that their children can be cared for in safe, and nurturing after-school centers. I have met women in South Africa who helped lead the struggle to end apartheid and are now helping to build a new democracy. I have met with the leading women of the Western Hemisphere who are working every day to promote literacy and better health care for children in their countries. I have met women in India and Bangladesh who are taking out small loans to buy milk cows, or rickshaws, or thread in order to create a livelihood for themselves and their families. I have met the doctors and nurses in Belarus and Ukraine who are trying to keep children alive in the aftermath of Chernobyl.

The great challenge of this conference is to give voice to women everywhere whose experiences go unnoticed, whose words go unheard. Women comprise more than half the world's population, 70% of the world's poor, and two-thirds of those who are not taught to read and write. We are the primary caretakers for most of the world's children and elderly. Yet much of the work we do is not valued—not by economists, not by historians, not by popular culture, not by government leaders.

At this very moment, as we sit here, women around the world are giving birth, raising children, cooking meals, washing clothes, cleaning houses, planting crops, working on assembly lines, running companies, and running countries. Women also are dying from diseases that should have been prevented or treated. They are watching their children succumb to malnutrition caused by poverty and economic deprivation. They are being denied the right to go to school by their own fathers and brothers. They are being forced into prostitution, and they are being barred from the bank lending offices and banned from the ballot box.

Those of us who have the opportunity to be here have the responsibility to speak for those who could not. As an American, I want to speak for those women in my own country, women who are raising children on the minimum wage, women who can't afford health care or child care, women whose lives are threatened by violence, including violence in their own homes.

I want to speak up for mothers who are fighting for good schools, safe neighborhoods, clean air, and clean airwaves; for older women, some of them widows, who find that, after raising their families, their skills and life experiences are not valued in the marketplace; for women who are working all night as nurses, hotel clerks, or fast food chefs so that they can be at home during the day with their children; and for women everywhere who simply don't have time to do everything they are called upon to do each and every day.

Speaking to you today, I speak for them, just as each of us speaks for women around the world who are denied the chance to go to school, or see a doctor, or own property, or have a say about the direction of their lives, simply because they are women. The truth is that most women around the world work both inside and outside the home, usually by necessity.

We need to understand there is no one formula for how women should lead our lives. That is why we must respect the choices that each woman makes for herself and her family. Every woman deserves the chance to realize her own God-given potential. But we must recognize that women will never gain full dignity until their human rights are respected and protected.

Our goals for this conference, to strengthen families and societies by empowering women to take greater control over their own destinies, cannot be fully achieved unless all governments—here and around the world—accept their responsibility to protect and promote internationally recognized human rights. The international community has long acknowledged and recently reaffirmed at Vienna that both women and men are entitled to a range of protections and personal freedoms, from the right of personal security to the right to determine freely the number and spacing of the children they bear. No one—No one should be forced to remain silent for fear of religious or political persecution, arrest, abuse, or torture.

Tragically, women are most often the ones whose human rights are violated. Even now, in the late 20th century, the rape of women continues to be used as an instrument of armed conflict. Women and children make up a large majority of the world's refugees. And when women are excluded from the political process, they become even more vulnerable to abuse. I believe that now, on the eve of a new millennium, it is time to break the silence. It is time for us to say here in Beijing, and for the world to hear, that it is no longer acceptable to discuss women's rights as separate from human rights.

These abuses have continued because, for too long, the history of women has been a history of silence. Even today, there are those who are trying to silence our words. But the voices of this conference and of the women at Huairou must be heard loudly and clearly:

It is a violation of human rights when babies are denied food, or drowned, or suffocated, or their spines broken, simply because they are born girls. It is a violation of human rights when women and girls are sold into the slavery of prostitution for human greed—and the kinds of reasons that are used to justify this practice should no longer be tolerated. It is a violation of human rights when women are doused with gasoline, set on fire, and burned to death because their marriage dowries are deemed too small.

It is a violation of human rights when individual women are raped in their own communities and when thousands of women are subjected to rape as a tactic or prize of war.

It is a violation of human rights when a leading cause of death worldwide among women ages 14 to 44 is the violence they are subjected to in their own homes by their own relatives.

It is a violation of human rights when young girls are brutalized by the painful and degrading practice of genital mutilation.

CONCERNED WOMEN FOR AMERICA, *Final +5 Beijing Battle Centers Around Abortion* (2000)

According to Concerned Women for America (CWA), this pro-family organization promotes Biblical values and evaluates public policy in terms of Christian teachings. Actively lobbying against the women's rights as human rights agenda at home and in the United Nations, CWA combats not only abortion rights but also any women's rights reform that it believes undermines the primacy of marriage and motherhood. In monitoring feminist policy objectives, CWA particularly scrutinizes language such as "the role of women" and "gender equality," which the organization considers "feminist passwords." One CWA magazine article queried whether civilization would survive feminism. Claiming approximately half a million members, CWA appears to rival in numbers the progressive, change-oriented NOW.

The two organizations' diametrically different agendas exemplify the deep divisions over women's rights that polarize the nation at the beginning of the twenty-first century. In the following document, CWA describes its struggle to combat feminist strategies to win abortion rights at the special Beijing +5 session of the United Nations General Assembly held in June 2000. The PFA referred to in the article is the acronym for the Platform for Action, adopted at the Beijing Conference. What arguments does CWA advance that feminist gender equality is a threat to the family? How would you assess these views? What parallels exist between CWA negative views on feminism and those of Kilbreth (see Chapter 14)?*

Highlights
United Nations Beijing +5 Preparatory Conference
Friday, March 3, 2000

In 1995, 189 members of the United Nations (U.N.) met in Beijing, China, for the Fourth World Conference on Women. The purpose was to create a document, the Beijing Platform for Action, outlining a set of obligations for signatory countries to follow in 12 "critical areas of concern," in order to ensure "equality" for women. While this might sound good, the feminist-driven concept of "equality" is a significant threat to the family.

Today, five years later, delegates from most of these nations gather at the U.N. headquarters in New York City, from February 28 to March 17, to assess each country's progress in implementing the Beijing Platform for Action and to discuss plans for an even more radical agenda. The Preparatory Committee (PrepCom) must meet to review a draft resolution. The resolution recommends further actions to be made by governments, the international community, and nongovernmental organizations (NGOs) to address areas of concern in the Platform for Action. This takes place before the U.N. Special Session of the General Assembly, entitled "Women: 2000: Gender Equality, Development and Peace for the Twenty-First Century" (Beijing +5), convenes June 5–9, 2000.

- **"Women's rights are human rights"** is a recurring phrase at this PrepCom. According to the U.N., "women's rights" include the right to abortion, lesbianism and sexual and reproductive health. Up to this point, pro-life efforts have kept abortion as a "human right" out of U.N. documents. Now, the U.N. has a different strategy. It is trying to bypass the debate over abortion as a *human* right by defining it as a *woman's* right.

- **"Gender Equality."** The PFA [Platform for Action] calls for NGOs to influence all levels of the government, community and media to work together to achieve "gender equality" between men and women. This is called "gender mainstreaming." In the process, these NGOs and the U.N. want to erase traditional "stereotypes" and discriminatory attitudes toward women, such as the importance of motherhood. The U.N. also believes that religions may raise barriers to women's rights. In essence, the *government* would decide which religious practices are a "burden" for women.

- **"Sexual and Reproductive Health."** NGOs aim to ensure that the Beijing +5 document emphasizes that women of all ages, races, ethnic and religious backgrounds, "sexual orientation," or geographic location have full access to reproductive and sexual health services. This gives any woman of *any age* the "right" to contraceptives and abortion-on-demand without fear of "discrimination."

Furthermore, the U.N. targets adolescent girls as young as *age 10* with

* From "Highlights of the United Nations Beijing +5 Preparatory Conference," March 3, 2000. Reprinted by permission of the Concerned Women for America, Washington, D.C.

"information and services available to help them understand their sexuality and protect themselves from unwanted pregnancy. . . ." In doing so, the U.N. assumes that 10-year-old girls have mature decision-making skills regarding their sexual health. In fact, G.H. Bruntland, Director-General of the World Health Organization (WHO), stated at a briefing on March 2, "Giving young people [sexual health] information does not encourage promiscuity; rather, it fosters mutual respect and shared responsibility."

Last week, at the Health Caucus' meeting on March 1, a representative stated that "fundamentalists have been lobbying hard to remove any language in the main document that gives any woman the right to abortion." As a result, this caucus of radical NGOs pledged they would fight hard to strengthen language that ensures a woman's "right" to an abortion. The U.N. hides behind its claim that "every attempt should be made to eliminate the need for abortion. . . ." Meanwhile, it vigorously works to legalize abortion and to make it available to all women upon demand.

- **Convention on the Elimination of All Forms of Discrimination Against Women, CEDAW.** One goal of the U.N. and most NGOs is to achieve universal ratification of CEDAW. CEDAW was the first international human rights treaty to address specifically the needs of women. It has become a legal instrument for addressing women's "rights"

and "equality." Once ratified, CEDAW serves as a framework for legal and policy changes at the local, national and international levels. When a country ratifies CEDAW, it can make the Convention a part of national law or use it to aid in interpreting existing law. As typical with U.N. documents, CEDAW contains vague language. So, it is up to the courts to interpret the meaning of concepts such as "gender" and how it should apply to specific needs in their country. The language could allow some courts to use CEDAW to push special rights for individuals according to their "sexual orientation."

Because CEDAW is an international document, it serves as a lever to implement so-called "human rights" within governments' national levels. Under the guise of "human rights" and "equality," CEDAW creates international norms and standards for women, and then requires governments to protect and promote these rights. These "rights" would include sexual and reproductive health for women of all ages (such as unlimited access to "contraceptive" drugs and devices, quotas for hiring women in the work force, and comparable worth—equal pay for unequal work).

Over the years, it has taken the collaborated efforts of governments and NGOs to implement changes at all levels of society and government. Although the United States *has not* ratified CEDAW, we are not protected from NGOs' commitment to implementing these so-called human rights.

SENATOR BARACK OBAMA, *Statement on the 35th Anniversary of Roe v. Wade Supreme Court Decision* (Jan. 22, 2008)

During his Democratic presidential campaign, Senator Barack Obama (b. 1961) issued strong statements of support for the *Roe v. Wade* 1973 Supreme Court decision that made reproductive choice and access to abortion constitutional. During the Democratic primary campaign, both Hillary Clinton and Obama supported the right to choose. The *Roe v. Wade* decision has become a litmus test for presidential candidates and also has played a role in nominations for the Supreme Court. Not too long after his election, President Obama nominated Sonia Sotomayor for the position left vacant by the retirement of Supreme Court Justice David Souter. In nominating Sotomayor, President Obama supported the first Latina nominee to the Supreme Court. Although her record on reproductive rights remains inconclusive, supporters of the *Roe* decision hope she will uphold the pro-choice decision. How did Senator Obama in his 2008 campaign pledge on the 35th anniversary of *Roe v. Wade* address the controversial Supreme Court decision?*

"Thirty-five years after the Supreme Court decided Roe v. Wade, it's never been more important to protect a woman's right to choose. Last year, the Supreme Court decided by a vote of 5–4 to uphold the Federal Abortion Ban, and in doing so undermined an important principle of Roe v. Wade: that we must always protect women's health. With one more vacancy on the Supreme Court, we could be looking at a majority hostile to a women's fundamental right to choose for the first time since Roe v. Wade. The next president may be asked to nominate that Supreme Court justice. That is what is at stake in this election.

"Throughout my career, I've been a consistent and strong supporter of reproductive justice, and have consistently had a 100% pro-choice rating with Planned Parenthood and NARAL Pro-Choice America.

"When South Dakota passed a law banning all abortions in a direct effort to have Roe overruled, I was the only candidate for President to raise money to help the citizens of South Dakota repeal that law. When anti-choice protesters blocked the opening of an Illinois Planned Parenthood clinic in a community where affordable health care is in short supply, I was the only candidate for President who spoke out against it. And I will continue to defend this right by passing the Freedom of Choice Act as president.

"Moreover, I believe in and have supported common-sense solutions like increasing access to affordable birth control to help prevent unintended pregnancies. In the Illinois state Senate, when Congress failed to require insurance plans to cover FDA-approved contraceptives, I made sure those contraceptives were covered for women in Illinois. In the U.S. Senate, I've worked with Senator Claire McCaskill (D-MO) on a bill that would make birth control more affordable for low-income and college women, and introduced the Senate version of Representative Hilda Soils' bill to reduce unintended pregnancies in communities of color. As President, I will improve access to affordable health care and work to ensure that our teens are getting the information and services they need to stay safe and healthy.

"But we also know that Roe v. Wade is about more than a woman's right to choose; it's about equality. It's about whether our daughters are going to have the same opportunities as our sons. And so to truly honor that decision, we need to update the social contract so that women can free themselves, and their children, from violent relationships; so that a mom can stay home with a sick child without getting a pink slip; so that she can go to work knowing that there's affordable, quality childcare for her children; and so that the American dream is within reach for every family in this country. This anniversary reminds us that it's not enough to protect the gains of the past—we have to build a future that's filled with hope and possibility for all Americans."

---

* In the public domain.

INDEPENDENT WOMEN'S FORUM, *Opposition to Lilly Ledbetter Fair Pay Act* (2009)

The Independent Women's Forum (IWF) has followed a conservative agenda against gender-based legislation, including the Lilly Ledbetter Fair Pay Act that reaffirmed women's right to equitable pay. Founded in 1992, the IWF, under the leadership of current president and CEO African American Michelle Bernard, advocates the view that women are not victims and do not need special gender-based government assistance. The organization supports a limited government role as best for the economy and women. Arguing that women as individuals need to make choices that will lead to greater workplace success, the IWF opposed the Lilly Ledbetter Fair Pay Act signed by President Obama. What are the major points of the argument against gender-based pay equity legislation?*

Gender warriors are not wasting any time in 2009. Two pieces of falsely titled "gender equity" legislation, the Lilly Ledbetter Fair Pay Act and the Paycheck Fairness Act, are set to be the first votes of the new House. Both bills are touted as protecting "equal pay" but, in reality, do nothing of the sort. The Equal Pay Act of 1963 already requires equal pay for equal work. So, whenever modern day politicians use the term, something else is usually afoot. The recent push for pay equity is no different.

Both pieces of legislation have popped up before. The Paycheck Fairness Act passed the House in the last Congress, but was never sent to the Senate floor. The premise of the legislation is that American workplaces are systematically hostile to women and that the government must therefore intervene to provide more protection for women.

The Paycheck Fairness Act would take significant steps toward the idea of "comparable worth," aka government intervention (rather than market mechanisms such as supply and demand) in determining salary levels for different jobs to ensure "fairness." Under the bill, the Department of Labor would issue guidelines that compare the wages of different jobs to give employers an idea of what is considered a fair wage. It would also subject employers to unlimited compensatory and punitive damages, even for unintentional pay disparities. As if that doesn't leave employers vulnerable enough, the bill would also prevent employers from defending differences in pay as based on factors other than sex (for example, productivity, years in the workforce, education level, etc.). In other words, the bill is a trial lawyer's dream come true. The potential for costly litigation is endless, which is likely to raise the cost of employment and discourage workplace flexibility, both of which are bad news for women.

Another bill inviting lawsuit abuse is the Lilly Ledbetter Fair Pay Act, which passed the House in the last Congress, but was blocked by a Republican filibuster in the Senate. The bill's namesake, Lilly Ledbetter, gained notoriety when she lost her equal pay case against Goodyear Tire and Rubber Co. before the Supreme Court. Ledbetter lost her case due to statutory timing limits, and the bill seeks to extend those statutory limits for future pay equity cases (giving employees more time to file a suit for wage discrimination).

Maybe the current standard doesn't give people enough time to file suit—that is an issue on which there could be a healthy debate. But surely there should be a reasonable limit to dredging up old grievances. The Fair Pay Act would so dramatically expand the statute of limitations that companies could face suits

---

* Allison Kasic, "Gender Equity" gets top billing in Congress. *Opposition to Lilly Ledbetter Pay Equity Act from Independent Women's Forum.* Copyright © Allison Kasic.

over pay decisions made forty years ago, with relevant employees long since moved on. A company shouldn't have to face lawsuits about those decisions—there is simply too much room for abuse.

Politicians invariably point to the existence of the "wage gap" in pushing for these, and other gender equity bills. Women earn just 77 cents for every dollar a man earns, they say. In their view, this proves discrimination and justifies government intervention. However, a closer look at the wage gap reveals a much different picture.

That much-cited statistic simply compares the wages of the median full-time working man and the median full-time working woman. It tells us nothing about the existence or nonexistence of wage discrimination. The wage gap ignores a myriad of other relevant factors including education level, years in the workforce, and type of occupation. Once these other factors are taken into account, the wage gap shrinks. So should we really be basing policy decisions on a simple statistic that doesn't take into account relevant information? To do so hardly seems prudent.

OPEN LETTER TO OBAMA, *Feminist Historians for a New, New Deal* (2009)

Some of the nation's leading feminist historians wrote this letter urging the Obama administration to remember to include gender equity in the administration's economic recovery package and not to repeat the gender-biased recovery policies of the New Deal of the 1930s. What evidence do they give that the Roosevelt administration's New Deal economic recovery programs discriminated against women? How do they describe New Deal policies with reference to gender-based workplace equity? What gender-based assumptions about married women historically supported inequitable government resources and wages for women's work? What specific gender-based work issues do women still face today?*

Dear President-elect Obama,

As students of American history, we are heartened by your commitment to a jobs stimulus program inspired by the New Deal and aimed at helping "Main Street." We firmly believe that such a strategy not only helps the greatest number in our communities but goes a long way toward correcting longstanding national problems.

For all our admiration of FDR's reform efforts, we must also point out that the New Deal's jobs initiative was overwhelmingly directed toward skilled male and mainly white workers. This was a mistake in the 1930s, and it would be a far greater mistake in the 21st century economy, when so many families depend on women's wages and when our nation is even more racially diverse.

We all know that our country's infrastructure is literally rusting away. But our social infrastructure is equally important to a vibrant economy and livable society, and it too is crumbling. Investment in education and jobs in health and care work shore up our national welfare as well as our current and future productivity. Revitalizing the economy will require better and more widespread access to education to foster creative approaches and popular participation in responding to the many challenges we face.

As you wrestle with the country's desperate need for universal health insurance, we know you are aware that along with improved access we need to prioritize expenditure on preventive health. We could train a

---

* Open letter to Obama from Feminist Historians for New, New Deal. Copyright © 2008.

corps of health educators to work in schools and malls and medical offices. As people live longer, the inadequacy of our systems of care for the disabled and elderly becomes ever more apparent. While medical research works against illness and disability, there is equal need for people doing the less noticed work of supervision, rehabilitation, prevention, and personal care.

We are also concerned that if the stimulus package primarily emphasizes construction, it is likely to reinforce existing gender inequities. Women today make up 46 percent of the labor force. Simple fairness requires creating that proportion of job opportunities for them. Some of this can and should be accomplished through training programs and other measures to help women enter traditionally male-occupied jobs. But it can also be accomplished by creating much-needed jobs in the vital sectors where women are now concentrated.

The most popular programs of the New Deal were its public jobs. They commanded respect in large part because the results were so visible: tens of thousands of new courthouses, firehouses, hospitals, and schools; massive investment in road-building, reforestation, water and sewage treatment, and other aspects of the nation's physical plant—not to mention the monumental Triborough Bridge, and the Grand Coulee and Bonneville dams. But the construction emphasis discriminated against women. At best women were 18% of those hired and, like non-white men, got inferior jobs. While some of the well-educated obtained jobs through the small white-collar and renowned arts programs, the less well-educated were put to work in sewing projects, often at busy work, and African American and Mexican American women were slotted into domestic service. This New Deal policy assumed that nearly all women had men to support them and underestimated the numbers of women who were supporting dependents.

Today most policy-makers recognize that the male-breadwinner-for-every-household assumption is outdated. Moreover, experts agree that, throughout the globe, making jobs and income available to women greatly improves family well-being. Most low-income women, like men, are eager to work, but the jobs available to them too often provide no sick leave, no health insurance, no pensions, and, for mothers, pay less than the cost of child care. The part-time jobs that leave mothers adequate time to care for their children almost never provide these benefits.

Meanwhile the country needs a stronger social as well as physical infrastructure. Teachers, social workers, elder- and childcare providers and attendants for disabled people are overwhelmed with the size of their classes and caseloads. We need more teachers and teachers' aides, nurses and nurses' aides, case workers, playground attendants, day-care workers, home care workers; we need more senior centers, after-school programs, athletic leagues, music, and art lessons. These are not luxuries, although locality after locality has had to cut them. They are the investments that can make the U.S. economically competitive as we confront an increasingly dynamic global economy. Like physical infrastructure projects, these jobs-rich investments are, literally, ready to go.

A jobs-centered stimulus package to revitalize and "green" the economy needs to make caring work as important as construction work. We need to rebuild not only concrete and steel bridges but also human bridges, the social connections that create cohesive communities. We need a stimulus program that is maximally inclusive. History shows us that these concerns cannot be postponed until big business has returned to "normal." We look to the new administration not just for recovery but for a more humane direction—and in the awareness that what happens in the first 100 days and in response to immediate need sets the framework for the longer haul of reform.

MELANNE VERVEER, *Written Testimony before Congress* (2009)

The following address expresses the Obama administration's position on the need for the nation to assume a key role in the UN crusade to end global violence against women and promote gender equality and rights. Melanne Verveer's (b. 1944) appointment as the U.S. Ambassador-at-Large for Global Women's Issues adds support to the global movement for worldwide women's rights. Congress will decide whether the United States will support the International Violence Against Women Act. (IVAWA). Verveer testified in support of this act. Prior to this appointment, Verveer served as First Lady Hillary Clinton's assistant chief of staff and subsequently co-founded an international, nonprofit organization to advance women's leadership roles and rights.

What does Verveer mean by her claim that violence against women is not just a women's issue but also a human rights violation? What evidence does she offer that zones of armed conflict escalate sexual violence against women?*

I am honored to appear before you this afternoon, in this groundbreaking hearing in full Committee, to address one of the most serious global challenges of our time: violence against women. Thank you Chairman Kerry, Ranking Member Lugar, and Distinguished Members of the Committee for taking the time to address this Important issue and for holding this hearing that builds on the May 13 Subcommittee hearing, chaired by Senators Boxer and Feingold, on rape as a weapon of the conflict in the DRC [Democratic Republic of the Congo] and Sudan. The momentum is building for us to be able to make a clear and concrete difference in the lives of women and girls who are affected by gender-based violence or who are at risk of violence. The President, Vice President, and Secretary of State are committed to incorporating women's issues into all aspects of our foreign policy. Just yesterday, Secretary Clinton spoke about this topic in the UN Security Council, where a U.S.-sponsored resolution that will more effectively address sexual violence against women in armed conflicts was adopted by unanimous consent. The unprecedented creation of the "Ambassador-at-Large" position to head the State Department's Office of Global Women's Issues demonstrates the Administration's deep commitment to women's issues, and preventing and combating violence against women is a top priority for my office. We have before us a new opportunity to intensify our efforts and to make effective progress against this global pandemic.

Violence against women cannot be relegated to the margins of foreign policy. It cannot be treated solely as a "women's issue," as something that can wait until "more pressing" issues are solved. The scale and the scope of the problem make it simultaneously one of the largest and most entrenched humanitarian and development issues before us; they also make it a security issue. When women are attacked as part of a deliberate and coordinated strategy, as they are in Sudan, the DRC, and Burma, and as they have been in Bosnia, Sri Lanka, and elsewhere around the world, the glue that holds together communities dissolves. Large populations become not only displaced, but destabilized. Around the world, the places that are the most dangerous for women also pose the greatest threats to international peace and security. The correlation is clear: where women are oppressed, governance is weak and terrorists are more likely to take hold. As the Secretary has said, you cannot

---

* In the public domain.

have vibrant civil societies if half the population is left behind. Women's participation is a prerequisite for good governance, for rule of law, and for economic prosperity—and gender-based violence and the ever-present threat of violence prevents women's participation in these sectors of society.

The violence against women and girls that we're currently seeing is a global pandemic. It cuts across ethnicity, race, class, religion, education level, and international borders. It affects girls and women at every point in their life, from sex-selective abortion, which has culled as many as 100 million girls, to inadequate healthcare and nutrition given to girls, to genital mutilation, child marriage, rape as a weapon of war, trafficking, so-called "honor" killings, dowry-related murder, and the neglect and ostracism of widows—and this is not an exhaustive list. This violence is not "cultural," it is criminal. It is every nation's problem and it is the cause of mass destruction around the globe. We need a response that is commensurate with the seriousness of these crimes.

The statistics that tell the extent of this humanitarian tragedy are well-known. One in three women worldwide will experience gender-based violence in her lifetime, and in some countries, this is true for 70 percent of women. A 2006 United Nations report found that at least 102 member states had no specific laws on domestic violence; others that do have laws too often fail to fully implement or enforce them. The United Nations estimates that at least 5,000 so-called "honor" killings take place each year around the world and two to three million girls and women each year are subjected to genital mutilation. Working from normative projections of sex ratios, we know that there are millions—some estimate as many as 100 million—girls who are missing from the world because of sex-selective abortion, infanticide, or because they're denied the nutrition and healthcare they need to survive past the age of five. In some parts of the world, girls are subject to

having acid thrown in their faces when they try to go to school or when they reject suitors. Millions of girls and women are bought and sold as commodities and trafficked into prostitution or purchased as indentured servants or sweatshop workers. The International Labor Organization (ILO) estimates that there are at least 12.3 million adults and children in forced labor and commercial sexual servitude, and the majority of forced labor victims are women and girls. Around the world, they are the worst-affected by HIV/AIDS, with rape and the fear of relationship violence adding fuel to women's rising infection rate.

The problem of violence against women and girls is particularly acute in conflict zones, where legal and social norms fall away and armies and militias act without fear of accountability or judicial penalty. This is especially apparent in places such as the Democratic Republic of the Congo, where, by some estimates, more than five million people have died since 1998 because of the ongoing conflict. Women and girls have been particularly brutalized, as rapes are perpetrated by security forces and rebel groups and have become pervasive throughout society. Some 1,100 rapes are reported each month in the DRC's eastern provinces, with an average of 36 women and girls raped every day. In Burma, which has long-standing internal conflicts with ethnic minorities, women and girls are subject to sexual violence and other forms of assault, including rape by members of the armed forces that targets rural ethnic minority women. The displaced women in Sudan's Darfur region risk rape when they leave camps to collect firewood—rape by some of the same perpetrators that caused their displacement and by other militia and bandits. In refugee camps in eastern Chad and in Kenya, women risk attack by local people protecting their resources as well as by armed groups. Rape is used in conflict situations as a purposeful strategy to subdue and destroy communities, and an atmosphere of impunity prevails.

Children in these war-torn areas are especially vulnerable. While boys may be pressed into service as child soldiers and trained to kill, girls are often raped and may be forced to become sex slaves. The Lord's Resistance Army (LRA), a Ugandan rebel group, operates in the DRC and Central African Republic and is among the perpetrators of these vicious acts. As the Secretary said before in her opening remarks to the UN Security Council on September 30, "Even though women and children are rarely responsible for initiating armed conflict, they are often war's most vulnerable and violated victims."

Behind all these statistics are stories of actual people: girls such as Nhkum Hkawn Din, a 15-year old student in Burma who was allegedly raped and murdered by one or more Burmese soldiers last year. According to Burmese news reports, she was bringing food to her brother in the paddy field where he worked when the soldiers saw her and started following her. Three days later, her clothes and shoes were found alongside the basket she had been carrying. Her body, naked and mutilated, was found 200 meters away from a Burmese Army checkpoint.

Or the story of 13-year-old Shan girl, Nang Ung, who was detained by Burmese troops on false charges of being a rebel. According to a 2004 report by the Women's League of Burma (WLB), she was tied up in a tent and raped for 10 days by five to six troops each day. The injuries she sustained from the repeated rapes were so severe that she never recovered. She died a few weeks after she was freed.

Or story after story of the rape of women and girls in the eastern part of the Democratic Republic of the Congo. In August, I traveled with Secretary Clinton to Goma. The residents of the camp we visited talked about how difficult their lives were each and every day, because the camp provides no real security. If you venture out, as too many of the girls told us, for water or firewood, you put your life at risk.

In a Goma hospital, we met a woman who told us that she was eight months' pregnant when she was attacked. She was at home when a group of men broke in. They took her husband and two of their children and shot them in the front yard, before returning into the house to shoot her other two children. Then they beat and gang-raped her and left her for dead. But she was not dead. She fought for her life and her neighbors managed to get her to the hospital which was 85 kilometers away.

In so many of these cases, especially when security forces themselves are involved, no serious legal action is taken against these criminals.

These stories represent a humanitarian tragedy. The abuses not only destroy the lives of individual girls and women, families, and communities, but also rob the world of the talent it urgently needs. There is a powerful connection between violence against women and the unending cycle of women in poverty. Women who are abused or who fear violence are unable to realize their full potential and contribute to their countries' development. There are enormous economic costs that come with violence against women. In the United States alone, an estimated loss of $1.8 billion in productivity and earnings is associated with gender based-violence on an annual basis. These types of losses are repeated around the world. Ending violence against women is a prerequisite for their social, economic, and political participation and progress. Girls in Afghanistan cannot get an equal education if they are subject to acid attacks and their schools are burned down. Women can't succeed in the workplace if they are abused and traumatized, nor can they advance if legal systems continue to treat them as less than full citizens. And female politicians can't compete for office on an equal playing field when they receive threatening "night letters" or fear for their families' safety. Beyond the tragedy of actual violence, countless other women constrain their lives and withdraw from civil society because of the even larger problem of the ever-present *threat* of violence. In this way, even beyond the victims, violence controls women's lives.

Preventing violence against women isn't just the right thing to do; it's also the smart thing to do. Multiple studies from economists, corporations, institutes and foundations have demonstrated again and again that women are key drivers of economic growth and that

investing in women yields enormous dividends. We know from these studies that women reinvest up to 90 percent of their income in their families and communities. And yet none of these benefits are possible unless girls are able to learn without fear and women are able to have autonomy and decision-making over their own lives, and those are the very things that violence and the fear of violence take away.

EQUALITY NOW, WOMEN'S ACTION, *United States: Female Genital Mutilation and Political Asylum—The Case of Fauziya Kasinga* (1995–1996)

The following excerpt focuses on the immigration asylum case of Fauziya Kasinga, who fled Togo in Africa for political asylum in the United States in an effort to avoid the compulsory ritual of female genital cutting or circumcision. In August 1995, Philadelphia, Pennsylvania, Judge Donald V. Ferlise denied Kasinga's application for asylum. The practice of female genital cutting is practiced in a range of African countries and to a lesser degree in other areas of world. The practice also crosses borders as immigrants to the United States continue to adhere to this culturally sanctioned custom. U.S. immigration authorities initially rejected Kasinga's asylum request, and she was imprisoned for a year for illegal entry. Rejection of her plea for asylum meant that she would be returned to her country of origin. Fortunately for Kasinga, human rights and women's rights groups intervened and provided pro bono legal assistance. There was a successful appeal, and in September 1996, the Board of Immigration Appeals reversed Judge Ferlise's decision and granted asylum.

This was a precedent-breaking decision and the first time the issue of compulsory female circumcision was considered adequate grounds for granting asylum. Previous asylum requests had focused on men escaping unjust political persecution. The Kasinga case resulted in gender-based abuse as a reason for asylum. In the twenty-first century, the practice of female genital cutting remains the center of a controversy that places the integrity of community and cultural rituals in opposition to a universal standard of women's rights. What arguments based on female identity did Judge Ferlise use in denying asylum? What role did cultural values play in the rejection of Kasinga's asylum request? How would you evaluate this asylum issue?*

Fauziya Kasinga has been in detention since 17 December 1994, the day she arrived in the United States seeking political asylum. She was seventeen years old, and had fled her home country of Togo immediately following a forced marriage to a 45-year-old man with three other wives. Although Fauziya refused to sign the marriage certificate, she was declared wed and confined to a storage room to await

the arrival of a circumciser who would subject her to female genital mutilation (FGM). Fauziya's father had protected her and her sisters from the practice, but upon his death, Fauziya's mother, originally from Benin, was effectively banished from the Tchamba-Kunsuntu tribe, and control over Fauziya passed to her father's family. Fauziya managed to escape before the circumciser arrived and

---

* Copyright © 1996 Equality Now.

made her way to the United States, where she has a cousin who lives in Washington, DC. When she arrived at Newark International Airport, Fauziya Kasinga requested political asylum and was immediately detained by the Immigration and Naturalization Service (INS).

On 25 August 1995 in Philadelphia, Pennsylvania, Judge Donald V. Ferlise denied Fauziya Kasinga's application for political asylum. In his decision, Judge Ferlise stated that even if he believed Fauziya, which he did not, the record "does not reveal any past or future or present persecution" because she could not be characterized as being persecuted for membership in a particular social group. He found that as all women from the tribe she belonged to are pressured into circumcision, she was "not being singled out for circumcision." The case of Fauziya Kasinga is currently pending before the Board of Immigration Appeals. Meanwhile, Fauziya remains in detention at York County Prison in Pennsylvania, where she is suffering from severe depression. Following Judge Ferlise's decision, a request for parole pending appeal was denied by the INS on 15 November 1995. On 13 March 1996, a writ of habeas corpus was filed on behalf of Fauziya Kasinga, detailing the harsh conditions of her detention and petitioning for her release.

There have been several recent decisions by immigration judges relating to FGM. On 28 April 1995 in Baltimore, Maryland, Judge John F. Gossart, Jr. denied an application for political asylum in the case of a woman from Sierra Leone, identified as DJ. In his decision, Judge Gossart described circumcision as "an important ritual" which "binds the tribe." He noted that the applicant "cannot change the fact that she is a female, but she can change her mind with regards to her position towards the FGM practices. It is not beyond [her] control to acquiesce to the tribal position on FGM." The immigration judge ruled that fear of FGM was not persecution under the Refugee Act. He observed that "while some cultures view FGM as abhorrent and/or even

barbaric, others do not." However, on 23 March 1994 in Portland, Oregon, Judge Kendall Warren ordered the suspension of a pending deportation order against a Nigerian woman, Lydia Oluloro, on the ground that her two daughters would be at risk of FGM, which he described as "cruel, painful and dangerous." In another case, decided in August 1995 in Arlington, Virginia, Judge Nejelski granted political asylum to a woman from Sierra Leone, identified as MK. In his decision, Judge Nejelski held that "forced female genital mutilation clearly merits being recognized as a form of persecution."

Fauziya Kasinga's appeal represents the first case in which the Board of Immigration Appeals will consider whether FGM constitutes persecution for the purposes of refugee status as defined by Section 101(a)(42) of the Refugee Act. This definition, drawn from the United Nations Convention relating to the Status of Refugees, requires that the asylum applicant must demonstrate an unwillingness or inability to return to his or her country because of "persecution or a well-founded fear of persecution on account of race, religion, nationality, membership in a particular social group or political opinion." On 26 May 1995, the INS introduced guidelines for asylum officers in adjudicating gender-based asylum claims. The guidelines include a reference to genital mutilation as a form of mistreatment directed against girls and women which can serve as evidence of past persecution. These guidelines are not binding, however, on immigration judges.

Representative Patricia Schroeder, together with twenty-five other Members of Congress, has appealed to the Attorney General for the release of Fauziya Kasinga and expressed concern that in her case the immigration judge did not accept the principle that FGM constitutes a form of persecution that qualifies someone for political asylum. The Members of Congress have stated that "FGM is a human rights violation, and it would be a grave injustice for our political asylum process to indicate otherwise and knowingly send women back to their countries of origin and face this cruel and degrading practice."

An estimated 100 million girls and women around the world have undergone female genital mutilation—the partial or total removal of the clitoris (clitoridectomy), the removal of the entire clitoris and the cutting of the labia minora (excision), or in its most extreme form the removal of all external genitalia and the stitching together of the two sides of the vulva (infibulation). For those who survive the cutting, which is generally done without an anaesthetic, lifelong health consequences include chronic infection; severe pain during urination, menstruation, sexual intercourse and childbirth; and psychological trauma. An extreme form of many traditional practices used around the world to deny women independence and equality, FGM is defended as a rite of passage and a social prerequisite of marriage. It is used to control women's sexuality by safeguarding virginity and suppressing sexual desire.

LAURA BUSH, *Radio Address on Afghan Women* (Nov. 17, 2001)

Laura Bush (b. 1946) served as the chief Bush administrative spokesperson, linking the U.S. war against the Taliban and the search for al-Qaida as an opportunity to protect women and children from Taliban oppression. In November 2001, she became the first First Lady to give the weekly radio presidential address, an event timed to coordinate with a State Department report dealing with the same issue of Taliban oppression of women and children. Over the years of the war in Afghanistan, Laura Bush retained her outspoken advocacy , and on the eve of stepping down as First Lady, she reiterated her commitment to the role of the United States in fostering rights for women in Afghanistan. In actuality, U.S. intervention has meant backing warlords who have no commitment to women's rights and some of whom have also committed acts of violence.

RAWA, the Afghan-based women's rights organization that first publicized the Taliban brutality against women, does not believe that U.S. intervention has resulted in expansion of rights or cessation of violence. RAWA cites U.S. escalation of force and coalition with warlords as detrimental to women's rights. In a rare display of agreement with the Bush administration, American feminist organizations also hoped U.S. intervention would end Afghani women's oppression. What are the major reasons given by Laura Bush that the United States has an obligation to help Afghan women and children? How does she link this issue to the fight against terrorism?*

Good morning. I'm Laura Bush, and I'm delivering this week's radio address to kick off a world-wide effort to focus on the brutality against women and children by the al-Qaida terrorist network and the regime it supports in Afghanistan, the Taliban. That regime is now in retreat across much of the country, and the people of Afghanistan—specially women—are rejoicing. Afghan women know, through hard experience, what the rest of the world is discovering: The brutal oppression of women is a central goal of the terrorists. Long before the current war began, the Taliban and its terrorist allies were making the lives of children and women in Afghanistan miserable. Seventy percent of the Afghan people are malnourished. One in every four children won't live past the age of five because health care is not available. Women have been denied access to doctors when they're sick. Life under the Taliban is so hard and repressive, even small displays of joy are outlawed—children

---

* In the public domain.

aren't allowed to fly kites; their mothers face beatings for laughing out loud. Women cannot work outside the home, or even leave their homes by themselves.

The severe repression and brutality against women in Afghanistan is not a matter of legitimate religious practice. Muslims around the world have condemned the brutal degradation of women and children by the Taliban regime. The poverty, poor health, and illiteracy that the terrorists and the Taliban have imposed on women in Afghanistan do not conform with the treatment of women in most of the Islamic world, where women make important contributions in their societies. Only the terrorists and the Taliban forbid education to women. Only the terrorists and the Taliban threaten to pull out women's fingernails for wearing nail polish. The plight of women and children in Afghanistan is a matter of deliberate human cruelty, carried out by those who seek to intimidate and control.

Civilized people throughout the world are speaking out in horror—not only because our hearts break for the women and children in Afghanistan, but also because in Afghanistan we see the world the terrorists would like to impose on the rest of us.

All of us have an obligation to speak out. We may come from different backgrounds and faiths—but parents the world over love our children. We respect our mothers, our sisters and daughters. Fighting brutality against women and children is not the expression of a specific culture; it is the acceptance of our common humanity—a commitment shared by people of good will on every continent. Because of our recent military gains in much of Afghanistan, women are no longer imprisoned in their homes. They can listen to music and teach their daughters without fear of punishment. Yet the terrorists who helped rule that country now plot and plan in many countries. And they must be stopped. The fight against terrorism is also a fight for the rights and dignity of women.

In America, next week brings Thanksgiving. After the events of the last few months, we'll be holding our families even closer. And we will be especially thankful for all the blessings of American life. I hope Americans will join our family in working to insure that dignity and opportunity will be secured for all the women and children of Afghanistan.

Have a wonderful holiday, and thank you for listening.

ELEANOR CURTI SMEAL, *Keep Pledges to Afghan Women and Girls: Build Lasting Peace* (Dec. 1, 2009)

Before founding the Feminist Majority Foundation in 1987, Eleanor Curti Smeal (b. 1939) had a key leadership role in NOW. The Feminist Majority's deeply rooted commitment is to foster feminist objectives on a global as well as a national level. In the following document, Smeal reaffirmed the organization's policy of support for continued U.S. intervention in Afghanistan. What aspects does Smeal's statement urging support for Afghanistan women share with that of Laura Bush? What differentiates Smeal's appeal?*

We must not forget the horrific human rights abuses toward women and girls that have been and are being committed by the

Taliban. In the past several years, hundreds of girls' schools have been destroyed. Teachers have been murdered—some right in front of

---

* John T. Woolley and Gerhard Peters, *The American Presidency Project* [online]. Santa Barbara, CA. Available from World Wide Web: http://www.presidency.ucsb.edu/ws/?pid=24992.

their students. Girls are being attacked with acid thrown in their faces on their way to or from school. Atrocities are regularly committed by Taliban forces against women. And we cannot forget, when Afghanistan was ruled by the Taliban, women and girls were not allowed to be educated, employed, go outside their homes without the company of a close male relative, go to a male doctor (female doctors were forbidden to work), or go to a hospital. Girl babies were even forbidden treatment by male doctors. Women were beaten and killed for violations of intolerable restrictions.

President Obama announced in March a comprehensive new strategy for Afghanistan and Pakistan that will provide not only military assistance, but also "a greater civilian commitment to the Afghan people." He pledged we will "support the basic human rights of all Afghans—including women and girls."

We believe for any campaign to bring lasting peace to Afghanistan humanitarian and development programs of education, health care, and employment, especially for women and girls, who compose the majority of Afghans, are essential.

We believe that the new strategy about to be announced must increase the humanitarian and development programs for Afghanistan. To establish the conditions for a lasting peace, Afghanistan must be rebuilt and the basic building blocs of a civil society must be restored. President Bush promised a Marshall Plan for Afghanistan. In the long run, rebuilding Afghanistan is not only the moral solution, but also the more economical solution.

Providing jobs with adequate pay will drain the recruits for the Taliban. Moreover, adequately paying Afghan soldiers, police, civil servants, teachers, and health care workers is essential to stopping corruption and Taliban recruitment. Until recently, for example, the Taliban has been paying its militia recruits significantly more than the Afghan police or military. According to the Afghan National Army's website, trained soldiers receive $120 a month, compared to $200 to $500 a month for the Taliban (NYTimes 10/19/2009 and Afghan sources). Afghan experts estimate that a subsistence wage is $300 a month. No wonder Afghanistan is having difficulty with recruitment and attrition rates in the military and police.

Current Situation in Afghanistan:

Nearly eight years have passed since the Taliban's fall from power. Despite some progress in restoring the rights of Afghan women and girls, the situation in Afghanistan is dire. Due to the shift in U.S. attention to Iraq, the Taliban has made a comeback. Since 2005, deadly attacks on Afghan civilians, relief workers, teachers, and private contractors have been increasing. Women aid workers, elected officials, government employees, and journalists have been especially targeted by extremists with the Taliban often claiming responsibility. Suicide bombings are increasing. Most Afghan citizens live without basic necessities, including sufficient food, clean water, electricity, roads and healthcare.

Dr. Sima Samar, the chairperson of the Afghan Independent Human Rights Commission (AIHRC) has told us that no place in Afghanistan is safe. We remain extremely concerned about the increase in severe violence against women in Afghanistan. For example, today some 35% of the 6 million school children (some 55% of all children) are girls, but in the southern province of Kandahar, where the Taliban insurgency is strongest, some experts estimate only 3% of the school children are girls. Nearly 1,000 girls' or co-ed schools have been attacked, arsoned, or destroyed by Taliban insurgents or militia. Teachers of girls as well as women political leaders have been assassinated; most recently a Kandahar woman provincial council member who was a fighter for women's rights was shot and killed.

Yet, despite the struggle and danger, millions of courageous Afghan women and girls go to school and work. Their drive for education is so great that several girls who had acid thrown in their faces for attending school in November 2008 were back in school just two months later in January 2009.

The FMF Campaign for Afghan Women and Girls, chaired by Mavis Leno, which began in 1997 to stop gender apartheid under the Taliban, galvanizes women's groups, campus and community activists, as well as ordinary citizens and conducts a public education campaign to ensure that Afghan women and girls will not be forgotten in the public debate concerning US policies toward Afghanistan. We have raised money for Afghan girls' and women's education, clinics, and employment training and have supported US programs for Afghan women and girls.

DORCHEN A. LEIDHOLDT, *Demand and the Debate* (2004)

Dorchen A. Leidholdt helped found the Coalition Against Trafficking in Women (CATW) in 1988. Since that time, she has served as co-executive director of the organization. CATW is an international organization with roots in the 1980s American group Women against Pornography. CATW supports the eradication of prostitution on the national and transnational levels. In the following document, Liedholdt describes why CATW opposes the legalization of prostitution and its redefinition of prostitution as sex work. With the surge in trafficking of women across national borders, the debate about whether prostitution is a choice or coercive trafficking has grown more complex. Opponents of CATW make a distinction between voluntary prostitution and coercive trafficking. They maintain that prostitutes who migrate across borders in search of greater economic opportunity are sex workers and entitled to rights. Pro–sex worker advocates portrayed the Bush administration as furthering right-wing moral and religious positions that refused to acknowledge the issue of female agency.

Why does the CATW believe prostitution is inseparable from international trafficking in women? In what ways do the objectives of CATW express continuity with nineteenth-century moral reformers? How does this debate relate to the 1980s feminist divide that resulted in the so-called "sex wars"?*

It is a tremendous honor to be speaking here. And a little daunting. When I looked at the list of participants, I saw the names of so many people I have worked with since the '70s and '80s in the movement against prostitution and pornography. So many people who have raised my consciousness and taught me unforgettable lessons—Meg Baldwin, Twiss Butler, Melissa Farley, Ruchira Gupta, Norma Hotaling, Donna Hughes, Laura Lederer, Linnea Smith, Morrison Torrey, and many others here. It is a privilege to be here with you. And what a pleasure and relief not to have to try to convince another audience that trafficking and prostitution harm women.

I'd like to talk about our history—the journey, politically speaking, that has brought us to this conference. It's a collective history, but we've had different experiences—we have different battle scars, different successes. I'd like to speak personally, about my experience in this movement and in the debate that has brought us to this conference. And I'd like to explain how, in my view, the subject we are focusing on at this conference—the demand for commercial sexual exploitation—helps resolve the debate and enables us to make a real difference in stopping the commercial sexual exploitation of women and children.

---

* Dorchen A. Leidholdt, CATW, "Demand and the Debate." Copyright © Dorchen A. Leidholdt.

I first encountered the debate in 1978. I was part of a little cadre of feminist activists in New York City that made up the NYC groups of Women Against Violence Against Women. WAVAW, as it was called, was working against images in the popular media that eroticized and promoted violence against women. I was also working with New York Women Against Rape. In the fall of 1977, there was an incident that stunned and galvanized us. A young woman was thrown out of the window of a building onto the pavement below. She was brutally murdered. But because she was in prostitution and the window was that of a brothel, the police were not taking her murder seriously. She was, as the media put it, "a hooker." We were outraged. We called an emergency meeting. We spray painted signs that communicated our anger. I typed up a leaflet and used the xerox machine of the publishing company where I worked to run off hundreds of copies. This woman was our sister, we declared, and her murder was a crime against all women. We sent out a press release to announce that we would be picketing in front of the brothel.

WAVAW and New York Women Against Rape were not the only groups to show up, however. Members of another group were there. They were British-based and called themselves Wages for Housework. Whereas our message was simple and feminist, theirs was more sophisticated and complex. The media turned out in droves, and our Wages for Housework comrades hogged the mikes.

"Prostitution is a job like any other job," they insisted. "Some women prostitute their fingers as secretaries; others prostitute their minds as college professors." "It's all the same." "If we unionized brothels and recognized sex work as a job, this never would have happened." "There's no difference between prostitution and marriage: hookers and housewives unite." . . .

As a young feminist in the early 1970s I had worked as a rape crisis counselor. Now I began to understand that what those women had endured as a one-time assault was the ongoing condition of women and girls in prostitution—a prolonged, numbing series of sexual violations carried out by multiple violators. And this was being done to women and girls, the vast majority of whom had already endured sexual abuse as children. Sarah [a former prostitute] called prostitution "bought and sold rape." But in reality it was gang rape, and not just a single gang rape, but gang rape carried out day after day, for years. The money exchanged—which the sex industry defenders pointed to as proof that prostitution is work—only deepened the violation to the woman or girl and her feelings of culpability. I became convinced that the labor paradigm COYOTE [Call Off Your Old Tired Ethics] and Wages for Housework were promoting was wrong, and that, like rape, prostitution was a practice of gender-based violence.

Sarah left Women Against Pornography to found the first organization of prostitution survivors to fight the sex industry. I wanted also to challenge it—not just the pornography it produced— but, working now with Kathleen Barry, the author of Female Sexual Slavery, I was thinking globally.

In 1987, colleagues from Women Against Pornography, the Minneapolis-based WHISPER, and I began to organize a conference entitled, "Trafficking in Women." I articulated the primary goal of the conference in a letter to Twiss Butler in January 1988: "What we hope to accomplish is to get feminists and others to rethink the pornography and prostitution issues from the vantage point of the women who are most victimized by the institutions and simultaneously flaunted and made invisible."

The conference took place in October 1988, one week short of fifteen years ago, in Martin Luther King, Jr. High School in NYC. It was the first international conference on "Trafficking in Women." Laura Lederer, a leader in the anti-pornography movement, was now a program officer at the Scaggs Foundation. Laura provided the seed money that made the conference possible. It was organized on a shoestring, but without Laura's critical support, it would not have been possible.

Speakers included the founding mothers of the global movement against the sexual exploitation of women, in addition to Kathy Barry and Diana Russell, international leaders like Yayori Matsui, the Japanese feminist extraordinaire and founder of the Asian Women's Association, who tragically died this year; Jyotsna Chatterji, the director of the Joint Women's Programme in New Delhi, India; Agnete Strom of the Women's Front in Norway; Aurora Javate de Dios, the director of the Women's Resource and Research Center in the Philippines; Rosa Dominga-Trapasso, founder of the Movimeiento el Pozo in Peru; British lesbian-feminist author and anti-pornography activist Sheila Jeffries; and Zimbabwe's leading women's rights scholar Rudo Gaidzanwa. Survivors participated on panels and in a three-hour speak out.

The conference organizers understood trafficking in women as a broad, umbrella concept that encompassed all practices of buying and selling women's and children's bodies. Trafficking as we understood it included American pornography, temple prostitution in India, military prostitution in the Philippines, street prostitution in Peru, sex tourism from Europe to Asia. It moved from the micro—"Trafficking within the Family"—to the macro—"Trafficking in Women: A Global Perspective." It exposed mainstream institutions that support and benefit from prostitution: "Military, Government, and Corporate Trafficking in Women." The conference looked at the sex industry as an instrument of the socialization of both men and women: "The Social Production of Prostitution"; "On Sale Everywhere: The Social Reconstruction of Women's Bodies." It exposed connections between sex trafficking and surrogacy, marriage, and adoption. It focused on violence against prostitutes, called for services and shelter for victims and survivors, and examined international legal strategies on trafficking in women.

Please forgive me if I dwell on the content of the conference, but I just received a program for a conference on "Human Trafficking" that will soon take place in New York City. You would never know that trafficking has anything to do with gender, sex, or women.

It was clear by the end of the conference that an international feminist organization combating trafficking in women in all of its forms was desperately needed. We began organizing the Coalition Against Trafficking in Women. Many of the conference participants took on key roles. Aurora Javate de Dios from the Philippines became our President.

We conceived of the Coalition as an umbrella with connected but autonomous networks in each world region to address its unique challenges. Within the next five years, there was a strong Coalition Against Trafficking in Women, Asia-Pacific, with Aurora at the helm; a newly formed Coalition Against Trafficking in Women, Latin America, coordinated by Zoraida Ramirez Rodriquez in Venezuela, whom we lost to breast cancer last year; and an incipient African Coalition being developed by Fatoumata Diake in Mali.

Not everyone was happy with the inclusive and feminist understanding of trafficking that was promoted at the 1988 Conference and embraced by the Coalition Against Trafficking in Women. Representatives from the Center for Women's Global Leadership observed the proceedings without participating, whispering among themselves. Representatives from the Dutch Foundation on Trafficking in Women arrived uninvited and did their best to foster dissent among the participants. However, it was not until 1991 during a seminar on trafficking in women in Strasbourg, France, sponsored by the Council of Europe and the Dutch government, that the opposition's agenda and strategy fully surfaced.

Sister Louise Akers, *Cincinnati's Pilarczyk Bans Nun from Teaching* (Sept. 2, 2009)

Sister Louise Akers (b. 1943), Sisters of Charity, Cincinnati, Ohio, is a proponent of women's rights policies within the framework of dedicated service to Catholicism. Over the years, she has advocated ending the suppression of women in male-centric religious institutions. Supporters of Sister Akers believe the archbishop's effort to silence her is a manifestation of the wider Vatican goal of bringing resistant and defiant sisters who advocate women's rights back into conformist and submissive roles. Although Sister Akers has officially been banned from teaching, she refused to repudiate her views about the ordination of women and stated she would continue to uphold "the value, dignity and equality of women in the church." The Vatican currently is conducting two investigations of American nuns and has decreed the ordination of women to the priesthood a "grave crime." The following excerpt deals with the actual silencing of Sister Akers and presents arguments in her defense. How would you evaluate Sister Akers' behavior? How does her defiance relate to women's rights?*

The visitation, which will take more than a year to complete, is an investigation into American nuns that is welcomed by many Catholic conservatives but feared by liberals and others wary of a Vatican crackdown.

Pilarczyk told Akers his decision was unrelated to the investigation, but the timing raised concerns about future actions against nuns and religious orders that sometimes are at odds with the Vatican.

Akers, 66, said she asked for a meeting with Pilarczyk last month after she learned he was concerned about comments she made about the ordination of women. She was teaching a class for religious educators at the time and said she wanted to clarify "what was expected of me."

She said Pilarczyk gave her an ultimatum: Remove her name from the web site of the Women's Ordination Conference, which supports the ordination of women, and publicly renounce her support of women priests.

She told him she was willing to take her name off the web site, but she could not reject her strong belief in the ordination of women and embrace the church's male-only doctrine.

"For me, it's an issue of justice within the church," Akers said Wednesday. "To make a public statement in support of the doctrine would be to go against my conscience, and I can't do that."

Akers, who has spoken out on social justice issues for years, said the ordination of women is both a practical and a fairness issue. She said allowing female priests would help address the shortage of priests in the United States and would put women on equal footing with men in the church.

"The primary motive for taking the stand I've taken is the value, dignity and equality of women in the church," Akers said.

Andriacco confirmed the meeting with Akers took place last month, but he said the archbishop would not publicly discuss personnel matters. He said the archdiocese has a vested interest in making sure its educators follow church teachings.

He said church doctrine clearly states that because Christ chose only male apostles, the church must allow only male priests.

---

* Sister Louise Akers, "Cincinnati's Pilarczyk bans nun from teaching" Cincinnati Enquirer, 9/2/09. Copyright © 2009. Used with permission.